Roads To
Jewish Survival

Roads To
Jewish Survival

Essays, Biographies, and Articles
Selected from The Torch *on its 25th Anniversary*

EDITED BY

Milton Berger

Joel S. Geffen

M. David Hoffman

National Federation of Jewish Men's Clubs

Bloch Publishing Company

New York

Library of Congress Catalog Card Number: 68-17689

PRINTED IN THE U.S.A

First Edition

FOREWORD

DR. LOUIS FINKELSTEIN

About ten years ago, I wrote an article, later published in *Fortune* magazine, in which I spoke of business morality, and of the tendency in our society to look to business men for ethical leadership. As the reader may imagine, that article stimulated a great deal of discussion. If memory serves me, I received several thousand letters from all over the world—most of them from men and women who shared my concern, but a substantial number from people who understandably challenged my expertise in business affairs.

It is incontrovertibly true that in an industrial society like ours, the customs and morals and attitudes of business leaders pervade the national life. Because business success is a national ideal, the values and skills which apparently help men to attain it are widely admired. Our real problem is to determine when achievement is illusory and when real, and to distinguish the patterns of behavior which will help us to eschew the illusion and attain the real.

Being human, we shall never be able to make these distinctions with complete certainty. But what we can and must do is develop the habit of worrying about them. If our every decision were a thoughtful decision—if we could learn to think through the pros and cons of each proposed course of action, examining all the dimensions of our problem—then, while our decisions would not always be right, neither could they be completely wrong.

This habit of thoughtful decision-making is not an easy one to acquire. Our tradition teaches that study is a way of worship, and constantly reminds us that thoughtful perusal of ancient texts is an invaluable guide to wisdom and the good life. In the day to day world of the Seminary, where we train rabbis and scholars, it might fairly be said that when we inculcate in young people this habit of study we succeed, when we merely impart knowledge, we fail. As if our task were not sufficiently difficult, we must also be concerned as to whether those graduates who have adopted the pattern of study for themselves are able also to win others to this way of life.

This anthology from *The Torch* is one of the indications of possible progress. *The Torch* is a magazine for business and professional men—the much respected "doers" in our society. In this anthology from *The Torch,* we find a selection of articles which your readers—members of The National Federation of Jewish Men's Clubs—have found worthwhile over the past quarter century, and which they wish preserved in a more permanent form, so that they can reread them themselves, and share them with their friends. Yet these are not "practical" articles. They speak of such matters as patterns of Jewish living, Jewish education, the relation of the American Jew to Israel. The authors include many of the intellectual and spiritual leaders of the Conservative Movement.

The business men who read these articles, who are concerned about the problems they raise, have taken an important step toward responsible decision-making. They have identified themselves with their tradition; they are forming the habit of thinking about problems which transcend their daily concerns. It seems to me reasonable to hope that they are also concerned about the fundamental ethical problems of our age, and that they will continue on the path, from concern to reading to study, which will ultimately enable them to live richly, and to contribute as Jews to our troubled society. The Men's Clubs and their leaders, both rabbinic and lay, are to be congratulated on their achievements, among which this volume is certainly to be counted. Readers of *The Torch,* and other devoted laymen of our Movement, have cause to be grateful to the editors of this book—to Dr. M. David Hoffman, Milton Berger, who conceived of *The Torch* and has been its editor for 25 years, and to Dr. Joel S. Geffen, whose services as spiritual advisor to the National Federation during the past quarter century have extended into every area. May the Federation continue to grow in spiritual stature in the decades ahead, so that its members may provide the ethical leadership which our civilization needs so desperately from its professional and business men.

CONTENTS

PART TWO

BASIC CONCEPTS

PART THREE

JEWISH EDUCATION

PART FOUR

ADULT EDUCATION

PART FIVE

AMERICA-ISRAEL

PART SIX

SIGNIFICANT FACTORS
IN CONTEMPORARY JEWISH LIFE

Part One

OUTSTANDING PERSONALITIES

"Na'eh doresh ve-na'eh meqayem (*He who preaches well and performs well*) *was the correct description of man's ideal behavior as viewed by our ancient sages. Such a combination of purposeful planning and careful execution is unfortunately not too often encountered in Jewish communal life in America.*"

—Salo W. Baron

INTRODUCTION

To appreciate fully the significance of the outstanding personalities portrayed herein one must understand the situation in American Jewish life at the time their influence became most pervasive. Dr. Schechter, Dr. Ginzberg, Dr. Adler and Miss Szold were contemporaries. Somewhat later Dr. Kaplan, Rabbi Steinberg and Maxwell Abbell came into prominence, and more recently still Dr. Heschel.

Early in the twentieth century Jewish life in the United States faced a critical situation. The vast tides of immigrants from Eastern Europe settling largely along the Eastern seaboard met a difficult struggle to obtain an economic foothold and showed less concern for the maintenance of their religious traditions and practices, while they sought eagerly for general educational opportunity and readily accepted prevailing American standards and values in order to become an integral part of American life as soon as possible. Huddled together in ghettos they preserved many of the folkways and organizations of their country of origin. Their common mother tongue was Yiddish. To the more affluent and well-adjusted earlier immigrants the newcomers were potentially a source of religious strength, but immediately their political and economic ideology, and, in some instances, their hostility to religion were of great concern. The Orthodox group sought to maintain their institutions and practices literally without change and without recognition or understanding of the rapid changes in life and thought in America of the new century. The extremists had captured the Reform movement with their American Zion, their Sunday Sabbath, their repudiation of the authority of the Torah, their new prayer-book, their practical elimination of Hebrew in the Service and of *kashruth* in the home. The way to as-

3

similation was wide open. The Historical-Traditional or Conservative group was small, weak and unorganized.

It had, however, men ready to aid, who only needed the inspiration of a great personality to lay out a program and get a movement of the masses under away. The times required dynamic leadership. Fortunately, in New York, Philadelphia, and Baltimore there were men of affairs, men respected in their communities, who understood the situation. In New York, Louis Marshall, Jacob Schiff, Leonard Lewisohn, Daniel Guggenheim, as well as Dr. H. P. Mendes and Joseph Blumenthal, were anxious to meet the crisis in Jewish religious life. In Philadelphia it was Judge Mayer Sulzberger, Dr. Cyrus Adler, Dr. Solomon Solis-Cohen and Charles I. Hoffman who carried the torch after Dr. Sabato Morais passed away in 1897. In Baltimore it was the Friedenwalds and Szolds who were ready to join forces under a great leader. What was needed was one who would have wide appeal and be at the same time a conserver of tradition, a modern Jewish scholar, and an articulate spokesman of a way of life adapted to the American scene and part of the historical development of Jewish law and its interpretation.

The man who filled all these requirements was Dr. Solomon Schechter, then Reader in Rabbinics at Cambridge University in England. He had become world famous through his discovery of the Cairo Genizah with its marvelous collection of ancient Jewish manuscripts. Dr. Schechter had delivered a course of lectures at Gratz College in Philadelphia and his *Studies in Judaism* (Jewish Publication Society) had been well received. He was the ideal person to lead the Jewish Theological Seminary, founded by Dr. Sabato Morais, and since his death struggling for survival. The Seminary was designed to train Rabbis and teachers and to unite Jewry in the maintenance of Judaism according to the historical traditional school of Zunz and Frankel and *Judische Wissenschaft*.

It should be noted here that all the personalities here included are closely linked to the Jewish Theological Seminary—Dr. Schechter and Dr. Adler as presidents, Dr. Ginzberg as its most world renowned scholar, Dr. Kaplan and Dr. Heschel as members of the Seminary faculty making original and creative contributions to Jewish thought, Rabbi Steinberg as a Seminary graduate, spiritual leader, and writer of outstanding ability, Maxwell Abbell, lay leader and president of the United Synagogue of America, and Henrietta Szold, once a part-time student at the Seminary, a close friend of the Schechters, founder of *Hadassah,* and American Jewry's greatest contribution to Eretz Israel in the early days of its cultural and spiritual regeneration.

These great figures thought in terms of *K'lal Israel* and sought to bring together the varied elements in American Jewish life. Their familiarity with the American Jewish scene, its intellectual climate, its local customs and institutions, its social problems, its orientation toward Palestine as well as toward the European Jewish communities, its needs and responsibilities, is clearly evidenced by their lives as well as by their written and spoken words.

These leaders are representative of various phases of the Conservative Movement and were themselves exponents of traditional Judaism. Each one has made a contribution which is related to Jewish communal life and has won the esteem of the non-Jewish world as well. The learning and piety of the Jews of Central and Eastern Europe were a part of their heritage and qualified them for their leadership of the masses of immigrants from foreign shores.

The career of Dr. Schechter was one of great historical significance as well as of great human interest. His influence on his contemporaries, both Jewish and non-Jewish, was profound. He revived historical-traditional Judaism and gave it new impetus and purpose—clarifying its goals and relating it to modern philosophy, science and archeology, and to the contemporary American civilization. One will find his writings valid and inspirational for our times as well. Rabbi Herbert Parzen in his *Architects of Conservative Judaism* has set forth in detail Dr. Schechter's ideas. So also has Dr. Bernard Mandelbaum, President of the Seminary, in *The Wisdom of Solomon Schechter.* In *Tradition and Change* by Rabbi Mordecai Waxman, in *The Emergence of Conservative Judaism* by Dr. Moshe Davis, and in *Conservative Judaism, the Legacy of Solomon Schechter* by Rabbi Abraham I. Karp further elaboration of Dr. Schechter's vision and scholarship is to be found. Dr. Elias Solomon writes in this book from the point of view of friend and disciple. He was a President of the United

Synagogue of America which Dr. Schechter founded. Of his founding of the United Synagogue in 1913 Dr. Schechter said, "This will be the greatest bequest that I shall leave to American Israel."

When Dr. Schechter came to the Seminary he planned to make it the greatest center of Jewish learning and scholarship in the world. Men like Judge Mayer Sulzberger gave encouragement. The latter said, "He who has scholarship, talent and enthusiasm may be more appreciated for the first time in our history than he who leads a party." Dr. Schechter's efforts to secure a world renowned faculty and library were most successful. First and foremost was his selection of Dr. Louis Ginzberg, a descendant of the family of the Gaon of Vilna, then a young promising authority on Rabbinic literature, to occupy the chair of Talmud. According to Rabbi Herbert Parzen in his *Architects of Conservative Judaism,* "the role of Professor Louis Ginzberg in the history of Conservative Judaism in this country has been determinative . . . his sway has been subtle and controlling. His influence on the Seminary students from 1902 to 1954 was profound." He was approachable and considerate, and the students and alumni of the Seminary looked upon him with veneration for his scholarly attainments, his convictions, and his piety. The all-embracing nature of his scholarly interests and achievements gave him top ranking in the field of Semitics. From time to time he made public addresses, and for a brief period acted as President of the United Synagogue of America, but he preferred research and teaching and writing in his chosen field—*Halakha.* Dr. Ginzberg inspired respect for the law and its historical development. He showed its application to changing times and circumstances. Through his prestige on the Law Committee of the Rabbinical Assembly he was able to keep the Conservative Movement on an even keel, not foundering because of pressure from the left or the right. He was always the interpreter of the law—not the prosecutor, the judge, or the jury. He tried to keep the Seminary above the heat of the battle. His conservatism was an indication that he did not think the time propitious for radical change of philosophy or ritual without either wide popular support or the sanction of Jewish law and tradition. The writer of the sketch of Dr. Ginzberg's life, Dr. Julius H. Greenstone of Philadelphia, was one of the most scholarly Seminary graduates of the early years, sympa-thetic in point of view, and personally a friend and contemporary of Dr. Ginzberg.

Basic to an understanding of the development of Conservative Judaism in America is an appreciation of the role of Dr. Cyrus Adler, for fifty years one of its outstanding personalities. His importance in the movement stems in part from his background. He was American-born (Van Buren, Arkansas, 1863), educated in Philadelphia under the tutelage of Dr. Sabato Morais and the influence of David and Mayer Sulzberger, his uncles. He was always a devout and observant Jew—a member of the historic Mikve Israel Congregation. Upon graduation from the University of Pennsylvania he went to Johns Hopkins University in Baltimore and was closely associated with its leading Jewish families—the Szolds and Friedenwalds. It is almost impossible to comprehend the breadth of his interests in general American life, and his dynamic leadership in Jewish life. There was practically no area of Jewish endeavor in which he did not have a role of leadership—for example, The American Jewish Committee, the Joint Distribution Committee, The Jewish Welfare Board, The Jewish Publication Society, The American Jewish Historical Society, The Jewish Agency for Palestine. His part as an elder statesman with respect to Jewish rights here and abroad is a record of historical significance. He was a leader of the Philadelphia Jewish community and president of Dropsie College as well as active in public life in that city. Our special interest lies in his direction of the re-organized Seminary after having been the chief architect of its renaissance under Dr. Schechter whom he succeeded as president. He held this office for 25 years. He had the confidence of the men of affairs who led Jewish communal life—Jacob Schiff, Louis Marshall, Felix Warburg and others. They trusted and deferred to him. He was active in the creation of the United Synagogue, serving briefly as president after the death of Dr. Schechter, and continuously on its Executive Council. Along with Dr. Schechter and Dr. Ginzberg he preserved the Seminary's position as interpreter of the historical-traditional school of thought. He was a firm believer in academic freedom, permitting wide differences of opinion in the Seminary faculty. He was a man of strong convictions which he supported regardless of consequence. Not in sympathy with some of the nationalism of the early Zionist leaders and with mass movements they inspired, he met with much opposition and misunderstanding. In the light of history his restraining influence and conservatism may have kept the movement from precipitate action and enabled it to maintain its true character and independence. No one questioned his unique abilities and conscientious efforts in administration. The triumvirate of Schechter, Ginzberg and Adler have collectively determined the course of the Conservative Movement up to this time.

It is most appropriate that the biographical appreciation here included should be written by his successor at the Seminary, Dr. Louis Finkelstein.

Henrietta Szold has already become a legendary romantic figure in modern Jewish history. While she is most closely identified with the early development of Jewish life in Israel and the work of Hadassah, her spiritual and intellectual life and her staunch affirmation of Traditional Judaism are most significant in the history of this period. Her personality, her learning, her vision and her practical creative imagination have been an inspiration to countless numbers of Jewish women here and abroad. Trained by her saintly father, Rabbi Benjamin Szold, she became the most learned Jewess in the United States. Familiar with the writings of Dr. Schechter while he was still at Cambridge University, she delivered an address in 1899 before the Council of Jewish Women in New York City referring to "Catholic Israel," a concept of Dr. Schechter's which she helped to make famous. She became a member of Hebras Zion, Zionist Association of Baltimore, possibly the oldest Zionist Society in the United States, organized three years before Theodore Herzl published *The Jewish State*. Her concept was akin to that of Achad Ha'am. She rebuked Zionism without religion: "Racial Zionism is a revolting anomaly . . . Zionism is at once spiritual, philanthropic, and political, and in good time—diplomatic."

She moved to New York City to be near the Jewish Theological Seminary in which she enrolled as a part-time student while carrying on her arduous duties as Editor of the *Yearbook* and other volumes of the Jewish Publication Society. She lived across the street from the Seminary and was an intimate part of its inner circle. Her home became a center of brilliant and challenging discussion of Jewish books and ideas—of the dynamic group attracted by Dr. Schechter as faculty and kindred spirits. She helped Dr. Ginzberg by translating his *Legends of the Jews* and many of his lectures from German or unidiomatic English. With the Schechter and Adler households she maintained close ties of lasting friendship. It was on a visit to Palestine where she saw the need for a health program, that she found the field in which she could be of greatest service to her people. The account given here by Rabbi Charles I. Hoffman is one by a devoted life-long friend who shared most of her views on Zionism as well as her loyalty to the Seminary and what it stood for.

As we reflect upon the development of the Conservative Movement in this century we may characterize the first quarter as the Schechter era, the second as the Kaplan era, and the current one as the Finkelstein era. Dr. Mordecai Kaplan, a Seminary graduate of 1902, became the founder and head of the Teachers Institute of the Seminary and professor of Homiletics in the Rabbinical Department. He was an inspiring teacher who literally challenged his students to think for themselves, to study the original sources of Jewish tradition, and to face realistically the issues of their times. He himself was influenced greatly by the current intellectual ferment caused by the natural sciences, the social sciences and by philosophy, on the American mind and on society in general. His influence on Seminary students was enormous. They were thrilled by his insight and his creative thinking, and each through personal contact at some time or other came to venerate him and admire his courage, his range of knowledge, and his sincerity in his search for truth. Dr. Kaplan shaped the course of Jewish education by developing a leadership group, which, in posts of responsibility, established Bureaus of Education throughout the country. He likewise had a great influence in the field of Jewish social service and the Jewish Center Movement. The disorganization and fragmentation of Jewish communal life caused him to evolve a new concept of community organization, all embracing in nature and democratic in structure. Dr. Kaplan's unique contribution to Jewish thought stems from his *Judaism as a Civilization*. This monumental work and its later amplifications made Dr. Kaplan a controversial figure with many able supporters and champions as well as adversaries. His place in the

Conservative Movement is analyzed in Chapter 8 of Rabbi Herbert Parzen's *Architects of Conservative Judaism*. There is no question that whether one agreed with him or not he stimulated creative thinking in the American rabbinate and among lay leaders. His attitude toward Rabbinic authority, toward the supernatural origin of the Torah (Revelation) and toward the concept of the "Chosen People" created division in the ranks. However, though offered the presidency of the Jewish Institute of Religion he declined, and worked through the Society for the Advancement of Judaism which he created, and through *The Reconstructionist* magazine.

The appeal of Reconstructionism has been largely an intellectual one and has not captured the masses, who could not grasp its theological implications or were not prepared to accept the personal responsibilities it placed upon them—even though Dr. Kaplan has been an eloquent, convincing and popular protagonist. There was a storm of protest when the Reconstructionist Prayerbook was published, and there have been heated discussions in attempts to liberalize the Conservative position on interpretations of Jewish law in the light of contemporary needs. Today, however, Dr. Kaplan receives from all, the recogniton and homage due him as the most creative Jewish thinker of our times. Dr. Louis Finkelstein, chancellor of the Jewish Theological Seminary, says of Dr. Kaplan: "Today, the philosopher of Jewish survival has become a strategist for world betterment, a creator of a philosophy of peace and understanding among all men and the promoter of a program looking to human unity despite diversity."

Dr. Mortimer J. Cohen and Dr. Joel S. Geffen, outstanding disciples of Dr. Kaplan, discuss various phases of Dr. Kaplan's life and writings with critical perception and full appreciation of his vision and contribution to Jewish thought.

During the second quarter of the century the most distinguished leadership in the pulpit came from Rabbi Milton Steinberg. He was born in Rochester, New York, in 1903. He was influenced strongly by Professor Morris Cohen, while he attended City College, and Dr. Mordecai Kaplan, while he was a student at the Jewish Theological Seminary. Steinberg delved deeply into religious and philosophical issues to discover for himself the answers to problems of the day. His spiritual insight, his clarity of thought, his eloquence in both the written and spoken word, all caught the imagination and the ear of his colleagues and intellectuals seeking new interpretations of Judaism. Steinberg was closely identified with the Reconstructionist group and warmly espoused Dr. Kaplan's program. However, as Arthur A. Cohen, a friend and disciple says, "Although Milton was a programmatic Reconstructionist, an ideological supporter of the movement, he never became a supporter of its theology." Park Avenue Synagogue, New York City, became the forum in which Faith and Reason were preached to a host of followers. American Jewry suffered an irreparable loss in his early passing in 1950. At the end of his *A Partisan Guide to the Jewish Problem* Rabbi Steinberg summarized his faith thus: "Within Jewry today there glows even now a spark, as it were a smoldering ember, of the great flame kindled on high altars in distant days. The Jewish religion, ethic and culture will open up opportunities to Jews for more exalted self-realization, for broader service to mankind. What is required is the imagination, courage and will to keep again an old rendezvous with destiny."

The article by Rabbi Simon Noveck, comes from one uniquely qualified to evaluate Rabbi Steinberg's place in American Jewish life and the extent to which he has shaped the course of Jewish religious thinking.

No survey of the Conservative Movement is complete without reference to its impact on the laymen. The United Synagogue of America has throughout the years sought leadership of men qualified by training, dedication, and vision. None have achieved greater heights and have won wider acclaim than Maxwell Abbell. As he saw it: "The positive Jewish causes involving the education of our youngsters and Jewish religious life are far less acceptable to the so-called leaders. Nevertheless, I felt that if we were to survive as a Jewish group these were the activities that were primary and basic. And so I have dedicated my life to participating in my local synagogue affairs—I have been its president; to local Jewish education where I am a member of the Chicago Board of Jewish Education and chairman of the Board of Governors of the Chicago College of Jewish Studies; and to the Conservative Movement on a national scale. To me the survival of physical Jews is secondary to the survival of Judaism as a religion, and the Jews as a historic group living in the tradition of their ancestors as adjusted to American conditions."

In discussing the role of the Synagogue Abbell wrote: "What is required to make the Synagogue the force that would bring the Jewish traditional ideals into fruitful operation on the American scene? The answer is two-fold—first, a Jewishly educated lay leadership, and second, a breaking down of the isolationism of the individual synagogue . . . The synagogue must be, as it is increasingly becoming, a house of study . . . the synagogue must also become the modern version of the house of assembly, or community center . . . I envision the synagogue being the central Jewish communal agency but not the totality of such agencies . . . *and* still *more* important the spirit of the synagogue and the influence of its teachings should be incorporated into and be an active influence in the lives of the men and women, lay and professional, who guide the destinies of these other Jewish communal organizations and furnish the Jewish communal leadership . . . The synagogue deals with the ultimate values of life, is organized about the family and comprises the totality of personal life, community standards and our hopes for a better world."

As president of the United Synagogue of America he came to realize one of the dilemmas of the Conservative Movement: "There has long been a crying need for bringing our *Halakha* into compatibility with the needs of the modern, fast-changing world. The longer we delay, the more persons we discourage from remaining true to our religion."

His autobiography gives us a picture of his personality. It does not mention his generosity. As Rabbi Ralph Simon of Chicago in *Builders of the Conservative Movement* tells us: "He literally gave away his wealth before he earned it . . . He created the Maxwell and Fannie Abbell Seminary Endowment Fund into which he poured very large sums. His benefactions and personal services extended to Camp Ramah, the World Council of Synagogues, and the Seminary Library . . . In his home library he cherished a special shelf of books which were printed and made available to the world through his financial aid. He bestowed great benefactions upon the Hebrew University . . . he established the Harvard Law School project on cooperative research for Israel's legal development." In a housing settlement he created for religious Jews near Jerusalem, he erected a synagogue in memory of his father. President Eisenhower in 1955 appointed him chairman of the Committee on Government Employment Policy. His untimely death in 1957 left a great void in lay leadership. His personal life reflected the highest ethical standards of Judaism and his public life revealed his depth of compassion and love of fellowman. He truly belongs among the great personalities that have shaped the course of our Jewish contribution to America in this century.

The most recent luminary in the firmament of Conservative Judaism is Dr. Abraham Joshua Heschel, Professor of Ethics and Mysticism at the Jewish Theological Seminary. Descended from a long line of Hassidic leaders, steeped in Rabbinic literature, a man of great spiritual perception and conviction, Heschel possesses a rare grasp of modern philosophy and of contemporary social problems. His philosophy of religion contained in his *Man is Not Alone* is a far cry from the anti-intellectual faith and fervor of the Hassidic zealots in America or in Israel, now that the East European centers have vanished. He has given Hassidism new interpretation and significance for our times. The influence of *Judische Wissenschaft* and of Buber and Rosenzweig are apparent. His originality, his creative thinking, and the lyric quality of his English prose have attracted wide attention in Christian as well as in Jewish circles. His recent work, *The Prophets,* gives a fresh approach to the prophetic message. His strictures on Prayer, The Sabbath, Halakha and Agada, on Religion and Modern Society, all indicate the wide range of his writing. Among his books are *God in Search of Man, Man's Quest for God* and *The Earth is the Lord's.* His *Theology of Ancient Judaism* in two volumes was published in 1963 and *The Insecurity of Freedom* in 1966.

Heschel was born in Warsaw, Poland, in 1897, where he grew up in an atmosphere of piety and learning. His paternal ancestry goes back to Rabbi Dov Ber of Meseritz, successor of the Baal Shem, founder of Hassidism. On the maternal side he traced his ancestry to Rabbi Levi Isaac of Berditschev. At the age of twenty he went to the University of Berlin and the Hochschule für die Wissenschaft des Judenthums. After receiving his Ph.D. in 1933 and writing a biographical work on Maimonides (1935), he succeeded Martin Buber (1937) in the Central Organization for Adult Education and Judische Lehrhaus, founded by Franz Rosenzweig in Frankfurt on-the-Main. Upon the Nazi persecutions in 1938 he went back briefly to Warsaw and then to the Institute for Jewish Learning in London. In 1940 he became Associate Professor of Philosophy and Rabbinics at the Hebrew Union College in Cincinnati, and in 1945 joined the faculty of the Jewish Theological Seminary. He is not the cloistered scholar, but one profoundly moved by problems affecting the Jewish people, their plight in the Soviet Union, their position on human rights, their lack of a sustaining inner sense of security. An excellent book entitled *Between God and Man,* an interpretation of Judaism, contains excerpts from Heschel's writings, selected, edited and introduced by Fritz A. Rothschild (1959).

The writer of the article on Dr. Heschel is Rabbi Herbert Parzen, author of *Architects of Conservative Judaism.*

M. D. H.

SOLOMON SCHECHTER

Personal Reminiscences

ELIAS L. SOLOMON

This article cannot possibly aim to be a comprehensive study of the great man, scholar, teacher, author and leader whose many-sided personality, brilliant intellect, encyclopedic learning, unequalled mastery of Rabbinics, and prodigious contributions to Jewish letters were such that Israel Zangwill declared that he never met such a wonderful combination of learning, wit and spiritual magnetism as that presented by Schechter, and Joseph Jacobs wrote that if there was a Jewish genius in our time it was Solomon Schechter.

HIS REMARKABLE APPEARANCE

His very appearance marked the extraordinary man. The venerable presence, the handsome noble countenance, the flowing beard, the merry twinkle in his blue eyes—all this made him an unforgettable figure and impressed all beholders alike. When Harvard University honored him with a degree, a gentleman in the audience, struck by the majestic figure on the platform, turned to a lady sitting beside him and asked, "Who is that remarkable looking man?" The lady, whom he did not know and who was none other than Mrs. Schechter, replied softly, "Only my husband."

NO ARTIST TO PAINT HIM

To give a complete picture of the man would require volumes, in addition to the excellent one written by Norman Bentwich for the Golden Jubilee of the Jewish Publication Society of America in 1938. Abraham Yaari in the Preface to his little volume of Solomon Schechter's Letters (to Samuel Poznanski) printed in Jerusalem in 1943, laments: "Unfortunately, no Rembrandt was found to paint him." Once only did an artist, Mielziner, succeed in capturing and fixing on the canvas the characteristic mood of the sage, the beauty and nobility of his countenance, the quizzical smile of the master, when, arrayed in the red gown of a Cambridge University "Don," he presided at Seminary Commencements. Then Doctor Schechter presented indeed the "Mar'eh Kohen," the aspect of the High Priest so ecstatically described in Ben Sira, the Hebrew original of which apocryphal book was Schechter's great find—a discovery which led to the unearthing of the Cairo Genizah treasure trove of books and manuscripts, and which at once brought him to the forefront of world scholars by reason of the new light its treasures were to shed on many an obscure passage in Jewish literature and on many a period of Jewish history.

"Happy the eyes that saw that glorious vision!" Happy the ears that were privileged to hear the words of wisdom and brilliant wit that issued as an ever-flowing fountain from that Sage, "unique in his generation."

PERSONAL REMINISCENCES

This brief article only aims to give a few reminiscences of Doctor Schechter by one who had the inestimable privilege to know him during the last thirteen years of his life, which he spent in this country as President of the Jewish Theological Seminary, and towards the end of which period he founded the United Synagogue of America. The writer was in the first class of four students graduated by Doctor Schechter from the Seminary (1904), and enjoyed close association with the Master during that entire period. This circumstance afforded the writer the opportunity to observe the great teacher at close range, on occasion of his public appearances, as well as in the classroom, in his home, and at gatherings of friends. It is on the basis of this association that this article attempts to fill the outline of our Master, with a few intimate glimpses and personal reminiscences as well as some appropriate observations anent our leader's character and views.

His monumental contributions to all branches of Jewish literature, history, theology and lore as well as Halakha, his brilliant, graphic sketches of Jewish life and men, I do not attempt to appraise. As to these there is ample testimony of noted scholars both here and abroad. Professor Louis Ginzberg sums it up thus: "It is no exaggeration to say that there is hardly any branch of Jewish literature, the knowledge of which was not enriched, any period of Jewish history upon which new light was not thrown by Doctor Schechter's studies and his discoveries." Men of opposing schools of thought joined in this estimate. Dr. Kaufman Kohler wrote of him that he awakened a new zeal and love for Jewish learning and a new interest in Jewish literature in all circles, that he brought about a revival of Jewish learning in this country.

NEED OF A BOSWELL

I deeply regret that none of us who, as his students and friends, had the precious opportunity to serve as his Boswell, had the foresight to endeavor to preserve the wealth of wise and pithy sayings, the brilliant sallies, the innumerable bon mots that flowed incessantly from the lips of the Master. Norman Bentwich is correct when he says: "If ever there was a Jewish sage who should have had a Boswell to record his daily sayings, it was Schechter. The essence and genius of the man were shown as much by the table-talk and the explosive conversation as by the written work or the scholarly lecture."

His lectures on the platform as well as in the classroom coruscated with wisdom and were illumined and enlivened by lightning flashes of wit. His very digressions and side-remarks, and they were numerous, were a rich source of instruction and an endless delight. His ingenious word coinages will remain for us a precious heirloom. Amongst the most famous phrases of his invention are: Catholic Israel, Higher Criticism—Higher Anti-Semitism. Rebellion against being a Problem. "A great nation" (a Schechterian euphemism for "a big goy"). "Amateur Gentile." "Jews by profession only."

HIS WIT AND HUMOR

Even his table-talk, his ordinary conversation, his chit-chat, was interspersed with witticisms of a delightful and instructive kind. His humorous propensities he inherited from his father who he said was a saint and never uttered a harsh word. "I am a ruffian, my father was a gentleman."

ANECDOTES

Several anecdotes, selected at random and illustrative of Schechter's humor will no doubt be interesting:

A rather widely-known incident is that of his meeting with a young Reform rabbi. In course of the conversation, Schechter offered the young man a cigar. "Thank you, Professor," said the young man, "but I don't smoke." "You don't smoke," countered Doctor Schechter in pretended astonishment, "what do you do on Shabbas?"

On another occasion when introduced to an elderly member of the Faculty of a Reform rabbinical college, he said to him: 'I have heard of you. I always thought you were a young shaigetz, but I see that you are "ein alter goy."

While attending a meeting one time in the social hall of Temple Emanuel in New York, Doctor Schechter lit a cigarette. "Excuse me, Doctor," timidly whispered a shocked member present, "but we do not permit smoking on the Temple premises." "Well," nonchalantly replied Schechter, "this is not the first law of the Shulchan Aruch broken here."

The shafts of his sarcasm were directed impartially also against the so-called Orthodox, when occasion demanded. He criticized those of the older generation who were content to go their way and made no effort to imbue the youth with Jewish loyalty. "These people," he said, "are interested in their own selfish salvation." Men who stubbornly refused to listen to reason and become enlightened, he called "Zaddikim le'hachlis"—"saints out of spite." Arguing with an uncompromising Orthodox rabbi about the use by Jews of wine not specially prepared for ritual purposes, he humorously remarked, "I draw the line at good wine."

Many still remember the profound impression Schechter made on his hosts of the Hebrew Union College at Cincinnati at the dedication of their new building when, borrowing from English political life, he wittily referred to the Reform party as "his Majesty's Opposition."

To Doctor Cyrus Adler he once wrote: "Something should be

done to show people that ignorance is not the best accomplishment for a Jewish minister."

He severely condemned the non-religious secular Nationalists who while advocating the cultivation of Hebrew as an integral part of the National Jewish culture, yet were indifferent or even hostile to religious Judaism. "Bacon," he declared, "is just as *trefa* in Hebrew as in any other language."

A pietist once took him to task for reciting a short form of the Grace after dinner at a hotel where he was summering. Schechter retorted: "For such a dinner, it is enough." At the same hotel another guest bent on making conversation said with unwarranted familiarity to Prof. Schechter: "How is the old lady?" "What do you mean, old lady?" snorted Schechter. "Either you say, your wife, or Mrs. Schechter, or you don't have to say anything."

His absent-mindedness, a common trait of great men, was a constant source of amusement to those around him. In the dining room of a hotel one day, he suddenly reminded himself that it was Friday. "Boy," he called out to the porter, "here, polish my boots for Shabbas," and kicking off his shoes right there and then, he sat down in a chair in the center of the dining room and became absorbed in his book, oblivious of the guests still at the table.

On one occasion when the writer, at Schechter's invitation, read a paper before the Senior Class of the Seminary on the subject of the Synagogue in America, the Master with characteristic magnanimity said: "This is perhaps the best lecture on the subject I have heard." When the audience politely applauded the compliment, Doctor Schechter slyly added : "I said, perhaps." The effect of this sally on the audience and the speaker can be imagined.

The so-called "Painted Bible," of Paul Haupt, Professor at Johns Hopkins University, was dubbed by him, "the Jezebel Bible." The reference was to Ahab's Queen Jezebel, who resorted to paint to find favor in the eyes of Jehu.

STORMS AND SUNSHINE

His angry outbursts, and they were frequent, for he felt deeply, were brief storms immediately followed by sunshine, the sunshine of his delightful, disarming humor. All knew he was devoid of malice, harbored no grudge, but out of love for truth, for his religion and his people, was moved by righteous indignation, to protest and denounce on occasions. And his expletives surely were vivid and picturesque, a source of merriment as well as instructive.

His very idiosyncrasies and human weaknesses coupled with his charming good nature, his hearty, jovial laugh, infectious smile, Johnsonian humor and merry twinkle, helped to make him universally beloved. And he was humble. Whereas others would have been made vain and haughty by such honors as were heaped upon him by the greatest universities in the world like Harvard, Cambridge and London, he would remark with charming humility: "I am getting more honor than is good for me."

Prof. Alexander Marx, in an article quotes Schechter's friend, Sir James G. Frazer, famous author of the "Golden Bough," as saying: "It would be difficult to say whether he was more admirable for the brilliance of his intellect and the readiness of his wit, or for the warmth of his affection and the generosity and nobility of his character, but I think it was the latter qualities even more than his genius which endeared him to his friends."

Doctor Schechter was a wonderfully compassionate man and a wonderfully just man, the embodiment of "Chesed Ve'emeth" "loving kindness and truth," virtues for which he pleaded so eloquently. His kindness extended to young and old, to men of every rank, class and condition. His love for children was touching to behold. On Saturdays, he would be followed by a flock of children, for they knew that if they said "Good Shabbas, Doctor Schechter!", they would be rewarded with a piece of candy of which he always carried a supply for that purpose.

His helpfulness and generosity were shown also in his prodigal sharing of his vast knowledge with others. His friends and colleagues knew him as an "intellectual spendthrift," as a "general notebook for scholars."

As pater familias, as husband, father and brother, he was most resplendent.

THE PERFECT HELPMATE

Incidentally, I have in my possession copies of two letters which Schechter in his early manhood wrote a friend in Focsani, Roumania, his native town, in which he describes the kind of woman he would like to have as wife. The lady he ultimately married, Mathilde Roth, of Breslau, fully measured up to Schechter's ideal of the perfect helpmate. She it was who later founded and was first president of, the Woman's League of the United Synagogue of America.

THE UNIFIER

Schechter's great ambition as lover and champion of K'lal Yisrael, his "catholic Israel," was to be the unifier of his people. He rejected the proposal of Doctor Judah L. Magnes that a third party, the Conservative, be created in Jewry. He was averse to parties, cared not for partisan labels. He was interested only in catholic Israel. As Professor Louis Ginzberg expressed it, " 'catholic Israel' was with him more than a happy phrase—it reflected his soul." He was gratified, as he states in the Preface to his "Seminary Addresses," that "it will be found that the ultimate goal at which we are aiming is union and peace in American Israel. The union of which I am thinking is not one of mere organization . . . The union we are in need of is one of principle and the recognition of vital facts, decisive in our past and indispensable for our safety in the future, by which alone Israel can hope for a 'name and a remainder upon the earth' . . . The longer I live in this country, the more I am convinced that it is only such a thorough and hearty union which will enable us to deal with the great problems, spiritual and otherwise, confronting us. Parties come and parties go, but the word of our God shall stand forever. And so shall Israel."

THE GREAT CONSERVATIVE

Schechter was the great conservative, the foremost exponent of Conservative Judaism of his day. Doctor Kohler said: "He made enlightened Conservatism more powerful, more popular in the East, nay, fashionable." He was gratified by the conservative spirit that permeated the Seminary. "It is taught by the Professors in the classroom; it is expounded in the pulpit by the majority of our alumni; it is propagated by its friends both in writing and by word of mouth on every occasion." In the Preface to his "Seminary Addresses," he cautions against the danger of "incessant innovations which must in the end touch the very vital organism of Judaism." We can readily understand what his attitude would be towards the extreme radical and sensational views occasionally promulgated in our day.

In the light of his pronounced conservatism, it is safe to say that he would condemn most vigorously the vagaries of some of his disciples, with respect to certain fundamental doctrines of Judaism. He was, it is true, no heresy hunter. He would extend to anyone the freedom, religious, intellectual, academic which he demanded for himself (and his fearlessness, originality and independence of judgment were amongst his most noted characteristics). But he would undeniably repudiate with all his great force views and statements misrepresentative or subversive of doctrines fundamental to the historic Faith, of which he was the foremost champion of his day. For him no truckling to ill-digested, half-baked truths, new-fangled slogans on the lips of glib orators, "wind bags" as he denominated them, men in love with their own fine phrases, fascinated by a pseudo-scientific terminology, borrowed from Philosophy, Sociology, Pedagogy, Anthropology and what not—a modern sophistry, negative and destructive, which confuses, misleads and befuddles the simple-minded, naive and ignorant, flatters the vanity of the self-styled "intellectuals," while leaving the serious thinker, the thorough-going student, the well-informed, truly learned, irritated and disgusted.

WISE ADMONITIONS

His addresses to the graduates of the Seminary always contained admonitions with regard to the special virtues expected from the spiritual leaders in Israel such as humility, meekness, peacefulness and considerateness. These he constantly preached and exemplified in his own life. It is hard to believe that men who came under his brilliant tutelage and within the sphere of his benign influence could fail to make these virtues their own.

REORGANIZATION OF THE SEMINARY

The Seminary founded by Morais in 1886 did not succeed in gaining adequate financial support. Only when it was reorganized by a coterie of communal leaders consisting of Jacob H. Schiff, Judge Mayer Sulzberger, Louis Marshall, Felix Warburg and others, who succeeded in bringing Professor Schechter here from England to head the Institution, did the Seminary achieve its rightful place as a great institution of Jewish learning.

Doctor Schechter surrounded himself with eminent scholars like Prof. Louis Ginzberg, Prof. Alexander Marx, the martyred Israel Friedlaender, and the recently departed Israel Davidson. He created the great library, now the greatest Jewish library in the world. He established the Teachers' Institute. And, being a man of action as well as the scholar and teacher, he quickly perceived the importance of an organization, a movement for the promotion and preservation of traditional Judaism, and therefore founded the United Synagogue of America. Under the sainted Cyrus Adler and since then, under Professor Louis Finkelstein, the Seminary has grown and expanded so that it now includes the Museum of Jewish Religious Objects, the Institute of Religious Studies, the Academy for Adult Jewish Studies and the Laymen's Institute of Jewish affairs, and has come to be recognized as one of the foremost institutions of higher Jewish learning in the world, a veritable University of Judaism.

THE UNITED SYNAGOGUE

Similarly, the United Synagogue has grown from the small organization of 22 congregations which responded to Dr. Schechter's call in February 22, 1913, into an organization comprising 400 congregations, 350 sisterhoods, grouped together under the National Women's League, 76 Brotherhoods, comprising the National Federation of Jewish Men's Clubs, and the Young People's League, quite a substantial organization endowed with the potential power to prove itself the effective instrument for strengthening and preserving Judaism in America, which was envisaged by the Founder. In every direction, in every enterprise engaged in by the Seminary and the United Synagogue there is clearly manifest the guiding and inspiring influence of the peerless leader and teacher, the immortal Professor Solomon Schechter.

HIS BENJAMIN

I may be permitted, in closing, to stress the importance of the United Synagogue, the Benjamin of Doctor Schechter's old age, which Chief Rabbi Hertz considers "the culminating achievement of his life" and which Doctor Schechter expected would be his "greatest legacy to American Israel." This is well expressed in the following words penned by Joseph Jacobs: "Above all, he was the first president and the abiding influence of the United Synagogue which represents in the practical religious life the Richtung which he represented in contemporary Judaism and by the success or failure of which, his permanent influence in the religious sphere will ultimately be measured.

"There are many signs that the position of the United Synagogue is that which is being adopted by the lay public throughout the United States towards practical Judaism. There is certainly reaction from the extremes of Reform among the middle-aged who have seen how little the Reform services and principles attract the young members to its intellectualism and want of imaginative attraction. On the other side the more rigid forms of Orthodoxy are equally repelling the rising generation by its want of elasticity and general unadaptability to American conditions.

"Between the two, the position of the United Synagogue could steer its way with great effectiveness and appeal both to the Orthodox who are drifting from the sterner forms of the faith and the Reformed who are coming back to the more human side of ceremonialism. When this position of the United Synagogue is more clearly appreciated by the Jewish public, it will gradually become more and more popular and a permanent monument to the insight and influence of Solomon Schechter." It is incumbent on his friends and disciples to continue to build that monument to the sage, master and saint in Israel.

The Torch, September, 1945.

Dr. Solomon (1879–1956), a tireless exponent of Conservative Judaism, served as a Rabbi in New York City for fifty years. He helped to found the United Synagogue of America and was its president from 1918 to 1926. He also was president of the Synagogue Council of America.

LOUIS GINZBERG

An Appreciation

JULIUS H. GREENSTONE

"His work divided among a dozen scholars would make each one great. Half of that dozen would be busy a lifetime with various branches of Rabbinic literature—tannaitic, amoraic and geonic; the other half would have to divide themselves in the fields of Hellenic literature, the Midrashim, the liturgy, the sectaries, folklore and philology. Professor Ginzberg has made contributions of first magnitude to all these branches of learning with mastery of erudition, with originality of treatment and with profundity of critical acumen."

These words spoken by Dr. Louis M. Epstein at the Commencement exercises of the Jewish Theological Seminary last June, which inaugurated the celebration of Professor Ginzberg's seventieth birthday anniversary, were not merely the utterances of a devoted and intimate friend of many years' standing who was carried away by his affection and reverence to indulge in exaggerations and hyperboles. The statement is literally true and would readily be attested to by thousands of students here and abroad; and especially by a generation of disciples who sat at his feet and imbibed of his wisdom, whereby their horizon was extended and their knowledge deepened. The graduates of the Jewish Theological Seminary of the last forty years, as well as the much larger circle of Jewish and non-Jewish scholars, are not only grateful for Dr. Ginzberg's numerous contributions in the various fields of Jewish and related scholarship, but stand in awe and reverence before his genius and grasp of the wide and intricate fields of knowledge in which he has manifested his greatness and erudition.

Ginzberg's genius showed itself in his early childhood, when he was living in the limited spheres of the Lithuanian Jewish milieu and was given the intensive training, zealously watched over by a scholarly father and a number of distinguished relatives, all of whom discerned in him the great intellectual powers which became evident in later years. The training in the wide range of Rabbinic literature which he received in his youth permitted his native talents to develop in an extraordinary manner and the coveted appellation of *Iluy* (genius) was given to him by his teachers and fellow students. With the removal of his parents to Amsterdam, although they preferred to leave their son in Vilna where he had been immersed in his studies, young Louis eventually also found his way to Holland and the course of his life assumed a new phase. Without relinquishing his interest in the subjects to which he had devoted himself from his early childhood, he was initiated into secular learning, first in Frankfurt-on-the-Main and later in Berlin. Mathematics and Physics attracted him at first, but he soon recognized that in order to excel in the realm of his choice he would have to devote himself to the acquisition of an extensive knowledge in the oriental languages and literatures. When he reached the age of 21, he traveled to Kovno to discharge his military obligation, but was set free because of physical inadequacy. While tarrying in the environment of his childhood, he obtained the Rabbinical diploma (*Semichah*) from several eminent rabbis. Instead of returning to Berlin, he took up his further studies in Strassbourg, under the famous orientalist, Theodore Noeldeke. After four years of attendance at that university, he was given the degree of doctor of philosophy, cum laude, and then returned to his home in Amsterdam.

Ginzberg was not attracted to the rabbinical profession, either of the type of his native land or of the type of the German rabbis, although he might have been an outstanding member in either group. It was his ambition to lead the scholarly life and to devote himself entirely to research in the fields of Jewish learning in which he showed himself the expert already then. He continued his studies at Amsterdam both by himself in Jewish learning and also at the University there, waiting for an opportunity which would make it possible for him to utilize his vast erudition and his native faculties to the best advantage. Through the recommendation of Professor Noeldeke, he received an invitation from Dr. Isaac M. Wise, the President of the Hebrew Union College in

Cincinnati, to come to America and teach at that institution. Ginzberg accepted the invitation and proceeded to America, where a brother had preceded him. He arrived in New York in 1899, but as he stepped off the boat, his brother handed him a letter, written by Dr. I. M. Wise's secretary, informing him that the governing board of the college refused to endorse the recommendation of its president. He felt the disappointment rather keenly and this may have contributed to his breakdown which made him go to a hospital for several weeks to recuperate.

It was at that time that the project for a Jewish Encyclopedia in English was assuming form and the young scholar who had meanwhile become known and admired by a number of the Jewish scholars in America was asked to join the staff of writers. Dr. Marcus Jastrow, of Philadelphia, was the editor of the Talmudic department of that great undertaking and Ginzberg was naturally attached to that department. Dr. Jastrow, who was then completing his work on the Talmudic dictionary, entertained the deepest admiration for Ginzberg's extensive scholarship, his prodigious memory and his originality of thought. He often spoke to the present writer of the marvelous genius of the young scholar and he confidently handed over to him the work of editing the articles of others besides the numerous articles which were assigned to him. Some of these articles constitute regular treatises which displayed his extensive scholarship and skillful treatment.

With the reorganization of the Jewish Theological Seminary in 1902, under the leadership of Solomon Schechter, who was brought here from England, Louis Ginzberg joined the reconstituted faculty. A most favorable field of scholarly activity was thus opened to him in the association of congenial spirits such as Dr. Schechter, the versatile and recognized scholar whose reputation preceded him, and later Professors Israel Friedlander and Alexander Marx, who came to the Seminary at Schechter's invitation. He devoted himself with all his zeal to teaching and study and did both of these with happy eagerness and under most favorable circumstances. He devoted himself to research with his wonted assiduity and produced a series of works in every branch of Rabbinic learning, each of which was characterized by originality of thought, honesty of purpose and familiarity not only with the entire range of Jewish learning, but also with the classic literatures of the nations of antiquity.

The first serious study which displayed his marvelous powers of memory and originality of thought was in the field of the Rabbinic Agada, that large branch of Jewish productivity in which imagination and popular fancy are predominant. His doctorate dissertation was a study of the use made of the Agada by the Church Fathers, and this appeared serially in a scientific periodical in Germany. In this study, Ginzberg revealed his wide knowledge of the sources of the patristic literature in Greek and Latin, as well as Ethiopic and other languages, and showed his industry in unearthing the most obscure fragments and giving them vitality and pregnant meaning. This was not an amateurish work, as most doctorate dissertations are, but an original and important contribution to a subject which has engaged the Jewish mind for many centuries and in which are hidden the longings and hopes of a people. His interest in this branch of learning occupied his mind also in later years, as evidenced by his numerous articles on this subject in the Jewish Encyclopedia and in his monumental work, "The Legends of the Jews," consisting of four volumes of texts, two volumes of notes, and one volume of Indices, the last prepared by his disciple and now his colleague, Dr. Boaz Cohen. The main concern of the author was to make available to the average intelligent student the fanciful products of the Jewish genius as it dwelt on the events and the characters of the Bible. The arrangement is in accordance with the chronology of the Bible, the language is smooth and the contents are absorbingly interesting. The work, published by the Jewish Publication Society, has become the classic in its line, although many other attempts have been made in this direction before and after its appearance. The two volumes of notes will continue to arouse the admiration of scholars, for in them the real genius of the author, his wide range of knowledge of the sources and his originality of thought become most manifest. Other more technical studies in the Agada were produced by him in his later writings, notably the two bulky volumes of Genizah texts and studies in the series of Ginze Schechter.

While the Agada reflected the emotions and the poetry of the

Jewish soul, it was in the Halakha that their life struggles, their economic and social relationships were truly mirrored. It is in this branch of learning that Ginzberg finds himself most at home. His keen historic sense and his familiarity with the most obscure sources make his studies in the Halakha most valuable and outstanding. He is never satisfied with secondary material and he never follows blindly the results of the investigations made by others. Staunchly conservative in thought, he still refuses to take the words of his predecessors, even the most recognized authorities, without first submitting them to analysis and criticism. Frequently, after much research and painstaking investigation, he comes to the conclusion that the traditional attitude was the correct one and that the doubts cast upon it by modern students are unreal and their theories have no basis in fact. In his studies of the Mishnah and of the early tannaitic texts, he often inclines to the adoption of the generally held opinions, but in his hands, these traditional views assume reality and force which they never had before.

His outstanding contributions in the field of the Halakha deal with the much neglected study of the Jerusalem Talmud, to which he was drawn, when still a youth, studying under the guidance of the great Lithuanian Rabbis, but the first manifestation of that interest was made after the discovery by Schechter of the Cairo Genizah, where a large number of fragments of the Jerusalem Talmud were found. The publication of a volume of these fragments with his comments made him at once the outstanding authority on the subject and at the same time turned his attention completely to that corner of Jewish intellectual production which has been a terra incognita even to some of the most prominent teachers and scholars of past generations. He was prompted to edit and comment on the Jerusalem Talmud, a gigantic enterprise, and the first three bulky volumes appeared about a year ago. The magnitude of the work may be gauged by the fact that these volumes do not quite cover the first treatise of the Talmud and that there are at least three more orders (Sedarim), including numerous treatises, in this version of the Talmud. We understand that Professor Ginzberg has practically the entire manuscript ready for the printer.

The discovery of the Genizah also stimulated him to delve into that important branch of Jewish literature—the Geonic Responsa. The two volumes of responsa fragments which he published cover numerous subjects of ritual, economics, history and law with which the Geonim had to deal in their endeavors to enlighten their brethren throughout the Diaspora for a period of more than five centuries. Of course, the Talmud was the main source of their decisions and one had to be thoroughly familiar with the Talmud and the other Rabbinic works preceding it in order to understand fully the Geonic arguments and conclusions.

Ginzberg has often been called upon to deliver popular lectures to mixed audiences. His erudition and skill manifested themselves also in these addresses, several of which have been issued in book form and enjoyed an extensive popularity. The originality of his mind and the depth of his great love for learning, as well as his powers of judgment in appraising personalities and events become patent in his popular studies even as in his scholarly works. The master mind is equally in action in either domain. A significant study was issued by him after the discovery by Dr. Schechter of a Genizah fragment which appeared as a sort of code of a Jewish sect of an early period. This manuscript was published and Ginzberg's study of it takes up a large volume, written in German, which deals with the entire subject of Jewish sectaries, especially during the waning years of the Second Commonwealth. With his wonted thoroughness and wide sweep of knowledge of the literature, he establishes the origin of this sect, its trend of thought and the reasons for its deviation from the established mode of religious life of that time.

Proclaimed by the scholarly world as the foremost student of Rabbinics in our generation, showered with honors by seats of learning here and elsewhere, Professor Ginzberg has maintained the modesty of the true scholar. He strives to help the humblest student in his work. His aid is in constant demand by students as well as by institutions of learning, and he is always ready to give of his time and thought to help others in their work. It is not always possible for a man whose powers of thought and judgment are so widely recognized and appreciated to remain entirely a closet student, but Ginzberg has succeeded in keeping out of communal squabbles and public works. He did not hesitate to make his point of view known, especially in matters relating to the basic philosophy of Judaism, but he kept clear from factionalism of any kind and is the spokesman of no particular ideology, except of the Jewish religious life and mode of thought of all the past ages. In his personal life he is observant of every Jewish custom and tradition and has been adamant in maintaining the traditional concept of Jewish religious philosophy. His relation to his pupils has been of the most cordial type throughout the two score of years of his connection with the Seminary and there is none of the graduates or the students who has not the highest regard and the deepest affection for him, even though some may differ with him in their interpretation of Judaism. His house is always open to them and his services are freely given to them.

On reaching his seventieth birthday anniversary, Dr. Ginzberg is assured of an important position in the gallery of Jewish scholars of all times and of the highest admiration and devotion of his contemporaries.

The Torch, November, 1943.

Dr. Greenstone (1873–1955), Rabbi, Scholar and Educator, was a key figure in the work of Gratz College, Phila., Pa. for fifty years and was on the editorial staff of The Jewish Exponent. *He was the author of* The Jewish Religion *and several Commentaries on books of* The Bible. *He founded and was first president of the Board of Jewish Education, Philadelphia Branch, United Synagogue of America.*

CYRUS ADLER

A Biographical Appreciation

LOUIS FINKELSTEIN

Nothing is more common in the western world than struggle and conflict. The strife among groups and nations which occupies the headlines of newspapers is only a small part of the total. There is even more widespread struggle among individual men and women. And the most universal of all is the struggle within the individual. Virtually all of us are heirs to conflicting influences, which have never been fully harmonized. Our personalities are rough mixtures of antipathetic elements. We are not only combinations of Dr. Jekyll and Mr. Hyde; each of us is a whole congress of Jekylls and Hydes; and most curiously few of us can distinguish the Jekylls from the Hydes who compose our particular congress.

Yet from time to time, the western world produces an individual in whom, to use the Shakespearean phrase, "the elements are so mixed," that he is a real unit. He is not a physical mixture, but a chemical compound. Each part of his personality is a miniature of the whole. Each of his actions reflects the sterling quality of the whole man. We know that no stress or trouble will break him, for the combined elements in him can no longer be separated. When he speaks, his words do not belie his character. The pressures of suffering may crush him, as the achievement of success may expand him; but neither can change him. Such a man was Cyrus Adler.

Cyrus Adler was the evolutionary product of a tradition of many centuries perfected in the light of American freedom. He was a thorough Jew, meticulous in his devotion to Jewish law and life. He was also a thorough American, equally meticulous in his love of his country. The element in his character which impelled him to summon his last energies, to rise from a bed of fatal illness to answer the call of the President of the United States, was precisely that which had moved him to ask that an appointment

33

which the President had fixed for the Sabbath be changed for a weekday.

The passion for accuracy and detail which made him so remarkable and effective an administrator was also reflected in the high standards of scholarship he helped maintain in the institution of learning which he headed. The common failing of our time— the double standard, one for others, and another for oneself, was quite lacking in him. He could not do unto others what he would not have others do unto him; for his judgment of what was right was not subjective and emotional, but as objective as any human decision can be. He approached each problem with all his intellectual and emotional resources. Since he was confident that his decisions had been taken in the light of the known facts and the moral standards fixed by untold generations of wise and saintly men, they were binding on him, despite the temptations which might move lesser men.

The rare consistency of Doctor Adler's character and personality is the key to the mystery of his life. No man in modern times who has been exposed to such fame has escaped so completely unscathed. Cyrus Adler at the climax of his career, in the last years of his life, famous throughout the world as educator, scholar, administrator, humanitarian, and diplomat, was as shy and self-critical, as astonished at words of commendation, and as hungry for affection as he had been in his youth. The man to whom President Wilson shouted an informal and affectionate, "Hello, Adler," when the President's triumphal party passed Dr. Adler's house on Broad Street, Philadelphia, was moved by this personal tribute of affection and friendship; but there was no glow of pride such as most men might feel at such recognition by the great and powerful.

Through his many associations, Dr. Adler for several decades was one of the most powerful figures in Jewish public life in America. But though power corrupts, as Lord Acton stated, Dr. Adler remained uncorrupted; for if he had power, he was utterly unaware of it. For twenty-five years he was president of the Seminary Faculty. During all the time that I sat on this Faculty with him, I do not recall a single decision which was taken against the will even of a substantial minority. The Faculty shared in the responsibilities for appointments and promotions; its members were consulted about major steps in administration and development of the institution; no honorary degree was conferred except by unanimous agreement. When at a meeting of the United Synagogue of America, a vote was taken which would have compelled him as President of the organization to act against his convictions, he resigned. But he remained a devoted worker in the ranks of the organization. He attended all the conventions of the Rabbinical Assembly, so long as his health permitted it; but only rarely would he comment on any of the issues which arose. He felt he belonged there as a lay observer, being the head of the institution which trained rabbis. But he came to learn, rather than to instruct.

His eagerness to benefit by criticism and his utter lack of any sense of humiliation in being corrected, became a source of great moral strength in a crisis. Thus I recall that at one of the meetings of the Rabbinical Assembly, an alumnus of the Seminary, angered at some failure of the institution, excoriated Dr. Adler in unmeasured terms. Not only was Dr. Adler's reply temperate and *cooly* didactic, but later in discussing the incident with me he remarked, "Young X is a man of great promise. His speech was excellent both in logic and in rhetoric." Mr. J. B. Abrahams (who was his secretary for many years), told me that in the first days of the re-organized Seminary, when Dr. Adler had served for a time as president of the Board, he received a visit from a man by the name of Joseph Silverstein. a former student of the Yeshiva of Slobodka, who had left Talmudic studies to engage in philosophical pursuits. This Joseph Silverstein was piqued at not having been appointed to the Faculty of the Seminary, and for forty-five minutes poured out vials of undiluted wrath on the head of Dr. Adler, whom he held responsible for the omission. When he finished his tirade, Dr. Adler simply remarked, "If you have finished, all I can do is to wish you good health and good morning."

Judge Mayer Sulzberger, who was Dr. Adler's uncle, and very proud of him, had remarked on this rare self-control, which he said he could not emulate. But the temperateness of Doctor Adler in the face of provocation was more than self-control. Dr. Adler was so eager to be set right that he heard the criticism, not the vituperation. When he read an angry letter, he was so concerned to

get the meat of the criticism that he overlooked the personalities
just as when he read a letter of commendation, he wanted too
much to get the constructive point to be moved by any flattery.

In the course of the years in which we worked together, there
were of course inevitable differences of opinion between us. But
they never divided us. The most serious of them developed at the
very beginning of our friendship. I had just completed the work
which was to be published as "Jewish Self-Government in the
Middle Ages." He read it, and made some minor criticisms, but
he disliked the title very much, because it might help to suggest
to the reader that the Jews today were seeking an *imperium in
imperio*. We talked over our differences of view, and neither of us
was able to change the other's opinion. The book was to be published under the imprint of the Seminary. I asked him whether,
in view of our irreconcilable differences on the subject, he was
willing to have the Seminary give its imprint to the book. "Of
course," he said, "Professor Marx has recommended it as a piece
of research. I have given you my advice. If you do not choose to
take it, that is your business, and not the Seminary's."

This passion for academic freedom was more than a rule of
thumb for convenient and efficient institutitional administration
in a democracy. He had the traditional Jewish respect for deviation from the norm, knowing that the deviation of one generation may well become the norm of the next. It is one of the para-
doxes of life that great scholars are the least angered by criticism
and correction; that just men are most responsive to reproof of
occasional injustice; and that men of the most profound faith are
the last to become vehement against the skeptical. Their awareness of the depth of their own convictions, gives them a sense of
security which leaves no room for emotional reactions to lack of
faith.

They know, too, that somehow, in the providence of God, even
deviation becomes ultimately a means for deepening the faith. He
could thus never be moved to denounce anyone, though he
strongly disagreed with that person's views. He would give his
own views constructively and emphatically, and then leave it to
the jury of Judaism and of mankind to give the verdict.

This faith in man and in the democratic process was destined
to cast a shadow on his last years, as Fascism and Nazism spread
over Europe. No catastrophe which had befallen him in all the

years that I knew him saddened him like the rise of Hitler, though he died before the worst evils of Hitlerism, the extermination of millions of people, became known. From January 30, 1933, when Hitler became chancellor until the day of Dr. Adler's death, March 24, 1940, I do not believe he had one day of real happiness. The sorrows of the world and of Israel lay on him like an unbearable load. He would have liked to see the door of every country in the world and of Palestine in particular, opened wide to the victims of Hitlerism. He was impatient with any suggestion that one person or another would "fall burden to the community" if he were brought here. "Is it better for him to rot in prison?" he once asked impatiently when the question of how a man would support himself in America was raised. With a keener eye than most Americans, Jewish or Christian, he realized that the history of the Jews in Germany had come to an end; and he wanted everyone who could escape the deluge he saw coming over Europe to do so.

But his hatred of totalitarianism did not begin with the rise of Hitler; he had recognized the symptoms of the anti-democratic trend in the rise of Mussolini. He had loved Italy in the days of freedom, and often visited Rome and Florence. But he only travelled there once under Mussolini. "I cannot breathe the fascist air," he said.

The Torch, March, 1946.

Dr. Finkelstein, regarded as one of the outstanding religious leaders and scholars on the American scene today, was born in Cincinnati, Ohio; and in 1919 was ordained as Rabbi at The Jewish Theological Seminary of America. He became Professor of Theology in 1931, Provost in 1937, President in 1940, and Chancellor in 1951. He is the author and editor of many scholarly works, including The Jews: Their History, Culture and Religion; Jewish Self-Government In The Middle Ages; The Pharisees, Their Origin and Their Philosophy; Akiba—Scholar, Saint, Martyr; *and* Beliefs and Practices of Judaism. *He is co-editor of:* Science, Philosophy and Religion Annual Symposia, *since 1942. Under his administration the Jewish Theological Seminary has become the foremost institution of its kind in the world.*

HENRIETTA SZOLD

Life and Letters

CHARLES I. HOFFMAN

Henrietta Szold was born into the Szold home in Baltimore in 1860, the oldest of eight daughters, three of whom died in infancy. This Szold home was the significant fact of her girlhood. Her Rabbi father combined Jewish learning and observance with modern German culture. To him she was daughter, disciple, confidant, and associate. He remained a permanent and dominant influence in her life. To her mother she was the life-long companion. Only after the latter's death was the daughter entirely free to find a new home in Palestine.

In her religious and secular school education Henrietta gave indications of precocious ability. The home influence was the prevailing and determining one. The opening of Johns Hopkins University brought scholarship and research to Baltimore and its Jewish reverberations were felt on Lombard Street, where the Szolds lived. Dr. Szold was a devout, observant Jew, but the service in Ohev Shalom Synagogue had admitted of some departures from the Shulchan Aruch. Henrietta once lamented to her father that she had not been brought up "Orthodox."

With her graduation from high school her school days were over, her real life education began. As a gifted, talented graduate, she was naturally designed to be a teacher in a private secular school and in a Jewish Congregational school. With marked qualifications as a writer, she drifted also into Jewish journalism as the Baltimore correspondent of *The Jewish Messenger* of New York. This gave an opportunity for an expression of her Jewish convictions and controversial ability. "Radical Reform" was the *bete noir* in those days, yet when she attended the first graduation of the Hebrew Union College in Cincinnati, she acted like Balaam of old.

The Russian pogroms and the consequent mass immigration of Jews to this country in the 80's of the last century was a great event in the life of Henrietta Szold, comparable in importance to the effect it had upon Emma Lazarus, though in a different way. Baltimore was not a main port of entry, but it received its proportion of newcomers, and their presence presented the problem of their adjustment. It was a little group that this young woman in her twenties gathered around her. She was to teach them English and the way of life in America, but they gave her much more—her life's mission, *Aruchas Bas Ami,* "the healing of my nation." She insisted upon the immigrant's self-dependence and they responded by converting her to Zionism. When she went out to preach the Zionist gospel to her fellows, the settled inhabitants of Baltimore, she declared they were unable to comprehend her message, so strange and unintelligible in its beginnings in this country. This "Philistinism" filled her with a kind of disgust. She condemned the assumption of superiority of the nation, even as she admired their philanthropic helpfulness to the newcomers.

All of this in its full significance was still in the future. The intellectual was still in the ascendant. Miss Szold was still a representative literary American Jewess. As such she was to present the paper at the Congress of Jewish Women at the Chicago Exposition in 1893, at which the Council of Jewish Women was founded. It was in this capacity that for many years she was to toil as executive secretary of the then newly formed Jewish Publication Society of America. Her work as editor, translator, chronologer, index-maker, was a valuable contribution to the life of American Jewry and Anglo-American Jewish literature. Her work in New York at the Jewish Theological Seminary, though brief, was important.[*]

The link that connected her literary career with that of executive direction was her visit to Palestine. It confirmed her Zionism, yet we are shocked to have her write in a moment of excess enthusiasm, "if not Zionism, then nothing—then extinction for the Jew."

Her return to America, marking the turning point in her work, saw the formation of the Hadassah organization and her accep-

[*] See Fineman, I.—*Woman of Valor* and Lowenthal, M.—*Henrietta Szold, Life and Letters*

tance of the secretaryship of the Federation of American Zionists. The latter was an onerous and disagreeable undertaking to straighten out the confusion that mismanagement had given rise to, in the direction of Zionist affairs in this country. The establishment of Hadassah, on the other hand, was a constructive work for Palestine, in which a correct path was opened, that led to important results in the life of the Jews in that country. Credit should be given to her mother, Mrs. Sophia Szold, for having struck the first spark. On their Palestine visit she called attention to the impoverished condition of the children and especially the eye-infection, trachoma, with which they were afflicted. In response to an inquiry at the Jewish Girls' School at Jaffa, why all the children in the school were perfectly healthy, while outside children were afflicted, the answer was—a physician visits us twice a week, a nurse comes daily. We take care of the eyes. Her mother said, "That is what your group ought to do."

Miss Szold turned a literary circle in New York, on her return, into a group to aid in practical health work in Palestine. In this initial undertaking she had the cooperation of Mrs. Richard Gottheil, a prominent figure in the early Zionist movement, and the latter's sister, Miss Eva Leon. The project was the establishment of visiting American nurses in Jerusalem. The matter dragged on for nearly a year; then something happened. Nathan Straus sent for Miss Szold, heard they wanted to send a couple of nurses to Palestine and offered to pay the expense of their transportation. Miss Leon raised a fund in Chicago for their support and two nurses were sent on. That was the beginning. Miss Szold traveled through the country establishing Hadassah chapters in various cities. Out of this grew the great development of the Hadassah organization and the splendid work accomplished through it in Palestine.

One other event was a determining influence. Some of Miss Szold's friends raised a fund that secured her future financial independence and enabled her to perform her work free from any reliance on any salary or organization's support. This, she declares, gave her an unique position free from rivalry and aspersion. Other large contributions were given her at important junctures of her work. With the $10,000.00 sent her by Justice Brandeis, malaria in the Emek was cleared out, but Baron Rothschild in Paris declined her request to contribute to what he considered American undertaking and obligation.

Finally Miss Szold cut loose from her work in America by resigning her post in the Jewish Publication Society, and accepted the call to Palestine.

It was in 1920 that she set sail for the land of the fathers and of her hopes for the future. She was in her sixtieth year, just recovered from a rather severe illness. She was to be the representative there of the American Zionist Organization to put in order the Medical Unit and other conditions that needed correction and direction. Her work was to be limited in duration like the Patriarch Jacob's stay in a foreign land to a "few days" or a couple of years; like his it has been prolonged for upwards of twenty years—a long, arduous, wonderfully effective work covering in its various developments the whole range of Jewish activities in Palestine. Her letters give a vivid reflection of these times and undertakings, of the uprisings of the Arabs, and her desire to secure an understanding with them; the relation to the government; the internal conflicts; and new duties to which she was called.

One of the primary difficulties was that of language. She had to possess herself of oral Hebrew speech. Her literary knowledge of Hebrew was insufficient to effect this. On her trip to Palestine, with characteristic thoroughness, Miss Szold devoted six hours daily to the study of Hebrew. When she arrived her first intention was to shut herself off in a Hebrew speaking environment. We note with interest her formal Hebrew address delivered at the corner-stone laying of the Hadassah University Hospital on Mt. Scopus; and her impromptu Hebrew addresses on other occasions. The result was, of course, her mastery of the language and her somewhat scornful attitude towards those who in the Jewish milieu failed to accomplish that result.

Language, however, was not a means to an end of bringing order out of chaos in her various undertakings. The first of these was the reorganization of the medical unit and the hygienic improvement of Palestine. The establishment of medical centres throughout Palestine, the extension of nurse service, the establishment of the school for nurses, the wrestling with the jealousies of physicians and the glorious establishment of the Hadassah University Hospital marks only one of her works.

As a member of the "Waad Haam" in charge of Jewish activities of the country, it was natural that the Jewish educational direction should be given in her charge, but it was a work surcharged with difficulties in which partisan politics was interjected. One incident may illustrate: Miss Szold is an observant Jewess, keeping Sabbath and dietary laws. Was football to be officially banned on the Sabbath? She would have preferred its voluntary omission, but could the Jewish official body prohibit its performance, and more than this, could it get the secular government to intervene and penalize the Jews for this infringement of Jewish observance? Miss Szold denounced such an interference in Jewish affairs on the part of the government and incurred the lasting opposition of the pietistic party. Nevertheless her work in the Jewish school direction was valuable.

The establishment and extension of social service was another of her great achievements, that brought succor to the poor and sick throughout the land.

Her last and greatest work was provision for the settlement of Jewish children in Palestine, the victims of Hitlerism in Europe. To find the colonies where these youths could be harbored and trained, to establish training for their integration into Palestinian life, to welcome and watch over them with maternal love and devotion—this is the crowning achievement of her splendid career. Miss Szold wrote in one of her letters, she ought to have been the mother of children; that was, she thought, a worthwhile employment of endless detail. Her wish has, in its own way, been abundantly granted.

Beside her work, Henrietta Szold has a personality. There is the story of the woman who came to her office to secure a position. When she came out she said I did not find a position, but I did find a human being. Her fellow-workers became her loyal adherents; her friends became her disciples and confederates.

In her letters we see events as in a panorama. There is the mixture of objective description with subjective analysis and introspection. The riots of the Arabs are described with the deep emotion of one who was in the midst of the melee. The oncoming of events are anticipated sometimes with striking accuracy. The beauty of the country is depicted with a lover's ardor. The death and burial of Bialik and Ussisonnchkin are recorded. The deep humiliation and dire desolation of the Jews in Germany is described as witnessed when Miss Szold was welcomed in Germany almost as deliverer of the children of the hunted and despised outcasts.

Henrietta Szold possessed a personality rich in intellectual perceptions, vision and compassion, religious by nature, and down to earth in practical constructive pioneering effort—an example and vindication of American Jewish womanhood.

The Torch, February, 1943

Rabbi Hoffman (1864–1945), friend and disciple of Sabato Morais and Solomon Schechter, was a staunch advocate of Traditional Judaism and its development in America through the Jewish Theological Seminary and the United Synagogue. He helped to found the latter and was its Secretary for twenty-five years. After a distinguished career at the bar and as community leader in Philadelphia, he was ordained at the Jewish Theological Seminary and served as Rabbi in Newark, N.J. for forty years. He was editor of The Jewish Exponent *and the* United Synagogue Recorder.

MORDECAI M. KAPLAN

Writer of Books

MORTIMER J. COHEN

Few men in history have made a great place for themselves as leaders of thought without having left to posterity writings that enshrine their creative thinking. To be a "writer of books" is to make a bid for immortality. To be sure, Socrates himself did not write, but his disciple, Plato, wove his philosophical dialogues about the Master, and so perpetuated his memory. Jesus of Nazareth did not write, but others, according to Christian tradition, wrote down his words to become the gospels for later ages. In Jewish tradition, from Moses down to our century, the great spiritual leaders of the Jewish people were primarily writers of books. The Jewish people itself came to be known as "the People of the Book."

Dr. Mordecai M. Kaplan, founder of Reconstructionism, teacher and guide to a whole generation of Rabbis and teachers, has created a rich inheritance of books whose spirit will nourish and inspire countless generations that lie ahead. Whether one agrees with Dr. Kaplan in his basic philosophy of Jewish life, or whether one reads him to refute him, he remains one of the most powerful intellectual and spiritual forces of contemporary Judaism. On the celebration of Dr. Kaplan's 75th birthday, it is eminently worthwhile to set down some of the books that he has written, discuss them briefly and, where possible, quote a characteristic sentence or two from them.

"JUDAISM AS A CIVILIZATION"

Dr. Kaplan's unique contribution to modern Judaism is his interpretation of Judaism as an evolving religious civilization. Civilization is "the accumulation of knowledge, skills, tools, arts,

44

literatures, laws, religions and philosophies which stands between man and external nature, and which serves as a bulwark against the hostility of forces that would otherwise destroy him." Furthermore, "each block of that accumulation is a civilization, which is sharply differentiated from every other . . . and each civilization is a complete and self-contained entity."

Judaism is but one of a number of unique national civilizations guiding humanity towards its spiritual destiny. Judaism . . . "is something far more comprehensive than Jewish religion. It includes that nexus of a history, literature, language, social organization, folk sanctions, standards of conduct, social and spiritual ideals, esthetic values, which in their totality form a civilization." A civilization over the centuries changes and evolves as new insights, new inventions, new experiences enrich the soul of a people. The quality of a civilization is found in its religion. And Judaism, for Dr. Kaplan, finds its uniqueness in being a religious— that is a God-conscious—civilization.

In his now classic work, *Judaism As a Civilization,* Dr. Kaplan presents the implications of his version of Judaism, especially for American Jews. Before he could present his affirmative views, he had necessarily to criticize the current versions of Judaism— Reform, Neo-Orthodoxy, and Conservatism. He had to preface this with his analysis of the nature of the crisis that had come upon Judaism in our times. In the remaining portions of his book, Dr. Kaplan discusses brilliantly and constructively the great themes of *Israel:* The status and organization of Jewry, *God:* The development of the Jewish religion, and *Torah:* Judaism as a way of life for the American Jew.

The secondary title of *Judaism As a Civlization* reveals Dr. Kaplan's whole aim and purpose which is: a reconstruction of American-Jewish life. Valiantly he writes: "In my search for a way to check the devastation of the Jewish spiritual heritage, I rediscovered Judaism."

"THE MEANING OF GOD IN MODERN JEWISH RELIGION"

To those who criticize Dr. Kaplan's version of Judaism as being secularist, no better answer can be made than his second major volume—*The Meaning of God in Modern Jewish Religion.* The richness of his learning, the wide and varied reading he has done, the intensive concentration he has given to the profundities of religious experience, find their expression in this volume which may in time prove to be Dr. Kaplan's most creative contribution to a vital Jewish religion. It is a volume that is an unfailing fountain of spiritual insights, illuminating the heart and giving new meaning and significance to ancient customs and ceremonies and revered texts of the Bible and Rabbinical literature.

After his introductory chapter on how to reinterpret the God idea in the Jewish religion, Dr. Kaplan discusses the Sabbath, the Holy Days, the High Holydays as they evince the divine power of God manifesting itself in human nature, social regeneration, Nature and history, public worship, the struggle for freedom and righteousness, and the challenge of Jewish survival.

For Dr. Kaplan, religion is a natural social process which "arises from man's intrinsic need of salvation or self-fulfillment." This need, he holds, pre-supposes that "reality is so patterned as to contain the means of satisfying it. This pattern of reality man has gropingly sought to envisage in his numerous and often absurd, conceptions of God." In the religious crisis of our times, the Jewish religion will have to transform itself from an other-worldly religion . . . "into a religion which can help Jews attain this-worldly salvation. It will have to accept without reservation the validity of the scientific rather than the authoritative approach to reality, and make its objective the achievement of such conditions on earth as will release the creative powers of man and enable him to realize the potentialities of ethical personality."

How shall the Jewish religion address itself to the modern Jew? What is the nature of this worldly salvation to which the Jewish religion will have to relate its conception of God? Through which of its principal institutions can Judaism best convey what God should mean to us? These are the questions that Dr. Kaplan here seeks to answer.

"THE FUTURE OF THE AMERICAN JEW" AND "A NEW ZIONISM"

However Dr. Kaplan envisages the world problem of Judaism, he directs his fullest attention again and again to meeting the spiritual needs of American Jewry. One might immediately add that, with the reality of the State of Israel, the relationship of American Jewry to the new State of Israel had also to engage his attention.

Spiritual descendant of Ahad Ha'am, Dr. Kaplan does not see the Jews who do not return to Israel as living in Exile. He is not a denier of Jewish life and values in the Jewries outside of the Jewish State. On the contrary, he regards the Jewish State as *potentially* the spiritual and cultural center of world Jewry and he regards world Jewry as the channel through which a revitalized Jewish message of hope and salvation for mankind can yet come. Dr. Kaplan is an Ahad Ha'amist in the fullest and deepest sense of the term.

In his *The Future of the American Jew* and *A New Zionism* Dr. Kaplan explores fully the possibilities of Jewish life in these United States and in Israel. What is even more important, Dr. Kaplan advocates the newly emerging concept of Jewish peoplehood as the rationale that best validates the relationship that should obtain between the fragments of the Jewish people throughout the world vis-a-vis Israel. Certainly, American Jewry must achieve its own Jewish way of life within the framework of the American democracy. This depends upon the ability of Jews to live in two civilizations, the American and the Jewish. Moreover, the concept of the peoplehood of Israel helps to resolve the question of political loyalty for American Jews without robbing them of the right to spiritual association with the Jewry of Israel.

In *A New Zionism* Dr. Kaplan faces the achievement and failure of political Zionism to answer the question of Jewish survival today. Political Zionism has been realized through the political State; but more is required for the Jews of the world. It is here that Dr. Kaplan turns again to Ahad Ha'amism as the truer direction in which to turn for the solution of the relation of the Jews of Israel and the remainder of the world, especially American Jewry.

"Zionism can emerge from its present crisis strengthened by the experience of challenge and danger. It can become the custodian of the Jewish future. It can lead to the fulfillment of the prophecy that 'from Zion shall go forth Torah.' But before the Torah can go forth from Zion, it will have to enter into Zionism."

ADDITIONAL WRITINGS

The volumes mentioned above do not exhaust the copious literary achievements of Dr. Kaplan. *Judaism in Transition and Ha-Emunah V'Ha-Musar* (based on Dr. Kaplan's lectures at the Hebrew University, Israel) are valuable contributions to a reinterpretation of Judaism. Innumerable articles, pamphlets, Random Thoughts, "Know How to Answer" responsa, and addresses continue to flow from inexhaustible well-springs of one of the most germinal and creative minds in Jewish life of our century.

* * *

We are so close to Dr. Kaplan that, in a very real sense, we cannot see the mountain that stands majestically in our midst. The snows of many winters crown his head, but his voice rings out— clear and strong and certain in these times of confusion and doubt. We thank God for the privilege of having lived in Dr. Kaplan's presence. We rejoice that we can render our humble tribute of gratitude to him for his guidance, his wisdom and his courage that have helped us to see more clearly the pathways to Jewish survival in our challenging days. In the spirit of Jewish tradition we pronounce the blessing enjoined upon us when we stand in the presence of a person of profound Torah wisdom: "Blessed art Thou, Lord our God, King of the Universe, who hast imparted of Thy wisdom to those who revere Thee."

The Torch, Winter, 1956.

Dr. Cohen, distinguished Rabbi and man of letters, has served the Philadelphia Jewish Community for forty-eight years. Under his leadership Beth Sholom Congregation of Philadelphia erected a new Synagogue designed by Frank Lloyd Wright. He has been editor of Jewish Bookland *and president of the Jewish Book Council of America. A frequent contributor to* The Reconstructionist, The Jewish Exponent *and* The Torch, *his most well known book is* Pathways Through the Bible.

MORDECAI M. KAPLAN

Architect of the American Jewish Community

JOEL S. GEFFEN

A basic problem facing the American Jewish Community is that of alerting each individual Jew to a greater feeling of identification with our people. Professor Mordecai M. Kaplan pioneered in plotting out the steps which have to be taken if American Jewry and if Judaism are to survive as a positive force in this land. Basing his thinking on the premise that we are living in two civilizations, he has made us realize that the Jewish Community must consider its many different component parts as well as the larger non-Jewish Community in which it finds itself.

A brief resume of his thinking in several areas of community life will help us to understand how Dr. Kaplan believes the American Jewish Community ought to function.

First of all he would have us think of ourselves as a "people"—AM—that is Am Yisrael. He contends that we are able to adjust ourselves in this free environment and to live in accordance with an ethical pattern which would help to save the soul of the Jewish group. When we accomplish this we will have launched a spiritual enterprise stemming from the will of the people and will thus lead to the establishment of a covenant dedicating ourselves to a common purpose.

As an Am Yisrael, a distinct group, we possess:

a.) a sense of common history;

b.) a common language and literature, common ancestral land, common folkways and a common religion;

c.) social cohesiveness imposed by those who dislike Jews.

From this Dr. Kaplan developed his conception of Jewish peoplehood whereby he sees unity possible despite the fact that Jews are scattered throughout the world. In the past when religious doctrines filled every nook and cranny of the human mind,

Jewish unity could survive the cutting off of each community of Jews from other segments of Jewry. That uniformity is no longer possible. Dr. Kaplan, therefore, proposes that Jews formulate a new convenant among themselves—and through their mutual love, strive to create a social entitity that will prove to be a blessing to mankind.

In the second place, Dr. Kaplan teaches us that our people need an organic Jewish Community through which to fulfill themselves. The *Kahal* or community organization of Eastern Europe which existed up to 1825 even in this country, was co-extensive with the synagogue. Gradually this changed and an attempt to set up an American *Kahal* in New York met with failure. Just as Dr. Kaplan saw no future for our people without a Jewish homeland Eretz Yisrael, so he visualized no hope for us without self-governing communities in the Disapora capable of cohesive and coherent thought and action. In his *The Future of the American Jew,* page 114, he states: "without an enduring social structure, such as only a well organized community can provide, being a Jew is like trying to live as a disembodied soul." Dr. Kaplan recommends an organic community, one in which "all matters of Jewish interest would in some way deeply affect lives of all who desire to remain Jews." (Idem page 114). This would require systematic correlation and co-operation of parts which will be regulative in some way or ways. The National Council of Federations and Welfare Funds, the National Community Relations Council, the Synagogue and local Jewish Community Councils are a few examples of trends in this direction.

A third example of Dr. Kaplan's influence on the American Jewish community has been his contribution to the Jewish Center Movement. Professor Oscar Janowsky in the *JWB Survey* (page 246) writes "in its broadest grasp, the view of the purpose of the Jewish Center as an affirmative agency has been championed by Mordecai M. Kaplan. He has envisaged a Jewish Neighborhood Center maintained by and for the total Jewish Community. He would endow it with all the *spiritual sanction* formerly enjoyed by the Synagogue. Its function would embrace every positive Jewish interest and need—religious, educational, cultural, philanthropic and social. He has placed particular emphasis upon the fostering of a spirit of neighborliness in order to weld the Jewish residents of an area into a "conscious communal unit" thus promoting the *we feeling* necessary for the perpetuation of group life.

Dr. Kaplan believes that we have made the mistake of setting up artificial barriers, between the religious and the secular, a mistake which he believes was not made in the past. That is why he urges us to look upon Judaism as a civilization in which "more, folkways and social institutions that have entered into the fabric of Jewish life possess as much of a religious character as prayer, worship and faith." (*Mordecai M. Kaplan—An Evaluation,* page 310).

His influence has been evident in the development and crystallization of the Jewish Center and its philosophy. That Dr. Kaplan provided purpose to this movement was symbolized by the award which he received on June 2, 1951, that stated: "from the earliest days of the Jewish Community Center Movement and of the National Jewish Welfare Board, he has helped to give education and purpose to the program."

The fourth area of comumnity life which has received impetus from Dr. Kaplan for positive Jewish living is that of Jewish social service. He has helped to provide a philosophy for Jewish living to thousands of Jewish social workers. For many years, Dr. Kaplan was a member of the Faculty of the Graduate School for Jewish Social Work which existed for some fifteen years, up to 1940. He has given serious study to the area of Jewish social service in our country and has offered many recommendations which have led to the incorporation of Jewish values in its work.

Thus we see a partial panorama of American Jewish community life which is taking on semblance and form because of the genius and creative thinking of the brilliant Mordecai M. Kaplan. In this way he has helped many individuals, both professional and lay, to strengthen their identification with our people and to assume a greater sense of responsibility for Jewish life in our community.

The Torch, Winter, 1956.

Dr. Geffen, devoted representative of the Jewish Theological Seminary in its service to the American Jewish community, served as Rabbi in Harrisburg, Pa. and Troy, N.Y. He is Director of Field Activities and Community Education of the Seminary and is a Research Associate of its American Jewish History Center. He is former Director of the New York Metropolitan region of The United Synagogue of America. Rabbi Geffen is Spiritual Adviser of the National Federation of Jewish Men's Clubs and has held this position for over 20 years. He is co-editor of The Torch and of this volume.

THE LEGACY
of
MILTON STEINBERG

SIMON NOVECK

The second day of Nisan which this year falls on March 23 marks the sixteenth *Yahrzeit* of Milton Steinberg, one of the best known and most beloved rabbis to graduate from the Seminary during the eighty years of its existence. Spiritual leader of the Park Avenue Synagogue in New York for eighteen years, author of several popular works on Judaism including an historical novel on Jewish life during the second century, popular orator and public lecturer, member of the editorial board of the *Reconstructionist* magazine and mentor to several national Jewish organizations, Steinberg passed away in 1950 at the age of forty-six in the midst of a very creative career.

In the sixteen years since his death conflicting opinions have been expressed about the nature of his contributions to Jewish life and thought. Will Herberg describes Steinberg as "one of the best informed and most penetrating theological minds that American Jewry has yet produced." The late Rabbi Barnett Brickner, shortly after Steinberg's death, referred to him as "the most creative mind in the rabbinate and its most able writer and thinker." Others like Ben Halpern and Eugene Borowitz while paying tribute to Steinberg as a human being and teacher of religion, have denied that he was an original theologian or that he made any special contribution to the development of American Jewish thought. Looking back after sixteen years, how shall we describe Steinberg's contributions? Living as we do in an intellectual climate so radically different from that of the 1940's, in an age characterized by distrust in reason, loss of faith in man and in society, inevitably a rationalistic, liberal, optimistic thinker like Steinberg will be evaluated differently than he was in a previous era. Nevertheless, in the opinion of this writer, Steinberg left a legacy of lasting importance which should be remembered by the present generation. In this article we try to sum up what seem to us to be the enduring aspects of his work and thought.

STEINBERG AS AN IDEAL RABBI

Milton Steinberg's major contribution to Jewish life lies in the unusually brilliant and gifted kind of rabbi he was—the combination of intellectualism and personal warmth he brought to his work, the unique quality of his preaching and teaching and his recognition of what should be the central concerns of the modern day rabbi. As American Jewish life has developed and become more complex, the functions of the rabbi have become increasingly varied. No rabbi can perform all the functions that theoretically fall within his scope. Some concentrate on communal activities or interfaith work; others emphasize pastoral and counselling duties, or devote themselves to administration and fund raising. Often, however, the rabbi becomes so involved in these activities that no time is left for the advancement of the religious and cultural life of the people he serves. Although Steinberg was drawn into the maelstrom of New York organizational life, he always took the religious, cultural or literary aspects as the focus of his interest. He recognized that the central task of the rabbi was to preach and teach and to do what he could to preserve the Jewish way of life.

Steinberg's sermons were a model of clarity, relevance and beauty, an exciting illustration of the kind of preaching a modern congregation should enjoy. His sermons covered a wide range of topics: problems of Zionism and Jewish peoplehood, aspects of Jewish tradition such as the Jewish concept of marriage and divorce or the teachings of Judaism on mercy killing, sermons on doctrines and beliefs and occasionally a review of an important book such as Ludwig Lewisohn's *Midchannel* or Mordecai Kaplan's *Future of the American Jew*.

While Steinberg agreed with his contemporaries that the social message needed to be asserted and that the synagogue had a responsibility to apply the ethical concepts of Jewish tradition to present day problems, he felt that ethics had to flow from a theology and Jewish preaching, therefore, ought to emphasize theological themes. Thus, he preached on such subjects as "The Jewish

Concept of God", "God and the World's Evil", "Existentialism—What Is Its Message for Religious People?", "The Mystery of Franz Kafka and Its Import", "The Distinctiveness of Judaism as Against Christianity and Paganism".

Though colleagues from the various wings of Judaism and rabbinical students from the Jewish Theological Seminary and the Jewish Institute of Religion often attended services in his synagogue most of his listeners did not have the philosophical background to understand many of his sermons. When Steinberg was asked why he persisted in speaking on such abstract philosophical themes, he replied that in his view there was no alternative except to try and sensitize people to issues of this kind. The pulpit to him was a place from which one should draw not only stimulus and courage, but knowledge and guidance. "If a congregation does not altogether understand the whole of a theological exposition," he said on one occasion, "something has been gained by its being put forth. A claim to attention has been advanced on behalf of the intellectual issues of the human spirit. A right has been asserted." Even if everybody did not understand everything, he felt "some people understand the whole, many more people understand a part and everyone experiences reassertion of the propriety of such interests in the pulpit."

The sermons which had the greatest impact on the congregation were those on personal themes some of which can be found in the posthumous volume *A Believing Jew.* These talks had a depth of emotional insight and reflected the quality of compassion, the ability to feel for others which was so characteristic of Steinberg. Several of these sermons "Indignation—A Lost Jewish Virtue", "When I Remember Seraye", "Telling Oneself the Truth" and "A Pity for the Living" are still being quoted. To him the recognition of the universality of suffering was the foundation of Jewish ethics. In Steinberg's view "to be pitiless was a grave sin, perhaps the gravest of which man is capable . . . He is a failure as a human being, no matter what his other traits and achievements whose heart does not hurt for his fellow man."

Steinberg's greatest sermon was probably the one he gave a few months after he had suffered a heart attack in Dallas in December 1943. He called it "To Hold With Open Arms." As a result of his illness, he told his congregation, he had come to realize how precious life was and had resolved to hold on to it as strongly as he could. But gradually he became aware that it is in the nature of things that we cannot hold on either to life or youth, our children or to any other thing in life. The great truth of human existence is always to be prepared to let go.

"For these things are not and never have been mine . . . They belong to the universe and to the God who stands behind it. . . . And I let go of them the more easily because I know that as parts of the divine economy they will not be lost. The sunset, the bird's song, the baby's smile . . . the dreams of the heart and my own being, dear to me as every man's is to him, all these I can well trust to Him who made them. There is poignancy and regret about giving them up, but no anxiety. When they slip from my hands they will pass to hands better, stronger and wiser than mine."

Steinberg's method of preaching was unique. He rarely denounced or excoriated the congregation. There was no sensationalism or superficiality in his talks. His purpose was less to inform than to awaken the mind, not so much to impart information, as to have the listeners learn by being intellectually active. In each sermon, he asked the listeners to participate along with him as he analyzed a concept, argued a thesis or presented alternate courses of action. These sermons reflected extensive knowledge of Jewish tradition, of Western philosophy and of contemporary religious thought and can still be read with great profit both for their content and as examples of the most intelligent, lucid Jewish preaching in the American Jewish community during the past few decades.

The same beauty of style and theological emphasis Steinberg gave to his sermons were evident in the adult education lectures he offered his congregation. These lectures were designed to introduce the student to broad areas of Jewish life and thought. They included a series of courses on Jewish history in ancient, medieval and modern times and on the causes and cures of anti-Semitism. His most successful courses, however, dealt with the problems of Jewish religious life. In these, he discussed the nature of religion and religious belief, the idea of God, the relationship of religion and intellectual life, the problems of morality, prayer, worship and the social ideals of religion. He also dealt with Jewish ethics and comparative religion with theologians like Paul Tillich and Reinhold Niebuhr participating as guest speakers.

As was true of his sermons, not all who attended his lectures were able to follow the intricacies of his philosophical discussion, but all enjoyed the experience of being in the presence of a warm, eloquent, erudite, urbane and sophisticated teacher of Jewish tradition. What James Russell Lowell once wrote about Emerson, could also be said of Steinberg: "that people do not go to hear what Emerson says so much as to hear Emerson." Steinberg, too, attracted people to his lectures not only because of the cogency and depth of his thinking, but also because of the fervor with which he spoke, the intensity and enthusiasm with which he presented his material. He loved people and had a charismatic effect on those who came in contact with him.

Those who got to know him also sensed the deep love he had for Judaism and for the rabbinate as a way of life. Although Steinberg had gone through an early period of doubt and hesitancy when he was a student at the Seminary and had seriously considered withdrawing on several occasions, once he had graduated and gone to live in Indianapolis, his first pulpit, the problem had resolved itself. "You may suffer from a sense of defeat and frustration, you may find yourself unable to effect your ends," he told a young theological student, "but you will never feel that what you are doing is not worthwhile." Steinberg always felt strongly that the rabbinate was eminently worthwhile as a life calling. "Dealing as I do with the deep problems of human beings at all levels and of all sorts and with all conditions of men," he wrote just a few weeks before his death, "I have a strong sense of the especial meaningfulness of the Jewish ministry." When his illness forced him to make a choice among his activities, some of his friends urged him to leave the rabbinate and not to squander his energies in visiting the sick and giving himself to all who called. While he gradually gave up most of his organizational involvements, he insisted on continuing as a rabbi, for it was here that he derived his greatest satisfactions.

It is this love for the rabbinate as well as his unique personality and gifts which inspired so many of his colleagues to look upon him as a "rabbi's rabbi", and made him the epitome of what they themselves would like to be in their life work.

Steinberg should also be remembered for the books he wrote which helped fill a great need for a pedagogic literature on the inner content of Jewish tradition. Unfortunately, few scholars are ready to devote themselves to this need of educating a generation. Steinberg was one of the few gifted and literate Jewish writers of the past generation who had both the knowledge and the willingness to give themselves to the historic task of interpreting Jewish values for the general Jewish public. He himself started out in the rabbinate with the intention of making a contribution to Jewish scholarship. He chose as the topic for his Ph.D. thesis at Columbia University *Hellenic Influences on Judaism,* but the many activities in which he was engaged—at the synagogue, the Reconstructionist Foundation, Jewish Welfare Board, Hadassah and Ninety-second Street Y and his schedule of public lectures left him little opportunity for sustained scholarly work. Gradually be began to feel that reaching the people was more important than scientific scholarship. As he wrote to Rabbi Joshua Liebman on the publication of *Peace of Mind* in 1947, "while all of us who have been extensively exposed to academic procedures tend to evaluate scientific work more highly than popular, I for one have increasingly freed myself of late of that obsession. That is why my thesis is still unwritten whereas other things have been finished and are in process."

Steinberg wrote three popular expositions of Judaism and Jewish problems. His first book entitled *Making of the Modern Jew* which appeared early in 1934 is a survey of the factors which made Jewish survival possible during the Middle Ages and during the period of emancipation when the Jew was catapulted headlong from medievalism into modernity. He describes the disintegrating effects of the collapse of the ghetto, the inner conflicts set in motion as Jews began to live on the fringes of two worlds—the Jewish and the European. In "Dusk Children," one of the most moving chapters of the book, he sketches the life stories of men like Heine, Mordecai Fierberg and Bialik who belonged to this transitional period of chaos when the boundaries grew confused. In the last section of the book on "The Modern Scene" Steinberg deals with the resurgence of anti-Semitism in Germany, the importance of Palestine and the "programs" or ideologies for Jewish survival in the Diaspora, such as Orthodoxy, Conservatism, Reform and Reconstructionism.

His second expository work entitled *A Partisan Guide to the Jewish Problem* was written in 1944. A logical sequel to the *Making of Modern Jew,* its tightly reasoned chapters deal with four types of problems which would confront the Jew in the postwar world: "Problems of Status" such as anti-Semitism, its causes and cures, "Problems of Self-Acceptance", that is, the trend to assimilation which Steinberg described as "the bitterest and most critical controversy in contemporary Jewish life"; and "Problems of Tradition" in which he describes through a series of case studies the varieties of Jewish outlook current at the time. He makes clear that to him the most tenable theory of Jewish life is Reconstructionism, the creation of his teacher, Mordecai Kaplan. The final section deals with "problems of Homeland", in which he presents the ideologies of Herzl, Ahad Ha'am, A. D. Gordon, and Max Nordau, which have served as the base for modern Zionism. In a particularly beautiful epilogue, "The Game is Worth the Candle", Steinberg replies to the question why be Jews, making an eloquent case for Jewish survival.

The work of most enduring value is *Basic Judaism* which appeared in 1947. Unlike his previous volume, *Basic Judaism* is nonpartisan in approach, presenting both the traditionalist and modernist viewpoints on what Steinberg regards as the seven component strands of the Jewish religion: a doctrine concerning God, the universe and man; a morality for the individual and society; a regimen of rite, custom and ceremony; a body of law; a sacred literature, and institutions through which the foregoing find expression.

The book has been criticized for its tendency to over-simplify the many different and conflicting interpretations of the Jewish religion and for its disregard of historical Judaism. His view that a thread of unity exists amidst the variegated expressions of Judiasm through the centuries was also questioned. However, as

Steinberg explained, the book was designed primarily as a primer for those who wanted a description of the common denominators of all the elements of Judaism. All three volumes, particularly the *Making of the Modern Jew* and *Basic Judaism* because of the clarity and lucidity of their style and the fairness of their presentation are still among the most widely used texts in adult education courses today.

Among Steinberg's popular works we must also include the beautiful and moving novel which he published in 1940 *As A Driven Leaf,* the story of Elisha ben Abuyah, the second century rabbi and member of the Sanhedrin who turned his back on Jews and Judaism. Steinberg's aim was not merely to tell the tale of the intellectual odyssey of a colorful figure in Jewish history. He wanted also to recapture a period in ancient Jewish history and the spiritual giants who peopled it and to set it in contrast with the brilliant pagan civilizations of the time. In addition, he was eager to put across through Elisha's struggle the message of "the indispensability of faith in all areas of human enterprise." Elisha in many ways symbolizes Steinberg himself. The quest for truth, the blunder in making intellect his only instrument, his final awareness of the need for faith and reason in an organic fusion— these concepts of Elisha ben Abuyah, Steinberg confessed, were central to his own thinking. Louis Ginzberg, the eminent Talmudic scholar and authority on this period, congratulated him on the book as did Alfred Kazin, who reviewed the novel in the *New York Herald Tribune,* calling it a "rare and moving book, creative in its thought, sensitive, scholarly, without being a document."

THEOLOGICAL ESSAYS

Aside from his books on Judaism, Steinberg left a number of brilliant, incisive theological essays which he published in various journals during his lifetime and which have appeared in book form since his death. These essays contain many insights expressed in the felicitous language which characterized all his writings. Although Steinberg was just at the beginning of his theological studies and had no chance to work out any system, the few essays he did write reveal him as a thinker who raised questions and wrestled with religious issues which still confront us today. In a period when theology was almost completely neglected in the American Jewish community Steinberg was one of the few who stressed its importance.

Religion to Steinberg consisted of four elements—a philosophy or *weltanschauung,* a set of rituals, a system of ethics and a focus of religious emotion by which he meant the need for a sense of awe or reverence, the awareness of the holy which a synagogue can produce. While he pleaded for a "balanced religion" insisting that all four aspects were important, his own essential interest was in theology or the "cognitive aspect of religion." To him men were "insatiably curious about metaphysics," and religion was basically a matter of cosmology, an interpretation of reality as a whole. Religious belief in the long run was a determinant of behavior and an understanding of the grounds for faith in God was as important as philanthropy and community issues. In this stress on the importance of theology Steinberg was almost unique in the American rabbinate of the 1940's.

Steinberg regarded himself as a religious rationalist and described his own convictions as "in great measure the consequence of a rationalist pragmatist metaphysics." He insisted that a case could be made for religious faith on the basis of reason and experience. He accepted the God faith because to him it was an interpretation of reality which met the tests of practicality, congruity and economy much better than did any mechanistic interpretation of the universe. "If a man will but think long enough, hard enough," he asserted, "he inevitably will come to such an affirmation." Steinberg recognized, however, that religion was more than a matter of reason and common sense. It included an awareness of mystery and poetry, a sensitivity to other realms beyond the intellect. He knew that the human intellect was not applicable to some realms of reality and was unable to provide intellectual certainty or give sure direction to man's activity. Faith and belief also play a role in the religious enterprise. In an address before the Institute of Religious Studies of the Seminary, he urged the rehabilitation of the word "faith," which among enlightened people had acquired an unpleasant taste.

An approach, however, based entirely on intuition, as he pointed out in a review essay of Bergson's *Two Sources of Religion and Morality,* is no substitute for rationalism. A religion or

morality which is entirely mystical is entirely personal and therefore not susceptible to logical examination and leaves no criteria
for judgment and evaluation. To him, a religious orientation unchecked by reason is "capable of all sorts of grossnesses and stu-
pidities." Reason may be a poor staff on which to lean but "it is
the only staff upon which man can rest his weight with some assurance that it will not break."

During the last years of his life when he had more time for
reading and study, Steinberg became increasingly familiar with
the new anti-rational trends in Protestant theology. He read the
works of Rheinhold Niebuhr, Richard Niebuhr and of Paul Tillich and became very much interested in Kierkegaard, the father
of modern existentialism. He met regularly with Professor Albert
Salomon of the New School for Social Research, a member of the
Park Avenue Synagogue, who introduced him to nineteenth century German thinkers like Dilthey, Simel, Max Weber and
Troelsch. They read together from their works as well as from the
works of Barth and Brunner, the continental theologians. Steinberg was also drawn to Will Herberg whose article in *Commentary* on his personal transition from Marxism to Judaism excited
his interest. Perhaps the comments of Irving Kristol, whose review of *Basic Judaism* had criticized Steinberg's failure to meet
the challenge of Existentialism, also stimulated him to read more
widely in this literature.

Out of this reading and reflection came a penetrating essay on
"Kierkegaard and Judaism" which appeared in the *Menorah
Journal* in January 1949, a masterful paper before the Rabbinical
Assembly Convention in June, 1949 on "The Theological Issues
of the Hour" and four lectures in January 1950 on "New Currents in Religious Thought." Some present day students see in
these essays a shift in Steinberg's point of view away from his earlier rationalism. They suggest that these later writings represent a
"turning point in his intellectual life" and that "the existen-
tialists toward whom Herberg leaned and for whom Salomon had
considerable sympathy had their impact on Steinberg's thought."

Actually, the fact that Steinberg surveyed the new theological
trends which began to appear on the horizon at the end of the
1940's does not indicate that he accepted these ideas. He saw a

value in the existentialist approach as a protest against a rationalism which had made the living God of religious faith into an ab-
straction and he recognized that this new philosophy had enabled
men to achieve a deeper understanding of human personality.
He saw virtues in Kierkegaard's approach—its "inwardness, mystical sensibility, a passion and groping for truths . . . imper-
fectly comprehended by conventional religion . . . a feeling for
the torments of human existence" and he expressed his indebted-
ness to Niebuhr for reminding him of "the depth and tenacity of
evil in the individual and society."

However, while Existentialism and the crisis theology had
deepened the religious consciousness of our time, as a program he
found it "an alluring but dangerous heresy," in the long run "adverse to clear thinking and wholesome feeling on religious matters and hostile to the entire enterprise of perfecting the world
under the Kingdom of the Almighty." Writing to Judge Simon
Rifkind in May 1948, Steinberg also indicated that he considered
the crisis theology "a dangerous doctrine, the contemporary ana-
logue of the Calvinist Lutheran dogma of total human depravity
and total human helplessness. It denies what is central to Judaism,
meliorism, the thesis that man can, if not perfect, at least better
his soul and his society. I regard it as near a heresy, Jewishly
speaking, as is possible to conceive." Reason, Steinberg insisted,
might be a "limited, unsteady, uncreative instrument," but to him
it was "the only one by which decisions can be made among sup-
posed truths in conflict, the sole pipeline for the communication
of ideas."

In one of his lectures two months before he died, Steinberg
seemed to temper his trust in reason by adding to the tests of
practicality, congruity and economy for the God faith "the existential act of faith." "Reason alone," he said, "will not bring man
to that point at which he is able to affirm with clarity and certi-
tude the religious answer." However, there is no evidence that he
abandoned his rationalism. He was rather reiterating what he had
written in the very moving last chapter of his novel a decade before, that "the light of man's logic is too frail, unaided, to prevail
against the enveloping darkness, that to reason faith is a prerequisite." This did not mean, as Elisha ben Abuyah puts it, the sur-

render of liberty of the mind to any authority, but rather "to go seeking now through faith and reason compounded, the answer to this baffling pageant which is the world."

Whatever be the merit of Steinberg's point of view, this can be said: if there has been a renewal of Jewish theological thinking in our time, it is in part, at least, because he opened the gates to theological speculation and paved the way for the new era.

STEINBERG AND CONSERVATIVE JUDAISM

Among Steinberg's interests was a strong desire to see the Conservative Movement define its position and work out its ideology. The Seminary for him was not only his alma mater but also his spiritual home. He felt there was no institution on the entire American scene more necessary to meaningful Jewish survival. Though some of the leaders of the Seminary had put forth their individual versions of a Conservative program, Steinberg was distressed that in the more than four decades since Solomon Schechter became President of the Seminary no progress had been made in evolving an adequate ideology for Conservative Judaism, in clarifying its theological position and in adapting Jewish law and observance to contemporary American circumstances.

Milton Steinberg regarded himself as a "traditionalist." When he first came to the Park Avenue Synagogue in 1932 the congregation was officially affiliated with the Union of American Hebrew Congregations. It was one of his proud achievements that he was able to veer the congregation from what he called "near Reform" to traditionalism. However, in a world which had undergone so many intellectual and scientific revolutions he thought some degree of elasticity and change in Jewish law were essential and he wanted the Conservative movement to overcome its "excessive caution" and adopt a bolder approach. He felt that if there was to be an orderly transition from old world Orthodoxy to a modernized traditionalism, the Conservative movement should not leave every synagogue and family to its own devices but rather furnish it with guidance in the field of doctrine and belief.

He urged that women as well as men be permitted to initiate divorce actions or that rabbinic courts be permitted to act in the case of recalcitrant husbands. "Unless we take such action very soon," he wrote, "what little is left of public respect for Jewish divorce laws will be irretrievably lost." Similarly, he thought it was still possible to save the Sabbath by working out "a defensible code of observance, one which sloughs off what is unimportant or impracticable, and puts forth new practices in the traditional spirit especially adapted to the American scene." Since in his opinion *Kashrut* in some form was indispensable to the Jewish future, he wanted the movement to set down a clear idea of what was required of Conservative Jews in this regard.

Steinberg also wanted a uniform Conservative prayerbook to be prepared which would eliminate outmoded elements in the liturgy and include the great treasures of worship materials that had been accumulating over the centuries. He was confident that these new materials would lend color and variety to the services and make possible a conservative form of worship worthy of the past and equal to the best in American and Jewish life.

Since the Conservative movement had not provided these materials, the Reconstructionist movement founded by Dr. Mordecai Kaplan had started its own publication program, issuing a new *Haggadah* and a Sabbath prayerbook of which he was one of the editors. Steinberg was one of the original group which had responded to Dr. Kaplan's call to establish a bi-weekly journal devoted to the spread of the idea of Judaism as a civilization. When the magazine was launched in January 1935, he served on the editorial board, contributed book reviews and articles and a few years later participated in organizing the Jewish Reconstructionist Foundation whose purpose was not to create a new movement, but to work through established movements in Judaism.

Steinberg remained a Reconstructionist throughout his life. However, he had certain reservations about the group's lack of interest in theology. In a letter to Rabbi Jacob Kohn he made it clear that his own interest in the movement was ideological and cultural rather than theological. "It is for its sociology of Jewish life that I am a Reconstructionist, not for the utility of Kaplan's theology." To Kaplan, "God is a concept, at least so he always speaks of God, rather than an existential reality, the reality of realities. Or to put it otherwise, Kaplan's God represents the psychological and sociological consequences of the God idea rather than the cosmic *ding an sich*. And yet," he went on, "with all my reservations as to Kaplan's theology, I am at home only in the Reconstructionist group. Conservative Judaism is for want of a philosophy jelly fish in character. Reconstructionism for all its inadequacies is to me an adequate sociology, the only one in contemporary Jewish life which takes cognizance of all aspects of Jewish tradition."

It was Steinberg's hope that the Reconstructionists would stimulate Conservatism to do something about the progressivism it professed and to begin to make Judaism creative once more. Accordingly, he agreed to serve on the Prayerbook Commission of the Rabbinical Assembly which during 1944 began to draft a new prayer-book for the movement. At meetings of the Commission he expressed the hope that the new book would have "the quality of elasticity in its treatment of the traditional text" and would be set up "to make possible varying choices in different congregations." He urged modifications of the traditional Hebrew text "whenever it was no longer consonant with what is common to our religious viewpoint and when in addition it could not be made such by reinterpretation as in the case of the restoration of animal sacrifices." He was anxious that the new prayer-book "reflect the fact that the world and Jewish life have changed in the past five hundred years." The majority of the Commission, however, did not agree with Steinberg's philosophy, preferring to move, as Dr. Robert Gordis, its chairman, put it, "with slow and cautious liberalizing."

In the sixteen years since his death a number of new developments have taken place in the Conservative movement—a daily prayer book has been issued as well as materials for adults and young people on various aspects of Judaism, a reorganized and more liberal law committee has come into being which has dealt with such questions as Sabbath observance, travel and the use of electricity on the Sabbath. A new type of *Ketubah* has been worked out to protect the woman in case of divorce, and *aliyot* for women have been approved by the majority of the committee. An anthology of readings entitled *Tradition and Change* on the development of Conservative Judaism was published and the official publication of the Rabbinical Assembly, *Conservative Judaism,* has been expanded and taken on a more exciting approach.

As we look back to the 1940's, it is clear that Steinberg helped prepare the way and made these developments possible.

His influence was recognized in the fall of 1946 when he was awarded an honorary degree of Doctor of Hebrew Letters by the Seminary. The citation summed up the position of prestige which he occupied not only in the ranks of Conservative Judaism, but in the larger American Jewish community:

"By your numerous writings you have brought many of our people and other Americans to a better understanding and appreciation of the nobility of the Jewish tradition, of the great and enduring contributions made by our sages to the culture of the world; of the place of the Jewish ethic and religion in uncovering new truths about life and new insights into the meaning of human existence;

Through your personal influence over all who have come in contact with you, your former teachers on the Faculty of this Seminary, your colleagues in the Rabbinate, the present student body of the Seminary, the membership of your congregation, and the vastly larger group throughout the country which looks to you as its Rabbi *par excellence,* you have greatly strengthened Jewish life in our time, bringing to it new forces for leadership, new energies for creativeness.

Through your personal self-dedication, you have set an example of devotion, which has a wide influence on the character of many of our people in this land, and have sanctified the name of God in the hearts of the whole community."

The Torch, Spring, 1966.

Dr. Noveck, Rabbi, Author and Educator, has occupied pulpits in Freeport, L. I. New York City, and, since 1961, in Hartford, Conn. He was Director of the National Academy of Adult Jewish Studies of the United Synagogue of America and of the B'nai B'rith Department of Adult Jewish Studies. He is the author of Adult Jewish Education in the Modern Synagogue *and has edited a series of books on* Great Jewish Personalities.

MAXWELL ABBELL

*A Jewish Business Man in
Contemporary America*

MAXWELL ABBELL

Recently I was invited to attend one of a series of dinners given at the White House by President Eisenhower. These were informal social dinners of small groups. At the one I attended there were sixteen guests, including three Cabinet officers, the National President of the A.F. of L. Carpenters Union, the President of the Massachusetts Institute of Technology, and leaders of industry, finance, education, and the professions. As I was flying to Washington to attend this dinner I could not help but think back to my early days as an immigrant boy, and the many struggles I experienced in the intervening years. I also could not help but think of the fact that here I was, a member of a minority group —a Jew, active in Jewish life—invited to dine with the head of our country, and with some of the nation's leading men, and I was grateful for this blessed land where a Jew, or a member of any other minority group, need not be ashamed of his race or religion, nor hide it, in order to attain success.

As the twig is bent, so the branch grows. And so I believe that I am what I am, and live as I do, because I am a fortunate beneficiary by precept and example of a great and noble tradition which guided and inspired the thoughts and the lives of my parents of blessed memory. For this fortuitous fact no credit is due to me. My parents inculcated in me a deep and abiding love for my people, and a reverent devotion to my faith. This outlook upon life became a part of me from as early an age as I can remember.

My parents were not only pious, deeply devout Jews; they were more than that. They constantly reiterated and emphasized, by formal teaching and exhortations, and by the example of their

68

own lives, the noble ethical principles enunciated by our Prophets and in our Holy writings. Thus, I became the fortunate possessor of a glorious heritage and a strong believer in the great teachings of our faith, and in living in accordance with these teachings from day to day.

While I have always revered my parents, it was only after the death of my father that I fully realized how strong-minded he was, how devout, how sensitive to moral and spiritual values; why, despite his meekness—originally a Jewish virtue, which some regard as a sign of weakness—he was such a strong influence in moulding my religious and moral life, as well as my professional and business activities. He had written down in Hebrew a few of the many sermons that he had occasion to preach on Holidays or special Sabbaths—not as a professional preacher, but as a learned and pious member of the Jewish community and of the Synagogue in which he worshipped. My own beloved Rabbi Morris Teller was impressed with these Hebrew manuscripts and urged me to have them translated into English and printed. I have followed this advice, and my father's work, "Sermons of a Maggid," has recently been published.

Like most Jewish immigrants fifty years ago, arriving without capital or occupational training, my father for a short while became a peddler. It would be an understatement to say that he was not successful in this occupation. But he carried into it those ethical principles which were a part, in fact the essence of his life. To him, the Biblical words "Love thy neighbor as thyself" . . . "Ye shall not steal; neither shall ye deal falsely, nor lie one to another" . . . "Thou shalt not oppress thy neighbor, nor rob him," (Leviticus XIX)—were not something to be recited on occasion, but a source of guidance in his everyday life. It is significant that in the same chapter, stealing, dealing falsely, and lying, are mentioned together. In order to fulfill even partially the commandment, "Love thy neighbor as thyself," one must first fulfill completely these simple, basic rules.

The exhortation of verses 35 and 36 of this same Chapter XIX of Leviticus: "Ye shall do no unrighteousness in judgment . . . in weight or in measure. Just balances just weights . . . shall ye have," was taken by my father most seriously and literally. Many businessmen think that they are not stealing or that they are acting properly, although in their business practice they flagrantly ignore and transgress the commandments contained in these sentences. Taking advantage of others' gullibility or weakness, "sharp practices," false weights or measures, misgrading, mislabelling, misrepresentation are in essence no different from actual stealing. Unfortunately, many people are not sensitive to this fact. Yet, according to the Bible the one is as wrong as the other. "Thou shalt not have in thy house diverse measures, a great and a small. A perfect and just weight shalt thou have; a perfect and just measure shalt thou have; that thy days may be long upon the land which the Lord thy God giveth thee. For all that do such things, even all that do unrighteously, are an abomination unto the Lord thy God." (Deuteronomy XXV, 13–16)

Bearing these great truths in mind, my father often sold his merchandise not only at no profit, but below cost. He always felt that there were others who were even poorer than he. He would no more think of overreaching anyone with whom he did business than of stealing money from that person's pockets. He later became a Hebrew teacher or *melamed,* a position which he fulfilled with devotion and earnestness the remaining years of his life.

To my parents, especially to my father, I owe two of my deep and abiding interests in life—my love of learning and my philanthropic interests. A few incidents of my childhood will indicate how their pattern of living engraved itself indelibly upon me.

As was true of most of the Jewish housewives who were contemporaries of my mother, the Sabbath was both a day of rest and a delight. On Friday afternoon, mother would tidy up our home in order to usher in the Sabbath with due reverance and dignity. We children would assemble about her as she dropped coins into a number of boxes representing different charitable institutions, a significant prelude to her lighting and blessing the candles. We were so poor that often these few pennies had to be borrowed from neighbors. Thus was instilled into my youthful consciousness the duty of helping others, not merely out of one's surplus, but even more so when it involved a material sacrifice.

This great truth was also taught to me by my father. For many years we lived in a four-room, stove-heated flat, with the fourth room closed off in the winter months as it could not be properly

heated. Indeed this was a substantial advance from our living ac-
commodations prior to that time. In three small rooms eight of us
lived, ate and slept—five sleeping in one room and three in another—the eight being composed of my parents, the four children
and two relatives who boarded with us. A couch in the kitchen,
which during the day was used instead of chairs, was often occupied at night by some itinerant wanderer whom my father had
met at Synagogue services and invited home, though there were
other people present with far more adequate sleeping quarters
who could have, but did not, volunteer to act as hosts. These
guests shared what little we had at our table.

We were so miserably poor that usually we could afford to buy
only stale bread returned to the baker; butter was a luxury; eggs,
fruit and vegetables almost unheard of. I was either a junior or a
senior in high school before I tasted a tomato. And yet there was
a wholesome, God-fearing spirit in this poverty-stricken home. It
was always meticulously clean, though after my birth my mother
was quite ill the remainder of her life. Yet despite her constant
pain, she did all the housework, including the laundry, which she
had to boil on the top of the coal stove in a tub, and then press
with an iron heated over the same stove. Into this home my father
would constantly bring strangers as guests in fulfillment of the
Biblical commandment to be kind to the stranger. These examples of my parents impressed me even as a child, and account for
the time and energy and means that I have since devoted to communal and philanthropic activities.

Though my mother could read and write both Hebrew and
Yiddish, it was from my father especially that I derived my love
of learning. Orphaned at a very early age, he was largely self-
taught, and could read, write and speak fluently, Russian, Polish,
Hebrew and Yiddish, and learned also to read and write somewhat in English, though never to any great extent. How he
scraped the pennies together I never could fathom, but he always
kept bringing home new Hebrew books. My mother often chided
him for thus literally taking the food out of his children's mouths,
but to no avail.

One incident particularly stands out in my memory. I was
about eleven years old. A representative of the Jewish Publication
Society had visited the Synagogue, and sure enough my father had

become a member, bringing three books home with him. I am sure he borrowed the membership fee, as he never had more than a few pennies on his person. These three books I still have and cherish. They were the foundation and the beginning of my present extensive Judaica library. They were the following: "Maimonides' Biography," "Selected Essays of Ahad Ha'am," and the revered Louis Ginsberg's first volume of "Legends of the Jews." These three books, which I have read and re-read, have both inspired me and increased my love for my people.

Besides my parents, the other great influence in my life was my Hebrew School, which I attended from the age of six until I was Bar Mitzvah. After public school I attended it thirteen hours a week. I went from four to seven Monday through Thursday evenings, one hour Saturday afternoon, and nine to twelve Sunday mornings. Nowadays, Jewish parents complain about taking three, four, or five hours a week from their children's playtime for this purpose. While at times I wished that I were playing outside with the other neighborhood children, yet on the whole I enjoyed going to Hebrew School. We managed to squeeze in a lot of fun alongside our serious study.

During my first years at Hebrew School, pedagogic methods were entirely old fashioned and inadequate. However, when I was about nine, we were fortunate in acquiring a new principal-teacher who, for the first time, taught us Hebrew Grammar, and used fairly modern teaching methods and procedures. From then on, I looked forward to my Hebrew classes and found them a source of joy as well as a competitive mental stimulant. A good portion of my later philosophy of Jewish life and values was derived from this teacher, both in class and as a frequent visitor at his home.

From my parents I derived a love for Palestine as the Jewish ancestral home. My father—as I have indicated, an extremely pious man—held the view of many orthodox Jews of those days, that in due course, in the Messianic era, Palestine would be restored to the Jewish people by the grace of God, without human intervention and assistance. In later years he changed his views and became a Zionist—too late, however, to influence me in this regard. My Zionism, which has been so major a factor in my outlook upon life and my Jewish activities, I owe largely to my Hebrew teacher. On the slightest pretext—and even without it— during our Biblical or Hebrew grammar studies, he would infuse us with the hope and the aim of rebuilding and re-winning the Holy Land as a Jewish home-land. For this inspiration, I owe him a deep debt of gratitude.

It was these childhood influences of home and parents, of Hebrew school and teachers, together with the influences of my dear wife that shaped my entire life as I shall relate.

At an early age—I would guess about nine or ten—I had resolved to acquire a good education. As I grew older and attended high school, living in a suburb of Boston, I gradually resolved that this education should be at Harvard. This aim I kept before me through years of bitter hardship and struggle.

When I graduated from grammar school at the age of thirteen, my parents reluctantly informed me that much as they desired to see me continue my education, their economic condition precluded their doing so. After much persuasion, I was given the opportunity of continuing in high school, provided I could support myself. For four long years I sold newspapers on the streets and delivered them to homes, arising early in the morning during the bitter New England winters, and often came home with my feet so frozen that I had to thaw them out in the oven of the coal stove on a pillow, while I was preparing my Latin or German lessons for the day. I not only purchased all my own clothes while attending high school, but paid board regularly and in increasing amounts. At the same time, I was able to save enough so that, together with a scholarship which I won, I was able to enter Harvard, where I earned my way by tutoring wealthier classmates, waiting on tables about thirty hours a week, and by doing sundry other chores. Despite this, I accumulated more than the necessary credits for graduation in three years, and graduated with honors.

One incident during my work as a waiter stands out in my memory. One day a student diner complained to the head waiter that I had not served him enough bacon with his liver. The head waiter reprimanded the chef, who insisted he had served enough, but that I must have eaten some of the bacon on my way from the kitchen to the dining room. (Some of the waiters did this, and the head waiter—himself a former waiter and a student—was not unaware of this practice) . I was called on the carpet and told my services were no longer required. This would have been a terrible blow to me, as without this job I would not have been able to continue in school. I pleaded that I could not have taken the bacon, as I never ate bacon, ham, or other pork products. I urged the head waiter, who regarded me with incredulity, to verify this fact with the other waiters. This he did, and then informed me that I could continue my job. Thus, quite accidentally, my Jewish way of living made it possible for me to continue my secular education.

On graduation from Harvard I was recommended to banks in New York City and Chicago by my teachers. Because of my religion I could not find an opening in this field. I had even been engaged by the Vice President of a Chicago bank and then, after my religion was ascertained, told that the bank did not need any trainees—although obviously this official had been sent to Cambridge for the very purpose of engaging graduates and did, I later learned, engage a classmate of mine whose academic record was much poorer. This experience did not leave me bitter; it merely strengthened my resolution to succeed regardless of such handicaps as my race and religion might impose upon me. In turn, in my own business dealings, I have always disregarded religion. A number of my close business and professional associates, as well as a vast majority of my employees, are men and women of the Christian faith. "Thou shall not oppress the strangers; remember that you were strangers in the land of Egypt."

Finding that even a Harvard education meant little in the business world, I became a social worker and then a factory personnel worker for a short while, at the same time studying accounting at night. Upon completing my studies and passing the Certified Public Accountant examinations, I accepted employment with a firm of public accountants, among whose clients was the Jewish Charities of Chicago and its affiliated agencies. While I was engaged in auditing these agencies, I was asked to join the staff of the Jewish Charities where I remained until September 1937, in charge of budgeting, fund raising, office and fiscal activities. The twelve years I spent at the Jewish Charities—now the Jewish Federation of Chicago—were years in which I matured in both my Jewish and general outlook.

These were the years when the ascendency of the German Jewish group was declining and the star of the East European Jewish group was rising. In the middle thirties conflicts which had been smouldering for years on the question of Jewish education broke out into the open, resulting in 1934 in the dis-affiliation of the Chicago Board of Jewish Education as a constituent agency. During this controversy I was often present at committee meetings of the opponents of Jewish education. The men present knew that I strongly favored Jewish education. I did not hesitate to tell them exactly where I stood on the subject. Instead of lessening their respect for me, my forthrightness increased it. One of these opponents of Jewish education several years later loaned me the funds with which I made my first purchase of real estate. It never occurred to me to curry favor with my employers and superiors by denying beliefs and principles I strongly held.

In later years I became very active in the field of Jewish education in Chicago, and in national organizations—despite the fact that until recently it was not too popular an activitity in the Jewish community.

For some years now I have been a Director of the Chicago Board of Jewish Education and Chairman of the Board of Governors of the Chicago College of Jewish Studies. This interest in Jewish education, plus the love which my parents gave me for my faith, led to my becoming increasingly active, as the years went on, in the affairs of the Jewish Theological Seminary of America, of which I am now a Director, as well as Vice-Chairman of its Board of Overseers. This combined interest in Jewish education and Jewish religion led to my intense activitity as a layman in both fields, which I have served during the past three years as President of the United Synagogue of America. My early training, both at home and at Hebrew school, has, however, impelled me to make my major contribution towards the perpetuation and reinvigoration of Jewish learning, toward creating a positive dynamic and meaningful Judaism in America.

There have been many times when problems arose because of my Jewishness. I have refused to attend civic and business meetings at downtown Chicago clubs where Jews are not admitted as members. Not only have I not sought to minimize my Jewishness, but have neglected no opportunity to call my interest in Jewish affairs to the attention of my non-Jewish clients and business associates. In numerous instances I have received from them, without solicitation, contributions to various Jewish institutions and causes as a tribute on their part to my interest in my faith, and as an indication of their respect for my attitude.

While, like other Jews, I have occasionally met with manifestations of ignorance and discrimination, on the whole I have found that Christians of character have regarded me with respect because I adhered to my faith, was not ashamed of it, and never attempted to hide or deny it. The few adverse instances I have related merely proved that it is possible to live Jewishly and to achieve, nonetheless, a measure of business and professional success. The obstacles that confronted me may well have been a challenge to greater effort.

My Jewish way of life, such as the observance of *Kashruth* in my home, praying daily, observing the Sabbath and Festivals, has been no real problem. To be sure, there have been conditions and situations where one or the other has been difficult. But so is life in general. That which is worthwhile is worth making a sacrifice for; and that which comes all too easily is often of little value, and less appreciated.

When, a number of years ago I opened my own public accounting and law office, I resolved to conduct myself in both professions in accordance with the highest standards of ethics. Some may think it unbusinesslike for me to say that the reputation for integrity which I have endeavoured to build up has, in many ways, enabled me to attain some measure of financial success. I claim no particular credit for my rule of honesty in business affairs. I was merely applying in practical life the teachings of my parents and my faith.

There have very often been times when, in my professional practice, clients have come to me with tax saving schemes and devices which I did not sanction. They have asked me to certify financial statments with incorrect figures or to make illegal and improper deductions on income tax returns. Sometimes I lost clients by refusing to become a partner to such mal-practices, even when I had just opened my office and could hardly afford to do so.

There were instances where I have gone beyond contractual obligations to protect the investments of friends and clients who have participated with me in my ventures. Once I arranged for the purchase of a valuable piece of property and, as sometimes happens in the world of business, virtually the entire investment was lost. Though I was not bound legally or even morally, I made good the money which had been invested by my friends and clients, for I felt that these people had invested because of their faith in my integrity and judgment and therefore I could not let them down. While momentarily this involved restriction of credit and the incurring of very substantial financial losses, in the long run it has created on the part of the banking institutions and insurance companies with whom I do business greater confidence in my integrity, which has enabled me to embark upon enterprises that would otherwise have been impossible. It has also created faith and confidence in my character and judgment on the part of those who have invested in my enterprise; thus demonstrating that in the long run high ethical principles in business not only need be no deterrent to financial success, but can in many ways further such success.

It has often been said that the Jewish religion is different from others in that it does not emphasize belief in formulas and doctrines, but insists rather on a program of day-to-day living. Judaism is a way of life and not merely a set of doctrinal beliefs. This awareness has been bred into my bones, and so it has been to me a matter of course to have lived in accordance with the great ethical principles handed down by our teachers and sages. Strange as it may seem, I firmly believe that by adhering to these great teachings I have added immeasurably to my professional and business successes.

It is as businessman, a Jewish businessman in Twentieth Century America, that I have come to understand the tremendous significance of the eighth Commandment, "Thou shalt not steal." It has always had in my eyes a far wider application than the usual narrow limitation to theft and robbery. To my mind, it forbids every illegal acquisition of another's property. There may be transactions which are legal and do not involve any breach of the law which are, however, base and disgraceful—such transactions in which a person takes advantage of the ignorance and embarrassment of another for the purpose of increasing his own profit. These methods I have eschewed as contrary to the eighth Commandment. To me it has always been very significant that proper standards of business conduct are considered so important that they are stressed by being mentioned in no less than four of the five Books of Moses. These truths were taught to me in Hebrew school and by the example of my parents.

While my formal Jewish education ended when I was Bar Mitzvah, the noble Biblical teachings I learned prior thereto have nevertheless been my guide ever since in my daily life. I have often gone back to the Pentateuch, and have always found new inspiration, new guidance, new stimulus, and new encouragement in my daily activities. Without this background and heritage I may have been less successful—certainly less happy. How any Jew can drink from the never-diminishing fountain of spiritual sustenance and inspiration that is our age-old legacy, and not be aided in his daily living; how any Jew who has had such inspiration can ever depart from the path of righteousness, decency and honesty; how a Jew can even think of foreswearing his ancestry and his spiritual heritage, hiding his Jewishness—or even worse, deserting his people—it is difficult to comprehend. As for me, my Jewish faith has been a source of joy and happiness, of light and guidance, of peace of mind as well as peace of soul.

The Torch, Winter, 1954.

ABRAHAM JOSHUA HESCHEL

A New Teacher and Personality in the
Conservative Movement

HERBERT PARZEN

The Conservative movement has, concededly, quickened Jewish life in America by pouring into its currents vital men with vital ideas who have sought to control runaway and disintegrating tendencies, foster creative trends, forge and formulate healing and healthful prescriptions for the community.

These men of distinction and learning, each in his own way, hoped to press beauty and joy, vitality and meaning, into Jewish tradition in order to harness that tradition to the purpose of preserving the historical continuity of Jewish life in the New World. And by historical continuity they did not understand changelessness. Indeed, they have exerted their influence and employed their talents to adjust, to adapt, to reconstruct Judaism into a pulsating pattern of life, to instill into American Jewry love and loyalty for the Jewish heritage, and understanding of their position and function in the modern world. The difficulties inherent in the task account for the limited goals so far gained. Nevertheless, the direction has been demarcated. Solomon Schechter and Israel Friedlaender, Louis Ginzberg and Mordecai M. Kaplan, each in accordance with his own understanding, have spent their mature lives in the effort to survey and to map the conditions essential for a creative Jewish community in democratic and industrialized America that should be comparable to earlier Jewish centers of significance.

Within recent years a fresh and rather unnoticed ferment, engendered by a resourceful figure, has been at work within the Conservative movement, especially in the halls of the Seminary. Because of his trenchant ideas and his personalized presentation of them, he has attracted extraordinary attention at the last convention of the Rabbinical Assembly of America, and at the subsequent summer sessions arranged for its members at the Seminary. At these occasions the man and his purpose have assumed injunctive importance.

Abraham Joshua Heschel, Associate Professor of Jewish Ethics and Mysticism at the Seminary, is by no means an unknown personality. His writings and public lectures have aroused keen debate and partisanship ranging from applause to dispraise. However, his program and purpose were hitherto not clearly appreciated. Now it is patent that he proposes to participate dynamically in the intellectual wrestlings that are so characteristic of the Conservative movement due to its continuous quest for solutions to problems confronting Judaism in modern America without surrendering its historical foundations. He has decided to share in shaping its future course. And he is entitled to do so because of his learning and way of life and, above all, because his imagination and poetic ideas are a refreshing antidote against the lackadaisical and lackluster milieu stifling the Synagogue.

As Dr. Heschel surveys the religious scene he finds it shallow, unimaginative, drab. Worship is without fervor or awe or reverence; is without joy, exaltation, aspiration. Observance, to the extent that it exists, is external routine, without stirring or awaking the chords of faith. Observance is considered an end in itself rather than an instrument to serve God, to experience the Divine. The mitzvot are performed without intent and thought, without devotion, without spiritual glee, and without affecting the soul.

Because the Jewish religion is stigmatized as "discipline," so contrary to modern conceptions of freedom and education, it is considered outmoded. *Tikun hanefesh,* the improvement of the soul, is seldom in consciousness. Personal religion—communion with God through prayer, study and meditation—is neglected or ignored. A confused folk faith is operative, incapable of stimulating the individual spiritually or shepherding Jewish group life.

Pervading the Synagogue is a superficial and unreasoned rationalism. The sense of wonder is missing; poetry, music, the stuff woven of the soul and spirit, are relegated to the incidental. Neither faith nor Torah is at home; neither the heart nor the mind is nourished.

Against this state of affairs—"religious behaviorism" he calls it —against the unimaginative, the mechanical, the uninspiring, he seeks to initiate a crusade. He wants to restore devotion, faith, the sense of the marvelous and wondrous in the religious life. He pleads with the Jew to reestablish a place in the religious sun for God, for his personal God.

In this connection, it becomes relevant to note his views of Conservative Judaism. He concurs that it is the only modern interpretation that has retained respect and reverence for the authority of the *Halakha,* the Law, and is concerned to recover its dynamism for Jewish life. He upholds the Conservative teachers in the assumption that Judaism is inconceivable without the discipline of the *Halakha,* and would be false to its history and genius to forego the regimen of the *mitzvot.*

However, he contends that the spokesmen of Conservatism have been unable to counteract the tragic trend toward "religious behaviorism," cumulative in its effect, because they have permitted the *Halakha* to be considered an end in itself, formal and punctilious; its operation random, uncontrolled, without understanding. The reason is clear. To breathe meaning and vibrancy, zeal and vitality, into the halakhic discipline by means of halakhic hermeneutics is a herculean task, well nigh beyond the spiritual strength of our Movement. The contemporaneous effort to adapt the Law is, therefore, largely artificial and in vain. In the final analysis, no change can be effected until the hearts of the people are changed. And Judaism, he insists, has the historical means to change their hearts, to lead them to discover their souls. These means must be brought to the fore in order to flower Jewish hearts and souls. Jews must be taught to recognize the inalienable bond between their hearts and their faith, the immediate relationship between their souls and serving God.

According to him, the Conservative movement is thus confronted with a great opportunity to meet unflinchingly the corrosive challenge of "religious behaviorism," and to influence the religious and spiritual rebirth of American Jewry. How? By developing techniques and arts to thaw the existent frosty atmosphere in the Synagogue. By imbuing the Movement with meaningful zeal, gleeful enthusiasm, poetic imagination, fervent faith. By teaching that the primary duty of religious men is to be servants of God. The *mitzvot* must be interpreted as tools to attain these ends. Accordingly, the *Halakha* must be made to function as an inspiring, heart-pulsating, soul-stirring agent in the service of Jews to prepare and train themselves to serve God, the God of Israel, who is concerned that every Jew obey His will. Overarching and underlying the *mitzvot* is *Emuna*, faith, in the traditional sense of the idea, with emphasis on *Ha'shagha Pratit*, God's care for every individual person. We must help our people to find that faith, that kind of faith.

This proposed program stems, naturally, from his experience and is based on his convictions. Both are rooted in rabbinic Judaism and in several aspects of Hassidism, but devoid of the Tzaddik cult. His secular studies in German universities have contributed his philosophies of idealism and esthetics, and in no way interfere with his Jewish *weltanschaung*.

He denies that he is orthodox; he certainly is not the conventional traditionalist. Nonetheless his theology is largely rabbinic, punctuated with ideas from Jewish mystic and moralistic (*musar*) literature. He considers the opinions of these authors as authoritative as the views of the halakhic sages. He warmly advocates the use of this literature in the education of Jewish personalities, particularly in institutions of higher Jewish learning, in order that their perspectives of Jewish tradition may be broad and deep and rounded.

Like the sages of Judaism throughout history, Dr. Heschel pursues the principle of selective emphasis in determining the doctrines which require extraordinary affirmation and accent at a given time—the trends of every era point to the teachings which must be stressed and raised to first position in the hierarchy of doctrines in order to keep strong and solid the structure of Judaism. Accordingly, he believes that the present status of Judaism in America demands emphasis on *Haggada*, the non-legal rabbinic literature, referring particularly to its inspirational and educative materials, its moral and ethical values, not to damage or weaken the *Halakha* but to bolster its authority. Thereby Jews will realize and recognize the Law's spirit and value. Therefore he wants due weight given to *Kavanah*, intent, thought, conscious concentration, during religious exercises rather than to *Kevah*, the fixed and formal observance in detail and in time. In sum, the moment calls for a change in method in order to instruct and inspire devoted Jewish living by emphasis on the soul of Judaism, its poetry, its sense of wonder, its exultation in searching for God.

I must add at once that Dr. Heschel does not underrate the significance of the *Halakha* and the principle of *Kevah*. He believes, however, that these must be transfused with fervor and charged with inspiration in order to destroy the prevailing "religious behaviorism," insidious in its effect. He is convinced that American Jews can be influenced to love and to do the *mitzvot* when their import will be focused on the emotional, the artistic, the wondrous.

In the history of Judaism, according to his reading of it, the polarity of the *Halakha* and *Haggada* are clearly manifest. This reading has always been in dispute. No conventional tradition accepts this viewpoint. He rather insists that the *Halakha* has been the normal, the dominant and authoritative force in Jewish history; the *Haggada* the personal, momentary, homiletic opinions of individual preachers.

Dr. Heschel, it appears, merely contends that the *Haggada* as a parallel stream in Jewish thought may be rightfully utilized at the present time in America to discredit the current behavior patterns and to substitute genuine and impassioned religious faith anchored to *Halakha* perceptively motivated, and not performed by rote but with rapture.

In the effort to establish the polarity of the two aspects of rabbinic literature Dr. Heschel is hewing out a road which leads away from the trodden and the usual. In striving to persuade the Conservative movement that its principal opportunity to vitalize Judaism lies in introducing the soul and spirit of the *Haggada* into the *Halakha* and its daily practices, he points to an approach tested in Jewish experience and not contrary to Jewish thought. Moreover, he is convinced that it must and can be achieved. His work, accordingly, assumes significance.

Whether one agrees or disagrees with Dr. Heschel's postulates is irrelevant to the fact that a vivid personality with intense convictions and intriguing ideas is at work in the ranks of the Conservative movement. He advocates his ideas with vigor and assurance. He is frankly committed to fertilize and fructify the thinking and living of Conservative Jews specifically, and American Jewry, in general.

Thus another vital teacher with a vital message is grappling with the problems of Judaism in America within the frame of the Conservative movement. He has indicated a current which is bound to endure and to carve its own distinctive channel in contemporaneous Jewish thought. This is in complete accord with the tradition and genius of Conservative Judaism. And it is a good omen for American Jewry.

Five decades ago, Solomon Schechter, at the very beginning of his labors in America, formulated the principle of freedom of thought and discussion for the guidance of the infant institution that has become the spiritual and the intellectual fountainhead of Conservative Judaism. Mystic and rationalist, traditionalist and radical religionist, as long as they speak with the voice of Jacob and their source of inspiration is Sinai, have their legitimate place in its ranks and free play for their ideas. History has fully vindicated this wise policy.

Professor Heschel has chosen wisely to explore his proposals and to realize his hopes within and by means of the Conservative movement.

The Torch, Spring, 1954.

Rabbi Parzen is a well known contributor to Jewish periodicals as well as an author and educational administrator. He has occupied pulpits in St. Paul, Minn., Portland, Ore., Freeport, L. I. and New York City. He is now attached to the Theodore Herzl Institute in New York. He has been Director of Programs, United Synagogue of America, and Executive Director of The Reconstructionist Foundation. His writings include Architects of Conservative Judaism, A Short History of Zionism *and* Herzl Speaks.

Part Two

BASIC CONCEPTS

"A critical reassessment of religion is necessitated by the very situation of our thinking. We cannot continue to employ our critical faculty in all our endeavors and at the same time abstain from raising questions in regard to religion. Our age is the age of criticism to which everything must be subjected. The sacredness of religion, and the authority of legislation, are by many regarded as grounds of exemption from the examination of this tribunal. But, if they are exempted, they become the subject of just suspicion, and cannot lay claim to sincere respect, which reason accords only to that which has stood the test of a free public examination."

—Abraham J. Heschel

INTRODUCTION

The articles which appear in this part reflect the thinking which was going on during the past twenty-five years in the minds of men of action—rabbis, scholars and lay leaders who were concerned with the thrust of Judaism in this transitional period. Many of the ideas propounded in these pages have already taken root in the life of our American Jewish community. While the search was directed toward the shaping of a particular movement it could not be thought of apart from the evolving form of the total Jewish community.

In this brief introduction reference will be made to some of the thoughts which are expressed by the writers. The impact and influence of the newly established State of Israel was recognized by them. Yet they were unanimous in asserting that American Jewry has a permanent abode and must seek out its own method of survival.

The late Solomon Goldman, a leading and ardent Zionist, expressed this when he wrote, "America is not for the Jew a boarding house. It is a home." Dr. Robert Gordis affirmed it by saying, "Jewish life is here to stay. In our day, at least, American Jewry is incurably survivalist." He continued, "it is no particularist loyalty which impels me to restate my conviction that it is Conservative Judaism in particular which should take the initiative in undertaking this life-saving function for American Jewry."

Both of these men suggested patterns for the strengthening of American Jewish religious life. Goldman advocated the establishment of a National Synagogue through the coordination and merger of several thousand congregational units, linking the individual synagogues to their national bodies in every way. Gordis, on the other hand, stressed the voluntary community dedicated to organic Judaism. His belief was that "on the local level the synagogue center would ally itself with other synagogues and form a local synagogue council. These would then be organized into the *Congregation of American Jewry.*"

Interestingly enough the suggested patterns outlined by these men have taken shape on the American Jewish scene through the Orthodox, Reform and Conservative national synagogue bodies. On a local level, synagogue councils have not flourished as much as was anticipated. On a national scale the Synagogue Council of America has succeeded thus far in keeping the three branches of Judaism together in a unified body made up of its national constituencies. It has been lacking in real effectiveness because a unanimous vote is required to adopt resolutions for action. Another weakness has been that there are sectors of the Orthodox community which have refused to participate in the Synagogue Council.

As the American Jewish community evolved there emerged a greater emphasis on the centrality of the synagogue. Dr. Simon Greenberg expressed it this way—"What made it possible for our people to defy what otherwise seems to be the inexorable law of history after exile from land to land? There is but one answer to this question. The Jewish people while living upon its soil, and during eras of spiritual and political autonomy, brought to fruition an absolutely unique institution, the synagogue. It proved to possess unprecedented powers of adaptation."

Taking cognizance of the impact of Israel on contemporary world Jewry, Dr. Greenberg makes the interesting observation, "assuming an extended period of peace and growth, the magic of the miracle of the State of Israel is bound to wear off. Jews in the Diaspora are bound to emphasize more that their attachment is not to the State of Israel as a political entity, but to the land of Israel in which the State of Israel happens to be located and to the Jewish community of the State of Israel insofar as it and they share common spiritual treasures. These common spiritual treasures have by our history been associated primarily with and concentrated in the synagogue."

Rabbi Jacob Agus stressed this further by stating that "the

only philosophy which is capable of lending to American Israel consistency and vigor, pride and purpose is the philosophy of the synagogue—not the philosophy of the spurious synagogue which ruthlessly breaks with tradition and cruelly cuts into the roots of Jewish loyalty in the name of an emaciated ghost called Judaism."

Mere "Jewishness" or being a Jew by nationality was not enough of an identification according to Rabbi Agus. The role of the synagogue had to be proclaimed forthrightly if it was to become the major instrument for the preservation of Judaism in the Diaspora.

The leaders of the Conservative Movement faced a two-fold challenge—to make tradition relevant to the majority of the people in modern day life and to enable them to accept it and not to encase it.

Dr. Max Arzt characterized it in this way: "thus our tradition lives by the dual process of historic continuity and organic growth. Conservative Judaism makes explicit that which is implicit in the behavior of those who are essentially loyal to Judaism. The widespread religious lawlessness is due to indifference rather than to defiance. There is thoughtless treading on the sacred. We must redirect modern Jewish life in the paths of the Halakha by establishing in each congregation fellowships of *Haverim*. Our age needs the kind of a convocation called by Ezra when the people stood as it were a second time at Sinai and publicly renewed their allegiance to the Torah."

However, the late Rabbi Morris Adler was more direct in his evaluation of the situation. He insisted "we must move forward to a stage in which Conservative Judaism revolves about an axis of positive and unambiguous affirmations." Adler went on to say "the Jews for whom we are called to devise a Jewish philosophy and rationale are not Jews whose conceptions of Judaism have become out-dated and are in need of revision, but are individuals with no conception of Judaism." He stated that "observance is not for us a supernaturally ordained regimen, but the vehicle of Jewish discipline and unity and the stimulus to refinement of our spiritual life."

The late Maxwell Abbell, a distinguished lay leader in the Conservative Movement, asked for more than learning. He pleaded for bringing "our Halakha into compatibility with the needs of the modern fast changing world and for a more simplified, more relevant, more meaningful, more feasible, more livable regimen of conduct that can be observed with integrity."

What specifically are the features of Conservative Judaism? Dr. Abraham Halkin described them as follows:

"It is cognizant and takes note of the conflict between a number of accepted religious dogmas and the position based on present day science and thought. It chooses to be intellectually honest. It does not entertain the least desire to break with traditional practice and behavior for the sake of breaking. As a general rule, the Conservative Movement recognizes fully and emphasizes the importance of loyalty to tradition, loyalty to the Jewish people and recognition of the importance of Hebrew in our religious culture. It makes a serious effort to treat the practice of the moral precepts with the same earnestness with which it approaches any other precept in our religious tradition. It teaches that religion must participate in contemporary events. People are no longer Conservative by defection because they left the ranks of the Orthodox. They are Conservative by choice, because they find it better suited to their convictions and to their attitudes."

Dr. Halkin concludes by urging that "our personal lives and our family life be governed by a calendar of the Sabbath and Jewish holidays (which emphasize our historical and spiritual values), that we be consciously and intelligently active in behalf of our brethren in the rest of the world and that we look upon the State of Israel and its welfare as an integral part of our Jewishness."

A broader and long range approach to the future of Judaism was taken by Dr. Mordecai Kaplan. Dr. Moshe Davis quotes him as follows: "in every aspect of its life our people is reeling under the impact of the great social and human revolutions in civilization. These crises can be met only by a process of metamorphosis, by transformation to a new stage of Jewish development." To do so, Dr. Kaplan proposed that The Jewish Theological Seminary of America become a University of Judaism. He said that "the program of the University must be based on the primacy of scholarship, the Hebrew character of Judaism, the abundance or plenitude of Jewish living and the acceptance of the American environment as permanent. The foundation or content of these principles is, of course, the religious tradition."

Jewish education is the indispensable ingredient to the survival of Judaism. Dr. Israel Kazis expressed the thought that only by producing dedicated custodians of our heritage could Judaism survive in the Diaspora. He asserted that "the development of such Jews requires above all an intensive pursuit of Jewish learning for only in the rich soil of knowledge can the seeds of appreciation and love of our heritage flourish." The priority of Jewish education from the elementary religious schools to higher institutions of Jewish learning has finally been conceded by most Jewish communal leaders on the North American Continent. Jewish all-day schools are growing in number and are receiving increasing financial support in many cities from their Community Welfare Funds.

Speedy action is needed as the hour is very late for salvaging the youths and adults who can still be imbued with a rich understanding and love for the cultural and religious values of Judaism.

Judge Simon Rifkind calls upon the laity to "develop habits of learning and to exemplify standards of conduct which we can proudly call Jewish, and to resume the initiative in the field of action by expanding and perfecting our educational institutions, particularly those like The Jewish Theological Seminary of America which are training the scholars and personnel for American Jewry." He also added, "to me it seems inevitable that should the synagogue long continue as an institution in which a learned Rabbi ministers to an uninstructed laity, it will cease to be a synagogue and become a church."

Conservative Judaism has thus emerged in these twenty-five years as a positive constructive movement, emphasizing the centrality of the synagogue, seeking to build a bridge between tradition, historical Judaism and modern thought, rooting itself in Halakha and yet adjusting to the times. It recognizes its tie to the Jewish people everywhere and particularly to Eretz Israel and looks upon the Hebrew language as indispensable to its existence. To achieve all of this the community must have Jewishly educated laity possessed of a sense of responsibility for the goals of Conservative Judaism.

J. S. G.

JUDAISM TODAY AND TOMORROW

SOLOMON GOLDMAN

All of our efforts in the United Synagogue, Seminary, and Rabbinical Assembly are predicated on the assumption or credo, if you will, that we neither look upon the United States as being our temporary asylum nor regard ourselves as lodgers for the night, resting from the weariness of the day's journey so as to continue more briskly on the morrow toward a beckoning haven. We suffer from no illusions, nor are we disposed to join in the councils of those who heal the breach of the people lightly. We are disturbingly aware of the offensive *numerus clausus*, unfair employment practices, crack-pot frontist organizations that so frequently receive support and encouragement from Christian industrialists, scholars, artists, statesmen and clergymen. We know of the prickly and poisonous barriers that bar a Jew's way to his rights, and, indeed, even to his duties, but we no more mistrust America because of the rash of prejudice that often breaks out upon the body politic than we despair of our own future destiny, because of our habitual backsliding. We have an abiding faith in America. Its early history parallels our own. Its founding fathers disengaged themselves from their country, their kindred, and their father's house even as did our forefathers in order that they might breathe the air of freedom.

America is not for the Jew a boarding-house. It is home. We have dug roots here and have harvested fruit aplenty. There is no doubt but that a small number of American Jews will settle in Israel. A somewhat larger number will forever be on their way there, at least by word of mouth, but for some mysterious reason will never get there. Many American Jews—do not ask me how many—will dissolve into thin air and disappear from our midst. Most of us, that is, the largest number of American Jews, will have the pride of heritage and the love of peoplehood, will sense vaguely the blessedness in both for ourselves and humanity as a whole, and possess the resolution, fortitude, wisdom, and consecration to preserve our self-identity and assure our creative continuity. You ask for how long? I do not know. The curtain of history is not only wrought of iron, it is lined with triple brass, and encased in granite. Yet I make bold to predict that the grandchildren of your grandchildren will be known as Americans and Jews.

It is not our understanding that this sense of at-homeness or feeling of belonging here impels us to erect a wall between the American Jewish Community and Jews elsewhere. To the contrary Jews who are proud enough to own a common background are men enough to want to face a common destiny. Those who seek to extricate themselves from the latter will end in reading themselves out of the former. Or maybe this is the beginning of their unwisdom. Most of us, that is those of us who wish to remain Jews, realize that the reality of our peoplehood is ineradicable. The attempt to bring about its end, if under the compulsion of anti-Semitic charges, is to mate folly with cowardice; if by virtue of religious liberalism, is to surpass the Bourbons in stubbornness as in ignorance. It is too late in our history to have to remind anyone that anti-Semites despise Judaism more than they do Jews and apprehend it the more. Nor is it anything but trite to point out that to divorce the Jewish religion from the Jewish people is to distort it. No, we seek no such divorcement, no such separation, either from our historical self or from the far-flung Jewish communities the world over. We refuse to equate patriotism with isolationism and Americanism with narrow nationalism. We refuse to believe that it ever was the intention of the United States to extend the privilege of citizenship only to those who deny or distort the nature of their being or background. We are satisfied that our desire to be linked to our people has the understanding and sympathy of America.

Need I add, after having said this much, that I have followed for the past three years the ebb and flow of life in Israel as one interested and implicated in all that is happening there. I have thrilled to the emergence of the State, its buoyancy, self-assurance, daring, and dignity, the recognition and esteem it has won in the conclave of nations, and, above all, to the ingathering of exiles, and the regeneration of many thousands of the victims of human bestiality, even as I have been saddened by the narrowness of its religious hierarchy, the fanaticism of its zealots, and by such other tensions and strains that accompany growth.

It is high time that the Synagogue pronounce both the spiritual unity of the world's Jewries, including Israel, and the absolute political independence of these Jewries vis-a-vis Israel as being undebatable first principles. Neither is it too soon to reject with contempt the futile, vain, mischievous and ultimately harmful debate on dual allegiance and priority and to underscore our faith in the creative continuity of American Jewry.

Now let us turn to another matter and inquire what it is that has disinclined most of the members of constituent congregations, if not indeed most Jews, toward religious services and Jewish observance. It is important that we solve this riddle, not only for the good of Judaism but even more for the sake of preserving our self-respect and integrity. Are Americans generally non-attendant and non-observant? Or are we alone an irreligious community? If we are, then why is it that Mr. X, and he is one of many, many thousands, pays a thousand dollars a year for the right of occupying a seat in the Synagogue three days a year? Why is it that he is so frequently among the first to contribute generously toward the expansion of the Synagogue's facilities and program? Why does Mr. X make such an ado about his boy becoming Bar Mitzvah, and why, when the happy event occurs, does he start off the Bar Mitzvah feast with shrimp cocktails? Shall we say that he is ignorant and confused? The fact is that he is passably intelligent and clear-thinking, no less than were his father and grandfather. If we deny this to be the case then what we are actually doing is condemning seventy, in many instances ninety, per cent of our own members and most American Jews with them. If we say that Mr. X's Rabbi is incompetent and derelict in the performance of his duty then we are condemning the whole American Rabbinate.

Now that of course would be no reason why we should call a spade a shovel. The truth, it has often been urged, is no respecter of persons. Neither need it be of classes and masses. If it is our considered opinion that American Jews are confused and ignorant and their Rabbis incompetent and derelict in their duties, then we are duty-bound to say so. The fact is that that is exactly what we have been saying for nearly half a century. We have shouted at Mr. X without abatement, with anger and indignation. But we have never stopped taking his money or doing him honor. Nor have we either driven him from our midst or regenerated him or provided him with a more competent and faithful shepherd.

How long shall we play at make believe? How long shall we pretend that these breaches of which I speak can be healed lightly? Are we really so wanting in dignity and self-respect—think we so little of our tradition—as to wish to lead Jews back to observance and Synagogue attendance by means of distributing awards and citations, gold stars, blue stars, and green cheese? Are we so unintelligent as to employ such techniques and think our people so infantile as to be allured by them? Are we so naive as to believe that the taking of a pledge, a kind of instant aid remedy, currently in vogue, will heal a body at which disease has gnawed for decades? Are ritual and worship basic in the tradition of the Synagogue? Then why have we never thought of examining the fact of their desuetude to its very roots? Why have we remained the prisoners of routine methods, techniques and slogans?

My purpose is to alert this Convention that has confidently chosen as its theme Judaism Today and Tomorrow, to the gravity of the situation and the absurdity of our wonted procedure, and to urge upon it to shake itself free from fixed routine, to act maturely, spurn easy solutions, distrust the promises of quick returns, and instead call into existence, once and for all, a commission of experts in a variety of fields—say economics, education, sociology, psychology, psychoanalysis, history and law—to search out thoroughly the wilderness in which we have now wandered for so many years. Perhaps such a commission might be fortunate enough to determine the causes of the general desuetude which we have not ceased to discuss and bewail, and which has by now engulfed most American Jews, if not the majority of Jews the world over.

I beg leave to put before you a number of questions that importune an answer. I have, for example, been wanting to learn whether my members had ceased to pray after joining the *Anshe Emet* or whether their present behavior has by any chance a long history? Is it possible that they actually never prayed, even when as children they accompanied their parents to "shul"? What are the facts in regard to this matter with respect to their parents and grandparents? When and where did the practice of *iberhippen*, that is, skipping over parts of the prayer-book or of galloping across its pages in double quick time begin? Does perhaps the break-down in our midst of the habit of worship have a history? If so, may it not be that the length of the Jewish service, its repetitiousness, its intermittent laboriousness and eruditeness, and its strange imagery and allusions, I speak not of its linguistic idiom, but of its cast and mood, have been operative for a considerable time in making prayer a lost art among our people? I say not yes, I say not no. I long for light. I beg this Convention to take at long last the steps that might lead to clarification and enlightenment.

The question here raised with respect to worship applies likewise to ceremonialism. Why do we persist in giving American Jewry a bad name? Why have we considered Jewish non-observance as a kind of fungus growing out of the putative unconcern and impiety of American Jews or America as a whole?

It is obvious that non-observance, no more than the neglect of prayer, is not exactly an American product, certainly not exclusively so. The former, like the latter, appears to have thrived in a variety of climates.

May it not be that our stubborn, unswerving insistence on the sacrosanct, unchanging character of the totality of our tradition has cost us too dearly?

It has been contended that we have no choice in the matter, that the immutability of Judaism is an eluctable fact, that its essential nature, its goal and mission are to affect and shape life, but itself to remain unaltered. Liberal Rabbis, it has been recently asserted by would-be theologians, have confused the history and essence of religion with those of science. Science, it has been argued quite correctly, is not science if its activities are not cumulative, progressive, constantly changing, and ephemeral. Scientific truths become antiquated and are superceded by new truths. The closer they are to us in time the more valid we assume them to be. Those removed from us in time we know to be obsolete, and curious for the historian, but having no claim either on the scientist or average man. A bright industrious freshman whose hobby is the physical sciences need not peruse the dusty pages of Archimedes. The chances are that he is familiar with more theories, theorems, and inventions than the old Greek could possibly have dreamed of. But no bright freshman or senior or any of their teachers can ever dispense with Moses, Isaiah or Amos, or ever claim to have superseded them or excelled them in insight. And why so? Because actually the scientific student can only boast of possessing more knowledge than Archimedes, he would not presume to put himself up as his equal in intelligence. Men busy like ants pile up facts, but they do not alter their mental processes, improve their faculties, or augment their brain-stuff. The quality of intelligence has remained the same in historical times. Even so have man's spiritual and esthetic powers. The sensitivity, delicacy of perception, insight, inspiration with which the creative genius is endowed are no different from what they ever were. No one today excels Phidias in sculpture or Raphael in painting or Shakespeare in literature, and, most certainly not the fashioners of Judaism in prophecy. Consequently religion, like art, is non-progressive and eternal.

All this may be sound reasoning, but it is a far cry from establishing the uniformly sacrosanct character of our tradition and its immutability. It is certainly not true of law or the Halakha. Here we are back again in the realm of science, where the phenomena are observable, where certain economic, political, and psychological factors can be seen to be operative. Take, for example, the Sabbath. To have conceived of it as the culmination of creation and its very purpose, as a day of complete rest and spiritual delight, as linking Israel to God, to His function as Creator and their emergence as a free people may have had nothing to do with the extension of knowledge, the accumulation of facts, or with any evolutionary process. It may all have erupted in Moses' mind of a sudden, unpremeditated, a gift of Divine Grace. But that does not alter the fact that the Sabbath, as we know it, is a far more elaborate pattern than its Biblical prototype. The few ancient injunctions and restrictions have been expanded into thousands of minutiae of rules and practices. How did that come about? Very simply. Our Sabbath is a product of a long history, of a complex of faith, poetic fancy, extreme promptings of the imagination, legal acumen, theological speculations, excessive piety, crushing poverty, bitterness of humiliation, exile and persecution, good common sense, and the sheer love for life. It was inevitable that in view of all these searchings, yearnings, and hard realities that the original should be overlaid or even encumbered with the genuine and spurious, precious stones and gewgaws, and to have been hedged about with barbed wire. The Rabbis were wont to say that the Sabbath was made for men. That is good Pharisaic doctrine and did not emanate from Galilee. But it is also true that men made the Sabbath, more correctly the conditions under which men lived man made. The question that arises whether any such product, the multiplicy of specific laws, is also unchanging and immutable. I say not yes, I say not no. I ask only that this Convention ponder the matter, and do so tenaciously, so that future conventions should not have to begin again at the *Aleph Bet,* and do so not alone *sub specie Americae,* but with full awareness of the fact that more than half of our people and the largest number of its creative men, to say nothing of most gifted youth of our own day, have either abandoned traditional Judaism or at any rate have seriously questioned whether it is uniformly sacrosanct and need be preserved in its entirety.

Should I not, for example, have urged upon you to make peace with the idea that American mores and folkways of today are playing a significant role in molding the Judaism of tomorrow, that Judaism in this land is destined to be no less American than was Judaism in Moorish Spain Arabic, that the Declaration of Independence and Lincoln's Second Inaugural might find their way into our liturgy and certain national holidays into our calendar of festivals; in a word, that the American folk religion, which is itself now in the making, will affect our own religious life?

Does it not come within the comprehension of my subject to remind this Convention that if Judaism tomorrow is to be less confusing, controversial, competitive, and wasteful, then the United Synagogue and other Synagogal bodies in the land will have to regain and reclaim their rightful place in the Community? But to do so I would have to put before you an endless number of proposals, most of which many of you would dismiss as fantasies. I should, for example, have to propose:

One, that our several thousand congregational units, or to begin with, our own several hundred, be coordinated and merged into the National Synagogue. That is, to develop a form of Synagogal organization, which, avoiding the dangers and evils of bureaucracy, would link the individual Synagogues to their national bodies in every way, at least as are the B'nai B'rith lodges or Hadassah chapters to their respective national organizations.

Two, that the objectives, goals, and tasks of the major Jewish organizations should be studied with a view of determining whether they are so at variance that they could not be made the responsibility of one properly organized and departmentalized body.

Three, that we re-examine the training the American Rabbi receives in relation to the duties and tasks that await him in the Community, to determine whether it is humanly possible for him to perform them all, whether or not a multiplicity of functions have not tended to make him the best third-rater in the land.

Four, to consider these and other steps as preliminary to bringing into existence the united Jewish Community, without which braggartism and controversies, competitiveness and wastefulness, whirl and confusion, disintegration and dissolution will be the beneficiaries of our toil, sweat, and generosity.

And could this Convention deliberate on Judaism Today and Tomorrow without being impelled to quadruple its efforts in behalf of Jewish education, learning, and every form of cultural expression. What are we? What is our life, distinction, value of our continuity, if it is not to ply Torah? What does it mean, if it is not to educate young and old, to afford every opportunity to the scholar, man of letters and artist; to add to the Seminary curriculum a variety of subjects and to its faculty a considerable number of men; to bring its library up to date in every department of Jewish life and thought; to make it possible for it to continue revealing to the world the secrets of its Genizah of manuscripts; to publish the Ginzberg *Yerushalmi*, the Marx *Catalogue*, the collected works of Professor Kaplan; to restore Dr. Finkelstein wholly and completely to the book, the love of his childhood; to make us sufficiently self-respecting and proud not to wait for translations of the Mishnah, Talmud, Midrash, and Zohar to come to us from a handful of Jews in England; concordances of the Mishnah, Tosefta, and Talmud and dictionaries of the Bible from nascent, hard-pressed Israel; to learn Hebrew, to learn Hebrew, to learn Hebrew, to cherish it as the language that is a quiver full of steel arrows, a cable with strong coils, a trumpet of brass crashing through the air with two or three sharp notes, that pours floods of anger and utters cries of rage against abuses of the world, that was heard above Sinai's peels of thunder, that bewailed Zion's destruction and celebrates its rebirth, that trumpeted forth liberty, and called upon the nations to beat their swords into plow-shares. Hebrew, friends, that might well be the trebled cord of world Jewry—the link, embodiment and symbol of its unity.

The Torch, Spring, 1951.

Dr. Goldman (1893–1953) was one of America's outstanding Rabbis for twenty-five years, from 1929 to 1953 in Chicago, Illinois. He was President of the Zionist Organization of America, Vice-President of the American Jewish Congress, and Co-Chairman of the United Palestine Appeal. He was the author of A Rabbi Takes Stock, The Jew and the Universe, Crisis and Decision, The Golden Chain *and* The Book of Books, *an Introduction.*

TOWARD A CREATIVE
JEWISH COMMUNITY IN AMERICA

ROBERT GORDIS

THE POTENTIALITIES OF
AMERICAN JEWRY

For all its undoubted weaknesses, there are several characteristics of American Jewry which may serve the Jewish future well. First is the widespread desire of Jews to be identified as such. Without knowing how, or even why, the vast majority of American Jews wishes to perpetuate itself Jewishly, and regards the extinction of the Jewish identity as an unalloyed tragedy. To be sure, the most overtaxed organ of American Jews is the "heart." Nevertheless, it remains true that this genuine desire may serve as the basis of a richer Jewish life in the future.

Second is the tremendous physical extent of the American Jewish community. Five million Jews in the United States are nearly ten times as large as the largest community in Western Europe in the heyday of modern liberalism, for at its peak, German Jewry numbered only six hundred thousand. As a result, American Jewry will be able to sustain far greater defections through assimilation than other communities without being exposed to biological extinction.

Third is the proliferation of Jewish organizational life and institutions. National organizations, synagogues and centers are all too often superficial in their approach, but they have the virtue of keeping the Jewish life before the eyes of a large segment of the community. Approximately one million Jews belong to the synagogue and about the same number are officially enrolled Zionists. The Jewish centers from coast to coast have at least one-half million members. Many hundreds of thousands more are affiliated with fraternal orders and other groups. All these have voluntarily accepted some form of identification with the Jewish people beyond the accident of their descent. It may not be much, it surely is not enough, but it is considerably more than nothing.

The fourth factor is the recognition by the general population, not merely by the anti-Semites, of the existence not only of individuals of Jewish descent, but of a distinct Jewish group. The inner factors making for Jewish survival are of course substantially strengthened by the existence of anti-Semitism. Anti-Semitism of itself does not create a Jewish cohesiveness. It may drive out completely many who are on the fringe, but for those in whom the Jewish spark is not dead, it often fans it into a mighty flame. This factor, unfortunately, shows little sign of disappearing.

The fifth factor is the existence of a living, heroic, vital Eretz Yisrael, which is a source of pride and a symbol of unity for nearly all American Jews. It has already demonstrated, however modestly, its capacity to inspire and enrich Jewish life in America. It stands, however, only on the threshold of its historic role as the heart pumping blood into the arteries of world Israel.

These factors guarantee, as well as anything can in our uncertain age, that Jewish life in America is here to stay. Both those who welcome assimilation and those who lament it are both dedicated to an outlook unacceptable to American Jewry. In our day, at least, American Jewry is incurably survivalist.

PRINCIPLES OF A CREATIVE
COMMUNITY

The organic Jewish community of tomorrow would not seek to win universal assent, nor would it presume to speak in the name of all American Jews, as is the all-but-universal custom of Jewish organizations today. It would be the spokesman of those Jews, however, who share a common outlook, expressed in some such platform as these *Ten Principles:*

1. The unity of Israel as a people, the world over, expressing itself in a common religious and cultural tradition;

2. The centrality of the Jewish religion as the heart of Jewish expression and the essence of Jewish brotherhood;

3. The role of the land of Israel as offering not only a secure home for the millions of oppressed Jews in the world today, but an

all-Jewish environment to further Jewish creativity and thus enrich the life of all Jews everywhere;

4. The survival of American Jewry as a vital and active element in the Jewish people, able to make its creative contribution to Jewish life and thought;

5. Simultaneously, the position of American Jewry as an integral element of the American people, since group loyalties, morally conceived and culturally expressed, are not mutually exclusive;

6. The duty and destiny of Israel, as yet incompletely realized, to advance the Messianic ideals of one God and One Humanity, embodied in a world order of social justice, individual and group freedom and universal peace;

7. The right of all Jews, affirmed by Jewish tradition, to fellowship in Israel, however far removed they may be at present from an acceptance of an affirmative attitude toward Jewish tradition;

8. The welcoming of participation, in one or another phase of Jewish life, by such individuals and groups as are unable to give their assent to Jewish religious practices and ideals, with the recognition of the proper role of their activities in the overall pattern of organic Jewish life;

9. The establishment of cooperative relations, wherever possible, between the *organic Jewish community* as here envisaged, and those elements of the Jewish people remaining outside its scope; and

10. The recognition that Jewish education, both for children and for adults, conceived in the broadest terms and based on the three pillars of faith, culture and people, is the central concern and basic enterprise of the organic Jewish community.

PROBLEMS OF ORGANIZATION

What organizational pattern would the *voluntary community dedicated to organic Judaism* take? On the local level it would be the *synagogue-center*. It cannot be sufficiently stressed that a synagogue which is not a center is as inadequate as a center which is not a synagogue, in doing justice to the organic character of Judaism. Only the synagogue-center, vitalized and active, reflects this conception of the integrity of Jewish life in all its phases.

But more is needed than the addition of club and recreation facilities to the synagogue and the school house. Each congregation must become a *kehillah ketanah,* a cell of the organic Jewish community, accepting and implementing the standpoint "I am a Hebrew, and nothing Jewish is alien to me." Hence, in addition to the various committees that give practical direction to the affairs of the congregation, committees should be created to study the situation and recommend attitudes and action by the congregation in all areas of Jewish life, such as philanthropy, civic defense, higher Jewish education, overseas relief, and cultural activity.

Members of the congregation, who by virtue of their interests or experience in special organizations are more familiar with one field or another, would serve on these committees. For it will be freely conceded that most, though not all, Jewish organizations perform useful functions and have their place in the ideal structure of Jewish life. But they must no longer be permitted to usurp the monopoly of power and influence which they now possess. Putting first things first and last things last is the beginning of wisdom.

The reports and recommendations of these committees would make meetings of the congregation town-meetings of the organic Jewish community and incidentally supply the content often woefully lacking in congregational meetings. Instead of the synagogue being perpetually exploited for every cause, good, bad and indifferent, the congregation would now assess the role of each, applauding its achievements, criticizing its short-comings and thus help to develop an informed as well as a loyal constituency.

In each community where there is more than one synagogue, the initiative should be taken to organize a *local Synagogue Council,* to coordinate their study of these issues and to speak with a united voice on the problems, and they are legion, where agreement exists among all who cherish the Synagogue as the central and all-embracing sanctuary of Jewish life.

These local units of *Keneset Yisrael* would be organized into the *Congregation of American Jewry.* Ideally, such an agency already exists on the American scene, the Synagogue Council of America.

THE ROLE OF CONSERVATIVE
JUDAISM

It is no particularist loyalty which impels me to restate my conviction that it is Conservative Judaism in particular which should take the initiative in undertaking this life-saving function for American Jewry. From its inception our Movement has always stressed the peoplehood of Israel and given wholehearted loyalty to Zionism, while emphasizing the basically religious and cultural character of Jewish tradition. We are no recent penitents, in whose presence, as the Talmud tells us, the truly righteous cannot stand!

Undergirding our specific interpretation of Jewish tradition as a moving and growing stream, Conservative Judaism has steadfastly maintained and often at a high price, the doctrine of the unity of Israel, formulated as "Catholic Israel" by Solomon Schechter. Our Movement should accordingly be the spearhead in this effort to create a structural pattern for the religious household of American Jewry, through the Synagogue Council, if possible, without it, if necessary. This effort will surely win the enthusiastic support of groups outside our own, as well as of individuals who have not in the past found their place in organized religious life, but who are increasingly sympathetic to the necessity for a religiously-oriented, creative relationship to the Jewish people.

This proposed plan for organizing the American-Jewish community through the medium of local Synagogue Councils is not the only possible mode of encompassing our goal, especially in communities where the religio-cultural-ethnic concepts of Jewish peoplehood is already widely accepted in the thinking of men and women. Here an already existent Community Council might be transformed in such a manner as to reflect this conception and to advance the religious and cultural aspects of Jewish life, which are all too often ignored and minimized at present.

Thus the Community Council might be set up in bi-cameral fashion, with a Council of Synagogues and a Council of Organizations. The Council of Synagogues would express structurally the central significance of the religious and cultural life of the community as well as the totality of Jewish activities conducted by the synagogue-centers. At the same time, the experience and special interests of non-synagogue organizations would not be dissipated, but would find a forum of free-expression in the Council of Organizations.

Community action would be contingent upon agreement by both Councils. Where differences would emerge, these would be reconciled by "conference" and compromise, as happens in the two houses of the American Congress.

Community Councils of this type would find it possible to consider and take action on the central, and not merely on the peripheral elements of Jewish life. With the passing of time, the religio-cultural-ethnic character of Jewish peoplehood would be all but universally accepted in practice, and not merely in theory, as is now generally the case. It would then be possible to simplify the community organization and utilize it with even greater effectiveness, in order to enhance the cultural creativity and religious vitality of American Jewry, which constitute its only true reason for being.

INNER TASKS OF CONSERVATIVE
JUDAISM

These undertakings do not replace the necessity for our Movement to strengthen the vitality of Conservative Judaism. Many important projects are crying out for implementation by the Rabbinical Assembly and the United Synagogue, as representing that view of Jewish tradition which understands the modern temper, while cleaving fast to the Torah.

Concrete steps toward *the liquidation of the Sunday School* should be taken. The establishment of *Jewish day-schools* by our congregations, especially at the primary level for the first three years to serve as a firm basis for an educational structure are necessary, by the side of such valuable projects as our Summer Camps and the Leadership Training Fellowship.

The creation of small groups of *Haberim* in our congregations, devoted to Torah, both as learning and as practice, can revitalize the spiritual life of our people.

In our metropolitan centers there is need to set up *Centers of Jewish Information* where brief daily services might be held, and where information on Judaism and religion generally would be made available to Jews and non-Jews, whether they might be men and women seeking knowledge on one specific detail of Judaism, or would-be proselytes who deserve adequate preparation for Jewish living. There is need for *Clinics for Personal Guidance,* staffed by a panel drawn from the rabbis of the area.

The Rabbinical Assembly should call a *National Conference on Kashruth,* with particular emphasis on the economic aspects of the situation, particularly the exorbitant prices of Kosher meats, which is undermining home observance. Such a project would win the respect even of those who have surrendered their adherence to the Dietary Laws.

There is need for direct activity by our movement in connection with *Israel.* We have had the testimony of Prof. Ernst Simon as well as others, that a vital religious life in Israel awaits the dynamic yet traditional approach toward Jewish religion, coupled with the socially progressive attitudes characteristic of Conservative Judaism. The present situation in Israel demands specific projects looking toward bringing the message of our movement to the youth in Israel, as well as to many of their elders who have no spiritual anchor in the forms of Jewish religion they see about them. Nor can we close our eyes to the problems of religious freedom in Israel.

The day is short and the work manifold; the workers dare not be indolent.

The Torch, January, 1950.

Dr. Gordis, Rabbi, Scholar and Author, holds a unique position of leadership in the American Jewish Community. For over thirty years he has occupied the pulpit of Congregation Beth El of Rockaway Park, N. Y. He is Professor of Bible at the Jewish Theological Seminary of America. He is past president of the Rabbinical Assembly and of the Synagogue Council of America. Among his writings are Judaism for the Modern Age, The Root and the Branch, Judaism in a Christian World, The Jew Faces a New World, The Wisdom of Ecclesiastes, A Faith for Moderns *and* Leave a Little to God.

THE ROLE OF THE SYNAGOGUE
IN JEWISH LIFE *

SIMON GREENBERG

Our feet are standing within thy gates, O Jerusalem;
Jerusalem, that art builded
As a city that is compact together,
Whither the tribes went up, even the tribes of the Lord,
As a testimony unto Israel,
To give thanks unto the name of the Lord.

(Psalms 122, 2–4)

The words which I have just read to you were first spoken by pilgrims who came to Jerusalem more than two thousand years ago. How grateful we should be that they have been preserved, for how perfectly they express the sentiments which are in our hearts today. As we read these words, so utter and complete a sense of identification between us and our ancestors suffuses our whole being that the intervening millenia become even for us as "yesterday which is past and as a watch in the night." We too experience that undefinable, unbelievable wonderment which moved the Psalmist to exclaim עוֹמְדוֹת הָיוּ רַגְלֵינוּ בִּשְׁעָרַיִךְ יְרוּשָׁלִָם : "Our feet are standing within thy gates, O Jerusalem." Like the Psalmist, we find it hard to believe that we are in truth standing on the holy soil of this sacred city. And yet here we are, a group of the שִׁבְטֵי ה׳, members of various tribes of the Lord, representatives of the communities of the people of Israel living on four continents. Our coming is, as it were, an עֵדוּת לְיִשְׂרָאֵל, a testimony that we humbly and gratefully claim our place in the household of the Jewish people.

We come for essentially the same reason that our forefathers came to Jerusalem thousands of years ago. We come לְהוֹדוֹת לְשֵׁם ה׳ ,

* This address was delivered by Dr. Greenberg at the First Convention of the World Council of Synagogues held in Jerusalem, Israel.

to give thanks unto the Name of the Lord for the imperishable historic memories bequeathed to us by the city of Jerusalem; to give thanks for the exalted, eternally valid moral and religious instruction that has gone forth from Jerusalem to us and to all mankind; and to give thanks for the privilege of beholding today ירושלם הבנויה‎Jerusalem that is builded כעיר שחברה לה יחדיו‎, as a city *in* which and *through* which the scattered remnants of the tribes of Israel are again united into one people. כי שמה ישבו כסאות לבית דוד כסאות למשפט‎—Here there are again gathered the chief symbols and the highest instruments of the sovereign authority of the third Jewish Commonwealth—the modern State of Israel.

The Psalmist reminds us, however, that it is not enough to come to Jerusalem to give thanks unto the Lord. He enjoins us rather שאלו שלום ירושלם‎, to seek the peace of Jerusalem. We readily and gladly respond to his imperious admonition. We are profoundly solicitous about the welfare of Jerusalemלמען אחינו ורעינו‎, "for our brethren's and companions' sakes." We are deeply concerned for the physical and spiritual welfare of the non-Jews as well as of the Jews who are citizens or residents of the State of Israel.

Though we have always had this concern, I am sure that as a result of this visit each one of us will be moved to do even more than he has ever done before in order to advance the just and high interests of the State of Israel—to support with unprecedented generosity those great enterprises whereby barren hillsides are re-afforested, disease-breeding swamps drained, scorched deserts irrigated, industries enlarged and commerce expanded, so that the homeless may have homes, the laborer an opportunity for self-respecting and productive labor, the student the means to pursue his studies, the scholar the leisure to increase knowledge and the statesman the confidence to pursue justice and seek peace.

And like the Psalmist we, too, are anxious about the "peace of Jerusalem" למען בית ה׳ אלקינו‎, *because of* and *"for the sake of* the house of the Lord our God." For the Psalmist, the house of the Lord was the Temple in Jerusalem. For us it is the Synagogue.

For many of us, this is not the first visit to the State of Israel. We were here before either on personal pilgrimages or as members of some Zionist or philanthropic or business or professional group. Now for the first time we have come as members of a world synagogal group.

We hope that we shall have been helpful in setting a pattern for regular and frequent conventions in Jerusalem of representatives of world-wide synagogal federations. It is high time, we believe, that through such gatherings we establish and dramatize the fact that the bond which forever unites Jews everywhere with the Jerusalem of Yesterday, Today and Tomorrow is the spiritual heritage which has been most passionately preserved and most fully exemplified by the Synagogue.

There has always been a very close association between Jerusalem and the Synagogue. It was in the Synagogue that the meaning of Jerusalem for our destiny as a people was kept vividly alive during some two thousand years of forced separation. Most of us first came to know about Jerusalem via the Synagogue, for it was in its liturgy and in the messages that were spoken from its pulpit that the place of Jerusalem in the memory and in the hopes of our people was first brought to our attention. Hence Jerusalem and the Synagogue are inseparable. We cannot think of the one without thinking of the other.

Insofar as we as a group are concerned, Jerusalem and the Synagogue are inextricably intertwined on the deepest levels of our subconscious and upon the highest levels of our conscious thought for yet another reason. The great scholars, thinkers, teachers and builders whose words and deeds have molded us as a group were indefatigable in their insistence upon our loyalty to the totality of our spiritual heritage. The cultural treasures accumulated by our people over the millennia include many institutions, ideas and sancta, each one of which is endowed with vast potentialities for spiritual growth. Hence there is the ever-present temptation to attach oneself to one or more of them, and by exploring and exploiting its or their spiritual potentialities, to fashion a pattern of life which is then claimed to be the authentic continuation of the totality of our spiritual heritage.

It is the identification of the part with the whole which is of the essence of sectarianism, and sectarianism is the mortal enemy nestling at the heart of every great spiritual heritage. It is the pitfall of sectarianism that we as a group have ever sought to avoid.

Hence, the emphasis in our thought and deed has ever been upon the totality of our heritage rather than upon any fragment of it, regardless of how substantial a fragment it may have been. We have sought ever to associate ourselves with those elements which we believe to be the warp and woof of all the overall pattern of our spiritual heritage, to nurture and sustain them not only for the preservation of the integrity of the heritage, but also for the richest and noblest fulfillment of our lives as Jews and as human beings.

Though I speak entirely in my own behalf, yet forty years of continuous association lead me to believe that I speak also for a very large, and perhaps even the preponderant, segment of our group when I express my conviction that the ingredients which comprise the total Jewish spiritual heritage inhere in three phenomena. These partake simultaneously of the characteristics of the most abstract of concepts and the most tangible of realities. I refer to *Eretz Yisrael,* the Hebrew language and the Synagogue. These constitute the very life-breath of our heritage as a whole. They endow it with endurance and suffuse it with grandeur. Should any one of these three phenomena ever be completely lost to us, or its functioning seriously impaired, our spiritual heritage as a whole will not merely be impoverished; it will disintegrate. And we cannot as a people long survive anywhere the disintegration of our spiritual heritage.

Until comparatively recent times no one suggested, much less ventured, to disengage any one of these three from the other two upon the assumption that either it alone or the other two alone can preserve the essential integrity of our heritage and meaningfully sustain our people. It was only in the last century and a half that there appeared Jews who, while protesting their loyalty to the Jewish people and to Judaism, repudiated *Eretz Yisrael* or the Hebrew language or the Synagogue. Each of the dissidents in his time and place mustered impressive logic and factual support for his position.

In the halcyon days of European liberalism and nationalism both fact and logic seemed to sustain the Reform movement's repudiation of *Eretz Yisrael* and the Hebrew language. Reform took its position on the side of what gave every evidence of being the irresistible wave of the future. At a later period, there was also much that commended the position of the Territorialists who broke away from the Zionist movement. The land of Israel never was the most ideal spot upon this globe upon which to build a home for a people. And when Eliezer Ben-Yehuda first broached the thought that Hebrew must again become the spoken language of our people, he could point to very few of the realities of his day to validate his position. The overwhelming majority of Jews spoke Yiddish. The most reasonable thing to do seemed, at that time, to adopt either Yiddish or a modern European language. But Jewish history and He who determines the course of all history have determined that *Eretz Yisrael* is the only land in which the Jewish people can and should hope to enjoy the privileges of exercising political sovereignty in the same measure as other peoples do in other lands; and that Hebrew is the only language in which the Jewish people can and should corporately articulate and preserve its spiritual heritage.

We who are here gathered have, thank God, been among those who have from the beginning recognized and wholeheartedly accepted these dictates of the historic experiences of our people. We have always tried to the best of our ability to enlarge the role of *Eretz Yisrael* and of the Hebrew language in our lives. But we did not stop there. To us the Synagogue and all that it symbolizes and embodies was always an inseparable companion of the other two. Hence we have over the decades been sorely distressed by the hot hostility or the cold indifference to which the Synagogue has been subjected not by those to whom *Eretz Yisrael* and the Hebrew language are anathema, but primarily by those to whom both are as dear as they are to us. It is their very love for *Eretz Yisrael* and the Hebrew language which makes their hostility or indifference to the Synagogue spiritually all the more distressing. Nay, more. It is not merely spiritually distressing. We believe it to be a real and present danger to the welfare of the Jewish people.

For there are aspects to the role of the Synagogue in Jewish life which make it more than merely one of the three basic pillars of the Jewish spiritual heritage. In the first place it incorporated both the Hebrew language and *Eretz Yisrael* into the very core of its structure and functioning so that both were able to retain extraordinary vitality even though they were for centuries deprived of much that they needed for their full flowering.

Frequent repetition has dulled our sensitivity to the miracle and the mystery which inhere in the fact that history offers no example, other than that of the Jews, of a people who succeeded not only in preserving, but even in enlarging its spiritual and cultural heritage centuries after it had been exiled from its land or ceased to speak the language in which that heritage first found expression. What made it possible for our people to defy what otherwise seems to be an inexorable law of history? Insofar as it is given to us to comprehend at all the mystery of Jewish existence, there is but one answer to this question. The Jewish people, *while living upon its soil, and during eras of spiritual and political autonomy*, brought to fruition an absolutely unique insitution, the Synagogue. It proved to possess unprecedented powers of adaptation. It could be successfully transplanted in any social and political environment which had the least modicum of regard for a human being's right to live and to think. This is not the occasion for a comprehensive presentation of the role of the Synagogue in Jewish history nor for an analysis of its structure and functioning. We shall make but brief references to those aspects which are of most immediate concern to us.

The Synagogue by its insistence upon the need for at least ten men in order to conduct a formal service vividly preserved the sense of community at the very center of the consciousness of its communicants. The fact that anyone who had the knowledge and the skill, and was religiously eligible for membership within the fellowship of the Synagogue, could conduct its services, made it for all times the most democratic of religious institutions. The role of the Torah in its service of necessity required the training of men who could read and expound the Torah to the congregants. Hence the association of the Synagague with the study and the exposition of the Torah became well-nigh inevitable, so that practically from its very beginnings there flourished, under its wing and within its shadow, the Beth Midrash, the school for the more advanced student, as well as the school for the תינוקות של בית רבן, for the young.

Side by side with the Torah, the Synagogue developed its own distinctive book, the Siddur. The language and the contents of both these books of the Synagogue assured the preservation of the Hebrew language and the memory of *Eretz Yisrael* in our midst. Thus the genius of our people succeeded marvelously, intricately, subtly, intuitively, in incorporating into the organizational structure and the day-to-day functioning of the Synagogue the other two indispensable ingredients of our spiritual heritage.

Had the Synagogue served no other purpose, its place in the life of our people would have been permanently assured. But it did do more, very much more. As a בית מדרש, a House of Study, and as a בית תפלה, a House of Prayer, it spoke to and for the heart and mind of the Jew. It confronted him with the ultimate, the eternal inescapable problems of life and death, good and evil. It taught him how to think of God, how to pray, how to discipline his passions. It sustained and invigorated that still small voice within him, which ceaselessly reminded him that he is worthy of being designated as אדם, as Man, only insofar as he strives to indentify himself completely with the צלם אלקים, that quality of the divine which our Creator vouchsafed unto us. And in so doing it bestowed dignity upon the individual Jew. It taught and buttressed the faith that each human being is precious in the eyes of God, that a man's status in the world is not determined by the hates and the hostilities of his fellow man but by the extent to which each man through his own efforts preserves the purity of the divine image stamped upon him by his Creator. Though the Jew was denied citizenship in man-made kingdoms, even the mightiest could not deny him citizenship in the Kingdom of God.

Eretz Yisrael endowed Jewish life with the dimension of space. It roots our people in a soil, gives it geographic locale, bestows upon it the substantial reality associated only with phenomena firmly attached to the very stuff of the globe upon which we live. *Eretz Yisrael* enables us to think of the Jewish people as a widespreading tree that has withstood for millennia the blast of cyclones and hurricanes because it has deep roots in the rich, congenial soil in which it was planted some 3,500 years ago.

The Hebrew language endowed our people with the dimension of time. Our whole history is wrapped up in its words, phrases, sentences and books. It is not the ideas alone contained in such words as השופט כל הארץ לא יעשה משפט, *shall not the judge of all the earth do justly,* or in לא ישא גוי אל גוי חרב, *nation shall not lift up sword against nation,* or in שמע ישראל, *Hear, O Israel,* that established at the deepest level of our subconscious the sense of unbroken continuity between us and Abraham, Isaiah and Akiba. That sense of unbroken continuity we experience primarily because of the vehicle wherein those ideals have been preserved for us, namely the Hebrew language. And to experience a sense of unbroken continuity is to experience history, and to experience history is to be rooted *in time.*

To these dimensions of space and time the synagogue *adds the dimension of eternity.* It is for the Jew a territorial enclave of the Kingdom of God upon this earth. The soil upon which it stands is that bit of ארץ, of holy soil, upon which Jacob's ladder stands in every Jewish community in the world, beckoning each Jew heavenward and bidding him to link his life with the Divine. This unique aspect of the Synagogue, this inherent quality which to so marked a degree emancipates it from complete subservience to space and time, was what enabled the Synagogue to be the visible, tangible embodiment of the spiritual bond which has preserved whatever meaningful unity there existed among the scattered remnants of our people from the days of the first Babylonian exile unto our day. No institution which we have created during our history ever compared with the Synagogue in endurance, in meaning and in power, as the bond that identified us and kept us as one people. And nothing that has happened in the last century or the last two decades has changed or from all appearances will change this situation.

Nothing can or will change the basic fact that only one who is eligible for membership in the fellowship of the Synagogue can be recognized as a member in good standing of the Jewish people. Citizenship in the State of Israel does not bestow upon one membership in the Jewish people, nor does a perfect knowledge of the Hebrew language. And one who is born of a Jewish mother does not dissociate himself from the Jewish people by being a citizen of a state other than Israel or by speaking a language other than Hebrew. To the extent that he can dissociate himself at all from the Jewish people, he does so by joining the fellowship of another institution whose ostensible purpose is to provide its membership with an opportunity for prayer, for worship and for meditation within the framework of a conception of the universe and a regimen of personal behavior which differ from that identified with the Synagogue. On the other hand, anyone born of a non-Jewish mother and living anywhere in the world can become a fullfledged member of the Jewish people in only one way. He must conform to the requirements that make him eligible for membership in the Synagogue.

Moreover, nothing can change the fact that the Synagogue has remained the only institution transplantable from *Eretz Yisrael* to any part of the world. Unpalatable as the truth may be to some, it is nevertheless a fact that we did not as a people preserve amongst us widespread knowledge of the Hebrew language except as the language of the Synagogue service. It was to the best of our knowledge never the language of daily intercourse in any Jewish community of the Diaspora.

We have heard it said repeatedly that the Synagogue as a bond of unity among the Jews of the world has greatly weakened in the last few generations. It may be so. But assuming that to be true, what should our reaction to this situation be? Should we then proceed to abandon it and place our faith upon another bond? And what shall it be? Shall it be the Hebrew language? Are there any who are of the opinion that it is easier to revive the use of Hebrew in the secular life of Jews throughout the world than it is to reinvigorate the Synagogue? Nothing that has happened even during the height of enthusiasm engendered these past fifteen years by the rise of the State of Israel can be offered in support of such an opinion, while much that has happened during these fifteen years, particularly in the United States, can be offered to support the hope that the Synagogue may be restored to its place of preeminence in Jewish life. Indeed, if Hebrew is to be preserved at all in the Diaspora in the future, it will be primarily through the Synagogue, even as it was in the past.

Can we expect the sense of kinship between Jews of the Diaspora and the Jews of the State of Israel to replace the Synagogue as a primary bond of unity among the Jews everywhere?

This sense of kinship has indeed worked miracles in our day. But assuming an extended period of growth and peace, the magic of the miracle of the State of Israel is bound to wear off. Jews in the Diaspora are bound to emphasize more and more that their attachment is not to the State of Israel as a political entity but to the land of Israel in which the State of Israel happens to be located and to the *Jewish community of the State of Israel insofar as it and they share common spiritual treasures. Those common spiritual treasures have by our history been associated primarily with and concentrated in the Synagogue.* Should the Synagogue ever cease to be the distinguishing institution that identifies a Jewish community, then as far as we can judge by all of our experiences of the past and the available data of the present, we shall have reached the end of the road, first as a world-wide people and then as a people maintaining an unbroken continuity with its past. That will be true for a Jewish community regardless of where it resides. A Jew who is a stranger in the Synagogue, regardless of where he lives, is one who is well on his way to being a stranger to the Jewish people.

It was in Jerusalem that, in the past, the totality of our spiritual heritage experienced in every one of its three chief components the grandest triumphs of vision and articulation. We believe with a perfect faith that it is in the Jerusalem of tomorrow that the totality of our spiritual heritage will be enhanced and will attain its noblest embodiment in the life of our people. We believe this first because we have faith in the divine promises given to us by our inspired prophets. And we believe it because in our day our faith has in large measure already been vindicated in the case of *Eretz Yisrael* and the Hebrew language. After some 1,600 years of only tenuous physical association between the land and the people, unsurpassed heroism, cooperation, generosity and skill have succeeded in establishing upon its soil an independent State of Israel, the home of some two million Jews. This physically small, young and besieged state is striving valiantly and, thank God, thus far with extraordinary success to establish an order of justice, of freedom and of equality within its borders and to raise its voice in the world council of the nations in behalf of universal peace and brotherhood. The well-nigh miraculous events which have occurred upon the soil of *Eretz Yisrael* in our own day renew our faith that *Eretz Yisrael* shall in due time fulfill its role as the promised land not only of the Jewish people but of all mankind; when "the mountain of the Lord's house shall be . . . exalted above the hills, And all the nations shall flow unto it," and shall in triumphant and exultant accord respond to the call that came forth from Jerusalem "to beat their swords into ploughshares and their knives into pruning hooks" and "to learn war no more."

As for the Hebrew language, never in human history has any language which was not used as a daily vernacular for some 1,800 years experienced so remarkable a renaissance. When during these past two thousand years has Hebrew flourished as gloriously as it does today in *Eretz Yisrael,* where it has again become the language of the child at play, of the statesman, the engineer and the industrialist at work on vast enterprises, of the philosopher and the scientist reporting upon the loftiest flights of the intellect, and of the poet struggling to articulate the finest nuances of the heart?

But while these two of the three indispensable components of the Jewish spiritual heritage have been rejuvenated by the events that have transpired during these past six decades in and outside of the land of Israel, the Synagogue in *Eretz Yisrael* is still biding its time. In the Diaspora, and particularly in the United States, there have been evidences that something is stirring within the soul of the Jewish community which is expressing itself in an effort of rejuvenate and re-invigorate the Synagogue.

If we are to think helpfully and constructively on the role of the Synagogue both in *Eretz Yisrael* and in the Diaspora, we must rid ourselves of two widely held fallacies. One is that the Jews of the Diaspora look to the Synagogue merely or primarily to satisfy their need for belonging. The other is that the Synagogue is in essence a Diaspora institution and only a sort of decorative appendage to Jewish Life in *Eretz Yisrael.* Neither of them is, in my opinion, even a half-truth. Rabbinic literature is replete with statements testifying to the central importance of the Synagogue in Jewish life. None of these statements directly or indirectly implies that the Synagogue is meant primarily for the Diaspora. That the Rabbis considered the Synagogue as central to Jewish life everywhere is reflected in the fact that the Beth Haknesset—the primary name for the Synagogue—and the Beth Hamidrash—the House of Study—are almost invariably linked in rabbinic literature, so much so that the most recent and the most complete anthology of rabbinic Aggadic literature lists references to both institutions under the same rubric (*Otzar Haagada,* Mosad Harav Kook) . Of the 154 passages therein listed we shall quote only two. The first is the frequently quoted statement כל עיר שגגותיה גבוהים מבית הכנסת לסוף חריבה—*any town whose roofs rise higher than that of its synagogue is destined to be destroyed.* This statement is not limited to Jewish communities of the Diaspora. The second statement records that before its destruction by the Romans, Jerusalem had 394 courts and an equal number of synagogues and houses of study (*Ktubot* 105a) . There is therefore not the slightest element of historic truth in the oft-repeated assertion that the Synagogue ever was or was intended to be a Diaspora institution exclusively or primarily.

Nor is there any more truth in the statement that the Jews of the Diaspora, particularly those of America, build synagogues primarily because they want to satisfy their need to belong. Insofar as the Jews of the United States are concerned, there are innumerable fraternal organizations, philanthropic societies, social clubs and recreation centers, all of which are as completely divorced from synagogal affiliation as they are completely composed of Jewish members. Hundreds of thousands of Jews in the United States today find that affiliation with one of these organizations satisfies all of their needs for Jewish identification and for belonging. They do not need the Synagogue to identify them as Jews. Their American citizenship certainly does not require it of them. Nor does social pressure make it necessary. Jews are building synagogues in the Diaspora not because they need social identification, but because they are consciously or subconsciously seeking what Jews have sought throughout their history, the ultimate purpose and meaning of life as individuals and as Jews. It is only as that search is profound and widespread among us as a people that our existence as a distinct group among the peoples of the world takes on a grandeur and a glory that is in no way related to our numbers or power. And for the Jew, history has decreed that the institution par excellence through which and in which that search finds its communal as well as its personal expression is the Synagogue.

No one knows more poignantly than we do all of the weaknesses of the Synagogue in the Diaspora in our day—the tenuousness of the relationship between it and the majority of its affiliates, the spiritual shallowness, the intellectual mediocrity, the ethical vulnerability, not only of its rank and file, but also of much of its leadership. But with all that, it remains the seminal institution around which a meaningful Jewish community can in time develop. Remove the Synagogue from the Jewish community, and what is there left around which a meaningful Jewish existence can be sustained? We know now beyond a reasonable shadow of doubt that in a democratic order of society no purely ethnic or linguistic group can long sustain a significant identity. Hence our efforts in the Diaspora to revitalize the Synagogue, by whatever means appears to us to be appropriate and in conformity with its essential character. That is why we are seeking to find within its organizational structure and program of activities room for both sexes, for all ages and for the largest possible variety of spiritual, intellectual, social and recreational needs.

We do not maintain that we have found the ultimate answer to the question of how the Synagogue can best function in our day. We merely say to our brethren in Israel, both to those who have found no place whatsoever in their lives for the Synagogue, and to those who find complete satisfaction with the Synagogue as a house of prayer exclusively, that they are wittingly or unwittingly abandoning or neglecting the very life-cord of our people and the one tangible and yet intangible bond whereby our scattered communities can continue to experience a real sense of kinship with one another and with the Jewish community in the State of Israel. No other bond of equal validity, significance, practicality or robustness is conceivable.

We come with no specific programs or suggestions. But we do harbor a hope which we want on this occasion to articulate. It is the hope that by our coming now and again and again in the future under the aegis of the Synagogue, we shall contribute toward a widespread and thorough study and re-evaluation of the role of the Synagogue in the life of our people today and tomorrow. Such a study, if it be objective and thorough, will, we believe, lead to the inevitable conclusion that the Synagogue, like *Eretz Yisrael* and the Hebrew language, is and must remain the precious, inalienable heritage of the whole people, a heritage in which every Jew should want and know how to claim his share.

Neither *Eretz Yisrael* nor the Hebrew language could be of maximum helpfulness to our people today in the condition in

which they were a hundred years ago. Endless effort and ingenuity, infinite love and sacrifice were poured into both of them to
make them most serviceable to the Jewish people today. It is a rejuvenated *Eretz Yisrael* and a rejuvenated Hebrew language that
we now have. The unbroken continuity between these and the
Eretz Yisrael and the Hebrew language of all of Jewish history is,
however, clear and unmistakable.

Proportionate effort, ingenuity, love and sacrifice must now be
brought to the Synagogue so that it too may serve us at its best in
a new age and under new circumstances. We speak למען בית ה'
אלקינו *in behalf of the House of the Lord our God,* because we believe that in doing so, we are speaking most effectively למען
אחינו ורעינו *in behalf of our brothers and companions,* and because
we know no better way of responding to the call of the Psalmist:
שאלו שלום ירושלם, *seek the peace of Jerusalem.*

The Torch, Winter, 1963.

*Dr. Greenberg, Rabbi, Administrator, Educator and distin-
guished interpreter of Jewish Values, is Vice-Chancellor and
Vice-President of the Faculties of the Jewish Theological
Seminary of America. He was Rabbi of Har Zion Temple,
Philadelphia, Penna. from 1925 to 1946. He has served as
Provost, Acting President, and Professor of Homiletics and
Education at the Seminary. He is the chancellor of the
University of Judaism, the Seminary's West Coast Branch,
and Executive Director of the United Synagogue of Amer-
ica. He is currently a member of the Executive Committee
of the Jewish Agency and the World Zionist Organization.
He is author of* Living as a Jew Today, Ideals and Values of
the Jewish Prayer Book, *The Harishon Series of Hebrew
Text Books, and a series of brochures on the Conservative
Movement.*

THE SYNAGOGUE IN THE COMMUNITY

✳

JACOB B. AGUS

To an outside observer, the typical Jewish community appears to be a beehive of activity and excitement. The number of meetings of all sorts, both great and small, the flood of mail and propaganda between meetings, the strange organizational pastime of blowing one's own horn that is the favorite theme at so many gatherings—all testify to the extreme dynamism of the average Jewish community. It is constantly on the go, at times quite agog with the multiplicity of functions and affairs, so much so that it is as difficult to introduce a new function into the crowded calendar of most communities, as it is to squeeze the proverbial camel into the eye of a needle. It has become necessary to have central clearing offices, whose thankless task it is to crowd the steadily expanding plethora of meetings and affairs into the rigid span of a yearly season's duration. For a man or woman of consequence to spend a quiet evening at home during the season is almost certain to be an act of disloyalty to one cause or another. So hectic is the pace of organizations dedicated to the "saving" of Judaism that virtually no time is left for the practice of the Jewish ideals of prayer, study and quiet contemplation.

But, while Jewish communal life impresses the outside observer with its feverish round of "doings," its inner hollowness and emptiness cannot easily be concealed. Almost it is as if the surface tumult and bivouac were a transparent screen intended to hide the subsurface stagnation and petrifaction. To penetrate beneath the misleading exterior, it is sufficient to inquire, what is the net gain from the round of luncheons and banquets, programs and installations? Do all these motions produce heat to suffuse with the warm glow of pride and the calm contentment of dignity the consciousness of being a Jew?—Light, to illumine the place of the Jew against the background of the general scene and to chart the path of survival?—Stored energy, to run the wheels truly in future contingencies?—Above all, how is all this activity related to our raison d'etre, as a Jewish people? How do they combine to answer the question, why and wherefore we are Jews?

Most "Jewish leaders" prefer to ignore these questions as irrelevant to the practical programs of their favorite organizations. They find it much more convenient to massage the body of Judaism than to face the challenge of its soul. But, clearly, of what use are all the comforts of the flesh, if the soul, the central purpose of existence, is allowed to ebb away?—Doubtless, it was a situation similar to the one of American Jewry that elicited the following sage observation of the Talmud, "because of the noise of the multitude of the city, the cry of the soul leaving the body is not heard."

A famous anecdote has it that a man once jumped into a taxi in evident haste and told the driver to get going at top speed. The driver obeyed, then turned to ask his impatient "fare" where he wanted to be taken. "I don't care where you drive," was the reply, "but get me there as soon as you can." The American Jewish community is not clearly aware of whither it is that it desires to go—but it drives there at breakneck speed.

If Jewish communal life is to have meaning and purpose, it must be related to the central purpose of the continued existence of the Jewish group. Time there was when this central purpose was known, felt and cherished by the most humble of our people, who could identify themselves at all times with the simple words of the prophet Jonah, "I am a Hebrew and I fear the Lord, the God of heaven, who hath made the sea and the dry land." To be a Jew is to belong to a people that has made the service of the Lord, the vital focus of its aspirations and ambitions. Today, the stage of Jewish leadership is unhappily crowded with those who no longer know why they are Jews and who still presume to set the tone for the rhythm of Jewish life. This is the source of the tragic paradox of modern Judaism—the magnificent surge of restless energy on the surface and the slow starvation of the soul within.

To say that many of our leaders do not know the purpose of Jewish existence is to take an optimistic view of the situation. For ignorance is only an inert burden, not a destructive force. Actually, the problem is complicated by the prevalence of hollow slogans, which provide illusory goals for our people "hardening their hearts" and hastening the process of decay.

The two philosophies which are presently most effective in confounding the purpose and content of American Judaism may be designated as being respectively, "Judaism by default" and "Judaism by politics." The former is really a racist philosophy. It begins and ends with the argument, "Hitler did not make any distinctions among Jews. Why should we?" It is held and advocated by people who are Jewish, only because they cannot be classified in any other category. They do not adhere to our cause by reason of any positive attachment to our faith, culture or aspirations. They are pushed toward us, but are not pulled by us. They are Jews by default—by default of being Gentile or Christian. Their spokesmen—and they are legion, especially in the fields of Jewish education and social work, speak of "Jewishness" rather than of Judaism or of "ethnic culture" rather than of the Jewish faith. These men, who are especially powerful and vocal in the community center movement, are as little Jewish nationalists, as they are Jewish religionists. The vision of Bialik and the spiritual travail of Ahad Ha'am are as foreign to them as the songs of Halevi and the yearnings of Israel Baal Shem Tov. Unconsciously they compare the American Jew to the American Negro, in inner self-consciousness as well as in extreme status, so that "Jewishness" means to them "gefillte fish" or "bagel and lox," not the distilled essence of millennia of Jewish intellectual toil and achievement.

To describe the high priests, votaries and vested interests of the organizations centered round the philosophy of "Judaism by default," would take us too far afield. Suffice it to say that this intellectual monstrosity is organizationally very powerful, though it is very obvious that it cannot serve as a raison d'etre for American Israel, unless indeed, chas v'sholom, the position of the Jew deteriorates to the point where a force of cohesion becomes unnecessary. It is a philosophy of despair, the bastard product of anti-semitism—sans heat, sans light, sans glory, sans hope this side of group suicide.

The other pseudo-philosophy active on the American scene is the American offspring of a worthy European forebear. Unfortunately, the philosophy of Jewish secular nationalism which spelled life, dignity and creativity for the Jew in the Russian Pale of Settlement, spells nothing but extinction for American Israel. This philosophy, operating with the concept of "the Jews as a nation in being" finds expression in the mania for the trappings of national organization and the symbols of political activity. The Jews of the world should seek to achieve full national status in Palestine, while the Jews of America should so organize their communal structure as to reflect the same concept. Now, Zionism, in its cultural and spiritual aspects, is part and parcel of Judaism. But, the secular nationalist philosophy with which it is sometimes associated, is totally inadequate as the theoretical base of American Israel. For if the Jews of America are essentially of the same category as the Italians and Poles of the metropolitan "little Italys" and "little Polands," then "Jewishness" is and should be no more than a transitory phenomenon in American life. America has evolved out of the commingling of European races and nationalities. The "melting pot" is not a theory, which may or may not be accepted; it is an ineluctable fact of American life, an actual phase of American history and experience, that cannot be controverted by the abstractions of Louis Adamic and the like. There is no getting away from this basic argument: if Judaism is nationality, then an American of Jewish ancestry has no more reason to identify himself with and preserve the Jewish group and its sancta, than an American of Italian ancestry—and this means something perilously close to absolute zero.

The only philosophy which is capable of lending to American Israel consistency and vigor, pride and purpose, is the philosophy of the synagogue. Not the philosophy of the spurious synagogue, which ruthlessly breaks with tradition and cruelly cuts into the roots of Jewish loyalty in the name of an emaciated ghost called Judaism, but the authentic philosophy of the historic synagogues, as expressed in the ideology of the United Synagogue, American Israel, is, to us, fundamentally a religious community, though the term religion is, in our usage, coeval with life and not a set of abstract dogmas. We do not evade the central question of the American Jew, nor do we content ourselves with the sterile substitutes of race and nation. We say to the young American Jew as follows:

"You are the bearer of an ancient and glorious tradition, which is the congealed expression of the word of God in the hearts and minds of generations of saints and sages. This tradition is truth and holiness, beauty and dignity, high-minded aspiration and strong-minded tenacity. To you, as a Jew it is the opportunity to share in an eternal spiritual adventure, to cleave unto a tree of life that is nobler by far than the individual leaves which sprout from it at any one generation. To you, as an American, Judaism is the opportunity to keep Americanism on the high level of conscience and spirituality, to help preserve and to replenish those springs of faith, from which Americanism, at its best, perennially draws its inspiration."

Judaism, in this full-blooded sense, is something to live for and to sing about. Conceived in spiritual terms, it calls upon every Jew to become a soldier in the ranks of God, Who is renewing the world daily, bringing it nearer to the perfection of the Messianic Era. Every faithful Jew knows himself to be, *shutaf b'maasei b'reshith,* a partner in the work of creation. In this perspective, antisemitism is divested of its ominous mystery and is seen to be a disease of the mind and heart, one phase of those Augean stables which we must help clean out. In a word, a faithful Jew, rooted in our historic tradition is the only kind of Jew who can retain his mental balance in this chaotic age, look the world straight in the face, know himself as a Jew and desire himself and his seed to share in Jewish destiny. We do not rule any one out of the fold, but neither do we take the marginal Jew to be the norm of "Jewishness," for a Jew without faith is as a body without a soul.

If religion is the central concern of Jewish life, then the synagogue should be the central institution in the community. It is nothing but hypocrisy to render lip service to the Jewish religion, while encouraging the organization of Jewish life on a nationalistic or racistic basis. For organization is the form in which the collective group speaks to its own members and to the outside world. If ninety per cent of the collective energy of the community is spent for secular purposes, and only ten per cent of effort is devoted to spiritual purposes, then something very definite is being said to those who will hear, concerning the scale of values that is really cherished by the Jewish community. If when all religious groups are invited for consultation, as was the case in San Francisco last year, the Jewish group is represented by three or more groups, all avowedly secular, then a very definite confes-

sion is made to our own thinking youth and to the outside thinking world. If the secular interests of Jewish people receive the unlimited and united support of the community, while the religious
and educational concerns are left to the "private judgment" of
individuals, then we permit it to be proclaimed from the house-
tops that religion is only a sectarian sideline in the community.
Religious ideas can be *expressed* in words, but they are *conveyed*
to the public only through the forms of social organization. Judaism will restore spiritual health to the Jew only when it is really
taken seriously, when the synagogue comes to assume its place as
the fountainhead of all that is positive and meaningful in Jewish
life.

The Torch, September, 1946.

*Dr. Agus, Rabbi of Beth El Congregation of Baltimore,
Maryland, is a distinguished scholar and interpreter of contemporary Jewish thought. He is the author of* Modern Philosophies of Judaism, Guideposts in Modern Judaism, The
Evolution of Jewish Thought, The Meaning of Jewish History *and* The Vision and the Way.

CONSERVATIVE JUDAISM AND THE LIVING TRADITION

MAX ARZT

Life refuses to be governed by logical syllogisms or to be confined to the restricted area of a definition. The living reality, the dynamism of life will not be petrified into a formula of precision. It will not submit to analysis under the microscope of exactness. Truth follows no party line. It resides between the extremes of controversial contentions.

As a movement that stands between two extremist camps in Jewish life, Conservative Judaism avows that ours is a *Torat Hayim*—a living Torah which, like all that has vitality, will not be strapped in a strait jacket of exact classification. Reform Judaism minimizes the authority of Jewish law and therefore ignores it. Orthodox Judaism declares that the law is fixed and final for all time. It thus disregards the studies of Krochmal, Zechariah Frankel, I. H. Weiss and Schechter which irrefutably prove that the applied Halakha always reflected the collective soul and conscience of Israel. Conservative Judaism asserts with Orthodoxy that Judaism is a legalistic, Halakhic system, that loyal Jews must sensitively react to the requirements of the law. But it also affirms that the law is a live, a growing and continuous process.

The pioneers of the Reform movement denied the validity of tradition. Leopold Stein, a guiding spirit of early Reform in Germany, uttered the following emancipation proclamation: "The Talmud is for us in no wise a source of divine communication. It must be completely divested of any higher authority." (Quoted in Strack's Introduction to the Talmud, p. 91). A similar pronouncement was made by Isaac M. Wise, the organizing genius of Reform Judaism in America. He said, "American rabbis have declared in various conferences, the authority of the Talmud abrogated. It could only be considered as an historical record to show how the ancient expounders of the law understood this or that passage of the Bible." (ibid.) The Pittsburgh platform of 1885, among other negations, repudiated the authority of the oral law. Had it not been for the influx and influence of rabbis and laymen whose love for tradition vetoed the rationalized conclusions of the early Reformers, the amputation of tradition would have continued unchecked. The Columbus declaration of principles adopted in 1937, is in part a repeal of the Pittsburgh platform. It pays homage to the oral as well as written law and speaks with great feeling about the need for traditional religious observances. In recent years many Reform rabbis have welcomed the Tallit, a plenitude of Hebrew prayers, the Sukkah, Lulab and Ethrog, Sabbath Candles and Kiddush as friends which had been undeservedly banished. Attempts have even been made to produce evidence that Reform Judaism reckons with the Halakha. But we must not confuse a longing for "beautiful customs and ceremonies" with an acceptance of the Halakha. Loyalty to the Halakha calls for a discipline of resistance to the reckless violation of that which breathes with hallowed significance. Reform Judaism may encourage numerous religious observances, but it does not decry violation of these observances. It now considers the kindling of the Sabbath lights to be an edifying practice, but such observance is not regarded to be spiritually mandatory. It counsels the recital of the Kiddush and underscores attendance at public worship on the Sabbath. But it regards virtually no act or activity to be a desecration of the Sabbath. One may smoke, write letters, fix a tire and begin a journey on the Sabbath without fearing that the sacred has been defiled. It is regarded as an admirable act of self denial to fast on Yom Kippur. But one cannot say it is forbidden for a Reform Jew to partake of a light breakfast or a light lunch on the Day of Atonement. I cite these examples not with the intent of carping criticism, for the day of acrimonious religious controversy has happily passed. I am merely endeavoring to indicate how Reform has abrogated the discipline of the Halakha. Tradition is not recognized where its indiscriminate violation is not deemed to be an act of religious unconcern and disavowal.

Conservative Judaism recognizes the authority of our tradition and at the same time reckons with the living process whereby the

Halakha retains its fluidity and vitality. The history of the Halakha evidences its viability in meeting unprecedented situations. The living Halakha is not necessarily that which is recorded in the codes. It is the resultant of the requirements of the law and the collective conscience of Jews who live under the law. This is what is implied in Schechter's phrase, "Catholic Israel." The law grows through a democratic process. That which a law abiding people allows to become obsolescent in its life ceases to be the norm for all. Though it may linger in the life of individuals endowed with an extra measure of piety, it has been put into desuetude by the people who "if they are not prophets, are the sons of prophets." (Pes. 66a) Where the rabbinical authorities are alert to the needs of their time, they re-interpret the law to meet the demands of reality. Where they are timid and cautious, they at least maintain a discreet silence following the Talmudic principle, "It is better for the people to err unwittingly rather than (through our condemnation) to be made defiant transgressors." (Shab. 148b) A severity which has not been accepted by the masses of the otherwise law-abiding community is not considered mandatory. "One must not impose on a community a rigor which is beyond its power of fulfillment." (B. K. 79a B. B. 6ob) It is the duty of the religious teacher to teach the law and foster its observance. But he must teach the observance of the *living* law, "Just as it is a duty to give instruction to the people concerning that which they will accept and obey, so it is a duty not to exhort them on that which they will reject and refuse to obey." (j. Terum. ch. 5 end) This remarkable Talmudic principle reflects the fluidity of the Halakha in each age. Of course it presupposes the people's acceptance of the law as the standard of their religious life. But once that acceptance is there, the people determine the norm and direction of the law by the manner in which the law impinges on their life. Thus our tradition lives by the dual process of historic continuity and organic growth.

The divergence from the written code resulting from the fact that the law is vital rather than static in nature, is manifest even in Orthodox circles. True it is that in certain Agudath Israel circles there is a limited group of pious adherents who are tenacious in their observance of the letter of the Halakha. The growing of the *peoth,* the prohibition against shaving the beard and the complete separation of the sexes in social life as well as religious life, are punctiliously kept. But such is not the case in neo-Orthodox circles. There, many departures from the codes are permitted or condoned. Thus the *Shaatnez* prohibition is disregarded by many "modern Orthodox" rabbis. Then again, there is great laxity in the matter of mixing the sexes in social and even religious functions. No liberal interpretation of the Shulchan Aruch would permit mixed dancing. Yet "strictly Orthodox" synagogues such as affiliates of Young Israel and others conduct such dances, often in the vestry rooms of their synagogue buildings.

The Mishna ordains that a woman may not teach children. (Kid. 82 a cf. Eben Haezer end of 22) Orthodox schools overlook this explicit law. In recent years a still small voice has been speaking with faltering inaudibility against family pews. In increasing numbers young orthodox rabbis seek and occupy pulpits in synagogues with mixed pews. Thus even in Orthodox circles, the norm of conformance depends on public acceptance or public disregard. Conservative Judaism makes explicit that which is implicit in the behavior of those who are essentially loyal to tradition. Granted that those who wish to live a meaningful Jewish life must be heroes of the spirit, there are situations where in a conflict of values undue rigidity may cause the Halakha to lose its viability. Hence Conservative Judaism prefers to delineate not a regimen but a pattern of religious observances to be retained in the face of changes necessitated by the intellectual and spiritual climate of our time. The preamble to the constitution of the United Synagogue worded by Solomon Schechter, outlines this pattern of traditional Judaism. It calls for observance of the Sabbath and holidays, stresses *Kashrut* and the home observances, underlines the importance of Hebrew as the key to Jewish learning and as the dominant language of Jewish worship. It insists that the hope of the restoration of Palestine ever remain a major motif in our prayers. Congregations which distort this pattern of tradition have ventured "out of bounds" into a perilous "no man's land" where Judaism is in danger of losing its form and substance.

Were the United Synagogue to comprise congregations of every degree of conformity and non-conformity, it would be a union based on a lowest common denominator. It would not evince direction nor be capable of decisive action. A United Synagogue allowing for no diversity would be guilty of authoritarianism and religious regimentation. It would then defy the principle that in each age those who live under the Halakha determine the slow but steady process of religious development and enrichment. Within the United Synagogue are congregations which Doctor Kaplan has aptly classified as rightist, centrist and leftist. The centrists and the leftists have introduced changes and innovations which divert from the traditional code. Some have organs and mixed choirs. All have family pews and conduct supplementary "late" Friday night services. These changes have been introduced in the belief that our times necessitates some or all of these divergencies from tradition. Yet in the "leftist" congregations as well as in the centrist congregations the essential pattern of our tradition is visibly discernible. From their pulpits the rabbi teaches reverence for *Kashrut,* the indispensability of Hebrew, the love for Palestine, and furthers the practice of an optimum of *Mitzvoth Maasiyoth* (religious observance) as means of serving God "when thou sittest in thy house, when thou goest on the way, when thou liest down and when thou risest up."

The fact that in some respects the Halakha becomes inoperative does not militate against a sense of obedience to the Halakha. Maimonides, the great codifier of Talmudic law, did not fail to list the prohibition against living in Egypt as one of the "negative commandments." Yet he wrote that code in Egypt and expressed his regret that he was constrained to violate that law. (Yad Ha-Hazakah Meloklim 5:7)

Living as we do in a period of transition and much needed adjustment, it would be unwise to validate by official action all the innovations and changes that have been introduced. It would also be ludicrous to proclaim a modern "Shulchan Aruch" in our time, when most American Jews have loosened the bonds of loyalty to the Halakha. As Doctor Gordis puts it, we are passing through a frontier stage of general disregard of Jewish law. The widespread religious lawlessness is due to indifference rather than to defiance. There is thoughtless treading on the sacred. To stabilize the status quo would be to surrender all hope for a return to a pattern of Jewish observance organically related to our basic tradition. The conscience of "Catholic Israel" first has to be activated before it can dependably function as the democratic determinant of the norm of Jewish living.

Our age needs the kind of a convocation called by Ezra when the people stood as it were a second time at Sinai and publicly renewed their allegiance to the Torah (Neh. Ch. 8) That historic reaffirmation of fealty to the Torah did by no means petrify Judaism. On the contrary, it paved the way for the Pharisees and gave impetus to the Talmudic process for the progressive development of the law. We must redirect modern Jewish life in the paths of the Halakha by establishing in each congregation fellowships of *Haverim*. These groups would be dedicated to a maximum observance of our tradition, with due allowance for insurmountable personal situations. These consecrated laymen would, without obnoxious belligerency, but with fervor and zest, through persuasion and personal example inspire others to a heightened respect for tradition. Such groups would eventually constitute the alert conscience of K'lal Yisrel and help reclaim "the children who have wandered away from the table of their fathers."

There is decided merit to Doctor Kaplan's plea for unity in diversity. The rightists in our movement must learn to accept the leftists with brotherly understanding. On the other hand the "leftists" must respect the scruples of the sincere rightists and must not insist that others must be as "liberal" as they are. Both groups must prize peace above all and avoid denominationalism and schisms. For the sake of peace the majority in each congregation should determine the particular alignment of the congregation within the framework and pattern of Conservative Judaism.

There are areas, however, which call for decisive action. The segregation of the sexes in worship, though rooted deeply in Jewish practice and sentiment through the ages, is no longer tenable. It disregards the status attained by womanhood in our time and its retention in the synagogue causes many to sever their affiliation with traditional Judaism. The elimination of this aspect of our tradition is a means of preserving other values of greater magnitude. There is a desperate need for "action now" on the troubled problem of the inequity of some of the Jewish divorce laws. Because action has not been taken, our marriage laws are on the verge of complete collapse and abandonment.

In other areas of departure from the Halakha, such as the use of the organ in worship, the time is not ripe for a categorical decision. It is true that some congregations which have had organ music for decades have been among the staunchest in resisting the wanton violation of our tradition. But we are not yet certain whether the organ induces a heightened mood of devotion in prayer. Jewish worship calls for a participating congregation rather than a listening audience. A careful study must be made of the effect of the organ on the participation of the congregation in worship. Till such a study is made, it is best to leave the situation in a state of flux and to make congregations contemplating the introduction of an organ aware of the considerations that warrant the cautious delay of a final decision.

I have forewarned the reader that he could not expect definitiveness in an exposition of Conservative Judaism. That which is living cannot be dissected into categorical segments. The living body has vital organs as well as atrophied muscles (such as the muscle behind the ear). It develops most fully those limbs and capacities which express its will to live. Conservative Judaism strives to imbue our people with the will to live as religious Jews —as a people of the Covenant. When that will to live will be fully aroused, Judaism will develop naturally and organically. Our times call for the affirmation of Judaism. Only those who affirm Judaism can be trusted to evince that collective conscience of "Catholic Israel" which makes for continuity in the midst of wholesome change.

The Torch, January, 1948.

Dr. Arzt, Vice-Chancellor of the Jewish Theological Seminary of America and its Professor of Practical Theology, has been for over forty years an outstanding spokesman for Conservative Judaism. He served as Chairman of the Joint Prayer Book Commission of the United Synagogue and Rabbinical Assembly and is now one of seven scholars preparing a new translation of the Bible for the Jewish Publication Society of America. He is the author of Justice And Mercy: Commentary on the Liturgy of the New Year and the Day of Atonement.

NEW GOALS FOR
CONSERVATIVE JUDAISM

MORRIS ADLER

We have seen in our day, in the case of the United Nations and Palestine, a dramatic and tragic instance of what follows when a resolve, however worthy, is divorced from the machinery requisite for its implementation. When we speak of goals, it is not with the desire to overlook but rather to emphasize the need for strengthening the instrumentalities and agencies of our movement so that they may serve effectively the ends we strive for.

The Seminary, the United Synagogue, the Rabbinical Assembly, and each of the congregations that comprise our total movement, must be transformed into large and potent means for the realization of our common purposes. In the clarification of our goals we should find the inspiration for fortifying and improving the agencies which are their instrument.

The primary motivation out of which Conservative Judaism arose and became organized was the necessity to negate prevailing conceptions held by the camps to the right and left of us. We reacted against existing movements. Orthodoxy was unacceptable and Reform undesirable. It is a useful function at specific points in the historic process to question, to challenge and to refute philosophies that have become embodied in movements and organizations. Partisans of either extreme may scoff at a viewpoint that seems to subsist on denials. But consciously or not, the Conservative movement made a notable contribution when it refused to be impaled on the horns of the dilemma of either wholesale acceptance in its entirety of an unchanged and unchanging body of Jewish tradition, on the one hand, or such a diluted and distorted interpretation on the other, as worked violence upon the historic pattern and integrity of that tradition.

Denials and negations play a fruitful part in the history of ideas. Every idea involves both affirmation and denial; acceptance and rejection; inclusion and exclusion. No apology or defense is necessary for the negations which were implicit in our position from the outset, although our positive formulations were by comparison pale and feeble. We spoke of the process of development which courses through all of the recorded history of our tradition, and meant thereby to negate the viewpoint of a static and immutable law, on the one extreme, and to reject the doctrine that the authority of Jewish law had completely lapsed on the other. We stressed the integrity of the Jewish motive in refutation of those who favored an easy and convenient capitulation to the environment. In the same breath we spoke of the flexibility and fluidity of our social heritage as Jews, in opposition to those who desired to congeal it and keep it insulated against all interaction with modern life. We spoke of modern Judaism and by it expressed our objection to a Judaism that was not modern, and a modernity that was not Jewish. Our affirmations were more apparent than real. They could be fully comprehended only in terms of a frame of reference constructed largely of our negations.

We must face the truth that we have been halting between fear and danger; fear of the Orthodox, and danger of Reform. We have set our watches by their time-pieces. The time has come for our emergence from the valley of indecision. We must move forward to a stage in which Conservative Judaism revolves about an axis of positive and unambiguous affirmations. This will require a measure of boldness and vision on our part which as a movement, I am sorry to say, we have not thus far manifested.

For one thing, there is a growing grass-root demand for such an exposition and clarification of our position as cannot be achieved by reliance on the eloquence of our denials and disavowals. There is a growing impatience on the part of our people, the members of our congregations—a growing impatience with the timidity or reluctance which inhibits our forward movement.

For another thing, the struggle with both Orthodoxy and Reform has lost much of its intensity and much of its meaning. Indeed, the whole battle has shifted to a new ground. The formulae of three or four decades ago no longer address themselves to the immediate or central problems of American Jewry.

Leaving for the moment the aspect of those who escape from

Jewry and concentrating upon Jews who live within the framework of our organized community, we shall have to conclude that our chief work must be to combat the inertness which, like a spreading paralysis, has settled in vital areas of American Jewish life. Inertness in our midst is of two varieties. First, we have the inert multitudes.

Multitudes of our people are untouched, uninformed, uncovenanted. They have not enough Judaism to live it, nor enough interest to reject it. Their personal lives are uninfluenced by the fact of their Jewishness. They take their values from the circle in which they move, from the business they operate, from the fashions in thought and action that are current about them. These and these alone serve them as Decalogue and Torah, the inheritor of and substitute for their tradition. Uncommitted, they represent a prehistoric and pre-Sinaitic tribe in our midst. Some of these we shall probably never reach. Others may yet be stirred if somehow we could devise the challenge and establish the organization that is electrically endowed with resurrecting powers.

There are others just as inert, but on the side of Judaism. You find them crowding the membership rolls of our numerous organizations, synagogues and Zionist districts. Instead of running membership campaigns, let us spend a month dropping members who have not lived up to our traditions. It is not non-Jewishness that is routine but Jewishness. Judaism has become for them a glacial heirloom which they have strangely fallen into the habit of guarding. On the surface they are affiliated, but theirs is a frigid and uninspired affiliation. There is about it no glow, no incandescence of the spirit. It does not have the compelling warmth, the transforming power of a great experience. Unimpassioned themselves, they communicate but little to their children. Theirs is a creed without color, a faith without fire.

Nor can we face our new obligations without an abiding and vivid awareness of the overwhelming cataclysm which, in our day, has deprived us of the most potent and creative source of Jewish vitality and content in the Diaspora. The hope of Goluth Judaism lies with us, and the challenge to our understanding is written largely on the very surface of contemporary Jewish life. It is a challenge which cannot be met by stepping up our techniques of fund raising or consolidating defense agencies. The statistics of our loss do not suggest the enormity of the cultural and spiritual depletion we have suffered. The millions who were done to death had maintained a society rooted in rich Jewish feeling and in the manifold variety of Jewish experience and expression. Their death marks a crisis in the conscience of mankind. It also marks the death of an epoch in Jewish history, midst horror and agony.

When we spoke of re-interpreting or reconstructing the tradition, we were placing a superstructure of interpretation upon a base sufficiently solid and strong to support our revisions. Whether we were aware of it or not, our amendments to Judaism had as their background that fullblooded Jewish center with its Volzhins, Vilnas, Odessas and Warsaws—the home of Gaon, Baal Shem, student, scholar and saint. Today our adaptations have as their background inertness, flatness and a process of pervasive corrosion and disintegration. Ours is the God-like task of creating a world to supplant the world that has gone down in destruction and ashes. Ours is not simply the task of reforming alone, but also of forming; not solely of reconstructing but likewise of constructing; not merely of re-interpreting but more importantly of interpreting Judaism to Jews. The Jews for whom we are called to devise a Jewish philosophy and rationale are not Jews whose conceptions of Judaism have become outdated and are in need of revision, but are individuals with no conception of Judaism at all. Our approach to the problem must therefore be seen in this new perspective.

Nor must we fall into the error of placing unreasonable reliance for our salvation as a Jewish community upon Eretz Yisrael. The role of Eretz Yisrael is secure and central in the economy of Jewish life but its influence is not exclusively the co-efficient of its own spiritual power. Thus Eretz Yisrael may practice affluence without exerting influence. The ability to export currents of cultural power must be matched by the ability to receive them. Ours must be a spiritual absorptive capacity. This quality depends upon the kind of Jewish attitudes that dominate our own community, the character of Jewish personalities that we develop, the caliber and effectiveness of our leadership and institutions in creating a climate hospitable and congenial to an influx of incoming, enriching, positive influences streaming from Eretz Israel.

American Judaism, if it is to enrich the lives of Jews, must be inextricably related to the conditions and circumstances of our society. Our life is marked by a greater involvement on the part of masses of Jews with the cultural, political and social forces and forms in the larger group in the midst of which we live. Our relationship to that larger group and its milieu is characterized by a community of interest and an identification of purpose which were never shared by as large a portion of a Jewish settlement in any previous period. Many needs hitherto filled exclusively by Jewish instrumentalities and outlets are now filled by American life. Less time, energy and need for specific Jewish experience is the inevitable result. There can be no iron curtain dividing our Jewish from our American lives.

This revolutionary impact upon the daily course of our lives is likewise felt in our attitudes, ideas and conceptions. It is not only the behavior of Jews that has changed, it is their mentality. To meet that impact it will be necessary to achieve a pace of adjustment to it, which corresponds to the rapidity with which change has come into our lives. No gradual and slow process of interpretation or geologic rate of adaptation will suffice either to evolve a Judaism compatible with our needs and our new mode of existence, or with effecting a narrowing of the growing gap between Jews and Judaism in this country.

Lloyd George once said that the most dangerous thing in the world is the attempt to leap a chasm in two jumps. That is what we have been trying. There have been other periods when the historic dislocations were so great that the customary process of interpretation geared to a slow moving, normally developing society had to be abandoned, although legally the procedure of change followed, or seemed to follow, the traditional legal pattern. The change from sacrifice to prayer, from temple to synagogue service, the transformation of the study of *Kodshim,* and later *Nezikin* to an academic exercise constituted basic changes which were more than orderly re-interpretations within the framework of the tradition. Life made imperious demands which Judaism could not deny.

It is not within the province of this presentation to deal with method or extent of change. Laymen have a great stake in it. We are talking about the pattern of Jewish living. However, if the above analysis has any validity, it implies that we must exert pressure through our congregations and through our rabbis. That in such spheres of Jewish law as Sabbath, dietary laws, divorce laws, laws relating to the problem of the *Agunah*, laws touching the priesthood, we cannot any longer be content with revisions by the strict, slow process of law. Nor can we transfer that responsibility to any other community, not even to Eretz Israel.

We must clearly and unambiguously articulate our conception of ritual observance as it is implicit in our philosophy and our behavior. The standards, insights and values which are permanently naturalized in our outlook as modern men cannot be segregated when we deliberate upon our problems as Jews. Observance is not for us a supernaturally ordained regimen, but the vehicle of Jewish discipline and unity and the stimulus to refinement of our spiritual life. We must deal with the system of practice in the light of such a view of it and stop hiding behind double meaning phrases. Nor should there be fear that any change is dangerous, since it will lead to a flood of changes. Such a fear simply means that we leave change to the haphazard environmental influences or to the anarchic will of any individual. It means a perpetuation of a chaotic status-quo and the elimination of human control and will from governing men's affairs.

If our faith is so feeble that it may catch its death of cold when we open the slightest aperture, then we must surrender all hope of preserving it under the present conditions of our life. The trouble with our Movement is that we have good brakes but we lack an accelerator. Our own paralysis in effecting a bold and reasoned adaptation, both to the inner world of our own ideas, needs and feelings, and to the outer world in which we live, is not equalled by a comparable paralysis on the part of the forces of life. They continue to nullify, destroy, revoke, erase with frightening thoroughness, the laws we cherish. We owe it to our people to guide them in energizing Jewish practice so that it serves contemporary purposes.

And we must seek a clarification of our basic philosophy of Judaism which once again in unambiguous and unmistakable language will express those views which among ourselves and at our conferences we do not hesitate to affirm. The fact that there are differences of view in our midst does not mean that there is not a body of concepts upon which there is widespread agreement. We can, I feel sure, unite on a statement which need not be final or dogmatic on such basic elements in our tradition as "Nature of Torah and its Origin," Messiah, Chosen People, Resurrection of the Dead, Reward and Punishment, Providence. Such a statement would not alone organize our common views, but also begin to prepare those cohesions which can unite our individual synagogues into a single movement. Thus far we are united only by an organization and by a school. We must develop that inner cement of a common practice and a common conception—else our movement for all of its techniques will disintegrate or become impotent.

We must seek to make of our Movement a factor and force in another transition, the transition of American Jewry from aggregation to center, from settlement to community. Obviously, the very existence of a large aggregation of Jews acts as reinforcement to the powers of survival and as a dam upon the corrosive and disintegrating impacts upon our group integrity.

Aggregation, however, is a physical fact, a statistical phenomenon, whereas a community is the product of historic, cultural and spiritual forces. An aggregation is in a sense a pre-historical, subconscious society which rises to the threshold of historic power when proximity and numbers are translated into an inner cohesiveness. The common descent of individuals becomes fortified in the case of a community by common activities, interests, loyalties and an inner sense of social and spiritual togetherness. The very recency of the settlement of large numbers of Jews in our land is, of course, a factor in our failure to reach the level of community status. The responsibilities which world conditions thrust upon us to engage in welfare activities on a large scale since World War I for the relief and rehabilitation of Jews in other lands have given a one-sided direction to our collective Jewish life.

But the confusions and timidities of our official leadership, and the inadequacy of our formulated conceptions, play a not unimportant part in the retardation of our communal development. A conscious goal of our activities must be the achievement of a community life, marked by self-acceptance and self-identification as Jews, and the placing of ourselves in the line of historic continuity and progress. American Jewry in its present immaturity still suffers from a type of isolationism in time, not viewing itself under the aspect of Jewish history.

We can and should contribute to the attainment of the larger perspective. A settlement, functioning on the sub-community level sees its primary functions in terms of elemental motivations, such as fear and pity. Neither of these is a healthy base for community organization. They breed a paternalistic leadership regarding itself as the guardian of a constituency composed of waifs and dependents. The Jewish community must become democratically organized and admit to representation the masses of Jews who are presently disenfranchised. We must give evidence of greater thought on this problem and seek to play our part in the establishment of such a community.

The tempo and temper of modern life have brought about emotional disturbance, spiritual confusion, personal instability. While a community is more than the sum of its individuals, it has of course no meaning apart from the life of those individuals. The malaise of numbers of such men, victims of the stresses and tensions of contemporary society cannot but react on the soundness of the whole community. In a more organized and planned manner must we equip ourselves to deal with the personal problems of our people. The rabbi must be trained in handling insecurities, fears, loneliness, guilt complexes and other symptoms of basic maladjustment of men and women. Our synagogues cannot overlook this field, and should accept as not the least of their functions, the obligation consciously to aid in bringing about better emotional balance and more wholesome attitudes towards self, towards others, towards the whole of life on the part of those in the community who need guidance and psychological reinforcement. I believe that if we are aware of the problem and accept our responsibility with regard to it we shall muster the wisdom necessary for meeting it.

The age in which we live confronts us with a spiritual challenge and opportunity which we cannot over-estimate. Our locale is the American scene, though as Jews the range of our responsibility and zealous interest extends far beyond it. We are, however, part of American life in more than any accidental or even physical sense alone. We are woven deeply into the fabric of America and live a considerable part of our lives in the wide area of mutuality common to all Americans. The spiritual problems of America are our problems, and the perplexities and conflicts of our time touch us deeply.

We do not touch the root of the problem of our time, until having probed beneath its economic and political expressions we come to the real and basic malady which is spiritual and moral in essence. We have not the ethical sensitivity adequate to the new conditions of life. There is an interrelatedness into which we are perforce thrown with all the people of earth, an immense skill for destructiveness which we wield—and here I might mention that it was my doubtful privilege to walk amidst the ruins of Hiroshima. It wasn't the ruins that depressed us then, because by the time we came to that fateful city, we had seen much of the Orient in shambles. We had seen Tokyo, one of the greatest cities of the world, reduced to ashes, but as we walked through the streets of Hiroshima we were aware that something had entered human life, a new dimension of destruction, a new havoc, global in its scope had now come into human history for the first time. And we wondered whether that power would be used to destroy us so that even historians would not survive to write a decent epitaph on the collective grave of mankind.

These new facts in our life require a larger vision and larger loyalty than we have attained. There is needed a moral revitalization, a spiritual reinforcement of our political policy, an ethical wisdom with which to make economic decisions that are wise and just. These problems must re-echo in our life and we must seek through our religious tradition to add to the strength of the mortal forces of our land. Our faith in the possibility of ordering our lives through human intelligence and goodness, and the passion for justice with which our tradition is vibrant must flow through our movement into the mainstream of American life. Until we are well on the road to world understanding, world justice and world peace, we are "dead men on a furlough," "playing golf across the burned hills of hell."

To attempt a program of the magnitude that has been here suggested, we shall have to draw closer one to another. We shall have to join synagogue to synagogue in a disciplined, purposeful movement that becomes a spiritual force. We shall have to overcome parochialism, timidity and confusion within our own ranks.

Aristotle points out that the distinction between a craftsman and scientist is that the former develops skill in the "sphere of being," the latter in the "sphere of coming to be." We have a great opportunity to work in the "sphere of coming to be" of an American Jewish life, informed with dignity, spiritual power and Jewish understanding. May it never be said of us that faced by a great opportunity, we lacked the will and vision to meet it. May American Jewry, through us, fulfill the ancient prophecy, "And they that be of thee shall build the old waste places. Thou shalt raise up the foundations of many generations. And thou shalt be called the repairer of the breach, the restorer of paths to dwell in."

The Torch, October. 1948.

In 1966 American Jewry was suddenly and most tragically deprived of the leadership of one of its most inspiring religious personalities. Rabbi Adler was Rabbi of Congregation of Shaarey Zedek of Detroit, Michigan. He served as Chairman of the Law Committee of The Rabbinical Assembly of America, as Adjunct Professor of Agada at the Jewish Theological Seminary, and as Chairman of the Commission on Adult Jewish Education of B'nai B'rith.

THE BASIC TASK OF THE SYNAGOGUE IN AMERICA

MAXWELL ABBELL

What is the basic task that the Synagogue has to perform in America? In my view the Synagogue can, and must, bring the traditional religious ideals of Judaism into fruitful operation on the American scene.

For various reasons the American Jewish community has reversed the priorities that historically had held sway for many centuries throughout the Jewish world. Whereas in Eastern Europe, from which area most American Jews emigrated, the Synagogue was the most important Jewish institution and the very center of Jewish life; in this country other agencies seem to have superseded it. It is generally accepted that this reversal of priorities is indigenous to the American scene. That is not the case at all. Philanthropic and defense priorities in American Jewish community life are a development of late 19th century America. In the Colonial period and until the late 19th century the Synagogue was the center of Jewish life and education. Only later, as the result of the mass immigration and the great duress of our people abroad, philanthropy, and later defense, emerged as the major aspects of our Jewish communal life. As important as these endeavors may have been, the resulting fragmentation of the Jewish community and the shifting of centrality in the American Jewish experience has been a negative factor. It is only within the past fifteen years or so that both Jewish Education and the Synagogue have been—recently at an accelerated pace—regaining a position of primary importance in the American Jewish scene.

The struggle of the American Jewish community for economic rooting placed prime emphasis upon material needs. To cater to the material needs of our poverty-stricken immigrants, philanthropic organizations and institutions were developed first. Thus they were in a position to attract the leadership of successful business and professional men. Thus such leadership as appeared gravitated largely towards philanthropic or semi-philanthropic activities, local and national. This was true in many instances even in the case of deeply religious Jews who found no outlet for their communal interests in the Synagogue or in Jewish Education.

It is to the eternal credit of our people that, under circumstances disadvantageous to the emergence of Jewish religious lay leaders, there nevertheless did arise a group of men and women to whom spiritual needs were as important as the material. These leaders recognized that man does not live by bread alone, that a healthy soul as well as a healthy body was required to constitute a healthy, well-rounded person. These devout and devoted persons, few in number at first, have gradually increased until today there are many capable, college-trained professional and business men, successful in their respective fields of endeavor, who, as the result of mature thought, have decided that the primacy of the Synagogue, of Jewish Education and of Jewish religious life must be reestablished if the American Jewish community is to survive as a healthy organism. These dedicated laymen gave of their substance, of their time and of their energy to found Jewish institutions of learning such as the Jewish Theological Seminary of America. They included such revered men as Judge Mayer Sulzberger, Solomon Solis-Cohen, Jacob Schiff, Louis Marshall, Felix Warburg and Sol Stroock, of blessed memory. You will notice that I omitted the name of Cyrus Adler. This is omission by design for he represents the very epitome of lay leadership—a layman who through the spiritual might of learning and insight scaled the highest summit given to any person in our tradition, rabbi or layman, namely the Presidency of a Seminary for the training of rabbis and teachers. His remarkable career reaffirmed the basic precept in Judaism that learning and talent, rather than birth or power, confer true distinction. Of such men the psalmist spoke when he said: "Mark the man of integrity and behold the upright."

Within the past decade these great leaders have been succeeded by a large number of younger persons who have stepped forward to assume leadership in Jewish Education and in the Synagogue.

It is heartening to see the many new congregations being formed at present throughout the country consisting largely of young people, American-born and educated, who have moved into new neighborhoods and who select the Synagogue and the Hebrew school as the first communal insitutions to organize.

What is required to make the Synagogue the force that would bring the Jewish traditional ideals into fruitful operation on the American scene? The answer is two-fold—first, a Jewishly educated lay leadership and second, a breaking down of the isolationism of the individual synagogue.

Before the synagogue can make a real contribution to American spiritual life it must develop greater strength through a higher standard of leadership. It must develop leaders who will assume a positive commitment to live in accordance with the ideals of our tradition and who will exemplify in their own lives our ancient moral, ethical and spiritual values. While responsibility for such a re-development of the synagogue rests to some extent upon our spiritual leaders, a great portion of this burden rests upon the laity. In Jewish life the distinction between lay and religious leadership has never been sharp. We never have had and we do not have today any religious hierarchy. We have only an age old distinction between the learned, informed Jew—the Talmid Haham—and the ignorant and uninformed. The existence of a Jewishly ignorant laity is a reversal of ancient Jewish values and traditions. It devolves upon us to correct this perilous situation.

The Synagogue must be regarded as a national Jewish institution. Even though the local group finances, builds, develops and conducts the local Synagogue, they should regard it as merely a local expression of a national institution. This idea prompted Dr. Schechter to insist that the national organization should be called the "United Synagogue of America" rather than the "United Synagogues of America." As I have already mentioned, we Jews have never created a hierarchical organizational setup and we do not want to. It is our belief that strength lies in voluntary expression of individual local groups banded together in a national organization. The latter in turn is but the fountainhead and inspirational center composed of local representatives of the individual synagogues. It is a curious anomaly that in most communities the synagogue is a well financed and very strongly rooted organization while on the national level the synagogue has not been able to assume its proper place among the three great religious forces of this country, nor even attain the importance which it should have in the Jewish community, because the local synagogue leadership has had a myopic vision that did not extend beyond the scope of its own building and community.

Until recently the leaders of local synagogues have tried to be completely self-sufficient, calling upon the national organization only when they were in difficulty—when they required help and advice in financing, when they needed functionaries, teachers, cantors or rabbis. They have succumbed to an "edifice complex," attempting to outdo each other in the size and costliness of their physical plants, forgetting that not brick and mortar but the spirit within the structures breathes life into a synagogue. They have failed to see that the local synagogue by itself cannot be healthy or enduring, regardless of its financial soundness. Each synagogue is but a single link in a large chain. The strength of the local synagogue depends upon the strength of the national group—the United Synagogue. With some support from each local synagogue, the United Synagogue can become a tower of strength to the entire movement, reflecting back its influence and prestige upon its constituent local synagogues.

But in order to make the synagogue the spokesman for American Jewry and the central institution in American Jewish life, there must be certain developments in the synagogue and in the contents and concepts of the Jewish religion which the synagogue represents. Most American Jews recognize that many of the laws in the Torah and in Rabbinic literature were devised for a community so separated from the rest of the world as to be governable by Jewish law alone, and that many others apply to a stage of economic development and mode of life much more simple than our present complex civilization. As a result it is difficult to observe the innumerable commandments of the *Shulhan Aruch* either in the letter or in the same spirit as one's ancestors. There has long been a crying need for bringing our Halakha into compatibility with the needs of the modern, fast-changing world. The longer we delay the more persons we discourage from remaining true to our religion.

One element of a revivified and strengthened Synagogue, if it is to become the central focal point of the modern Jewish community, must be a more simplified, more relevant, more meaningful, more feasible and more livable regimen of conduct that can be observed with integrity, that will not offend our reason, that will offer emotional satisfaction and which will constitute a sound, defensible, explicable and understandable body of rules for ethical living and spiritual conduct, which will be attractive to modern Jewry. In this respect little has been done and much must be done and done quickly because every day's delay means the loss of many of our people who choose the easier path of deviation, non-observance and complete separation from our religious tradition and heritage.

In this connection, I am glad to note the important developments in the Law Committee of the Rabbinical Assembly in recent years. The Committee has been re-organized so that it can deal realistically with the crucial problems confronting our society. At the recent convention of the Rabbinical Assembly, a historic decision was reached. The Faculty of the Seminary and the Rabbinical Assembly together planned to take constructive steps to meet the vexatious problems which derive from the need to correlate Jewish civil and religious marriage and divorce laws. In their earnest desire not to further divide the American Jewish community, the Rabbinical Assembly and the Seminary faculty invited both the Orthodox and Reform groups to join in the establishment of a *Beth Din,* which in any event will be established with or without such participation. The United Synagogue congratulates its sister organization for this bold step. We laymen hope it will lead to further action. Such an approach in the area of law, on the part of our rabbis, will be of great influence in helping the synagogue return to a position of centrality in the Jewish scene.

In addition, to attract American youth and adults and to become once again the central Jewish institution, the synagogue must not be, as until recently it was, solely a house of prayer. Prayer, while important, is only one aspect of a person's life, only one function of the synagogue and only one form of religious expression. The synagogue must be, as it is increasingly becoming, a house of study as well. Though there is opinion to the contrary, many of us welcome the development of the congregational

school which ties in the members' children with the synagogue itself so that when the children graduate they automatically become members of other groups in the synagogue until they
marry, when they join the young married, and later the adult,
groups. We welcome also the development of adult Jewish study
in our synagogues so that the parents of the lost generation can,
albeit, belatedly, imbibe some of the Jewish spirit which their
parents neglected to furnish them, or which through force of circumstances they never developed themselves. This in turn will
help create closer relationships between parents and children.
There is nothing so discouraging to the child or so disconcerting
to the parent as to have the child taught to observe holiday and
Sabbath customs and ceremonies and then to find the parent
either ignorant of them or unwilling to join with the children in
celebrating them. The synagogue must also become the modern
version of the house or assembly, or community center, where the
boys and girls, after school or between classes, during the week-
end or during vacation periods, can meet in various groups, social, athletic, study and religious. In this area the congregations
can make use of the fine programs, guidance materials and organizational techniques that the United Synagogue have developed
and are anxious to make available to all member synagogues.
Thus children who are members of the Leaders Training Fellowship or who have attended a Ramah Camp during the summer
can become centers in their synagogues from which a genuine enthusiasm for things Jewish can radiate.

The thoughts I have expressed thus far flow from my conception of the nature of the centrality of the synagogue's position in
our American Jewish community. Permit me to elaborate a bit
further upon this concept.

By the centrality of the synagogue I do not encompass, as has
been suggested by others, the possibility that all philanthropic,
recreational and other activities of the Jewish community which
are now being conducted outside the walls and outside the organizational set-up of the synagogue should be included within the
synagogue framework. I envision the synagogue being the central
Jewish communal agency but not the totality of such agencies. I
do not have in mind the elimination of all other Jewish communal organizations or the making of such organizations sub-

sidary to some over-all synagogue organization. Such imperial designs are far from my mind. I regard the centrality of the synagogue in Jewish life not so much in organizational terms as in the implication that the synagogue become the basic and primary unit of Jewish organization. This means that every Jew, regardless of his other associations and activities, should associate himself with a synagogue in his community, *and, more important still,* that the spirit of the synagogue and the influence of its teachings should be incorporated into and be an active influence in the lives of the men and women, lay and professional, who guide the destinies of these other Jewish communal organizations and furnish the Jewish communal leadership. This is worlds apart from the present situation where both lay and professional leaders are often either ignorant of, or indifferent to, the Jewish tradition or openly and avowedly anti-religious and opposed to anything savoring of Jewish religion in the sphere of Jewish communal life.

When the synagogue is not basic, as is the case today in American Jewish life, we in effect proclaim that we Jews are not a religious community. It is unfortunate that the few among us who continually emphasize the fact that we Jews are *only* a religious community, are those who all too often are furthest from the synagogue and from the spirit and tradition of Judaism and who use the term "religious community or people" only as a smokescreen behind which they hide in their attempt to run away from Judaism completely. We are not a political community nor a racial or ethnic community. As Jews we have meaning only as a religious community. It is encumbent upon us to implement this proposition, symbolically and actually, upon the American scene by insisting that the lay leaders of the community, regardless of their other associations, associate themselves specifically with the synagogue and speak as Jews through the synagogue.

What do I mean when I say that the synagogue should bring the religious Jewish traditional ideals into fruitful operation on the American scene?

Hitherto the synagogue has not made the contribution as one of the great religious forces in American life that it can and should make to the spiritual life of America. Americans have always spoken of the Judaeo-Christian traditions as the basis of the religious life of the modern world, thus giving us Jews credit for the basic elements of this tradition. Americans have always spoken of the three great religions of this country as Protestantism, Catholicism and Judaism, despite the fact that we Jews number only about five million out of about 160 million population. It is a widely accepted proposition that Western civilization rests upon three basic pillars: religion from Jerusalem and Judea, philosophy from Athens and law from Rome. Matthew Arnold, in his essay on Hellenism and Judaism, goes further and points out that Judaism is one of the two great forces that molded all Western civilization.

Our non-Jewish friends have the right to expect the synagogue to bring the traditional Jewish religious ideals into fruitful operation on the American scene. That is the basic task the synagogue should perform for us and for America. The synagogue can and must influence the civic life of the country in the same way that all alert religious institutions do. Social, political and cultural problems which we share with our non-Jewish neighbors must be studied by the synagogue groups and their religious and ethical implications and conclusions put on the free market of ideas in friendly rivalry with the views of other religious and of secular groups. Thus the Judaic emphasis on ethical behavior should be utilized as a motivating force for raising the ethical and spiritual level first, of American Jewry, and through them, of the totality of American life.

Our spiritual contribution to America cannot be made through institutions or organizations which consider religion as being only of marginal importance. It is through the synagogue and only through the synagogue that we can become a vital and creative spiritual factor on the American scene. For the synagogue deals with the ultimate values of life, is organized about the family and comprises the totality of personal life, community standards and our hopes for a better world.

What criteria can we establish by which to recognize the successful functioning of the synagogue upon the American scene? What is it that we hope for in lay synagogue leadership in the future and what is it that we have in mind when we talk about the synagogue as being a spiritual force in American life?

We mean among other things that there should arise a generation of Jews in America whose lay leaders will feel that their spiritual, moral and ethical life is rooted in the teachings of the Bible, the Talmud and the Commentaries; that we should have an increased number of laymen who will feel at home in the writings of the Prophets and in the Ethics of the Fathers and whose conversation, public statements and public acts will be buttressed and enriched by the wisdom and inspiration of the five books of Moses, of an Isaiah, or an Amos, a Jeremiah or a Hillel, a Maimonides or a Rashi, a Vilna Gaon or an Israel Salanter; that it should become generally known, as it was in former generations, that the Rabbi is not the only one to whom the Bible and the Talmud are open books, but that there are learned laymen as well to whom these books are a daily delight, representing the fountains of living waters. Such personalities, once they appear upon the American Jewish scene, would make a profound impact upon American life generally. Even as great American Jewish businessmen, industrialists, lawyers, jurists, physicians, scientists and scholars have helped to shape the economic, legal, medical, scientific and sociological life and thought of America, so in the future may we hope that there might appear on the American scene a Jew who will be recognized as a great spiritual personality, not because he happened to be a rabbi or a scholar, devoting all his time to the spiritual or scholastic field, but because he is an outstanding business or professional man or scientist who at the same time lived and breathed and bespoke the unique Jewish heritage of our Fathers.

We American Jews have the right to aspire to an American Maimonides in scholarship or an American Moses Montefiore in Jewish public service.

The Torch, Winter, 1955.

THE SEMINARY:
AS A UNIVERSITY OF JUDAISM

MOSHE DAVIS and MORDECAI M. KAPLAN

A key word in the philosophical vocabulary of Mordecai M. Kaplan is *metamorphosis*. This concept runs through most of his writings as he applies it to his interpretations of religion, history and contemporary decisions. In the idea of metamorphosis, Dr. Kaplan finds the possibility of transformation of both self and group as a deliberate process. It is the law of spiritual selection as differentiated from the evolutionary concept of natural selection.

Jewish institution-building, too, Dr. Kaplan urges, should be guided by the principle of metamorphosis. Like the caterpillar— to use one of his favorite images—which enters its adult butterfly stage only by shedding its chrysalis, so must we learn to transform our institutions to meet the urgent needs of changing times and social conditions. Growth, in personal or group life, is measured not by what you are but by what you are becoming.

Most Jewish institutions which find themselves unable to cope with new challenges, continue in their accustomed manner and rationalize their outmoded programs by trying to find reasons for habitual patterns which they are reluctant to abandon. Others try to persevere in their being, by inventing substitutes for their original goals. Neither way, Dr. Kaplan warns, can solve the needs of our people, which in every aspect of its life is reeling under the impact of the great social and human revolutions in civilization. Only by a process of metamorphosis, of transformation, to a new stage of inner Jewish development, can these crises be met successfully today, as they have been met in the past.

This is the text of life Dr. Kaplan read to the assembly gathered at the Seminary in February, 1945, to celebrate the thirty-fifth anniversary of the Teachers Institute. He called his address "From Strength to Strength." After describing the past two stages in the history of the Seminary, he made his historic proposal for its transformation to the next stage: the Seminary must become a University of Judaism, if it is to continue to serve as nerve-center of Jewish life and thought in the new age.

The program of the University, he suggested, must be based on the Seminary's "definite organic pattern of values and assumptions which, more than any avowed theological creed, has constituted the animating spirit of the Seminary since its re-organization in 1902." These principles, or methods of approach to the content of Jewish living, he described as: the primacy of scholarship; the Hebraic character of Judaism; the abundance or plenitude of Jewish living; the acceptance of the American environment as permanent. The foundation, or content of these principles is, of course, the religious tradition.

In characteristic fashion, Dr. Kaplan plunged into the difficult tasks involved in bringing this idea into being. Joining Dr. Finkelstein and Dr. Greenberg, he visited Los Angeles several times to interest the lay leadership there in its establishment; he taught classes in the graduate school; and he is beloved throughout the West Coast today not only as the founder of the University of Judaism but as its mentor and symbol.

Ten years have passed since Dr. Kaplan delivered his address in the Library of the Seminary. The original student body of one hundred is now approaching the thousand mark, and the University, occupying at present a home given it by Louis M. Rabinowitz, is preparing to move to its new enlarged campus.

While we publish but a small portion of the address the reader will be quick to grasp why this essay has already assumed the quality of an historic document in the annals of American Jewry. And it will live as all great dreams and visions live. For it is built on the past and looks to the future, and therefore can be read every day. This is the lasting quality of the ongoing work of our master and teacher, *morenu v'rabbenu.*

From Strength to Strength BY MORDECAI M. KAPLAN

. . . While the Seminary has been increasing its centripetal and integrative influence on American Jewry in arithmetical ratio, the environment has been increasing its centrifugal and disintegrative influence in geometrical ratio. The overwhelming majority of unaffiliated and disoriented Jews exert on the minority of affiliated and loyal Jews a demoralizing influence which is even harder to resist than the challenge of the non-Jewish environment. If the Seminary wants to catch up with the forces that are undermining American-Jewish life, it must aim to reach out in its influence far beyond the limits within which it has been operating all these years. It must extend the scope of its research and teaching to include many other phases of Jewish professional service besides that of the rabbinate and Jewish education. It must be prepared to undergo a transformation that is tantamount to a metamorphosis in its setup and in its functions.

. . . The fundamental issue is: What does American Jewry need most today? I submit that the question which has come to obsess the growing number of our people is not: What must one do to be a *good* Jew?, nor even, what *kind* of a Jew should one be? but, whether to be or not to be a Jew at all. Throughout the centuries, from the destruction of the Second Commonwealth to the era of the Jewish emancipation, the Yeshiva was the academic institution that answered the question of what one must do to be a good Jew. When the Jew began to be westernized, he wanted to know what kind of a Jew he should be. He then created rabbinical seminaries and colleges to help him find an answer. But now that he has become more sensitive than ever to the liabilities of being a Jew, he wants to be sure that those liabilities are counterbalanced by genuine moral and spiritual assets. He is seriously asking himself whether he should remain a Jew, bring up his children as Jews and encourage the perpetuation of Judaism. No mere Yeshiva nor even a Jewish Theological Seminary as hitherto constituted, is qualified to meet such a challenge. Yet without an academic institution capable of training leaders who have the necessary knowledge, technique and moral courage to face the situation as it actually is, no future for American Judaism is conceivable. There is no reason in the world why our own Seminary should not become such an institution. The precedent of having undergone metamorphosis twice before in the course of its career, as well as the inner restiveness both on its own part and on the part of its graduates and lay adherents, should impel the Seminary to measure up to the need and opportunity of these new times, and become the kind of institution that would resurrect the Jew's faith in his people and its religion. In order to achieve this, the Seminary must avoid the pitfall of denominationalism . . .

. . . Though the Seminary has wisely abstained from identifying itself with any Jewish denominational program, it has stressed unremittingly that without which no Jewish denomination can long remain creatively Jewish. That element has constituted its dynamic *continuum*. There can be no meaning to metamorphosis, unless we identify the *continuum,* or dynamic constant, which may be counted on to connect its passing with its oncoming stage. Hence as well as envisaging the shape of things to come in the Seminary's career, it is necessary to identify the *continuum* or dynamic constant which is to bind its present with its future.

Long association with the Seminary has enabled me to experience at first hand the impact of a definite organic pattern of values and assumptions, which, more than any avowed theological creed, has constituted the animating spirit of the Seminary since its reorganization in 1902. The values and assumptions group themselves around four main principles, or methods of approach to the content of Jewish living. That content has always been the religious tradition. Since the advent of Dr. Schechter it has come to include Zionism, as set forth in his classic statement on Zionism, which he described as the Declaration of Jewish Independence from all kinds of slavery, material or spiritual.

The first principle is the primacy of scholarship. This is the principle that, if the knowledge of Jews and Judaism is to be employed in the services of Jewish survival and growth, it must be the result of a modern scientific approach to the historical sources of Jewish life. When over a century ago, Zunz, Frankel, Geiger and Graetz laid the foundation of Jewish scholarship, which they termed *Juedische Wissenschaft,* they deliberately departed from the traditional assumption that the kind of knowledge Jews needed was to be obtained merely through learning. Learning consists in mastering the texts as they have come down, regardless of the living or historical context in which they arose. Scholarship is the relativity theory applied to ancient sources. It insists that the true meaning of any text cannot be derived from the contemplation of the text itself apart from the social, economic, psychological and intellectual setting to which it belongs. No wonder Neo-Orthodoxy has had its face set against the application of scholarship to Jewish tradition. But since the advent of Schechter, no one in the Seminary has ever questioned the legitimacy of Jewish scholarship. On the contrary, it has become the *sine qua non* of any claim to a true understanding of Judaism.

A second principle is that Judaism must be Hebraic. When Schechter fulminated against what he called a Hebrewless Judaism, pointing to the disappearance of Alexandrian Judaism as a warning of what might happen to American Judaism, he had in mind essentially the use of the Hebrew in the synagogue as a medium of religious service. Since those days, as a result of the Hebraic renaissance in Palestine and of the consensus of the Faculties of the various departments of the Seminary that Palestine must be counted on to become the spiritual center of world Jewry, Hebrew has come to be regarded as indispensable to the achievement of Jewish consciousness. Such a consciousness reaches far more deeply into one's soul than mere ideas or symbols ever can. A Jewish consciousness formed on a knowledge of Hebrew gives depth to the ideational and institutional content of Judaism. With the wide diversity which exists in the acceptance of the content of Judaism, Hebrew has become indispensible to that kinship of soul without which Jewish unity is unthinkable. This consideration has prompted the Teachers Institute and Seminary College of Jewish Studies to make Hebrew the medium of instruction in all their courses.

A third principle is that Jewish life must have plenitude. Before Jews were admitted into the body of the western nations, they had only their own historic civilization to draw upon for everything that gave meaning and direction to their existence. They had no problem of how to prevent Judaism from being crowded out of their lives by the competing claims and interests of a non-Jewish civilization such as they now depend on for their health, security and happiness. Not even in the so-called "Golden era of Medieval Spain" were Jews expected, as they are now by virtue of their civic status, to be mentally and spiritually integrated into the non-Jewish culture of the majority. A Jew nowadays must ration his very time, to say nothing of his energies and capacities, so that he may find it possible to live as a Jew as well as an American, Englishman, or Frenchman. In this matter of rationing, the principle implied in the Seminary pattern has always been: Be a Jew to the maximum degree compatible with the legitimate claims of the non-Jewish national civilization. Being a Jew to the maximum means refraining from the tendency to reduce Judaism to the worship of solemn and sonorous generalities . . . The position taken by the Seminary has always been that Judaism must be lived with all the senses and not only with our common sense. It must be audible and visible and tangible. Hence the maximum ritual of observance is advocated not so much because of authoritative rule as because of the feeling that Jewish life, to have saving quality, must be abundant and not thin and ghostlike.

And finally there is the fourth principle that the American environment must not only be accepted, but accepted graciously, as capable of permanently harboring Judaism. This is addressed to the maximalists among us who contend that civilizations, cultures or religions cannot be rationed. They hold that civilizations or cultures are necessarily exclusive and jealous of one another, and will take nothing less than the whole of one's personality. Accordingly, some of our maximalists conclude that under the most favorable conditions, America can only be a way station for Judaism on its return to its homeland. This philosophy of Jewish life, known as the negation of *Galut,* though seldom aired publicly, exercises a distorting influence on more of Jewish activity than we suspect. In a quiet but effective way, the Seminary has counteracted this negative influence through its affirmative attitude toward American life. . . .

. . . If the Jewish people is to survive its present spiritual crisis it will have to employ consciously and deliberately the means it has hitherto employed intuitively, whenever its existence was challenged. Its principal means has always been the creation of the appropriate educational agencies to transmit its heritage from generation to generation and to foster the needed type of spiritual leadership. The crisis which has been developing in the inner life of our people since the beginning of the emancipation is now coming to a head. The reservoirs of creative Jewish life in the old world have been ruthlessly destroyed. The best of what has been salvaged of that life has found refuge in this country. If American

Jewry is to emerge from the present catastrophe strengthened instead of broken, it must forthwith create the appropriate educational institution for those who are to minister to its needs and to foster its powers of cooperation and creativity. There they will learn to see Judaism integrally and whole, and to communicate to those to whom they minister the necessary zeal and perspective for living a normal Jewish life. In Palestine the Jewish people has already created the Hebrew University as the instrument of higher education for the new life of Israel in its own home. It now devolves upon American Jewry to evolve and foster the University of Judaism which should become the main instrument of higher education for diaspora Jewry. With two such types of university to foster Jewish leadership, the future of Jews and Judaism the world over is assured.

The Torch, Winter, 1956.

Dr. Davis, formerly Provost of the Jewish Theological Seminary of America and Dean of the Seminary's Teachers Institute, has been the dynamic Head of the Institute of Contemporary Jewry at the Hebrew University, Jerusalem, and occupies the chair in American Jewish History and Institutions. He also is Research Professor of American Jewish History at the Seminary's Student Center in Jerusalem and Co-Director of its American Jewish History Center in New York. Dr. Davis was a pioneer in creating "The Eternal Light" TV Program. He is the author of The Emergence of Conservative Judaism, Jewish Religious Life and Traditions in America, *and* Israel, its role is Civilization.

MEETING THE CHALLENGE
TO JEWISH SURVIVAL

ISRAEL J. KAZIS

While the survival of the Jewish people throughout the centuries is indeed a remarkable phenomenon in the history of nations, it is not altogether unique because other peoples have also survived from ancient times. What is unique is the fact that despite the oppression to which they have been subjected, the Jewish people refused to become dehumanized and debased by the brutalities of their persecutors, and instead have emerged from their long encounter with hostility in quiet and dignified possession of a rich, humane tradition. This is an extraordinary spiritual achievement. People who have resided for centuries as outcasts and pariahs in India and elsewhere show the effects of their social condition in terms of their estrangement from the amenities, refinements and sensitivities of civilized living. A degrading environment can debase and desensitize human beings. Remarkably enough, however, the Jews as a group have succeeded in transcending the effects of the conditions which surrounded their existence and have survived as a significant spiritual and cultural force among the peoples of the world.

In his inspiring book, "The Earth Is the Lord's," Dr. Abraham J. Heschel quotes the following from a Christian scholar who recorded his observation of Jewish life in Warsaw during the First World War. "Once I noticed a great many coaches on a parking place but with no drivers in sight. In my own country I would have known where to look for them. A young Jewish boy showed me the way: in a courtyard, on the second floor, was the *shtibl* of the Jewish drivers. It consisted of two rooms: one filled with Talmud-volumes, the other a room for prayer. All the drivers were engaged in fervent study and religious discussion . . . It was then that I found out and became convinced that all professions, the bakers, the butchers, the shoemakers, etc., have their own *shtibl* in the Jewish district; and every free moment which can be taken off from their work is given to the study of the Torah." The pursuit of study among the Jews was not limited to the intellectual class. Jews from all walks of life and in significant numbers felt it their duty either to engage actively in some form of study or to listen to learned discussions presided over by the rabbis and scholars. Adult education thus has a rather long history in the experience of our people. Dr. Heschel relates the very moving fact that among the books saved from Nazi-occupied Europe is one that is now found at the Yiddish Scientific Institute in New York and which bears the following stamp, "The Society of Wood-choppers for the Study of Mishnah in Berditschev." One would be hard put to find in England or in the United States a society of wood-choppers for the study of Shakespeare or Walt Whitman!

The pursuit of study on the part of the Jew resulted not only in familiarizing him with the texts and ideas found in his literary heritage. It also produced a very significant effect upon his personality. Moving in the realm of ideas, the mind of the Jew developed a more subtle perception of the real value of things, his character came to reflect the refining influence issuing from religious and moral teachings, and his spirit grew as it reached out for those dimensions of faith, sturdiness and patience which animated the souls of his spiritual heroes whose way of life he reverently sought to emulate. In possession of this spiritual orientation, the Jew ordered his life in accordance with a discriminating sense of values, strove earnestly to place moral considerations above expediency in the conduct of his affairs, and above all approached life with its exigencies and contingencies in a spirit of affirmation and optimism.

Fortified with this philosophy of life, the Jews were enabled to face the challenge to their survival with conviction that Judaism as a noble way of life was eminently worthwhile preserving, with the courage to suffer in order to assure its preservation, and with the faith that in God's good time the challenge which confronted them would be met successfully. In our rabbinic literature we find an illuminating passage which seeks to capture the struggle which went on in the souls of men who lived under the yoke of oppression, the alternation of mood as faith and despair, courage and capitulation strove for mastery of their spirit. It is told that when Pharaoh decreed that every son born to a Jew was to be cast into the river, Amram, the father of Moses, said: "We take wives unto ourselves and beget children, and the Egyptians drown them in the Nile. Why should we toil in vain?" Thereupon Amram sent his wife away and others did likewise. Amram, a leader in his generation, and his fellow Jews were overwhelmed by a sense of futility. It remained for the women to revive the discouraged spirits of their husbands in their darkest hour: "The Egyptians will not keep us in bondage forever. The Holy One, blessed be He, will in the end redeem us." The men regained their composure and came to realize that faith meant not only the maintenance of a hopeful attitude toward the future. It required, in addition, the assumption of the responsibility, in the midst of sordid and oppressive conditions, of preserving and practising the basic human decencies, of keeping the religious and moral legacy of past generations alive and vital. Accordingly, rabbinic tradition relates that "the Jews in Egypt banded together and made a compact among themselves that they would be true to the covenant of Abraham, Isaac and Jacob and that they would perform deeds of loving-kindness." Living as slaves in a society which was tyrannized by its rulers, the children of Israel put up defenses about their spiritual inheritance, cherished and nurtured it, incorporated it in their way of life, and thus saved themselves from the debasing influence of their environment. Indeed the biblical words describing the plague of darkness, when interpreted allegorically, reveal a deeper significance regarding the spiritual condition of man in Egypt: "And there was a thick darkness in all the land of Egypt . . . but all the children of Israel had light in their dwellings." The darkness that settled on the land of Egypt was not the darkness which descends on earth in its appointed time in the rhythmic course of nature. It was the darkness of benighted souls and insensitive spirits, and under the cover of this darkness man's inhumanity to man had ample room for unrestrained expression and wanton play. In the midst of this black and interminable night, the children of Israel had light in their dwellings. Their lives were illumined by the spiritual light of their faith and of the basic human virtues which they sought to keep alive. They committed themselves to the preservation of their faith and to the practice of these virtues and, in so doing, lent quiet dignity to their being and secured the humane tradition for succeeding generations.

It was no easy matter for our ancestors to keep the light burning when all about them the lights had gone out. To keep one's faith when moral values are pulverized and to persist in one's humanity when men become beasts requires a stout heart, unshakeable convictions and a profound concern for the future of the human race. It is perhaps this kind of vision, courage and dedication which Lewis Mumford had in mind when he wrote of the supreme need "to prepare for the renewal of life" in the very midst of the crisis and the perils which prevailed during the insecure and turbulent periods in mankind's history. The affirmation of life and the determination to enhance it spiritually and culturally despite the grave pressure of discouraging and disillusioning conditions in the social situation have contributed above all other factors to the creative survival of man's humane and civilized tradition. In this respect the history of the spiritual and cultural creativity of the Jewish people represents a striking dramatization of the human capacity and will to perpetuate and to advance its noblest aspirations and achievements in sublime defiance of forces conspiring to overwhelm the spirit of man, if not to destroy it.

It was this kind of unyielding dedication which animated the being of Jochanan ben Zakkai 2000 years ago as he stood before Vespasian, the Roman leader, at a time of profound tragedy for his people, when the Temple lay in ruins and multitudes of his fellow Jews were slain or taken captive. His spirit shaken but not defeated, Jochanan asked that Jabneh and its scholars be spared. His request was granted, and as a result he and his colleagues secured the preservation of the humane tradition for the future. It was a similar commitment that possessed the creative spirits among all peoples who have contributed to the cultural advance of mankind. In the midst of the hostilities and anguish of a civil war, Milton added the fruits of his genius to the treasury of English poetry, and Keats at a later date did likewise when England and France were engaged in a devastating war. Goethe and Beethoven wrote and composed for the ages while the continent of Europe was held subject in the powerful grip of Napoleon.

The history of civilization thus presents us with a remarkable paradox. While powerful forces were engaged in destruction and death, other forces representing dedicated individuals or groups were engaged in the vital task of creating and building. In the early history of our country when the settlers were exposed constantly to attack and death at the hands of Indian raiders, Jonathan Edwards urged them, despite the threat to their security, to continue to plant their corn because he said "in the very planting thereof there is health." As we study the contemporary condition of mankind, we see the same paradox in operation. On the one hand, wars are being fought and the best scientific brains in the world are feverishly at work in the production of atomic weapons, and yet, on the other hand, we are building more schools to prepare our young men and women for the pursuit of the peaceful arts and professions and are intensifying our research in the social sciences in order to improve human and international relations.

How do we explain the operation of the positive element in this paradox? Some may say that the explanation is to be sought in the instinct of self-preservation, in the natural will to live. While this may serve to explain man's physical survival, it does not account for the preservation and enhancement of his culture. To find the answer to this question, one must turn to the souls of sensitive men and women in every generation, whose appreciation of the truth, beauty and worth of man's spiritual and cultural achievements was so profound that they were impelled by the highest sense of responsibility to keep the humane tradition alive, to add to it and to hand it on as a cherished and inviolate legacy to those who came after them. It was this kind of appreciation, conviction and loyalty which energized the souls of our ancestors, endowed their spirits in the face of suffering with such marked resilience, and secured the survival of the Jewish heritage. David's contest with Goliath was neither more remarkable nor more difficult than the perennial encounter of the Jews with the enormous forces mobilized against them in their valiant struggle to keep their spiritual inheritance alive. Throughout the ages dedicated Jews stood their ground bravely and said in effect: "We have studied the teachings and values of our faith and culture. We find them to be inspiring, beautiful and true. We lead purposeful

lives under their influence, and we mean to communicate this
elevating experience to our posterity for their ennoblement."

The challenge to the survival of Judaism in our country today
is different from that which confronted our people in former days
and in other lands. In the past and as recently as the Hitler period, the crucial question was: Will Judaism survive in the face of
persecution? In the United States where Jews live as free and
equal citizens in an open society, the question, paradoxically
enough is: Will Judaism successfully meet the challenge of freedom? Will the social and cultural forces making for assimilation
lead to such an alienation of Jews from Judaism and to such an
attenuation of the inherited system of Jewish values that Jewish
religion and culture will in time become museum objects with
very little if any influence or meaning in the lives of its adherents? If we are to address ourselves seriously to this great challenge to Judaism in our country, we must strive to produce, as
did our ancestors, dedicated custodians of our heritage who will
with equal conviction and devotion cherish it, enhance it and
transmit it with love and loyalty to their children and children's
children. The development of such devoted Jews requires above
all an intensive pursuit of Jewish learning for only in the rich soil
of knowledge can the seeds of appreciation and love of our heritage flourish. Now more than ever must we reassert and re-establish the primacy of study and learning in the life of our people. The
dictum *Talmud Torah K'neged Kulam,* the study of Torah takes
precedence over all other precepts, must guide and inform the
philosophy and policy of Jewish community life in America as it
did wherever our ancestors settled and lived in the past. Only
knowledgeable Jews are in a position to develop the intellectual
appreciations and spiritual affinities which are prerequisites for
the cultivation of an authentic and meaningful Judaism. Great
and important as our achievements in the field of philanthropy
and social work may be, the lasting significance and ultimate value
of the organized American Jewish community will be measured in
terms of the positive and creative Jewish life of its members. To
achieve this end there must be a reorientation in the thinking of
many of our community leaders as a result of which they will
come to see that priority must be given to our Jewish system of

education from the elementary religious schools to the higher institutions of Jewish learning. In a community as resourceful as ours, it is a mark of immaturity on our part to tolerate a situation in which the handful of higher institutions of Jewish learning in our country, which embody the hope and the promise of our future, are hard put because of inadequate financial support to discharge their time-honored responsibility of providing for the full flowering of the Jewish creative spirit. To economize in the spiritual and cultural economy of our people is to court disaster for the future. It is obvious that without the enriching and sustaining power of the creative impulse of Judaism, Jewish life in America would come to represent a sad and pale reflection of its inspired and vigorous prototypes in other lands in past generations. To prevent this from happening, it becomes a sacred responsibility to foster and strengthen that climate of opinion throughout the land which will engender a discriminating sense of values under whose influence Jewish education and learning will occupy their rightfull position of pre-eminence in the life of the community. Given the ample resources at the command of the Jewish people in the United States, we have it within our power, through proper orientation and with sufficient dedication, to develop and to maintain a center of creative Jewish living in our country which will enhance our lives as Jews and Americans, will result in a significant contribution to the long history of Jewish cultural productivity, and will qualify the American Jewish community to achieve a deserved place alongside the great centers of creative Jewish living of the past.

The Torch, Summer, 1957.

Dr. Kazis, eloquent preacher and exponent of Conservative Judaism, has served as Rabbi of Congregation Mishkan Tefila of Newton, Mass. for over twenty years. His articles have appeared in Conservative Judaism, The Reconstructionist, *and* Jewish Social Studies. *He is a member of the American Academy of Religion and Mental Health.*

THE RESPONSIBILITIES OF
THE JEWISH LAITY

SIMON H. RIFKIND

The words "Jewish Laity" are in a sense self-contradictory. Jewish tradition knows no such classification as that of clergy and laity. As far as I have been able to discover the Jews never had a word for it.

One would suppose that a civilization as old as the Jew's would have a well defined, generally recognized line of demarcation setting off the province of the rabbinate from that of the rest of the community. After all, the rabbinate is a hoary institution in Jewish life. Surely we would imagine that in the course of the millennia of our history the boundary between professional rabbi and lay public has been staked out. We know, of course, that much younger institutions show a sharp line of cleavage between their professional and lay participants. In our courts of law the separation between the professional judge and the lay jury is sharply defined. In the Catholic church there is an acknowledged and unbridgeable chasm between clergy and laity. Indeed, I think that it is from our Christian neighbors that we have borrowed the phrase.

It is a useful and convenient phrase, a handy tool for distinguishing between the professional and the non-professional participant in every important calling. Why then has not Jewish tradition made the distinction? I venture to suggest that the omission is not the product of accident. Scripture, we know, emphasizes the very contrary, the absence of such a distinction. The Jews were a "Kingdom of priests and a holy people." Ideally, all the Jews were conceived of as professionals. For a long time that ideal was substantially realized in practice. When the active priesthood vanished and religious life took on its modern appearance, Judaism in the Diaspora became a learned pursuit to which a multitude of followers gave lifelong and supreme devotion. That, by modern definition, is what we mean by a profession. In Jewish communities throughout the ages we had a vast number of learned men who pursued and lived Judaism with the single-minded devotion and zeal of the professional although they derived no livelihood therefrom. The rabbi was one scholar among scholars; one learned man among his peers. No wonder the Jews never invented a word for laity; but they did invent and used a host of words for a classification which interested them and which they regarded as important. They differentiated sharply and vividly between the learned and the ignorant.

The consequences of this circumstance upon Jewish life, until relatively very modern times, were of tremendous significance. It meant that the rabbis, unlike the functionaries of other religious organizations all about them, did not have a monopoly upon religious truth. They had power derived from knowledge which, of necessity, they shared with the learned laymen who were their neighbors. They labored before an audience competent to judge them, differ with them and collaborate with them. They were like poets reciting their lines to an audience of poets. Because of that fact the synagogue never became a hierarchical church. Because of it the Jewish community never became a theocracy. It was the wide distribution of learning and knowledge which sustained democracy in Jewish communal life. Out of that equal and respected association of rabbis, scholars, and learned men of affairs Jewish life evolved coherently, made its successful adjustments to the environment and insured the survival of Jews and Judaism.

One problem runs like a continuous thread throughout our history of the past 2,000 years: how to preserve Judaism in a non-Jewish environment. Because the environment interpenetrates the Jewish community more thoroughly and pervasively than it did before the Emancipation, the problem has become more difficult—but still not insoluble.

Surely we ought to master the art of living in a non-hostile, in a neutral, if not cordial, environment.

The route our fathers followed was the democratization of learning.

I believe it is needless for me to prove the obvious, that Jewish life in America has veered away from that route. Of the forms of democracy in the synagogue we see much more than our medieval ancestors ever dreamt about. Every proposition, whether momentous or trivial, is put to the vote of the congregation. But what of the essence of democracy, what of the knowing participation in the practical and spiritual life of the community? That seems to have escaped us. It has escaped us because in the average Jewish community the rabbi is, to all intents and purposes, the sole repository of Jewish tradition, learning and law. There are few in his congregation prepared to contest his view if they are in disagreement, few equipped to collaborate with him when they are in agreement. When the rabbi speaks to such an audience he necessarily speaks like an oracle because the audience is incapable of passing professional judgment. By default of the lay community, the rabbi is acquiring a monopoly upon religious knowledge. Such monopoly invariably leads to unchecked power. Unchecked power derived from the private possession of special knowledge is as unwholesome and dangerous as absolute power derived from any source. The Englishmen who fought for Magna Charta were right when they exacted from their King a promise to apply the law of the land which tradition had made their common possession. And Moses spoke with divine concern for the freedom of future generations when he formulated as one of his prime commandments that we shall diligently teach the Torah to our children so that it may be the common possession of all the people.

To me it seems inevitable that should the synagogue long continue as an institution in which a learned rabbi ministers to an uninstructed laity, it will cease to be a synagogue and become a church. When that happens, Judaism will not wear the face it has worn these thousands of years.

It is not my purpose to recite a Jeremiad. My object is to call attention to the danger of the present trend, to awaken our lay leaders to their responsibility and thus to help restore Judaism to its historic road. That it can be done I have no doubt. History is replete with examples of such recurrent revivals in Jewish life.

The indispensable prerequisite is that the lay leadership shall come to recognize its responsibility. That responsibility extends in several directions. First, lay leadership must undertake to see to it that the laity generally is better informed, that the laity develops habits of learning. That, I believe, is the central tenet of

Jewish life. I do not mean that such learning need be circumscribed by the boundaries of the sacred literature in which 17th Century Jewry was engrossed. If I grasp the significance of Judaism clearly it is not the knowledge of truth but the quest and search for truth which is the abiding principle of the Jewish way of life.

Second, Jewish lay leaders should in their own personal lives strive to exemplify standards of conduct which we can proudly call Jewish. I am not now referring to matters of ritual although they, too, play a role in the beauty, dignity and spirituality of Jewish life. I mean specifically that they ought to exert themselves so to order their ordinary affairs as to make evident that they regard the enoblement of the human personality as their principal aim, that they differentiate good from evil and have the character to prefer the good, that they exhibit courage in adversity, steadfastness in danger, humility when in power, manliness under oppression, magnanimity to friend and enemy, and integrity at all times; in summary, that they pursue their ideals not because they are profitable, not when they are profitable, but pursue them relentlessly even when they involve pain and travail.

In other words, I regard it as one of the obligations of lay leadership that they constitute themselves visible exemplars of how estimable life can be when enhanced and exalted by the application of Jewish traditional values. Manifestly, that is a task which the rabbi cannot perform for us. The rabbi's superior scholarship and more prolonged application may help us re-interpret Jewish tradition in modern terms, but the day to day task of living in the pattern of the high ideals of that tradition cannot be delegated, cannot be performed for us by proxy.

The direct consequence of the discharge of this responsibility would, of course, be felt in each of our own lives. The indirect consequences would also be enormous, for the unwarranted increase in our own self-esteem would inevitably bring an increase in the esteem in which we are held by others. Membership in the Jewish community would become a badge of honor. To be known as a Jew would amount to recognition as the holder of a patent of nobility. I can think of no more precious heritage to leave to our children.

Sometimes, in an idle moment, I reflect on the time, talent, money and effort which now go into activities for the defense of Jews against defamation. I wonder whether more would not be accomplished if a substantial proportion of this activity were directed toward the affirmation of Jewish life and values, toward the improvement of our common American life by the catalytic effect of Jewish ideas, by the enrichment and uplifting of Jewish idealism so that the Jewish community might indeed be a blessing to the American people. I think the answer is yes. I know that Judaism bids us wager our salvation on the assumption that the answer is yes. And I am sure that the execution of such an enterprise is not a rabbinical task but an undertaking for laymen.

The third step in the discharge of the responsibility of the Jewish laity is for it to resume the initiative. Are we not expecting too much of our rabbis when we look to them for deep scholarship and reflection and at the same time expect them to be dynamos of civic action, energizing and activiating the community? Generally speaking, we rarely find the two capacities united in a single individual. I am convinced that in the field of action the laymen ought to assume the initiative and develop the necessary staying power. The laymen must create and sustain those Institutions without which nothing of what I have spoken can materialize. Putting first things first, I say that the primary task calling for attention is the expansion and perfection of our educational institutions. In Jewish life they command top priority. They represent the indispensable condition to all other improvements in our communal life.

We need a tenfold increase in the number of our rabbis, a hundredfold increase in the number of our teachers. We ought to mobilize the hundreds and thousands of brilliant young women in our colleges and universities for careers in Jewish teaching and incidentally in Jewish homemaking. We have hardly begun to scratch the surface in providing continuous life-long education for our adults. Without it Judaism may become an empty ritual. No community of Jews, no matter how small or big, ought to be without its adult classroom, without some assembly devoted to the contemplation of the things that really matter. In the Jewish Theological Seminary we have the nucleus for the generation of such an expansion. The scholars there have pursued a noble work. Theirs is the task of continuing the manufacture of the uninterrupted fabric of our tradition. Nowhere else on the face of the earth is there collected in any one place so superb a body of Jewish scholars as in the Jewish Theological Seminary. It is the function of us laymen to carry their learning to the four corners of this continent. It is our assignment to provide the means, to create the channels, by which the learning which is here found in such abundance can flow out and irrigate the most distant of the Jewish communities.

Momentous events are taking place in Israel. Such is our faith in the fecundity of Judaism that all of us expect to see a great flowering of the human spirit in that benign climate of freedom.

I see many good reasons why the fruitful development in Israel should simultaneously be accompanied by a parallel development in the United States. The American Jewish community is still very young. Its history is not behind it but in its future. It poseses great talent. If Jewish laymen would only visualize the potentalities and possibilities of this, the greatest Jewish community in the world today, if they were willing to invest in this great reservoir of top-flight ability, there is good reason to expect that this continent would witness another golden age in the history of the Diaspora, an age that would rival Babylonia and Spain.

I, for one, choose not to forget that neither the Talmud Bavli, nor the Guide to the Perplexed, nor the Shulchan Aruch was a product of Eretz Israel. All, however, were products of the genius of Judaism which has flourished so richly in adversity and which I believe can grow even more luxuriantly in freedom.

If we persist in such endeavors we may yet recreate a society in which Torah is not the private possession of the selected few but the democratic resource of the whole House of Israel from which generation after generation of mankind, of all creeds and colors, will draw everlasting strength and happiness.

The Torch, January, 1950.

Judge Rifkind, Chairman of the Board of Directors of the Jewish Theological Seminary of America, has rendered dis-

tinguished service to his country in many capacities at home and abroad. Since 1954 he has been a member of the Board of Higher Education in New York City. He is a leading figure in the American Bar Association and is the outstanding lay spokesman of the Jewish Theological Seminary of America's role in American Jewish life.

A POSITIVE RELIGIOUS PHILOSOPHY

ABRAHAM S. HALKIN

In the last several decades, leaders of the Conservative Movement, rabbis and laymen, have given much thought to the platform of the movement. Much which is worth reading has appeared in periodicals and in separate tracts. Obviously the feeling is strong among the leaders that a well-defined position on the issues is highly desirable.

There is certainly no want of issues. American Jewish life is full of light and shade, of challenges and obstacles. Like Jewish communities in Western Europe, American Jews have reacted very favorably to the opportunities offered them by the American environment. They have immersed themselves wholeheartedly not only in the economic life of the country, but also in its education, and its culture, its outlook and its pursuit of destiny. They have become fully acculturated, so much so that there is no longer any self-consciousness about their Jewishness. I see a good many boys on the college campuses, evidently Orthodox, who practice their religion unhesitatingly in public and in private. It certainly convinces the interested onlooker to see them wearing their Yarmulkes in subway and on street, and it is demonstrative proof of the security they enjoy. They feel themselves entirely American, Jewish American.

But for the vast number of American Jews, the adjustment and transition proceeded without stopping to wonder what was happening to their Jewishness: their Jewish home, their Jewish education, their identification with Jewish causes. The lure of what they were achieving here was clearly too strong to allow for questions in their mind as to the relative values of the exchange they were making, the evaluation of the gains versus the losses.

Judaism, and, for that matter, religion in general, has also become a complex of many doubts and issues under the stress and strain of modern society. Apart from the practical religious obligations which have come upon bad times in present-day life, some of the fundamentals of the religious system have been endangered, if not shaken. They have been challenged by the overwhelming confidence man has won, in his ability to predict, to venture, and to achieve. The dependence on a superior power, with its demands and teachings, its promises and its rewards,—which satisfied the personal needs of many in times gone by, has had to yield to an indomitable self-reliance, an unlimited aggressiveness, and an enviable record of progress. Far from being the sheltering mother, religion must now discover persuasive arguments in order to attract followers.

At the same time, it is not difficult to discern a new ferment within the American Jewish intellectual group. The steady, phenomenal progress in science and technology, in communication and automation has not proved adequate to satisfy their moral and spiritual needs. They are sensitive to the negative by-products of the great material gains, of the remarkable strides in man's development of his talents. They are restless as a result of the anxiety which has been engendered, the fear of war and calamity which has been generated, the delinquency and the licentiousness which are on the increase.

These responses have created a climate for what is called religion. To be honest, it is not quite justifiable to equate these cravings with what have been taken to be the basic requirements of the religious attitude. Perhaps under intelligent guidance, their quest may be channeled to the domain of religion. But of one conclusion we need entertain no doubts. Except for the isolated few who represent special situations, these intellectuals are not ready to turn, or return, to fundamentalism, even if they adopt orthodox practice. They have learned too much, they have had too much contact with the various branches of culture, to find it possible to adjust to the strictly defined, and decidedly circumscribed world of Orthodoxy.

This is what has made the Conservative Movement timely. This is why it is experiencing an unprecedented growth. People are no longer conservative by defection, because they left the ranks of the Orthodox. They are conservative by choice, because they find it better suited to their convictions and their attitudes.

It will not, I hope, be superfluous to enumerate some of the features of the Conservative Movement which make it attractive, to a contemporary, seeking generation.

It is cognizant, and takes note, of the conflict between a number of accepted religious dogmas, and the position based on present-day science and thought. It chooses to be intellectually honest. It does not shirk the, to it, inescapable task of examining the religious dogmas, in the light of what intelligent people can now accept. Respectfully and thoughtfully it strives to find new meaning, where the old can no longer be maintained, to reinterpret the beliefs, so that the spirit remains, even if the body must change.

The Conservative Movement does not entertain the least desire to break with traditional practice and behavior for the sake of breaking. Those of our critics who chide our Rabbis for making an occasional adjustment in a law, or a practice, do not choose to understand that they do so, only out of necessity, because of their expectation that the change will result in some greater, and more desirable benefit. As a general rule, the Conservative Movement recognizes fully, and emphasizes the importance of loyalty to tradition. No matter what the view may be, of the theological rationale of tradition, we appreciate its value as a source of edifying content in our life, as a manifestation of the link between us and all the generations that came before us, between us and the Jewish people all over the world. Included in their loyalty, we have a sound recognition of the importance of Hebrew in our religious culture as well as in our life as a scattered, yet united people.

The Conservative Movement makes a serious effort to treat the practice of the moral precepts with the same earnestness with which it approaches any other precept in our religious tradition. We have learned well how easy it is to identify religious behavior with ritual practice; we know how much self-discipline is required to perform the right act of justice or of decency. But we have taken on this difficult task as a "must", and we want to lead a life which gains the approval of men and the reward from God.

Since the Conservative Movement realizes the function of religion as a vital force in human life, it teaches that religion must participate in contemporary events. As Americans and as Jews the Conservative Movement wishes to be an active participant in all causes which will improve the situation of people, whether it be labor or civil right, aid to our brethren abroad or the interests of the people in the State of Israel.

This is our program. I for one do not agree, with those who complain, that the Conservative Movement has no program. These criticisms are based on differences among its leaders, regarding certain practices, or other details of religious belief. But it is in fact quite unanimous in its agreement on the general principles.

However, I do not think we are quite ready to pat ourselves on the back. We seek, and it is not difficult to point to what we seek. It is—implementation. I cannot say that we have done all that can or should be done to realize the obligations connected with life as Conservative Jews.

We should strive to have our personal lives, and our family life governed by a calendar. I do not mean knowing the date. I mean the distinction between the six days of the week and the seventh. It extends even to the difference between Sunday of our free weekend and Saturday. Saturday should be Shabbat, a day on which the place of work is taken by prayer and relaxation, the place of activity, which makes us lose sight of ourselves, by reflection, reading and communion with God. It is a calendar which notes the holidays. They mark events in Jewish history which should be important to us as reminders of the past, and as symbolic of values and experiences which are significant to us. Even psychologically, let alone religiously, the alternation of days is a need. It adds color, it provides something to look forward to, it relieves the monotony of no change.

We should be consciously and intelligently active in behalf of our brethren in the rest of the world. The Conservative Movement has been quite emphatic in its claim that it attaches great importance to the unity of Israel and insists that the ties which bind us are stronger than personal prejudices, or preferences, which can represent a divisive force. Dr. Solomon Schechter's concept of "Catholic Israel" is an oft-repeated *desideratum* in our midst. We have been taught, both as Americans and as Conservative Jews—the many virtues of tolerance. Let us apply these doctrines in our daily life. We must seek and find means of doing, and of joining others in doing, all we can for Jews in Russia, in

South America and all other places where our help is needed and can reach.

We should be keenly aware of the great importance which living religion has always attached to the moral code, to the practice of the virtues, of *consideratenen,* concern, justice and mercy in our dealings with our fellow-men. All too frequently this fundamental contribution of religion is shunted to the background if not altogether disregarded. Religious literature, notably ours, contains a tremendous volume of writing in which authors complain of the neglect of these duties and the great harm which results to society and to our appreciation of religion by this neglect. We must live knowingly, remembering at all times to do and to behave in a way which will help, will reconcile, will afford aid, and comfort, and good-will.

We must learn to look upon the State of Israel and its welfare as an integral part of our Jewishness. There is great danger—many have called attention to it—of a growing difference between our community and the people of Israel. Our general ignorance of the language they speak, our failure to read their literature, our own steady development under conditions which must be different from the conditions under which they develop,—all these facts contribute to a growing separation, a fragmentation of the Jewish people. The natural trend is in this direction. To counteract it requires effort and determination. We must, all of us, seek ways to forestall this development. Visits to Israel, contact with its people, gathering information in other ways about cultural, religious, and economic life there, joining groups and efforts which others make towards this end—these are some of the means which we must adopt in order to give body to our contention that the interest in the State of Israel is a cardinal plank in our program.

There are undoubtedly other goals which may be included, other efforts which we must make. The purpose I have in mind is to remind ourselves that the very commendable atttendance at conventions, the praiseworthy resolutions and the speeches are only one-time occurrences, single occasions. Buildings, societies, are necessary instruments. But the task is to lead a Jewish life 365 days a year. The call is for all of us, individually and collectively, to take upon ourselves the assignments dictated to us by our Jewishness, by our Jewish conscience, by our membership in the brotherhood known as the Community of Israel.

If we can resolutely determine that we shall live as Jews with a religious commitment every day of the year, our lives will be richer, we shall introduce a healthier climate into the community, and we shall make the word Jew more meaningful and more respectable to ourselves and to our fellow-Americans. Let us live in such manner that we shall be able to say with Isaiah "God is with us."

The Torch, Winter, 1964–65.

Dr. Halkin, scholar and Hebraist, is Associate Professor of Jewish Literature and Institutions at the Jewish Theological Seminary of America. He has served as Vice President of the American Academy for Jewish Research, Director of Keren Hatarbut and editor of its publications, and a member of the Board of Directors, World Union of Jewish Scholars, Jerusalem. He is author of Muslim Sects and Schisms, Zion in Jewish Literature *and* Maimonides' Epistle to Yemen.

Part Three

JEWISH EDUCATION

"Without the beneficent influence of religious knowledge, the ignorant person remains color-blind to the finer implications of the spiritual life. In Judaism, ignorance is not the mother of devotion, only too often it is the mother of desertion."

—Joseph H. Hertz

INTRODUCTION

When Dr. Schechter came to America in 1902 to head the Jewish Theological Seminary he recognized the sad plight of Jewish education here. There were no qualified teachers and no adequate textbooks. Schools were usually held on a one session a week basis in Conservative congregations. Results were meager. There was no incentive to attract young people to prepare for teaching and no institution equipped to offer instruction. Subscribing to the principle, *Talmud Torah K'neged Kulam* (the study of Torah transcends all other precepts), Dr. Schechter took immediate steps to make the Seminary the center of Jewish educational activities, bringing to it Dr. Louis Ginzberg as the living example of modern creative Jewish scholarship, and Dr. Alexander Marx, the greatest Jewish bibliographer of his time, to teach history and create a library adequate for Jew and Gentile, for foreign and domestic scholars and students. In 1907 he picked a young graduate of the Seminary, alive to modern thinking in philosophy and education, Mordecai M. Kaplan, to head a new Teachers Institute. New York City at the time had organized a Kehillah under Dr. Judah L. Magnes, with Dr. Samson Benderly as director of its Bureau of Education. Along with Dr. Israel Friedlander of the Seminary faculty, these leaders jointly stimulated a band of devoted disciples headed by Alexander Dushkin.

But the way was not easy. Jewry throughout the country was not stirred. Vested interests were affected. Conflicting points of view emerged. Teachers Institute, however, received support from men like Israel Unterberg, Felix Warburg and Sol M. Stroock, as well as Jacob Schiff and Louis Marshall. The Seminary library flourished under the original impetus of the acquisition of the Judge Mayer Sulzberger Collection and that of Professor Moritz Steinschneider of Berlin.

Along with the Library and Teachers Institute (now including the Seminary College of Jewish Studies) came the establishment of the Rabbinical Assembly and the United Synagogue of America, organized to spread traditional Judaism throughout the country by means of educated lay as well as rabbinical leadership. In turn came the Women's League, the Federation of Jewish Men's Clubs and the United Synagogue Youth.

In more recent years the educational vision of the Seminary brought about the formation of:

1) The Institute for Religious and Social Studies
2) The University of Judaism in California
3) The Schocken Institute for Jewish Research in Jerusalem
4) The Seminary School of Jewish Studies and the Women's Institute
5) The Melton Research Center
6) The American Jewish Student Center in Jerusalem
7) The Cantor's Institute and Seminary College for Jewish Music
8) The Ramah Commission with seven Hebrew speaking summer camps throughout the United States and Canada
9) The Herbert H. Lehman Institute of Talmudic Ethics
10) "The Eternal Light" programs on radio and television in cooperation with the National Broadcasting Company
11) The World Council of Synagogues
12) The Jewish Museum
13) The American Jewish History Center

This formidable contribution to Jewish education is backed up by publications of each of the constituent agencies. The Commission on Jewish Education in which the Teachers Institute, the United Synagogue and the Rabbinical Assembly are partners, is producing textbooks and other valuable educational materials. The activities in the field of adult education will be referred to in Part IV. The formation of an Educators Assembly and the National Council of Synagogue Administrators was a logical result of the general educational program.

Educational services offered by the several organizations include:

1) Organization of local and regional Boards of Jewish Education composed of schools of congregations of the United Synagogue
2) Teachers registry and placement—including principals and educational directors
3) Curricula for congregational schools
4) A series of textbooks on different levels in the various subjects commonly taught
5) A traveling exhibit of articles in the Seminary Museum
6) A book and supply purchasing service
7) Solomon Schechter Day Schools
8) Summer Hebrew-speaking camps throughout the country
9) Local and regional educational conferences
10) Educational Travel experience for youth in Israel
11) Summer sessions to improve teaching skills
12) Information and organized social action on current issues

Encouraging developments in Secondary Education are the recent organized regional Hebrew High Schools supported jointly by congregations and community agencies.

A great deal of thought, effort and expenditure of funds has been involved. The effort has spread throughout the country and has involved a great many people in programming and fund raising. The Seminary also cooperates with other organizations, such as providing Chaplains for the Armed Forces, promoting the Associated Conference on Science, Philosophy and Religion, the Seminary—Israel Institute, the American Jewish History Center, and the Universal Brotherhood Program.

It is too soon to evaluate the effectiveness of this phenomenal and far-reaching effort. It is without parallel in our history. Other groups have contributed similarly on a smaller scale. It indicates the vitality and the optimistic approach of the movement to contemporary problems and needs. The congregational religious schools now include 80% of the children receiving weekday instruction, and have therefore a large measure of communal responsibility and are beginning to receive some aid from Jewish communal funds. The Jewish Day Schools are largely supported by the Conservative Movement. However, the increasing numbers of children and beautiful new school buildings may be deceptive. It remains to be seen whether there will be adequate financial support, adequate supply of teachers, and a holding power to give Jewish education in America the opportunity to create a pattern of living for succeeding generations in keeping with our great tradition.

The articles that follow are self-explanatory and illustrate the extent of the overall program for Jewish education in the Conservative Movement. Dr. Dushkin and Dr. Millgram have been outstanding leaders in the field in America and Israel. Dr. Mortimer Cohen's school has engaged in a forward looking experimentation. Dr. Potok writes authoritatively on the Leaders Training Fellowship as does M. Bernard Resnikoff who is Executive Director of the National Ramah Commission.

M. D. H.

EDUCATION FOR JEWISH LIVING

ALEXANDER M. DUSHKIN

In times of crises our purposes become clearer, our spiritual vision sharpened. Whatever other reasons the Jewish people have for continuing to survive, Hitler and his ilk have made one fundamental reason crystal clear: we must continue to live because evil men do not wish us to live, because the evil forces in the world recognize in the Jewish people their first and most persistent enemy. This is as it should be; as we should wish it to be. Likewise in education our aims have become clearer by contrast. Nazi education is described as "education for death," as preparation for "the day." Jewish education, like the democratic educations of our day, has always been education for life. Our Torah is the Tree of Life. Even death is conceived in Judaism, as in all religions stemming from it, as "life beyond;" so that even education for *Olam Haba* is education for "life." It is this life motive that is the leit-motif in Jewish education.

However, in American Jewish education we do not always put sufficient stress on this positive life motive, preparation for Jewish living. Too much is Jewish instruction motivated by negative motives—the "Kaddish" motive; "pleasing grandmother"; fear of anti-Semitism. What we must emphasize instead are the positive values to be derived; not only the social value of survival for the group, but even more so the personal values for the individual —the enrichment of personality, the expansion of interests and loyalties, the deepening of emotions, the courage, balance and sanity which the educated Jew can acquire for his personal life through self-identification with the compelling zeal of Prophets, the tender abiding faith of Psalmists, the mellow wisdom of Sages, the purposive suffering of Martyrs.

What is education for Jewish living? One way of answering the question is in terms of general education. All education can be

said to teach four kinds of knowledge: facts, skills, wishes and relationships. In all educational systems, children are taught those
facts of the physical and social environment which they must
know to live intelligently, and those skills which they need for
productive occupation and for their inner leisure life. But facts
and skill can be destructive unless the wish life of children is properly directed. The leaders of Germany, for example, may be able
scientists and accomplished painters and musicians, but their
education is bad when their wishes are directed to selfish over-
lordship through wilful deceit and planned murder. Facts and
skills must be directed and interpreted toward wished-for ideals.
Lastly, all education concerns itself with helping the child to
grow in his human relationships; for the life of the human being
is like the series of concentric circles made by a stone when
dropped into water—as the child grows, he forms ever wider and
wider circles of fellowship, with himself as the center and the
Infinite as the ultimate circumference.

These things Jewish schools also teach, but through Jewish me-
dia of expression. Jewish schools teach their pupils those facts
in their environment which they must know to live intelligently
as Jews; facts of history and background, facts of language (Hebrew), facts of literature, facts regarding customs, rites and prayers,
facts concerning Jewish life in America, Palestine and elsewhere,
facts regarding attitudes of non-Jews both friendly and hostile.
Jewish schools must also teach children the skills needed to participate in the customs of home life, particularly those dealing
with festivals, the Sabbath and vital events, as well as those skills
which are needed to be at ease in the synagogue. Good Jewish
schools recognize that the teaching of these facts and perfor-
mances must be directed into wishes; and Jewish teachers should
deliberately seek to imbue their pupils with those ideals which
stem from the Bible, from rabbinic wisdom, from the historic
struggle of the Jews, and from their present hopes to achieve for
their people a place of well-being and honor among the peoples
of the earth. Likewise, Jewish teachers should cherish in their
pupils their growing selfhood, which is served and enhanced by
having them accept gladly and understandingly their Jewishness
as membership in that widening fellowship which, starting from
Jewish parents and family, extends through congregation to the

local community, on to the Jewish people, and through it to the human brotherhood under God which has been that people's vision, and finally to the ultimate infinity of God.

From modern education we have learned three things regarding methods of educating for living: (a) The best way to prepare for life is by living; (b) The school is only one of the agencies involved in the educational process; (c) Education is a continuous life-long activity, not to be confined to childhood and youth only. These three ideas have influenced Jewish education and should continue to do so in even greater measure. The Jewish child must live happily as a child, and his Jewish relationship must be made significant to him in terms of his child relationships. The Jewish school should continue to emphasize activity, and particularly socialized activities such as junior congregations, dramatization of festivals, Keren Ami. In our curriculum-making and in writing our text-books, increasing attention should be given to the use of larger "units" of study rather than to fragmentized teaching of facts. The school should be conceived as a "school-community" and pupils should be trained to think and act in terms of their community. Parents must realize that the Jewish school is but one agency in the educational process, and that without the help of the home and the other influences in the life of the child, the school alone cannot train for living; it is as if the Jewish school were asked to heat the great out-of-doors.

There is current among us considerable talk of the necessity to increase the time allotted to Jewish education. This increase of time can take various forms. It may be increase in *hours,* as in the case of the Yeshivas and Talmud Torahs; it may be extended over more *months* during the year, as in the use of Jewish summer camps; or it may be extended over more *years,* by commencing Jewish education at the nursery school level and extending it upward through the high school level and through adult life. All of these are important, but the last is probably the most important. Unless Jewish education is continuous, the "years of forgetting" swallow the years of learning, even as the lean cows swallowed the fat cows in Pharaoh's dream.

Possibly the greatest problem confronting us in education for Jewish living is a confusion as to what sort of Jewish life we should prepare our children for. Here we strike a fundamental dilemma: on the one hand we need education for Jewish living, and, on the other, we cannot give Jewish education effectively unless we know for what system of living we should educate. It should be recognized that in the last analysis the "curriculum," which is "what we should teach," cannot be created by teachers. It is created rather by the thought-life of the adult Jewish community; by its thinkers, scholars, artists, literary men, community leaders. The teachers merely organize this "body of desirable knowledge and attitudes" into the specific school curriculum. The Conservative group more clearly than the others is committed both to the continuation of tradition and to the continuous need for change. Probably it is inevitable that there should be confusion in our day, because we are as yet in the early stages of the making of American Judaism—that Judaism of tomorrow which is based on our continuous tradition, but which will nevertheless suit American Jewry as integrally as the various stages in Jewish development suited the needs of Babylonian, Spanish, Polish and German Jewries.

As Conservative Jews we should stress four ideas in the teaching of our children:

First, *Historically*—namely, that Judaism is a developing way of life. Evolution, in its broad outlines as an idea, is something that we did not get from the outside only; it is in the very character of our history. Our children must be "conditioned" from early childhood to the conception of an evolving Judaism.

The second idea is that of *Community*—namely, that differences of Jewish opinion are natural, but that despite these differences there are common basic interests; and the possibility for common effort is not negated by such differences. This is the democratic idea. It, too, comes to us not merely from the outside but also from our own inner development. Our children should be taught the lesson of "unity in diversity" for their living in the Jewish community, and should also be prepared thereby for the greater lesson of relationship to humanity as a whole.

Third, is the idea of *Positiveness*. The joy of Jewish living must be emphasized, despite Jewish suffering and misery. This does not mean that we should take a "Pollyanna" attitude and avoid telling our children the sad truth. It does mean, however, that we must teach them that realistic optimism which is expressed in the classic term *bitachon,* for which a modern prose translation might be "faith in the possibilities of life." Just because reality is sad, we must compensate by stressing the bright aspects of Jewish life. In this endeavor, Palestine has been and will continue to be of immeasurable help by supplying both a positive practical ideal to strive for, as well as positive achievements which lend themselves to positive joyous teaching.

Fourth is the idea of *Partnership.* We must teach our children that a great partnership exists between American Jewry and the *Yishub* in Palestine in creating the new way of Jewish life in our day. In the days ahead the Jewish people is to be more than ever a "Jewish family of nations"; and in this "Jewish family of nations" American Jewry will provide, not a second-class Judaism, but a distinctive new strain. We shall not only take, we shall also give. Our children must therefore be taught that American Jews will and should be creative partners in shaping a better, fuller Jewish life for tomorrow the world over.

The Touch, May, 1945.

Dr. Dushkin, pioneer and leading authority in Jewish Education in the United States and Israel, directed the work of The Jewish Education Committee of New York, headed the Board of Jewish Education in Chicago for twelve years, and was a Professor in the School of Education of the Hebrew University in Jerusalem for fifteen years. He is chairman of the Israeli Government Commission on the Training of Teachers and educational advisor of Hadassah Youth Activities in Israel. He is author of Jewish Education in New York City, Jewish Education in the U.S.A. *(with Engelman) and* Studies in Education *(with Frankenstein). He was founder and editor of* Jewish Education.

A PRACTICAL APPROACH
TO JEWISH EDUCATION

ABRAHAM E. MILLGRAM

When the United Synagogue Commission on Jewish Education, representing the United Synagogue and the Rabbinical Assembly, issued its Statement on "The Objectives and Standards for the Congregational School," many a school board disposed of it with the devastating remark that it was "impractical." The very thought of eliminating the one-day-a-week school and demanding that all children who have reached their eighth birthday be required to attend a minimum of six hours per week was a revolutionary thought and therefore regarded as impossible of achievement.

The word "impractical" has also dealt a death blow to many a proposed Hebrew nursery school and to many an educational program for adolescents. Our experience, however, has established the fact that those congregations that took the Statement seriously and refused to relegate it to the realm of the impractical, succeeded in implementing these standards with relative ease.

The time has therefore come for us to reverse the process, and to point out how impractical and unrealistic many of our school boards are when they allow themselves to be guided by threadbare slogans and outworn shibboleths which mislead them in the formulation of their educational policies. It is a particularly discouraging fact, since these men are usually efficient and wise in their respective business and professional fields. If their practical know-how were transferred to the field of Jewish education, Jewish life in America would surely present a more hopeful prospect for all who are concerned with its future.

INTENSIFYING JEWISH EDUCATION

More than half of our school children start their Jewish education too late, at the advantaged age of 10 or 11. By the time these children register, their most promising and most fruitful years for personality development have passed. Their earliest years, particularly the pre-school years of 3 to 6, when sound foundations are laid for wholesome, integrated Jewish personalities and for an intensive, Hebraic Jewish education are far behind them. By that time Jewish education has missed its greatest opportunity.

But many of our school boards and school administrators have a compelling justification for tolerating the "too little and too late" program. They claim, with seeming logic, that something ought to be done for the masses of Jewish children who do not attend any Jewish school. These children, they say, should be attracted to our schools. The way to do it is to provide them with a course of study that is neither costly to the parents nor burdensome to the children. The one-day-a-week school ideally meets these requirements. The Sunday School is thus justified on the ground that "it is better than nothing." This "better than nothing" fallacy has often been demonstrated to be utterly false despite its seeming logic. It was Dr. Alexander Dushkin of the Jewish Education Committee of New York who properly pointed out that the registration of a school is never increased by lowering standards. The only way to attract children to a school is to engage an outstanding faculty and provide an equally outstanding program of studies. The only definitely proven effect of lowered standards is that of Gresham's law in the field of economics, namely, that bad money chases good money off the market. The establishment of one-day-a-week schools on the theory that they will attract large numbers of children who otherwise would not attend any school at all fails to achieve its avowed purpose. It only competes effectively and successfully with the more intensive Hebrew school.

Our attempt to cater to the children who are not enrolled in our schools fails in its primary objective and only serves to water down the standard of Jewish education in all our schools. In short, the whole process is one that makes our schools educationally less and less profitable and more and more ineffective.

FINANCING JEWISH EDUCATION

Our schools are often equipped with expensive educational materials, such as moving picture machines, costly furniture and ornate decorative effects. But the salaries of our teachers are usually determined by the tuition income. Many a school board is proud of its questionable success in balancing the budget, that is, of deriving the faculty's salaries completely from the tuition income. This policy of skimping on teachers' salaries has had its tragic results, which may well leave a crippling effect on Jewish life in America for generations to come. In this regard, we fare no better and no worse than the general American community which has similarly crippled its public school system, once regarded as the pride of America. About a year ago, Dr. Benjamin Fine, educational editor of the *New York Times,* published a survey on conditions in American education. He quoted some striking figures and pointed to alarmingly low standards in our schools. He showed that Americans spend seven billion dollars a year on liquor and three billion on tobacco, but spend far less than three billion dollars on education. His survey underscored the poor treatment accorded teachers, which has resulted in the loss of the best personnel. What has happened to our public schools has happened with more tragic consequences to the Jewish schools. The decline in the teaching personnel of the Jewish school is threatening the future of the American Jewish communities and is undermining the Jewish child's chance of developing an integrated, wholesome and happy personality.

To remedy this distressing situation we must start with the realization that no school can be better than its teachers, and that education cannot be bought at a bargain counter. Cheap teachers are invariably poor teachers. And poor teachers are not worth even the low salaries they get. Whereas the good teacher may succeed in developing a love for the Jewish school and for Jewish life, the poor teacher usually plants seeds of violent antipathy to and even hatred of everything for which the teacher stands, namely, Jewish life and Jewish learning. As a result of our utterly unrealistic approach to the problem of school finances, we have lost many of our most promising teachers and, what is worse, we have failed to attract promising young men and women to the profession. The prospects for Jewish education are therefore bleak indeed.

There is only one remedy which may avert the catastrophe, and that is the adoption of a new and realistic policy in regard to the financial structure of our schools. Such a policy would make it a routine practice of every congregation to give the school budget priority over every other expenditure, and to treat the Hebrew school teacher as a member of a noble profession, deserving of a respectable livelihood, of a feeling of security, and of a social status worthy of the name of *Talmid Hakham* and of "guardian of the fortress of Judaism."

COMMUNITY RELATIONSHIP

Finally, there is the widely accepted fallacy which is responsible for demoralizing strife and untold waste in the field of Jewish education. It is the "either or" logic which has crept into the reasoning of an ever widening circle of Jews, and has brought with it vehement conflict between people who should be united in the cause of Jewish education. The controversy is between those who insist that the communal school is the only institution that can save American Jewry from further disintegration, and those who insist that only the congregational school has the potentialities of meeting this crucial problem.

This "either or" approach, coupled with partisan heat, has blinded many of our leaders to the actual situation, and has caused them to see evils which do not exist, and to nurture antagonisms which should not exist. Actually, this "either or" approach is as fallacious and illogical in the field of Jewish education as it is in every other field. Our only logical approach is to examine these school systems objectively and impartially, to discover the strengths and weaknesses of each, and to develop a system of Jewish education which will incorporate the advantages and will eliminate the disadvantages of both systems. This logical procedure was adopted by several communities such as New Haven, Connecticut and Omaha, Nebraska. In each of these cities the Jewish community, represented by its Federation, accepted the basic fact that the congregational school is training its pupils not only for congregational membership but also for membership in the Jewish community at large. The loyalties that are fostered among the children also include a sense of responsibility to the local Jewish community, to Eretz Yisrael and to K'lal Yisrael. Hence the congregational school deserves the support of the community. The congregation, on its part, realizes that the community at large has a justifiable interest in the congregational school, since the children, when they grow up, will be members of the Jewish community as well as of the congregation. With this mutual good-will on the part of the congregation and the community, there inevitably developed a simple, logical and fruitful approach. The Federation assumed its share of responsibility for the pupils in the congregational school by subsidizing the congregational school in proportion to the children registered and the hours of attendance. Although the congregation alone decides on the personnel and the curriculum of the school, yet it recognizes the fact that the community at large has the right to determine minimum standards in regard to facilities and the professional training of teachers. This partnership of community and congregation holds out great promise for financial stabilization and the raising of standards in the field of Jewish education.

THE ATTITUDE OF THE UNITED
SYNAGOGUE COMMISSION
ON JEWISH EDUCATION

The United Synagogue Commission on Jewish Education has given these problems serious consideration. The Commission scrutinized the reasons for our failures, analyzed the thinking and reasoning behind our accepted procedures, and with firm resolution stated its position in regard to these challenging problems.
. . .

In the revised edition of the Statement there is a section dealing with the Bet Hayeled (the Foundation School). This section reads in part:

> The pre-school years of 3 to 6 represent an unusual opportunity in the field of Jewish education through the Bet Hayeled program. Modern psychology has recognized the importance of these early years in the molding of the character of the adult. In addi-

tion, Jewish parents readily enroll their children in a nursery school or kindergarten provided the child is safe and happy, and are willing to pay the fees necessary to maintain such schools. Experience has proved that given a well-trained faculty, the Bet Hayeled program offers the child a sound foundation, both in attitudes and knowledge, for happy living as a Jew in America. . . . Every congregation is therefore urged to explore the possibility of establishing a Bet Hayeled either alone or in cooperation with other congregations.

The Commission also delved into the problem of financing our schools. It examined the budgets of successful schools and compared them with the budgets of congregational schools that merely mark time. The Commission was aware of the difficulties involved. Nevertheless, it concluded that the only practical procedure in Jewish education is to shun the policy referred to as "penny wise and pound foolish." Again, I quote a telling paragraph from the Commission's Statement:

No educational program can be adequately financed from tuition fees alone. Experience has shown that the cost of instruction, exclusive of heat, light, secretarial and other overhead expenses, in a weekday school offering six hours instruction per week, and having an enrollment of 150 pupils, is approximately $70 per child per year. The Congregation must therefore provide out of its general funds the substantial sums necessary for creating a sound financial basis for the school. It must further empower the School Board to raise additional funds whenever necessary so that the school budget might be adequate for the proper conduct of the school in accordance with the standards herein set forth.

To solve the pressing problems of Jewish education, we must look for wise and bold leaders who will fulfill the prophetic vision by becoming "Shepherds according to My own heart, shepherds or leaders who will teach knowledge and understanding," רועים כלבי, ורעו אתכם דעה והשכל, knowledge of our pressing problems, and understanding of the ways to solve them.

The Torch, October, 1948.

Dr. Millgram rendered distinguished service to Jewish Education in America as Director, United Synagogue Commission on Jewish Education for sixteen years. He previously served as Rabbi in Philadelphia, Pa. and as Hillel Director at the University of Minnesota. His home is now in Israel, but he has been temporarily engaged in establishing a central agency for Jewish education in Kansas City, Mo. He is the author of Sabbath, The Day of Delight, *an* Anthology of Medieval Hebrew Literature, *and a* Handbook for Congregational School Boards.

ARE WE REACHING THE
SOUL OF THE JEWISH CHILD?

MORTIMER J. COHEN

In "The Objectives and Standards for the Congregational School"
published by the United Synagogue Commission on Jewish Education, the very first goal of an intensive Jewish education is
stated in these words:

> "To develop and enhance the child's spiritual and ethical sensi-
> tivity so that in act and attitude he may be governed by the reli-
> gious, ethical and cultural traditions of Judaism."

By implication, the remaining seven goals that relate to the Hebrew language, Jewish history, literature and culture, the practice
of traditional Jewish observances in the synagogue and the home,
the group activities and observances, the stimulation towards
higher Jewish education, the participation in local, national and
world Jewish affairs, and the harmonization of the ideals and traditions of American democracy and those of Judaism—these goals
are made to appear subsidiary to the very first. And rightly so.

It is a good thing to keep the ultimate goal of Jewish schools of
the United Synagogue always in mind. Unless we hold our goal
high and clear before our eyes, we will not be aware of the place
of all the rest of our schools' activities in the total curriculum. We
will, furthermore, not become aware of the urgent need to set up
standards to measure our progress towards, or our regress from,
the goal we project before us. Indeed, the whole process of evaluation is impossible unless we know the goal at which we are aiming.

In all education, Jewish and general, there are roughly two
points of view that might be called at their extremes: the "Factualists" and the "Attitudinists." The Factualists are people who
put major emphasis on the acquisition of information, whether it

be in the field of history, literature, customs and ceremonies. For the Factualists, evaluation is a simple process. One needs only give a test and, if the student can produce from memory the right answers, then the student is praised, the teacher is commended, and the educational process receives high valuation. There are many Factualists in the fields of General and Jewish Education.

The Attitudinists approach education from the opposite extreme. They are concerned over the inner life of the student. They wonder whether heaping up a lot of factual information makes any real difference in the attitudes of students towards life, Jewish life, their fellowmen, their duties towards the so-called "higher things" of life, the development of such qualities as reverence, piety, and the virtues that are the crown and glory of human character. It must be confessed that the Attitudinists are often regarded as emotionalists who are a bit on the batty side. The Factualists always come to the Attitudinists and say: "Show me! Give me a Curriculum! Set up a group and let us have the know-how!" And the Attitudinists grow somewhat red in the face and say: "You practical fellows! You live in a world of techniques. We are talking about inner, spiritual qualities beyond your ken!"

Surely, in the teaching of Concepts and Practices, or Customs and Ceremonies of Judaism we come to the heart of the whole matter, for here we seek to reach the inner, emotional life of the child. The merest tyro in education knows that out of the emotional resources of life are molded the character of the adult; in the emotional resources of life is anchored the sense of worthwhileness of the whole human enterprise; in the emotional resources of life we have the rootage out of which alone can grow those allies by which facts, skills, habits and acts gain meaning and significance.

Our problem, then, is how to measure the progress we are making towards molding the emotional, inner, spiritual attitudes of the child who, for an approximate period of nine years (from 7 to 16 years of age), is entrusted to us.

Lest we start out with a feeling that the problem is an overwhelming one, one that we cannot solve, let us remember that not only Jewish educators, but educators in general, have made little progress in this field of measuring the progress of spiritual growth in terms of techniques, methods and measurements. Some little progress has been made, of course, in at least understanding the problem and in formulating its difficulties.

In the first place, the Factualists and the Attitudinists, mentioned above, are of course caricatures of the extremes and not copies of the reality. For the truth of the matter is that attitudes and spiritual values cannot be taught apart from factual content. Indeed, the finest and noblest spiritual values are made real only through the context of facts, situations, activities. Jewish ethical values could actually be conveyed to children through a class in cabinet making, or a class in photography by imaginative and resourceful teachers. What we must first of all decide is that we are interested in developing or enhancing "the child's spiritual and ethical sensitivity so that in act and attitude he may be governed by the religious, ethical and cultural traditions of Judaism."

In the second place, should we not concern ourselves with the techniques needed to evoke such emotional and spiritual responses as will help children to hold as precious and worthwhile Jewish ideas, facts and behaviors? The following suggestions might well be explored:

a. Can we use the technique of the Children's Religious Services to get inside of the child's emotional apparatus more effectively? How can we do so? Could attendance at such services be used as a measurement of growth in inward, spiritual satisfaction?

b. Have we used the School Assembly to the best advantage of our purposes? Have we created sufficiently significant techniques so that the Assembly becomes or may become an experience that will move the heart and spirit of the child in the directions we want the child's inner life to grow? And can we utilize the Assembly experience in some way to make it a measuring-rod of growth of inwardness in the child?

c. What of the Summer Camp, either in the neighborhood or in the country, and its availability for two months as a place of religious, emotional experience of the right kind? What thoughts can be followed along this line? Is a new field of Jewish spiritual education opening up for us here? How can we begin to use it and how can it be used to establish standards of growth of inner spiritual change even in the short period of two months?

d. And, finally, what of the teaching of Arts and Crafts? Do not these provide experiences in which we work through imagination and creative expression open up new vistas, long and inspiring vistas, of reaching the inner resources of Jewish children so that they help to shape and mold their attitudes towards all things Jewish? Of course, by Arts and Crafts I mean not only painting, clay-modeling and other manual manipulation, but also dancing, dramatics, music, and the social arts of living together.

The teacher himself has been left to the very end. We all know that the teacher is indispensable to any scheme of education, but the teacher must himself be more than merely the messenger of a curriculum and the engineer of a technique. He may be excellent in carrying out instructions as developed in a curriculum, and he may be most skillful in handling educational techniques, but I think that for shaping and molding the characters and the spiritually sensitive inwardness of children more is needed. The teacher himself must be a liver of the attitudes he would convey. The old, now almost threadbare truth, that "Religion is caught not taught" still carries much valid authority. Herein the Jewish teachers in our Religious Schools are different from the Jewish teachers who are secularists in point of view, or nationalists who are concerned merely with the national survival of the Jewish group.

The Religious School must be conceived as an organic unit, with its specialized limbs, and its nervous system of techniques, skills and methods. The power that makes it move and gives it significance must be found in the realm of the spirit, the inner realm where live the emotions, the feelings, the dreams, the attitudes, the hopes and the fears of each Jewish child.

The Torch, January, 1949.

THE FUTURE OF JEWISH
EDUCATION IN AMERICA

ABRAHAM E. MILLGRAM

To discuss the future of Jewish education in America presupposes the gift of prophecy. Since prophecy ceased more than two thousand years ago, my task appears to be an impossible one. Yet I believe that the expressed wish of Moses, "Would that all the Lord's people were prophets," is not altogether unfulfilled in this regard. For all of us can make some sound prognostications regarding the future of Jewish education.

However, before making any prophecies, we must agree on the meaning of the term "Jewish education," particularly as it applies to the Conservative synagogue. To arrive at a logically cogent definition, we must realize that Jewish life and more particularly, Conservative Judaism, has no future without an adequate system of Jewish education for our children. Futhermore, a superficial Jewish education, such as the one-day-a-week school or Sunday school, spells ultimate death for our way of life, for children so educated cannot possibly feel at home in a Conservative synagogue where the core of the service is in Hebrew, and the character of Jewish life is traditional. Synagogues sponsoring such schools are faced with the sad prospect of ultimate extinction. Hence Jewish education for congregations affiliated with the United Synagogue must necessarily be defined as a program which is in consonance with the minimum standards as defined by the United Synagogue Commission on Jewish education. These standards call for a minimum of six classroom hours of instruction per week.

Another preliminary, but most relevant, statement is here urgently needed. It is crucial for us to bear in mind that the central responsibility for the future of Jewish education in America rests on our shoulders. Recent statistics published by the American Association for Jewish Education indicate that fully a half of the children attending Jewish schools are under the auspices of Conservative congregations. The other children are to be found in schools sponsored by Reform Temples, Orthodox Synagogues, Community Talmud Torahs and Yiddishist Schools. Moreover, since it is generally recognized that, at best, only a small percentage of our children will receive their Jewish education in all-day schools, the future of Jewish education is inevitably tied to the supplementary afternoon Hebrew school which is largely in the hands of the Conservative Movement. It is for this reason that we are troubled by the problem of the future of Jewish education. By learning something about its foreseeable future we may be able the better to play our proper role in developing the pattern of Jewish education, and we shall the better carry this responsibility which history has placed upon our shoulders.

CREATING A CLIMATE FOR
JEWISH EDUCATION

Now for the promised prognostications.

The future of Jewish education in America rests largely on our success or failure to create in our communities a healthy climate for Jewish education. Climate is generally understood to be a proper balance between several component elements of the atmosphere, such as heat, wind, moisture and vegetation. Similarly, a good climate for Jewish education is composed of several elements in sufficient quantity and in proper balance.

To begin with, our historic experience with Jewish education has been a happy one. For centuries Jewish education has been astonishingly successful. Its success is attested by many educators and scholars. Thus we read in Professor Frederick Ely and Charles F. Arrowood's *History and Philosophy of Education:*

The fact that it (Jewish education) has outlasted every other system whatsoever makes it the most successful educational experiment ever staged in the history of civilization.

What is it that made the old Heder such an outstanding success? To be sure, it lacked many of the modern accoutrements of good education. It lacked adequate physical facilities. It lacked basic tools such as textbooks. It lacked pedagogic knowledge. But it had a number of essential elements which are indispensable to successful education. It had a healthy climate in which to function.

The first important element of this favorable climate was the universal acceptance of the school's objectives, standards and curriculum. The objectives of the Heder were seemingly limited. Basically, they aimed at transmitting to the children the Jewish way of life, its faith and its Torah. The curriculum was correspondingly narrow but deep. It consisted of an educational ladder starting with the elements of Hebrew reading, followed by the study of the Bible and its commentary *Rashi,* and then the study of Talmud. The standards, however, were intensive, calling for nine hours of daily instruction, six days per week, twelve months per year. And the child was started on this intensive course of study at the delicate age of four or five.

THE ROLE OF LEADERSHIP

But it is not the curriculum, the standards, or the methods of instruction that I pose for emulation. It is rather the universal acceptance of this program of education that I am pointing up as one of the healthy elements in the educational climate of the old school. This universal acceptance was rooted in a long tradition dating back to the days of Moses. Leaders of every generation repeatedly urged universal and intensive education of the children because they equated it both with the key to Jewish survival and the key to spiritual fulfillment in this world and the next. Thus, our confession of faith which teaches to "love the Lord, your God, with all your heart, with all your soul, and with all your might," teaches with equal insistence that "thou shalt teach them (the Torah) diligently unto your children." This tradition continued through the Middle Ages up to the threshold of modern times when we hear the Vilna Gaon state categorically that "the Torah is to the soul of man what rain is to the soil." In our own generation, too, we hear the late Professor Louis Ginzberg, a member of the Vilna Gaon's family, make the telling statement:

> The school is the most original institution created by post-biblical Judaism—a magnificent institution, a veritable fortress unshaken by the storms of the ages. To borrow a simile from the

Midrash, the school was the heart that kept watch while the other organs slept. Ideals pass into great historical forces by embodying themselves into institutions, and the Jewish ideal of knowledge became a great historical force by embodying itself in the Jewish school.

The sentiments about teaching Torah, so repeatedly and insistently taught by Jewish leaders throughout the ages, were embodied not only in Jewish custom, tradition and belief, but also in Jewish law. They were thus made part of the official Jewish way of life. It was Maimonides, in his monumental legal work, the *Mishneh Torah,* who stated:

> It is obligatory to appoint teachers in every province, in every city. If there is a city which has no school for children, its inhabitants are to be excommunicated, and the ban is not to be lifted until teachers are appointed. If, despite the excommunication, the inhabitants fail to appoint teachers, the city itself is to be put under the ban, for the foundation of the world rests on the education of our children.

The outcome of this tradition has been that the Jewish school functioned in a favorable climate of universal acceptance, a climate of universal concern with the school and with the child's progress in his studies, a climate making for a flourishing, intensive program of Jewish education for all children.

THE SENSITIVE AREA OF THE
CHILD'S HOME

A second crucial element of the favorable climate was to be found in the sensitive area of the child's home. Mere living in the traditional Jewish home was in itself an intensive Jewish education. Not only were Sabbaths, holidays, dietary laws and other religious practices fully observed, but there was an atmosphere of deep faith in God and an unquestioning reverence for the sancta of Judaism. Jewish life in the home was absolutely normative and healthy so that neither parents nor children ever questioned the place of Hebrew in the scheme of Jewish life, or the peoplehood of Israel, or the holiness of the Land of Israel, or the ultimate coming of the Messiah and the redemption of the Children of Israel. God's justice and loving-kindness were accepted as absolute realities. No wonder that even the Jewish woman, who was generally given no formal Jewish education, was perfectly adjusted to Jewish life and was able efficiently to play her part in it. She knew exactly how to keep the home kosher, how to prepare for Sabbaths and holidays, and how the hundreds of minutiae of the law applied to the conduct of the household and to the daily life of every member of the family.

Educators today fully understand the power of the home as an educational force. They know that the child brought up in a Jewish home lives, thinks and feels Jewishly long before he experiences the formal instruction of the school. And the informal instruction of the home is usually deeper than that of the school. A brief discussion by parents at the family table on any Jewish theme makes a deeper and more lasting impression on the child than several good lessons on the same theme by an excellent teacher. Conversely, all the teaching in school about the central importance of the Fourth Commandment—to observe the Sabbath and keep it holy—will prove a mere academic discussion, unless the Shabbas is experienced by the child as a reality in his normal life at home. The congruity between the child's life at home and the school's program of studies is a vital element making for a school's success. It is the presence of this congruity in the old Jewish communities that made for the second favorable element of the climate for Jewish education and accounted, in great measure, for the success of the old school.

TWO BASIC EDUCATIONAL
INGREDIENTS

This favorable climate in the community and in the home produced two basic ingredients which are indispensable to successful education. First of all, to use educational jargon, it made for strong motivation. Motivation, our psychologists and educators tell us, is the lifeblood of learning. In plain English it means that you can lead the horse to water but you can't make him drink. Children who have no desire to learn may attend Hebrew school for years, and attend regularly, without learning much. The inner drive to learn, which the educators call "motivation," can in part be created by the school itself. But the best teachers and the best schools cannot begin to approach the motivation that comes from the natural climate in which the child lives.

This natural climate prevailed in the old Jewish communities and exerted a powerful influence on the child. Everyone in the community was concerned with and was interested in every child's Jewish studies. The successful pupil was given constant and universal recognition. The social approval often expressed itself in mere pinches of the cheek, or pats on the head. But it had a most profound effect on the child. Whether he was bright or slow, he was deeply aware of the great value that the adult community placed on successful learning. This produced in the child a strong desire to master his studies. With this motivating drive even poor teachers and backward schools were able to achieve remarkable results.

The favorable climate of the old Jewish communities was also productive of the second important factor in education—an ample supply of devoted teachers. There were no teachers' institutes, nor other facilities for pedagogical training. Technical preparation for the profession of teaching was unknown. What a teacher needed in those days was enough knowledge of the subject matter and an earnest desire to transmit it to the children. This type of person was to be found in large numbers in every community. Since Torah was prized above everything, it was inevitable that a substantial number of men were learned and thus equipped with adequate knowledge for the teaching profession. Further, by living in this climate, they derived their knowledge of the school curriculum and their conviction that the curriculum was practical and ideally adjusted to the needs of the children. Moreover, they were, as a rule, deeply imbued with the prevailing conviction that the teaching of children was nothing less than "God's work," a holy calling. To be sure, some were not suited for teaching by temperament. But their deep convictions and personal piety endowed them with enthusiasm for and devotion to their work.

In short, the old Jewish school, with all its shortcomings— untrained teachers, primitive facilities, and a total lack of pedagogic aids—is universally acclaimed as "the most successful educational experiment ever staged in the history of civilization." It was that because it was blessed with a healthy climate of Jewish education, a climate which produced well motivated students, devoted teachers, and, by common consent, an intensive program in terms of many classroom hours per week and many years of schooling.

THE OBVIOUS LESSON FOR MODERN JEWRY

The obvious lesson to be learned from these historic facts is that the future of Jewish education in America is largely in the hands of the Jewish communities, and more specifically in the hands of the leadership. If American Jewish leadership will be fully committed to the proposition that the proper Jewish education of our children is a matter of communal life or death, and, like our leadership of old, will transmit this feeling to the rank and file in their communities; if they will talk of it "morning, noon and night," "when they lie down and when they rise up;" if they will continuously paint the picture of the future of American Jewry as either bright or bleak, depending on the community's concern for and commitment to Jewish education, then our people will begin to respond with generosity and enthusiasm. They will begin to demand better schools and higher standards. They will begin to center their pride in the fine schools they have instead of in the costly structures they have built. They will begin to find rewarding satisfaction in their children's progress and in the spiritual promise it holds.

THE FAMILY-CENTERED SCHOOL

If our leaders will be committed to the priority of Jewish education they will make a special effort to penetrate the Jewish home and bring into it a new heart and a new spirit. This is not beyond possibility. I am convinced that the frequent complaints that the parents are indifferent to Jewish education are mostly unfounded. If the parents were indifferent they would not be making the many sacrifices that go with enrolling their children in Jewish schools. From experience I can testify that many parents are ready to assume responsibilities for their children's Jewish education beyond mere enrollment and tuition payment. But they need guidance. Our failure often lies in the fact that too many of our school boards and faculties are content with teaching the children. They little realize that when a river dries up at its source barrenness inevitably afflicts the whole country side. The source of Jewish life and ideology is the home. *And unless a proper climate for Jewish education is created in the home the very foundations of the Jewish school are hollow and brittle.* The Jewish school, if it is to thrive, must enlist the parents' active participation, and must inject a living Judaism into the child's home life. Otherwise, the education that the school provides is only academic, a mere fleeting shadow. *During the past few decades educators have been stressing the child-centered school. In Jewish education we must stress the family-centered school.*

With the creation of a favorable climate in the community and home, the child will cease to regard his Jewish studies as irrelevant and unrewarding. He will begin to respond with enthusiasm, because Jewish knowledge will be the essence of worthy achievement. Our children will come to our schools fully prepared psychologically and emotionally to learn.

MAKING HEBREW TEACHING
A DESIRABLE PROFESSION

The improved climate for Jewish education will not only imbue the child with a will to learn but will also affect the teacher problem which is plaguing our schools today. Our present plight, resulting from the critical lack of well-trained, devoted teachers is, in large measure, due to the barren climate in which Jewish education is cultivated. Many potential teachers choose other fields, while many in the profession leave it for more promising occupations. But if Jewish education were to rise in the esteem of the community, the teacher's status would improve. He would come to be regarded as an indispensable adjunct of the community's life. He would grow in the esteem of the people and, consequently, in his own esteem. The community would then want to give him an adequate wage as well as tenure, insurance, and an old-age retirement pension. His social status, too, would change to one of acceptance and integration. His present sense of isolation would be replaced by a sense of rootedness and belonging. Hebrew teaching would then be on its way to becoming a desirable profession, attracting enough idealistic young men and women to provide us with an adequate supply of devoted teachers.

HIGHER STANDARDS IN
JEWISH EDUCATION

Finally, our standards would inevitably rise. No longer would congregations and parents be satisfied with substandard schools. No longer would more than half the children, enrolled in Jewish schools, be attending one-day-a-week or Sunday schools. Even the standards set by our Commission would become antiquated, relics of an age when our people had temporarily forgotten how to prize the Torah. To be sure, school sessions would not be as lengthy, nor would the curriculum and methods of teaching be like those of the old Heder. But parents would expect the schools to be as intensive as is consonant with American Jewish life, and the teachers well-enough trained and devoted so as to be a positive force in our children's lives.

When God chose Abraham to be the father of our people, He justified that choice by saying: "For I am certain that he (Abraham) will instruct his children and his household after him that they keep the way of the Lord to do righteousness and justice." I cannot speak with the same certainty. I must add to my prophecy a number of "ifs." If the leaders of Conservative Judaism in America will be thoroughly imbued with the conviction that Jewish education must at all times receive first priority in all congregational activities, then I am certain that the people and the households of our communities, will instruct their children to keep the way of the Lord. Our efforts will in time transform the climate for Jewish education in our communities and in the children's homes. A new generation of willing students, devoted teachers, and an adequate school program will be the blessings of American Jewish life.

The Torch, Winter, 1956.

RAMAH—A THINKING CHILD'S CAMP

M. BERNARD RESNIKOFF

A man living in the Midwest, a normal, average American, traded in his 1957 Pontiac for one of 1951 vintage so that he would have the money to send his daughter to Ramah.

A pretty college co-ed spent a week-end at a Ramah camp visiting her brother, who was on the staff. Following this brief stay, she vowed to complete her professional training (nursing) as quickly as possible and go to Israel to practice there.

A nine-year-old girl wrote the director of the Ramah camp where she had spent the summer that she is teaching her parents Hebrew at the dinner table and had persuaded them to join her at Sabbath services.

All these events happened. They were incidents typical of many that rest in the files of the four Ramah Camps sponsored by the United Synagogue of America, lay arm of the Jewish Theological Seminary of America. They illustrate forcefully why the Seminary has joined forces with several regional groups of Conservative congregations to create and guide a summer camp program—an area somewhat removed from their usual interests.

These are the results, but what lies behind them? Why was Ramah created; what is it; how does it differ from the hundreds of good camps dotting the country?

Camping, as is commonly agreed, is practically the only childhood experience outside the family that provides a *total* living experience for 24 hours a day. It offers unprecedented opportunity to develop a child within the confines of his own world, to mold his character, to instill within him ideas, imbue him with ideals that have life-long effects.

It is these peculiar advantages of camp life that led to the establishment of Ramah. For Ramah is a concept as much as a camp. It is, basically, an educational institution, taking advantage of the distinctiveness of a camp program to buttress and supplement the Jewish education the child receives in school and at home. It is a fulfillment of intensive Jewish living for eight weeks, 24 hours a day. It takes place in a community geared in all its resources and guided by a dedicated staff to help these young American boys and girls know, understand, live and retain the values of our tradition.

By making this a *total* experience, the child learns to *apply* these values, bringing them alive with a wonder and excitement that can be achieved only in the all-encompassing activity of a summer camp program.

How is this done? First, by conducting the entire program in Hebrew, be it Red Cross instruction, dramatic pageants, classes, sports, discussions, nature study, etc., insofar as possible. The camper thus becomes familiar with the special sound and rhythm of Hebrew in addition to increasing his vocabulary astonishingly.

Second, by a study program. Not only every camper, but also every counselor, waiter and other members of the camp population studies every day. Depending upon the age and previous training, the subjects might be Bible, history, literature, Zionism, Talmud or, as requested by one group of seven boys at one camp, Hebrew grammar.

Third, by prayers. Whether daily (usually outdoors), or on the Sabbath with 200 white-clad children conducting and participating in their own service (with an incalculable emotional impact), before and after meals, *zemirot* in celebration of the Sabbath, special Tisha b'Av ceremonial, there is an aura of elevated morality and spirituality that lifts the child up with it in unforgettable communion.

Nor is this all, for each of these facets of the program are brought into play in discussions, both formal and informal, that deal with such subjects, on each child's level, as living as a Jew in America, Jewish values in everyday living, problems of a teen-ager in a small community and a host of others that are extremely close to home for the average American Jewish child.

All of this is accomplished, as proven by Ramah's experience, within the framework of the classic camping program. Far from neglecting those typical activities—pioneering, nature, swimming, dramatics, arts and crafts, sports, music and the entire gamut of interest-laden programs designed to give the camper a healthy, fresh and stimulating outdoor summer experience—Ramah utilizes them to the fullest. It merely assigns them an *added* role, and complements each of these living and learning experiences by capitalizing upon them for the sake of its educational goals.

RESPECT FOR THE INDIVIDUAL

Similarly, it would be a gross error to assume that the most touted aspect of camping—listed in almost every camp brochure as "personality development," "character growth and building" or "emphasis on individual"—are incidental in the Ramah program. On the contrary, it is only by emphasizing these factors that Ramah can achieve its own aims. It must—and therefore does—concern itself with the individual, his personality and his character, so that he may reap the full benefits that are offered. An unhappy or uncomfortable child cannot possibly learn; Ramah assesses each child according to his needs and capabilities so that he may garner the most out of what is available to him.

This, to spell it out a bit more, though briefly, is accomplished at Ramah by a dual approach—through mental hygiene, in the broadest sense, and with a cultural philosophy.

From a mental hygiene approach, we know that no two children are alike. Each brings to camp his own unique experiences, his needs, his anxieties, fears, aspirations, interests—all of which must be allayed, encouraged, satisfied, developed or met, as the case may be, and the measure of camp program success is the measure to which it fulfills all these.

How is it done at Ramah? Well, little Danny may be encouraged to go swimming, but he certainly will not be forced to do so; Judy may enjoy playing with her small group, but she may also wish some occasional solitude. The camper, Ramah feels, has the right to certain decisions—even, on occasion, the wrong ones, *provided the child learns by and from them.*

A mature, sensitized Ramah staff helps campers choose their own programs, tempering their teaching with understanding. Thus, while there are aims to the Ramah program, there is sufficient latitude to permit even daily changes in specific program aspects, decided upon by camper committees. Such committees set up schedules, plan divisional activities, organize the Oneg Shabbat and even share, to the extent possible, in formulating camp policy.

Visionary, anarchic? Not at all—experience has proven that it works—and works well. The fixed program is the easiest in the world to run; the Ramah method infinitely more difficult, but infinitely better, too. It requires truly reaching the child, and to do so that counselor must be constantly alert, poised on the balls of his feet, prepared to modify, re-direct, abandon, limit or expand program to meet developing needs. To have it any other way would spell miserable failure. Ramah, it must be constantly emphasized, is an educational institution, which means learning —and learning involves the *whole* person, the *total* personality.

The Ramah approach in this area can best be summarized by the fact that the winter training program for counselors this year has centered on mental hygiene for children.

LIVING A FULL JEWISH LIFE IN
AMERICA

Now, as to Ramah's cultural philosophy. Much has been written on the problems of a minority group in a host culture. Many leaders are concerned with deculturation (loss of Jewish values) of our youth as they become more attracted to the society they live in (acculturation). Some critics of Ramah, on the other hand, accuse it of trying to re-create the isolated and insulated community of the *shtetl* (not desirable) on the soil of America (not possible). This being neither the time nor the place for a full-blown argument on cultural anthropology, Ramah's position will be stated simply.

A leading sociologist, the late Kurt Lewin, pointed out that "the group to which an individual belongs is the (psychological) ground on which he stands, which gives or denies him status . . . security and help." And, further, "Loyalty to the Jewish group furthers . . . friendly relations with (other groups)." In other words, a member of a minority group reacts to outside stresses and strains in direct relationship to how he views his relationship to that group; and his security depends in good measure on his understanding and appreciation of the values of his group. This is Ramah's premise.

Social research has shown that by the time he is of camper age, a child has developed a sense of identity. We know also that delay in helping a child recognize the meaning of his Jewish group membership leads to difficulties in later years. Ramah, with its stated aims, serves to lessen the impact of those stresses and strains that are bound to come. It does so by providing a cushion of positive experience of Jewish living "in the round" and its concomitant understanding of the values inherent in it.

Finally, but by no means of least importance, Ramah provides an opportunity for the realization of the full potential of the child, without undue regard to "conformity." In other words, Ramah seeks to develop non-conformists in particular regard to Jewish life today, to have its children develop dissatisfactions with what they see and enable them to overcome these dissatisfactions, to replace them with vibrant, fulsome attitudes and practices. Thus, Ramah children have gone home to further, more intensive study; to assume leadership in their congregations; to pursue Jewish professional careers; to influence their families and friends, and to make an invaluable contribution to Jewish life in America. Over 100 are enrolled presently in the various Seminary schools.

The statistical success is equally heartening: in thirteen years one experimental program for 93 children has grown into four camps with 1,200 youngsters from every part of the country and Canada, coming from every economic class, from metropolis and hamlet. Operational budgets total over half a million dollars; a fifth Ramah will open in Canada in 1960; other United Synagogue regions press for their own camps; rejections for this summer could fill another camp (in a period of generally declining camp enrollments!) .

The vision that is Ramah owes its fulfillment to no one person or group—it is the end result of the educational supervision of the Seminary's Teacher's Institute; the efforts of Rabbinical Assembly members everywhere; funds given and obtained by United Synagogue leaders; involvement of Men's Club and Women's League representatives; assistance in manifold ways by educators and cantors. Each Ramah camp is sponsored by a United Synagogue region, with its board composed of representatives of all these groups. The National Ramah Commission, similarly representative, is the coordinating, policy-formulating body for all the movement.

The unique role of the men's club is to help provide the necessary leadership, seek out to share and help the most gifted candidates, provide scholarships, concern itself with the physical needs of the camp serving it and help in the many special ways that men can, and for which it is so well fitted by its connection with the L.T.F. program.

This, above all. If all who are concerned, not with merely an adequate, but with a maximum Jewish education, would strain and strive together, our time may yet see the launching of a Golden Age of Jewish life in America.

The Torch, Spring, 1959.

Dr. Resnikoff, noted educator and social worker, is Executive Director of the National Ramah Commission. He has been Executive Director of the Canarsie Jewish Center, Brooklyn, N. Y. and of the Jewish Community Center, Holyoke, Mass. He has also been associated with the Jewish Welfare Board and has served as Executive Director, Y. M. H. A. in Jerusalem, Israel.

LTF: A NEW IMAGE

✳

CHAIM POTOK

The Hebrew essayist Ahad Ha'am once wrote that the Jew never lives in the present but in the past or the future. As a people we have always lived with dreams in our eyes, dreams of the glory of our past or the infinite possibilites of our future. We are rarely satisfied with any given moment of time. There is so very much to be done. There is so very little time for complacency or lengthy self-congratulations.

The primary preoccupation and concern of certain segments of the American Jewish community today is with the future. We are the richest Jewish community in the world. We are one of the most benevolent Jewish communities in the entire history of our people. The aid we have given to oppressed Jews everywhere is a vivid testimony to the way we have spelled out in deed the Jewish concept of *tzedakah*. We have rendered this aid in order to enable Jews less fortunate than ourselves to achieve a better future. The many institutions in this country which bear Jewish names stand as clear examples of how we have concretized benevolence in stone and steel. These too, represent our investment in the future. We have every right to be proud of these aspects of our preoccupation with the future of our people.

Yet with all of this, we have thus far tragically neglected the single most significant problem confronting the American Jewish community. Because we have paid only token attention to this problem we have made no *real* investment in our future.

We are now at a point in our history where we are quite literally starving for leadership. There are not enough teachers, there are not enough educational directors, there are not enough rabbis. There are not enough informed laymen. We are reaping the whirlwind born of neglect.

There is an ominous dearth of Jewish "quality leadership" today. It need hardly be added that dearth of such leadership spells death of community.

The problem is even graver than appears at first glance. We have never had a surfeit of Jewish leadership in America, and yet somehow we have always managed to survive. We have limped from generation to generation. We are still limping today. The heart of the problem is that we can no longer afford to continue limping. The world of today is different *in kind* from the world of two decades ago. We are confronted by a dizzying array of mind-numbing problems. If as a people we have nothing to say about these problems, then we will continue our limping. And to continue our limping now is to lose the very best of our youth to those who *have* something to say about these problems. To continue limping into the next generation is ultimately to be unable to walk at all. We will have become a redundancy in the modern world.

We can no longer afford the laxity of limping. But we can begin to walk correctly only if we provide ourselves with adequate leadership.

And here we confront another aspect of this problem: it is not enough to build Jewish *leadership;* what is needed is *Jewish* leadership.

About fifteen years ago, when the world was not nearly as complex as it is today, the Teachers Institute of the Jewish Theological Seminary of America created a youth movement known as the Leaders Training Fellowship, or LTF. As the name implies, the purpose of this movement was to train future *Jewish* leaders. It was the belief then, as it is today, that study is a primary prerequisite for such leadership. So a certain number of hours of Jewish study per week became a basic requirement for membership in LTF. Service of some kind became another requirement. Service in those days meant service in the synagogue: Torah reading, leading a junior congregation, tutoring, assisting a teacher, and so on. The movement drew its membership from among the finest teenagers in the Jewish community. In particular, it drew members from among the teenagers who attended the Ramah camps. LTF came to be known as a kind of winter extension of the Ramah summer program. It remained a small, intense quality group within our Movement. It contributed locally and nationally far out of proportion to its numbers. To cite one example: more than eighty percent of the students in the Seminary today are former members of LTF.

LTF accomplished something else that was very significant. It created a climate of opinion in which Jewish teenagers who wanted to continue their Jewish studies and retain their Jewish loyalties could do so without fear of the mockery of others. This is not to say that the mockery disappeared. It *is* to say that there is strength in numbers: ten Jewish teenagers belonging to an LTF group are always better able to withstand the questions and raised eyebrows of others than is one Jewish teenager. It is important to remember this. LTF operated in a climate of opinion in which being a committed Jewish teenager became a mark of character. The LTFers themselves created this climate. For as it turned out, the teenager who was attracted to LTF was almost invariably the leader of his peer group *outside* of LTF. He became the one whom other Jewish teenagers wanted to emulate. It was in this way that LTF made its contribution to Jewish life.

With the rapid growth of other youth movements, the image of LTF began to blur. Quality always stands tremulously before quantity. The nature and the message of LTF were swallowed by the hard-earned and overwhelming successes of these other mass youth movements.

And the world changed, too. This is not the world of fifteen years ago. Now the teenager faces a world besieged by a host of overwhelming problems. The tone of the world has changed. The quality of its problems has changed. In an era of space exploration, racial explosions, horrifying poverty in the midst of unprecedented affluence, the swiftly rising star of China, and the proliferation of atomic weapons—in an era such as this the established goals of LTF, the goals of study and synagogue service, seem somehow insufficient. Notice: the word used here is *insufficient,* not *unimportant.* There is the feeling now that more than study and synagogue service is needed if the Jewish teenager is ultimately to make an adequate *Jewish* contribution to the world in which he will one day take his place as an adult.

What is needed is the new dimension that has now been added to LTF, the dimension of *action.* Without this dimension we will continue to lose our best teenagers to those movements that stress action. We will continue to lose them to those movements because they will grow up without being aware of this most important truth concerning Judaism; *the essence of Jewish creed is deed.*

Does the Jewish tradition have anything to say about the problems confronting man today? Can the teachings of the rabbis of the Talmud possibly be relevant to the dilemmas of twentieth century life? What would the rabbis have said about the racial revolution in which we now find ourselves? What would they have said about the nature of government. What would they have said about the awesome power that is now in the hands of labor and management? What would they have said about the culture of poverty that has now become part of the American landscape? What would they have said about our responsibilities to the Jews of Russia? What would they have said about the arms race and the search for peace?

These are the problems that LTF has now begun to explore in depth.

Notice the titles of recent and projected LTF publications: *The Ethics of the Individual, The Ethics of Human Relations, The Ethics of Labor, The Ethics of Management, The Ethics of Government, The Ethics of Law, The Ethics of Language, The Ethics of Social Welfare.* These publications contain rabbinic source material pertinent to the various subjects under discussion. Together with the source material there is a running commentary that attempts to explore the relevance of the material to today's world. The LTFers are partners in this exploration.

This is the kind of Jewish study that is now going on in LTF.

But study alone, it is now felt, is not sufficient. And here we enter the new dimension of LTF. This dimension is not only in its infancy. It is prevalent only in a few pilot groups throughout the country. It is this dimension that is now the ultimate goal of LTF. It is the dimension that fuses study with action.

Here are some examples of this new dimension. In Connecticut LTF is transforming itself into a kind of Jewish Peace Corps. LTFers teach Bible via Braille to the Jewish blind; LTFers undertake to work in slums; LTFers help mentally retarded youth in a recreational program (one such LTF project is linked to a Federal Government grant) ; LTFers are tutoring educationally deprived children. A similar program is now beginning in Chicago. In Philadelphia a group of LTFers has undertaken the task of "patterning" with brain-damaged children.

Using the rabbinic source material as focal points of study and as jumping-off points for action, LTF groups have begun to represent the essence of the Jewish fusion of creed and deed. They bring to life to the fullest degree possible the flexibility, universality, and potential relevance of Judaism to the modern world. They don't only study about this relevance. They *act* out this relevance. They translate this relevance into their lives.

These are the new goals of LTF: study and action relevant to the problems of our time. And this is the new image of LTF: a tradition-oriented group of Jewish teenagers with its feet firmly planted in the twentieth century.

No other youth group today is capable of undertaking this sort of task *en masse* because no other youth group is equipped to handle the technical vocabulary and conceptual wealth found in the rabbinic source material. This task is unique to LTF.

It should be repeated and stressed that this emphasis is new to LTF and that it will be a few years before all of LTF is reorganized along these lines. It should also be repeated and stressed that these goals are not intended as replacements for traditional Jewish study during classroom hours and for service to the synagogue. They are *additions to* and not substitutions for LTF's original goals.

It remains the task of LTF to help provide the coming generation of American Judaism with *Jewish* leadership—with the kind of Jewish leadership that has a full awareness of the enormity of the world's problems and how our tradition can contribute towards helping to resolve them.

It is this kind of LTF that the men's clubs now sponsor.

By undertaking the sponsorship of LTF, the men's clubs have joined in the vital task of helping to meet the crisis in Jewish leadership. The dream in the eyes of all of us is of a leadership that will be adequate to the words of Tennyson:

"The fire of God fills him. I never saw his like. There lives no greater leader."

The Torch, Spring, 1965.

Dr. Potok, editor, author and educator, holds the position of Editor of the Jewish Publication Society of America and has just published his first novel, The Chosen. *He was National Director, Leaders Training Fellowship and Director of Camp Ramah in California. He served as managing editor of* Conservative Judaism *and as a member of the faculty of Teachers Institute of the Jewish Theological Seminary.*

Part Four

ADULT EDUCATION

"Our aim goes considerably beyond that of imparting knowledge. We are not directly and especially interested in knowledge. We are interested in man. Man must have knowledge, too, but if knowledge becomes the center of the person, it is just the opposite of what we want. We want the wholeness of a person because only whole persons can influence others as we want to influence others. This particular conjunction of situation and person is Adult Education as I understand it. It is not instruction first of all but education of character, and character is not above situation but is attached to the cruel, hard demand of this hour."

—Martin Buber

"The formerly inexhaustible reservoirs of Jewish learning in Eastern Europe have been destroyed in our days, and it is our holy duty to find new ways and means for the propagation of Jewish studies. The modern method has revitalized the study of the Talmud and today it is possible to acquire a sound knowledge of our traditional literature without sacrificing the general education which is indispensable to the cultured man of today.

—Alexander Marx

INTRODUCTION

The development of Adult Jewish Education in the Conservative Movement has paralleled that of adult education in the general community. Its uniqueness lies in its emphasis on spiritual values and its use of Jewish traditional source material—Bible, Rabbinic literature, History and Ethics. It relates to the synagogue, the community and Klal Israel. It recognizes the need for Jewish cultural life for the purpose of Jewish survival and for making a contribution to American civilization. Its impetus came originally from the Jewish Theological Seminary through the establishment of the United Synagogue of America, the Women's League, and the National Federation of Jewish Men's Clubs. The leadership at the top came from Dr. Louis Finkelstein, Dr. Mordecai M. Kaplan, and Dr. Simon Greenberg. In the previous sections the whole gamut of the Seminary program, including its University of Judaism, the Seminary Library and Museum, the Eternal Light Program, the College of Jewish Studies, the Student Center in Jerusalem and most recently the Mathilde Schechter Dormitory for Women has been indicated.

The appalling lack of knowledge of things Jewish by Jewish laymen and the absence of qualified lay leadership in Jewish life made Adult Studies a vital necessity. A fine beginning has been made by all the constituent Seminary-United Synagogue organizations including its National Academy of Jewish Studies in providing literary materials—books, pamphlets, publications, mimeographed curricula, and records. *Conservative Judaism* and *The Torch* are informative and inspirational magazines—not merely house organs.

The range of Adult Education includes work with college age young people for communal get-together for study and spiritual revitalization. The results have been encouraging but constitute only a scratch on the surface. Much more sustained effort in depth is called for. It is one thing to set up high standards and another to carry them out. It is encouraging to note the increasing public demand for clarification of aims and objectives in Conservative Judaism and for relating it to Israel and World Jewry. More good books on topics relating to Judaism and Jewish life are becoming available and being read. More organized efforts by Jewish international, national and local organizations in this field are being developed.

There are some unique features in the remarkable development of Adult Jewish Education in our times. One is that it has grown out of felt needs of the people themselves, out of questions and doubts and fears, out of the uncertain ties of life, out of tensions, out of radical changes in environment and social mores, out of a world-wide shift in values and standards. The insecurity of life, despite an affluent society, has caused us to search for a new basis for faith and belief, for something that will transcend the phenomenal developments of science and technology and bring hope and happiness to a world torn asunder by violence and conflict and racial antagonism. We seek a new foundation for world understanding and brotherhood.

The articles by Milton Berger and Arthur Bruckman reflect what the Jewish Men's Clubs in America recognize as the needs of their members for intellectual and spiritual growth through Adult Jewish Education. Another factor of importance is the absence of fixed traditions that institutionalize or confine the movement. Experimentation does not have to fight against entrenched interests and attitudes. In fact our Adult Jewish Education is largely indigenous. We are a generation of men and women with a *secular* education through high school, and in many instances through college, and a *Jewish* education that has not gone beyond the bar mitzvah stage and has been forgotten, and at all events is totally inadequate to meet our needs as mature members of the Jewish community. It is for every Jewish home that Dr. Solomon Grayzel offers a wide range of books to meet individual interests and ability to comprehend. Happily Dr. Israel M. Goldman's article shows that the National Academy of Jewish Studies addresses itself to new approaches. The Jewish Theological Seminary has its

Institute for Religious and Social Studies and the article on Laymen's Institutes likewise indicates recent trends. Dr. David Aronson suggests new ways by which the Rabbis can make the Synagogue have a larger share in the program of Adult Jewish Education.

Dr. Bernard Mandelbaum in his article draws these conclusions: "To be committed to one's beliefs with enthusiasm, strength, fullness of heart—this is the great need of America today". . . . "We have neglected our education in responsibility". . . . "Education in the values of the human spirit, education in character is the most vital factor in our survival."

We all learn through experience. It is when we face reality— problems of intermarriage, immorality, bigotry, violence, cynicism, disrespect for law or the disciplines of home, school, or society in general, that we seek answers. We then become eager to be guided, look for the lessons of history, and try to discover what our spiritual heritage has to offer. We examine the pages of our Bible, our liturgy, our Talmud, our Rabbinic Literature—in the original Hebrew and in translation—to find ways out of our dilemma. The study of our classic literature can have direct bearing on our lives and those of our children and our community. When our prophets and sages become real personalities to us through our own understanding of what they have said and the way they lived we shall have found the road to survival—that is the objective of Adult Education.

M.D.H.

THE CHALLENGE WE FACE

MILTON BERGER

The modern Jew's interest in Judaism cannot be stimulated or maintained by an emotional appeal alone. The beauty and pageantry of our religious practices are not sufficient to capture the imagination of the secularly educated Jew. Scientific education tends to lessen the awesome regard for Torah which characterized the traditional Jew. Religion has ceased to be an all-consuming passion. While the mass of our laity maintain religious affiliations, these are, in many instances, of an occasional and sporadic nature. This situation may not be so dangerous now, but we must be concerned because the future of Judaism is at stake.

To those who are firmly convinced that Judaism must be preserved not alone for the sake of the Jew, but also because of its contribution to civilization and the happiness of man, the solution of this problem is urgent.

But, how can we meet the challenge of those who question the basis for religious practices? How can we establish the validity and efficacy of prayer to the satisfaction of those who refuse to follow blindly the ritual of religion?

These are the questions which must be answered, if we are to build a Jewish community in America which will endure, a community which is morally healthy and spiritually strong. Theological dissertations will not suffice. We must reach out to the mass of laymen and show them that Judaism is a way of life. However, until the intellectual background for understanding is established, we shall only be planting our seeds on barren soil.

The answer is education.

We must devise a system of study for adult Jews which will fit into the pattern of modern life. The assumption that the task is complete once our youth receive a Jewish education has been proven fallacious. Our leaders are beginning to realize this. They realize too that the religious impulses created in youth will not last throughout life. There is too much competition and adults are wont to succumb to the glamorous, the bizarre and the popular. This is a sad truth, but if we are to solve the problem, we must first face it.

What then can we substitute for the discipline to which youth is subject? We may assume that the interest is in our Jewish people—but in varying degrees of intensity. How can we revitalize those religious impulses which now are dormant?

It is submitted that this can be done by study and discussion. Once an interest is awakened in the rich storehouse of thoughts and ideas which comprise our heritage, the way to a solution of the problem will be in sight. There is sufficient virility in our spiritual and ethical ideals. There is strength in Judaism. The weakness lies in its adherents. This weakness has its roots in ignorance.

The challenge we face is to lead our laymen back to study. We have always as a people respected learning. Our thirst for knowledge is even today a pronounced group trait. Our task is to guide that thirst so that it seeks satisfaction in Jewish knowledge.

The foregoing analysis highlights the reasons which have caused the National Federation of Jewish Men's Clubs to launch a frontal attack on the problem of Adult Jewish Education. The Federation believes that it has a clear understanding of the difficulties which must be overcome. A call to formal classroom study may find only a limited response. Study courses in pamphlet form would, however, be more acceptable. The busy layman could and probably would work such a study course into his schedule. This would be especially true if the courses were sponsored partially or wholly by a lay organization of which he was a member. These pamphlets must be prepared for the layman. Once an interest is created, we may then expect our laymen to discover that time is available for regular attendance at adult study groups. We may then hope to re-establish that habit for Jewish study which has always characterized the observant Jew. Then, too, we may find a reawakened interest in Jewish books and learning. This interest may be directed into the establishment of a Jewish home library, and from such an undertaking we can expect our layman to exhibit an interest in the library at his Synagogue.

Another method for stimulating interest in Jewish culture is to arrange institutes for our lay leaders, preferably at Jewish institutions of higher learning. Imagine the impetus which a movement for adult education would receive if laymen could spend a week or more in the atmosphere of the Jewish Theological Seminary of America; there to listen to some of our foremost Jewish thinkers. These leaders would return to their communities spiritually inspired and intellectually refreshed. Such leaders would have a keener understanding of the standards and goals of Jewish life. From such leaders we could expect intelligent and courageous guidance.

The plans formulated by the Men's Club movement are by no means exclusive. Other lay and rabbinic organizations should also initiate programs or lend support to those already started. The united effort of all organized Jewry is needed if the interest, loyalty, and devotion of the Jewish People for their Religion is to be maintained. Our task is to establish a Jewish cultural background. Once this is achieved, we shall have an enlightened laity, possessed of a continuous source of religious inspiration, a great body of men who can be counted on to practice Judaism and to preserve it for posterity.

The Torch, February, 1944

Mr. Berger, a national leader in the Conservative Movement and B'nai B'rith, has been Editor of The Torch *since it was first published twenty-five years ago. He was President of the National Federation of Jewish Men's Clubs, Vice-President of the United Synagogue of America, and Treasurer of the World Council of Synagogues. He served as president of District Grand Lodge, No. 3 of B'nai B'rith and is National Chairman of its Vocational Service Commission. He has been prominent in the Boy Scout Movement. Mr. Berger is a lawyer and is Co-editor of this volume.*

JEWISH BOOKS FOR YOUR HOME

SOLOMON GRAYZEL

I

WHY A JEWISH BOOKSHELF

Jewish law and tradition contain no more interesting regulations than those which deal with the care and treatment of books. The custom, for example, of kissing a Hebrew book which accidentally dropped to the floor, or the prohibition to use a book as a prop for another object, or the stern warning against employing a book to shield oneself from flying missiles are indications of the respect in which books were held.* It was a respect based on the Jewish ideal of Torah, good books that add to Jewish knowledge and thus act as a guide to life being accorded some of the sanctity which attaches to the Bible itself. One may understand, therefore, why the Jews of former days, and many to this day, considered that a home without books lacked the dignity that a Jewish home should have.

"Atmosphere," however, is not enough. That books are decorative, that they lend "tone," is a modern discovery. To buy books for no better reason than that their bindings go well with the color scheme of the household represents a littleness of spirit of which no truly Jewish man or woman should be guilty. Jews have collected books because of the information they contained or because of their ability to afford spiritual comfort. The Jew purchased a book in order to make the author his guest—an honored guest—with whom he might converse on a subject of mutual interest. This is not to say that a Jewish library must be dull; Jewish books can also be entertaining; but the emphasis should be on the spiritually worthy and useful. The bookshelf within the Jew-

---

* See the very interesting pamphlet, "The People and the Book," by Joshua Bloch, reprinted from Bookmen's Holiday by the New York Public Library, 1943.

ish home must help in the fight against ignorance and against despair, for the preservation of the Jewish heritage and, through this, of the Jewish people.

SIZE OF BOOKSHELF

Space is the only limit to the number of books that a Jewish home should have, with interest as a limitation on the type rather than the size of the bookshelf. Dwellers in apartment houses are, of course, at a disadvantage as against dwellers in suburban homes. One must pay rent for books, so that their initial cost, as in the case of many other possessions, is sometimes smaller than their upkeep. This is one reason, among others, why a lending library is such a boon. But a lending library has one great drawback: it makes for casual acquaintanceship with books which should be friends and constant companions. One may use a lending library to borrow books which contain so little meat and inspiration that a single, rapid reading of them is sufficient. Such books, if purchased, should be read and disposed of, in order to make room for permanent inhabitants of the bookshelf.

No matter how small the home, it has room—or must make room—for a few books. We shall set the number of these at about fifty, small enough not to be a burden, yet large enough to permit variety and include basic volumes in many of the numerous phases of Jewish life. This, moreover, is to be a bookshelf for adults; a children's library requires a separate discussion.

NATURE OF THE BOOKSHELF

There are bookshelves in Jewish homes which are a drawback rather than a stimulant to further Jewish interest. This is the case where the bookshelf represents merely an accumulation of children's textbooks or story books, thus setting limits to the continued education of both children and parents. Sometimes bookshelves become cluttered up with old periodicals. There are, of course, periodicals which a Jewish home should receive; but, apart from an occasional article, they should not be kept. Finally, there are the multi-volumed works which, though very useful and culturally important, are forbidding in aspect and occupy so much room as to exclude more easily readable and more stimulating volumes.

Encyclopedias, for example, present a serious problem, and the advisability of purchasing them should be carefully weighed. There are two sets which, from the point of view of an American Jewish home, may be considered. *The Jewish Encyclopedia,* published in 1906 and consisting of twelve heavy tomes, is a very scholarly and supremely important work. *The Universal Jewish Encyclopedia,* published from 1939 to 1943 and consisting of ten handsome volumes, can also be very helpful; it is, in fact, more interestingly written than its predecessor. Were the discussion here concerned with a Jewish library, the purchase of both would be recommended. For a bookshelf in a home, however, where an encyclopedia will form 20 percent of the bookshelf's population the question is open to debate. Much depends upon the interest of the individual home. Some people have need for a constant reference book and can stand the dry, concise form in which encyclopedias necessarily present their information. Others have to have their information in more vibrant terms. Where there is room for the usual shelf over and above an encyclopedia, the possession of one or the other of them is highly advisable. Where the room is limited and the need for a reference work not too great, a collection of other, single-volumed works may be preferable.

A partial solution to the problem lies in one or the other of the existing one-volume encyclopedias: Cecil Roth's *Standard Jewish Encyclopedia* is the most inclusive. It offers the essential facts and dates on a large number of subjects in which the layman, as regards Jewish culture, may be interested.

What is true of encyclopedias is true to an even greater extent of other sets of books. In recent years the Soncino Press of England produced an excellent and attractively bound English translation of most of the Talmud as well as of the Midrash and the Zohar. It is impossible to overestimate the importance of such works. Every Jew who can afford the price and every Jewish home that can afford the shelf space should have them if only as reminders of our vast cultural treasures. In the great majority of cases, however, these sets will be purely decorative. In the competition for space on the bookshelf, their lure should be resisted.

The bookshelf should, on the whole, consist of such books as are: (a) purchased for a single reading and then disposed of; (b) useful for re-reading because of their inspirational value; (c) good for occasional reading and reference. Finally, few books on any subject deserve an absolutely permanent home on the bookshelf. To be sure, a new book is not necessarily a better book; but when a better book does appear, one must steel his heart, open his purse, and part with the old friend in exchange for the new. The bookshelf must be kept as fresh and useful as possible.

WHAT TO REMEMBER

The bookshelf in the Jewish home has a significance beyond the walls of the household. American Israel is now in process of developing personality and a culture of its own. It is possible for us, under existing circumstances, to inaugurate a Golden Age of cultural activity which may rival the famous Golden Age of the Jews in Spain. This means the encouragement of literary productivity. There will be no authors if there are no readers and no purchasers of books. Authors are human; they will turn their talents to fields where they are appreciated. A Jewish bookshelf, therefore, is not only an index of the Jewish foundations of the home, but also proof of its cooperation in the task of building an American Jewish community.

II

We turn now to the actual books which should find their place on the Jewish shelf. A warning is in order: the judgments offered below are subjective, at least to some extent, although the writer is trying hard to be absolutely impartial and to view the books from the standpoint of the prospective shelf-builder. It may be moreover, that, because of variations in interest and in preferences for style, readers will take issue with advice here given. That is as it should be. Literary criticism is not a science. Except for books of reference and scholarship, books are made to appeal to different tastes. All one can ask is that the books named below be given consideration as representing one man's judgment on what other people should read.

"MUST" BOOKS ON THE SHELF

The Jewish bookshelf must contain a Bible. It is our opinion that the shelf must have a Hebrew Bible in addition to one in English translation. Even if not a single inmate of the household reads Hebrew, a fair-sized, well-bound Hebrew Bible must be there for sentimental reasons and in the hope that sentiment may lead to curiosity and curiosity to action in the form of study. Preferably the English Bible should be the one translated by American Jewish scholars for the Jewish Publication Society (1917) ; a Leeser edition is second choice. But a copy of the new translation of the Torah (JPS, 1962) should also be there; and in time, when the entire Bible is translated, the new translation should replace the old. But under no circumstances should a Jewish home be content with a Christian edition of the Bible, with its insistence on Christological references. Thus, if the Bible is used—as it should be—whether to read two chapters a day, in accordance with the custom now urged upon Jews everywhere, or to read from it occasionally at random, an impartial interpretation of it will rest in the reader's mind. Those interested may also add the Pentateuch and Haftarahs with the charming commentary prepared by Dr. Joseph H. Hertz, Chief Rabbi of Great Britain. Every Jewish bookshelf must, as a matter of course, contain a daily and Sabbath prayer book. Those edited by Ben Zion Bokser or by Philip Birnbaum or the one edited by the late Rabbi Joseph Hertz, will be found easiest to handle and follow; there are others. The ideas underlying Jewish prayer are interestingly discussed in Evelyn Garfield's brief volume, *The Service of the Heart*. Even though the "Ethics of the Fathers" (Pirke Abot) may be found in these prayer books, it may be well to have it in separate form, so as to encourage the reading of this remarkable collection of wise counsel; the best in this respect is the edition by Judah Goldin, called *The Living Talmud* because Dr. Goldin used the Ethics of the Fathers to illustrate rabbinic thought and method.

A Jewish bookshelf should have a comprehensive history of the Jews. For many years, H. Graetz's *History of the Jews,* in six volumes, was the only work one could recommend to the non-scholarly reader. In more recent years a number of one-volume histories have appeared. If the *History of the Jewish People* by Margolis and Marx is found too dry because of its encyclopedic nature, one can turn to the single volumes with more or less the same title by A. L. Sachar, or Cecil Roth, or Solomon Grayzel. The last-named does not cover the biblical period. It makes mandatory the acquisition of H. M. Orlinksy's *Ancient Israel,* which should be on the shelf in any case.

BOOKS FOR OCCASIONAL
READING AND REFERENCE

Encyclopedic reference books have already been discussed, yet there is one book of that type, the *American Jewish Year Book,* which deserves separate discussion both because of its contents and because of the peculiar problem which it presents. It is the only volume in which a great variety of information about current Jewish life may be found. It contains statistics on Jews in the United States and abroad, lists of organizations, a calendar, and above all, a summary by country of important events during the preceding year. Obviously it cannot be an interesting book in the ordinary sense. Even though attempts are made to add to its interest by including articles on important subjects and men, the *Year Book* remains a book to consult, not to read. To a Jew conscious of his Jewishness and concerned with the process of Jewish life, it is invaluable. But it must be recognized for what it is—a reference book, ephemeral by its very nature , to be discarded as soon as the year is up and another volume appears. People hate to throw away a well-bound volume. The result is that an accumulation of *Year Books* becomes a burden, an annoyance, an occupant of space which could be put to better use. The only sensible procedure for the non-specialist is to keep the latest one or two volumes and give the others away to a library or relegate them to the subcellar.

The bookshelf should have something on Jewish legends. It is not enough to know what the biblical story relates about a hero, a villain, or an event; one should also know what later Jewish tradition taught about them. Professor Louis Ginzberg's *Legends of the Jews,* a work of peerless scholarship, reads easily. Again, it is a pity from the bookshelf's point of view that this work consists of four volumes of text, two volumes of learned notes, and one volume of index. The smaller bookshelf might perhaps be satisfied with the first four volumes or with their abbreviation into a single volume which is now obtainable.

A book or two on the Bible should find a place on the Jewish bookshelf. Max L. Margolis wrote a small but extraordinarily useful volume called *The Hebrew Scriptures in the Making*, which describes the process by which the Bible became what it is. Robert H. Pfeiffer was a Christian and something of a radical in Bible criticism; his *Introduction to the Old Testament* is, however, an exceptionally useful book. In this connection, it is well to take note of Moshe Greenberg's summarization in English in one volume called *The Religion of Israel*, of the seven Hebrew volumes by the late Ezekiel Kaufmann.

There are two books dealing with the rabbinic teachings which the bookshelf should contain. One is George F. Moore's *Judaism in the First Centuries of the Christian Era*, consisting of two volumes of text and one, not altogether essential for the average reader, of notes. Professor Moore was a Christian, but no Jew has written quite so comprehensive and understanding a description of the age and work of the Scribes and the Tannaim. The second book is *Everyman's Talmud* by the English rabbi, A. Cohen. It describes the contents of the Talmud topically and in simple, straight-forward style.

This section of the bookshelf should also contain a usable edition of Chief Rabbi Hertz's *A Book of Jewish Thoughts*, which makes excellent reading when one's spirits are low. Some history of the Jews in America also belongs here, but it is difficult to recommend any one specific volume. The usual bookshelf builder will have to be satisfied with Rufus Learsi's *The Jews in America: A History*. For a discussion of the Jews in America today, the reader must turn to Oscar I. Janowsky's *The American Jew: A Reappraisal*.

Whoever is interested in the growth of Jewish literature will want occasionally to look into the encyclopedic work, *A History of Jewish Literature* by Meyer Waxman, in four bulky volumes. It is a mine of information, becoming more detailed as it approaches modern times. There is as yet no one-volume history of the subject worth recommending, though portions of the field have been treated in single volumes, some of which will be mentioned below. One, however, must be noted at once. Shalom Spiegel's *Hebrew Reborn* is an exceptionally good and well-written discussion of the revival of Hebrew literature since the Mendelssohn era. Unfortunately, it stops with the 1920s, just when Hebrew literature entered upon a new era.

Till a generation ago every Jewish home was provided with a copy of the *Shulhan Arukh,* that famous code of laws by which Jewish life was regulated. It was consulted regularly. Nowadays, when problems of religious practice arise, it seems easier to telephone the rabbi. Whatever advantages this may have in saving labor, it has no advantages from the point of view of Jewish unity. We therefore list a number of books on the Jewish religion, leaving it to the reader to choose those which he considers most useful. As to the *Shulhan Arukh* itself, a number of translations of its abbreviated edition are in existence, the most easily available being H. E. Goldin's *Code of Jewish Law* (Hebrew and English in three volumes, English alone in one volume). Those who feel the need for discussion and motivation of Jewish observances, rather than for listing of them, might turn to the following: Levi and Kaplan's *Across the Threshhold: a Guide for the Jewish Homemaker,* which emphasizes the woman's part in Jewish home-building, and to either Ben Zion Bokser's *Judaism: Profile of a Faith,* or Arthur Hertzberg's *Judaism,* or Leon Roth's *Judaism: A Portrait.*

A worthwhile series of essays, with an orthodox Jewish emphasis, was edited and published in three volumes by Leo Jung, under the general heading of *The Jewish Library.* The Reform attitude is expressed in Kaufmann Kohler's *Jewish Theology.* Having considered these last two items, the interested person should make an effort to acquaint himself also with the views of the Reconstructionist movement, on which the best available are the works by Professor M. M. Kaplan, the most recent being *The Purpose and Meaning of Jewish Existence,* where the Reconstructionist approach is presented in historical setting among interpretations of Judaism.

It is a great pity that there is not, at least in the opinion of this writer, any simply-presented history of Judaism. Bernard J. Bamberger's *The Story of Judaism* presents Judaism historically from

the viewpoint of Reform. The volume *Great Jewish Ideas,* edited
for the B'nai B'rith by E.. A. Millgram, does so topically. Moshe
Davis' *The Emergence of Conservative Judaism* tells part of the
story for the United States. Sooner or later, however, the most
historical of religions will have a history written about it which
may satisfy the conservative reader.

The bookshelf should have representative titles in various
branches of Jewish religion, culture and history. It is only fair to
warn the bookshelf builder, however, that such books are usually
not written to be interesting, but to be informative. Thus Salo
W. Baron's two works—*A Social and Religious History of the Jews*
(of which ten volumes have appeared by 1966) and *The Jewish
Community* (three voumes) —though distinguished discussions of
their respective subjects, are too ponderous in content and approach for the usual reader. Much the same may be said about
the distinguished collection of essays edited by Louis Finkelstein
under the title *The Jews: Their History, Culture and Religion*
(two volumes) . Add to these Julius Guttmann's *Philosophies of
Judaism,* as a not-too-difficult history of Jewish thought. The
more scholarly-minded ought to have them. On the other hand,
every American Jew should want to know how his nation-wide
and local community functions, and therefore should have at hand
the history of his local community, if he lives in one of the dozen
or so Jewish communities about which histories have been written. The Janowsky volume has already been mentioned, and one
might add Bezalel Sherman's *The Jews Within American Society*
or Marshall Sklare's *The Jews: Social Patterns of an American
Group.*

The titles of the following very readable and useful books
clearly indicate their contents. Bevan and Singer's *The Legacy of
Israel* is a solid evaluation of what the Jews have given to the culture of the western world. Cecil Roth's *The Jewish Contribution
to Civilization* deals with the same subject topically: Letters, Art,
Scientific Progress, etc. Anti-Semitism, the other aspect of the
Jew's relation to the world about him, has brought forth an extensive literature, though from this writer's point of view, not a

very helpful one. H. Valentin's *Anti-Semitism, Historically and Critically Examined,* is the best concise study of the subject. By its side, as an interesting Jewish interpretation of anti-Semitism, one may place Maurice Samuel's little volume, *The Great Hatred.*

The historical foundations of current affairs will be found in the following. Marvin Lowenthal's *The Jews of Germany* and J. R. Marcus' *Rise and Destiny of the German Jew* deal with the same subject with slightly different emphases. Solomon Liptzin has given us a discussion of the German Jewish tragedy from the literary point of view. His *Germany's Stepchildren* is an engrossing story of an attempt at adjustment which American Jewry may take to heart. A. A. Neuman's *The Jews in Spain* tells of another famous Jewish community which came to a sudden end. It should be supplemented by Yitzhak Baer's *The Jews in Christian Spain.* Simon Dubnow's *History of the Jews in Russia and Poland* tells the history of the third community which, to a large extent, laid the foundations for our Jewish life in America. Unfortunately, it carries the story only to World War I. The volume in English on the East European Jewries which carries the story down to the present day is S. W. Baron's *The Russian Jew Under Tsars and Soviets.* There are many reminiscences, autobiographies and semi-fictional portrayals, but no inclusive single volume of this type of material that one can refer to for the tragic events in the 1930's and 1940's. One example of this that does come to mind is Alexander Donat's *The Holocaust Kingdom.*

The modern Jew also shows an altogether understandable curiosity about the rise of Christianity. Such a person might turn to the following three volumes: Joseph Klausner's *Jesus of Nazareth,* the same author's more recent *From Jesus to Paul* and S. Zeitlin's *Who Crucified Jesus?* Of exceptional importance, since we live in the midst of a Christian civilization, are Leo Baeck's *Judaism and Christianity* and *This People Israel,* as well as Abba Hillel Silver's *Where Judaism Differed.* One or another of these books, or all of them, or any of a growing number of others, may help clarify the differences between Judaism and Christianity and save the reader from the superficiality of assuming that all religions are alike and that Judaism has nothing distinctive to offer.

The following deal with narrower subjects in interesting fashion. Joshua Trachtenberg, in *Jewish Magic and Superstition,* analyzes the popular beliefs and fears of the medieval Jew. Zevi Idelsohn, in his *Jewish Music,* presents an interesting history of Jewish melody, chiefly religious. For modern Jewish song one should go to Coopersmith's *Songs of Zion.* Finally, this section ought to contain one or more books describing the holidays and their celebration. H. Schauss's *The Jewish Festivals* is the best all-inclusive book in the field. There are also interesting volumes, each dealing with a Jewish holiday: *Hanukkah, Feast of Lights,* by Emily Solis-Cohen; *Sabbath, Day of Delight,* by Abraham E. Millgram; *Purim, Feast of Esther,* by Philip Goodman, and the same author's *Passover.* They contain essays, poems, stories, art, humor and music connected with the occasions which they respectively describe.

The shelf should have a book or two on Israel; yet it is hard to choose any one that promises a degree of permanence. Since a visit to Israel is always either a pleasant memory or a hope, a guide book is desirable. Joan Comay's *Everyman's Guide to Israel* is currently most useful, although it bears only a vague resemblance to the usual guide to other countries. Walter Eytan's *The First Ten Years* (a diplomatic history) may already be somewhat antiquated, but it still offers a very useful picture of the turbulent beginnings of the State. The shelf-builder must be on a constant lookout for better and more up-to-date books in this area.

In the last ten years a new field of interest has been opened up through the literary discoveries in the caves along the Dead Sea. Books on the subject have been appearing constantly. The most useful reference book for the layman is Theodor H. Gaster's *The Dead Sea Scriptures.*

BOOKS TO BE READ AND RE-READ

A number of books and collections of essays on Jewish subjects deserve a place on the bookshelf because they are informative and inspiring. The contents of some of them have a high place in the history of Jewish thought. *The Essays of Ahad Ha'am* will prove fascinating to an intelligent reader. Also so each of the following anthologies contains material which will undoubtedly be read more than once: L. I. Newman's *Hasidic Anthology;* A. E. Mill-gram's *Anthology of Medieval Hebrew Literature,* and Leo Schwarz's *Jewish Caravan* and *Golden Treasury.* There is exceptionally little overlapping among these books. Original essays, whether collected into a full book or merely placed side by side, are the first two volumes of S. Schechter's *Studies in Judaism;* Robert Gordis's *The Root and the Branch,* and Stuart Rosenberg's *America is Different.* The discriminating shelf builder will not omit that wonderful collection of essays, poetry, fiction and art which appeared in the *Menorah Journal* and was anthologized by Leo W. Schwarz, under the title *The Menorah Treasury.*

BIOGRAPHIES

Biographies and autobiographies present a unique problem. No two people are likely to be interested in the same type of biography or the sort of subject whose biography was written. Jewish history is rich in personalities: warriors and martyrs, thinkers and men of affairs, statesmen and pioneers, law-makers and philanthropists. Consider Leo W. Schwarz's *Memoirs of My People,* or the more recent collection of excerpts from American autobiographies made by Jacob R. Marcus for the 19th century and Harold Ribalow for the first part of the 20th; you can have no better examples of the richness of Jewish personality. If one adds the biblical and medieval Jewish experience, the variety becomes staggering. Yet Jewish biographies can be a source of great inspiration. The only device one can give is for the reader to be alert for the appearance of new ones. It is hard to refrain from recommending as a more or less permanent denizen of the home shelf such a biography as Alex Bein's *Theodor Herzl,* who laid the foundations for a movement and a State. But there are literally dozens and dozens of other biographies from which to choose.

NOVELS OF UNUSUAL
SIGNIFICANCE

Much the same can be said about fiction. New ones constantly appear. What is more, it is beginning to be difficult to distinguish

between Jewish and general fiction in which Jewish character and
Jewish life are portrayed. All one can do is to offer an opinion as
to which novels of the past stand out and may deserve re-reading.
Israel Zangwill's *Children of the Ghetto* and *Dreamers of the
Ghetto* are already part of the modern Jew's heritage. So are Ludwig Lewisohn's *The Island Within* and Irving Fineman's *Hear, Ye
Sons,* and Sholem Asch's *Kiddush Ha-Shem,* Irving Fineman's *Jacob,* and Thomas Mann's trilogy about Joseph. Leon Feuchtwanger's three novels with Josephus as their hero are also historical and intellectual, but with more action and drama. At the
other extreme Abe Cahan's *The Rise of David Levinsky* and
Henry Roth's *Call It Sleep* are exceptional novels about America.

A number of books which could not be classified in the above
categories should also be on the bookshelf. Among them belong
the selected poems by each of the three poets of the Spanish Golden Age published in the Schiff Classics Series: Zangwill and
Davidson's *Gabirol;* Solis-Cohen and Brody's *Moses Ibn Ezra;*
and Salaman's *Halevi.* Among the unclassifiable is also the charming volume on *The World of Sholom Aleichem* by Maurice
Samuel.

There are other books, many of them. It is probably as much as
the writer's reputation, if not his life, is worth not to have mentioned them. Bad memory may account for some of the omissions
and bad judgment for the rest. May the authors, living and dead,
forgive me. There is, however, one consolation, namely, that reading is a habit; indeed, it can become an all-absorbing habit. It
creeps up unawares and then becomes a person's chief delight.
With surprisingly little practice, moreover, the reader learns to
criticize and evaluate. The books he has missed in the past bring
themselves to his attention, as though by magic. If this list, therefore, starts some people off on the beautiful and instructive journey through bookland, if such people learn to look to their bookshelf for aid in understanding and enjoying life, they will soon
learn to go beyond the advice given here. The important thing is
to find a bright and cozy corner, near a not-too-comfortable arm-
chair, and there fix the household's Jewish bookshelf.

BIBLIOGRAPHY

What follows is a list of the books mentioned above, with the necessary bibliographical information. It is well to repeat at this point that not all of these books need be purchased; nor should they be considered the only ones deserving the attention of the reader. Moreover, a fair number of them may be had in paperback. The advisability of having a paperback as a permanent denizen of the homeshelf is open to question; it is a matter of taste or of necessity. The volumes available in paperback at this writing are marked with an asterisk.

JPS is, of course, the abbreviation for the Jewish Publication Society, with its headquarters in Philadelphia. UAHC stands for the Union of American Hebrew Congregations, with headquarters in New York. The place of publication is given below only if it is outside New York City.

Ahad Ha'am, *Selected Essays*. Tr. by Leon Somon. JPS, 1912.

American Jewish Year Book, JPS, 1899– .

Asch, Sholom, * *Kiddush Ha-Shem.*

Baeck, Leo, * *Judaism and Christianity.* JPS, 1958.

Baeck, Leo, *This People, Israel.* Holt, Rinehart and Winston, and JPS, 1964.

Baer, Yitzhak, *The Jews of Christian Spain.* 2 vols. JPS, 1961, 1965.

Bamberger, Bernard J. * *The Story of Judaism.* Union of American Hebrew Congregations, 1957.

Baron, S. W., *The Russian Jew Under Tsars and Soviets.* Macmillan, 1965.

Baron, S. W., *The Jewish Community.* 3 vols. JPS, 1942.

Baron, S. W., *A Social and Religious History of the Jews.* 10 vols. Columbia University Press and JPS, 1951–1965.

Bein, Alex, * *Theodor Herzl.* JPS, 1940.

Bevan, E. R. and Singer, Charles, *The Legacy of Israel.* Oxford University Press, 1944.

Bible, Bible, Hebrew and English, tr. by Isaac Leeser. Torah, JPS, Hertz ed.

B'nai B'rith, *Great Jewish Ideas.* E. A. Millgram, ed.

Bokser, Ben Zion, *Judaism, Profile of a Faith.* Knopf and Burning Bush Press, 1963.

Buber, Martin, *Tales of the Hasidim.* 2 vols. Schocken, 1947–48.

Cahan, Abe, * *The Rise of David Levinsky*. Harper and Bros., 1917 (reprinted later).

Cohen, A., *Everyman's Talmud*. Dutton, 1949.

Comay, Joan, *Everyone's Guide to Israel*. Doubleday, 1962.

Coopersmith, *Songs of Zion*. Behrman, 1942.

Davis, Moshe, *The Emergence of Conservative Judaism*. JPS, 1963.

Donat, Alexander, *The Holocaust Kingdom*. Holt, Rinehart and Winston, 1965.

Encyclopedia, The Jewish. 12 vols. Funk and Wagnalls, 1906.

Encyclopedia, Standard Jewish, ed. Cecil Roth. Doubleday, 1959.

Encyclopedia, The Universal Jewish. 10 vols. 1939.

Dubnow, Simon, *History of the Jews in Russia and Poland*. 3 vols. JPS, 1916.

Eytan, Walter, *The First Ten Years*. Simon and Schuster, 1958.

Feuchtwanger, Leon, *Josephus* (1932); *The Jew of Rome* (1936); *Josephus and the Emperor* (1942). Viking Press.

Fineman, Irving, *Jacob*. Random House, 1941.

Finkelstein, Louis, ed., *The Jews, Their History, Culture and Religion*. 2 vols. Harper, and JPS, 1960.

Garfiel, Evelyn, *The Service of the Heart: A Guide to the Jewish Prayer Book*. Yoseloff, 1958.

Gaster, Theodor H., * *The Dead Sea Scriptures*. Doubleday (Anchor original), 1956.

Ginzberg, Louis, *Legends of the Jews*. 7 vols. JPS, 1913–1938; Simon and Schuster and JPS, one volume, 1956.

Goldin, H. E., *Code of Jewish Law*. 3 vols. (Hebrew and English); one volume (English).

Goodman, Philip, *The Purim Anthology*. JPS, 1949. *The Passover Anthology*. JPS, 1961.

Gordis, Robert, *The Root and the Branch*. University of Chicago Press, 1962.

Graetz, H., *History of the Jews*. 6 vols. JPS, 1898.

Grayzel, Solomon, *A History of the Jews*. JPS, 1953.

Greenberg, Moshe, *The Religion of Israel*. Chicago University Press, 1960.

Guttmann, Julius, *Philosophies of Judaism*. Holt, Rinehart and Winston, and JPS, 1963.

Hertz, Joseph, *A Book of Jewish Thoughts*. Jewish Welfare Board, 1943.

Hertzberg, Arthur, *Judaism*. George Braziller, 1961.

Idelsohn, Zevi, *Jewish Music in its Historical Development*. Henry Holt & Co., 1929.

Janowsky, Oscar I., *The American Jew: A Reappraisal.* JPS, 1965.

Jung, Leo, *The Jewish Library.* 3 vols. Bloch, 1928, 1930, 1934.

Kaplan, M. M., *Purpose and Meaning of Jewish Existence.* JPS, 1964.

Klausner, Joseph, *Jesus of Nazareth.* Macmillan, 1925.

Klausner, Joseph, *From Jesus to Paul.* Macmillan, 1943.

Kohler, Kaufmann, *Jewish Theology.* UAHC, 1943.

Learsi, Rufus, *The Jews in America: A History.* World, 1954.

Levi, S. and Kaplan, Sylvia, * *Across the Threshhold: Guide for the Jewish Homemaker.* Farrar, Straus, 1959. (Paperback, Schocken).

Lewisohn, Ludwig, *The Island Within.* Boni and Liveright, 1925.

Liptzin, Solomon, *Germany's Stepchildren.* JPS, 1944.

Lowenthal, Marvin, *The Jews of Germany.* JPS, 1936.

Mann, Thomas, *Joseph and His Brothers.* 2 vols. Alfred Knopf, N.Y., 1934; *Joseph in Egypt.* Alfred Knopf, 1938.

Marcus, Jacob R., *Memoirs of American Jews, 1775–1865.* 3 vols. JPS, 1955.

Marcus, J. R., *Rise and Destiny of the German Jew.* UAHC, 1934.

Margolis, Max L., *The Hebrew Scriptures in the Making.* JPS, 1922.

Margolis, Max, and Marx, Alexander, * *History of the Jewish People.* JPS, 1927.

Millgram, A. E., *Anthology of Medieval Hebrew Literature.* Burning Bush Press.

Millgram, A. E., *Sabbath, Day of Delight.* JPS, 1944.

Moore, George F., *Judaism in the First Centuries of the Christian Era.* 3 vols. Harvard University Press, 1927.

Neuman, A. A., *The Jews of Spain.* 2 vols. JPS, 1942.

Orlinsky, H. M., * *Ancient Israel.* Cornell University Press, 1954.

Pfeiffer, Robert H., *Introduction to the Old Testament.* Harper and Row, 1948.

Ribalow, Harold, *Autobiographies of American Jews.* JPS, 1965.

Roth, Cecil, *The Jewish Contribution to Civilization.* UAHC, 1940.

Roth, Henry, * *Call It Sleep.* Pageant Books, Paterson, N.J., 1960.

Roth, Leon, *Judaism, A Portrait.* Viking, 1961.

Rosenberg, Stuart, *America Is Different.* Thomas Nelson and Sons, 1964.

Salaman, Nina, and Brody, H., *Yehudah Halevi.* JPS, 1924.

Samuel, Maurice, * *The World of Sholem Aleichem.* Alfred Knopf, 1943.

Schauss, H., *The Jewish Festivals.* UAHC, 1938.

Schechter, S., * *Studies in Judaism.* JPS.

Schwarz, Leo W., *Jewish Caravan.* Farrar & Rinehart, 1935. *Golden Treasury of Jewish Literature.* Farrar & Rinehart, 1937. *The Menorah*

Treasury. JPS, 1965. * *Great Ages and Ideas of the Jewish People.* Modern Library, 1962.

Sherman, Bezalel, *The Jew within American Society.* Detroit, Wayne State University Press, 1961.

Silver, Abba Hillel, *Where Judaism Differed.* Macmillan, and JPS, 1956.

Sklare, Marshall, *The Jews: Social Patterns of an American Group.* Free Press, Glencoe, Ill., 1958.

Shulhan Arukh: H. E. Goldin, *Code of Jewish Law.* Star Hebrew Book Co., 1928.

Solis-Cohen, Emily, *Hanukkah, Feast of Lights.* JPS, 1940.

Solis-Cohen, Solomon and Brody, H., *Moses ibn Ezra.* JPS, 1934.

Spiegel, Shalom, * *Hebrew Reborn.* JPS, 1962. (1930)

Talmud; Judah Goldin, * *The Living Talmud: The Wisdom of the Fathers.* New American Library (Mentor), 1957.

Trachtenberg, Joshua, *Jewish Magic and Superstition.* Behrman, 1939.

Waxman, Meyer, *A History of Jewish Literature.* 4 vols. Bloch, 1930–1941.

Zangwill, Israel and Davidson, Israel, *Solomon ibn Gabriol.* JPS, 1923.

Zeitlin, Solomon, *Who Crucified Jesus?* Bloch, 1965 (1942)

The Torch, Winter, 1965.

Dr. Grayzel, Rabbi, editor, historian and educator, was Editor of the Jewish Publication Society of America from 1939 to 1966 and is now Professor of History at Dropsie College, Philadelphia, Pa. He taught at Gratz College in Philadelphia and became president of its Board of Overseers. He has served as President of the National Jewish Book Council and of the Board of Jewish Education, Philadelphia Branch, United Synagogue of America. He is a frequent contributor to the Jewish Exponent. *He has written* History of the Jews *and* History of Contemporary Jews.

"TO STRENGTHEN THE VALUES OF JUDAISM"

ARTHUR S. BRUCKMAN

If we were to formulate in one phrase the purposes of the National Federation of Jewish Men's Clubs, that phrase would be "to strengthen the values of Judaism." The "sine qua non" of a program to bring such purpose to fruition is adult Jewish education.

The National Federation has recognized this need and has for the past few years made adult education the keystone of its program. We have, however, only scratched the surface of our possibilities, and must now re-examine our program in the light of our past experiences. . . . .

The problem how to properly fulfill this function, however, is not a simple one. Our men's clubs for the greater part consist of second generation Americans. It is the group whose Jewish education has been most neglected. Their Jewish education, which usually ended at their Bar Mitzvah, took place in the old Cheder. This was not entirely the student's fault. The Jewish community was not properly equipped to provide the facilities for proper Jewish education, parents were too busy becoming Americanized, and very frequently the parent or the child associated Jewish education with something foreign and not compatible with American ways. The entire stress of Jewish education was on the children, with next to no provision for secondary Jewish education for the youth and for adult Jewish education. For a large group of our men's clubs are either entirely uninformed Jewishly or have smatterings of information picked up at random.

Education to most people is a means to an end; therefore, they associate study with work, something arduous and to be avoided. This must be borne in mind in planning that part of the program which is intended to create a desire for formal Jewish education.

Once this desire is created, then what would at first seem arduous and burdensome would no longer so appear.

Our program would depend upon what we deem most important for stress and emphasis and what our objectives are—immediate and ultimate.

Although our roots are three thousand years old, we do not live in the past. We are not ancestor worshipers. Our Jewish Education must be a relevant education, and our past only important to the extent it is a living past, an evolving component of the present and a guide to the future. Its function must be that of transmitting the social and cultural heritage of the Jew to sustain the present and future Jewish community.

Our objectives for an educational program are all inclusive. In addition to the general objectives of Jewish education for child and adult, we must educate the parents to take their place, as the teachers of their children, in the home. The synagogue and religious school should be regarded as the subsidiary agency in the religious educational process and the home the primary. If the parents are to provide conditions necessary for religious growth in the home, they themselves need have the necessary background for strengthening their own religious values. They need knowledge and Jewish attitudes so that they can develop a positive Judaism within their children. This will do away with Jewish self-hate, provide them with an inner security as a bulwark to anti-Semitism, and give a positive feeling of belonging to Klal Israel, and ability to live with dignity in a Jewish environment in a Christian world.

Dr. Luther E. Woodward of the National Committee on Mental Hygiene, known for his studies in psychology and religious development, interpreting mental health needs as revealed in military statistics, recently said that increased interest in religious education is necessary to make for greater personal stability. Religion must be portrayed and practiced as an integrating force.

Religious education and secular Jewish education cannot be segregated. Our educational program should tend to develop a greater desire to participate as a Jew, in the synagogue, as well as in the home and the community. Judaism is a totality. Our people cannot be educated merely for worship, or for philanthropy, or for Jewish nationalism, or for Jewish culture. Our past, the living past, was concerned with the people of Israel, its land, and its Torah. Our present and future must have the same trinity, and our Jewish education must be established on these fundamentals integrated with our American environment.

Our approach to adult education must not be merely indoctrination, education in things Jewish, but the integration of the totality of Judaism in our American environment. The confused Jew must be adjusted and prepared to live as a Jew in his American environment and the educational program should not only be for the purpose of transmitting the Jewish heritage to the next generation for the perpetuation of Jewish life and culture, institutions and ideals. It must have in view to provide the Jew with the means to interpret the past or our tradition in terms to be compatible with or relevant to contemporary American life, to understand the problems that the Jew has to face in a world that has changed from the time of Rabbinic literature; the Jew must be educated to become a lay leader in Jewish communal life. Adult education must include a study of civic and world problems to the end that we have an informed and intelligent American Jew able to assume his share of responsibility as an American, and to build a better America.

To carry out such a program is indeed difficult. It presents a two-fold problem. One is to create a desire or interest in adult Jewish education, and second to carry out the program itself.

The negative factors present in adult Jewish life makes the first problem more formidable. To overcome the apathy of our people and to awaken them from their lethargy and smug self-satisfaction is the immediate need. The men's club is a ready nucleus for the education program since it is a synagogue affiliate and we can assume the desire is there, either in a lesser or greater degree.

The educational program, however, in most men's clubs, seems to lack an orientation program. At the present time, the educational facilities are limited to speakers or forums or a course in Bible or Talmud by the Rabbi and an annual visit by a privileged few to a Layman's Institute. No consideration seems to be given to the background of the audience subjected to the lecture so that they can derive sufficient benefit from it.

It seems to me that there is need to orient the comparatively uninformed to the history of the Jewish People. Not political history, except where it affected subsequent Jewish life, but the stream of Jewish life, so that the present can be interpreted in the light of the past, so that present institutions, symbols, and conditions will have meaning. Religion, philosophy, literature, rabbinic teaching, Zion, economic and social conditions, Jewish and non-Jewish, Gentile influence and similar factors affecting Jewish life are part of such history and must be included. Such a course must be merely a bird's-eye view so the present can be connected with the past, and make such past relevant to the future. Such a course must be by necessity sketchy, leaving for future study those phases which have attracted the attention of the group or individuals. Some may desire to study Bible, Talmud, Zionism, Rabbinic literature, political or economic history of the Jew in America and elsewhere, post-war problems, anti-Semitism, American religious and secular institutions, etc. A complete syllabus should be prepared with reading and reference material, so that in the smaller congregation it can be led by the rabbi or qualified laymen. I believe such a course would lay the foundation and also inculcate a desire for further study.

The Layman's Institute forms a most important part of the program of men's clubs. However, it must be expanded on a regional basis to render it more accessible to the clubs.

The individual club should individually or in groups sponsor planned lecture series by qualified lecturers in lieu of isolated "name" speakers. Forums and seminars on questions of Jewish interest should be added to the program as well as the traditional groups to study Talmud and Bible.

Social functions can be utilized for educational purposes by having them revolve about a Jewish festival or holiday.

The men's clubs should urge the reading of Jewish books, listening to Jewish and Hebrew music, promote the use of Jewish art. Many interesting programs can be built up along these lines. The men's clubs should sponsor a program for Jewish Book Month and Jewish Music Week. They should sponsor in their congregation a library on Judaica. They should urge their members to listen to radio programs of Jewish interest such as the Eternal Light program.

This informal type of adult education, consisting of forums, discussions, music, radio programs, celebrations, and other cultural programs arranged by the men's clubs serve to keep the members at least partially informed on questions of Jewish interest and creates an awareness of their Jewishness.

These suggestions for a program hardly scratch the surface of what the men's clubs can do to further Jewish Adult Education. By a well-planned program, the National Federation of Jewish Men's Clubs will be instrumental in developing in and through the Men's Clubs the lay leadership which is so necessary for our Jewish Community.

The Torch, May, 1946

Mr. Bruckman, lay leader in Adult Jewish Education and communal affairs, is Associate Editor of The Torch. *He is a former president of the National Federation of Jewish Men's Clubs; of Temple Emanuel, Parkchester, N.Y., and of the Parkchester Y. M. and Y. W. H. A. He served as Vice-President of the Metropolitan Region of the United Synagogue of America and as president of the N. Y. Board of Education of the United Synagogue. He has been closely associated with the National Jewish Welfare Board and the Jewish Center Lecture Bureau. Mr. Bruckman is a lawyer and is currently Secretary of the Synagogue Council of America.*

THE PLACE OF THE PULPIT
IN ADULT EDUCATION

DAVID ARONSON

My subject is "The Place of the Pulpit in Adult Education." I
might have added a question mark to it. I am reminded of that
old winemaker who in his will to his children told them, "Remember it is possible to make wine out of grapes, too." We have
reached a stage where it is necessary to consider whether it is possible for the pulpit to be an educational instrument, too. As a
matter of fact, it is a real challenge. I have been thinking for
some time as to what is the place of the sermon, the *Derasha*, in
the set-up of the synagogue. I need not tell you that the sermon as
part of a service, sandwiched in the middle of the service, is relatively new in the old, old history of the synagogue. It came to us,
probably, from the Protestant-Lutheran churches. It was unknown in Eastern Europe. The rabbi was a teacher. As a rule he
conducted his teaching lessons Shabbas afternoon. In many cases,
since people went to shul every day, three times a day, he had an
opportunity to teach a select group in Talmud before the evening
service, every evening or a few times a week. Whenever a sermon
was given it was given not at a service, but in the afternoon. As a
rule, the rabbi delivered a *Derasha* only twice a year: on the
Shabbas before Pesach and on the Shabbas between Rosh
Hashana and Yom Kippur.

Those sermons represented a type of education that is unique.
The idea was to prove the scholarship of the rabbi. A great sermon was one where an ordinary man could follow for half an
hour and a scholar could not follow after the first hour, and it was
rare, indeed, if there was anyone who would know what the rabbi
was talking about at the end of the two hours. A sermon by the
rabbi was a scholastic exhibit. It was not meant for popular education.

Now, personally, I always assumed that when the rabbi gets up in the pulpit, he is teaching. To be sure, teaching from the pulpit has certain limitations. Two are common.

Many a sermon deals with abstractions, and the audience is not a graded audience. When you announce a study group in history, theoretically you get people who are interested in history or are conditioned in history; and since you get a small group, it is theoretically a selected group. Realistically it is not so. You may get fifteen people and you will get five who have no conception of history and several who know history very well and just enjoy studying it over and over again. You may have the same unconditioned and ungraded levels in the small group as in a larger group. Theoretically, however, the larger the audience the less graded it is. At the service you have some who hardly know what you are talking about, and some who have fine cultural background, and all the way in between.

Another problem in using the pulpit as a means of education is that there are no opportunities to ask questions. It is very important that people be given an opportunity to ask about some points which may not be clear to them, or which they think they want to challenge. Now, it seems to me that we can readily obviate the second difficulty—the first difficulty we must accept as inevitable, namely, an ungraded audience; but as I say, you meet that problem everywhere except on the campus—by either having a question period in the social hall (I know it is being tried by many of our colleagues) following the service; or perhaps still better—I may experiment with it—to have the sermon, the lecture period, or the study period, after the service. We may get through with the complete service, with the exception, perhaps, of the benediction, and then we can be informal. When you are in the midst of a service, and the Cantor has to get up with his sanctimonious *Kiddush,* and the mourners are waiting for a *Kaddish,* it is very difficult. At the very end of the service, just before the benediction, have an informal half hour study period, a half hour of Torah. After all, if a *derasha* is not Torah, it is not a sermon that is appropriate for the synagogue at a Sabbath service. Now whether it is going to be a *midrash haggada* or a *midrash halakha,* that is, a non-legal discussion or a legalistic rabbinic discussion, depends on local conditions. Historically speaking, you really cannot draw the line between the *haggada* and the *halakha*. Our master builders of Judaism used the *haggada* as a popular appeal to lay the moral foundation for implementing the legal part of Judaism. On the other hand, often you find the best sermon, the best moral ideals, in the actual way of life of Judaism, in the *halakha*.

Now, there is another criticism against the pulpit as an effective instrument for adult education, namely, that there is no continuity. The preacher jumps from subject to subject. Half an hour is not enough to present a pattern of thinking on any phase of study, but the rabbi, as a rule, changes his theme week after week, and there is no continuity. I think this criticism could be obviated—it is being done from time to time, but not as a policy—either by setting aside a season, or part of a season, to one theme.

Let's say you study history: critical periods in Jewish history. We are facing a critical period. We live in a changed world under radically changed conditions. What must we preserve as basic? What must be changed? Now there must have been other periods in our long, long history which are somewhat similar. Take, for example, the period after the destruction of the Jewish State, when they no longer had either a political center or a central force, or a spiritual religious center; but they continued and survived. Or consider the change from Babylonia to Europe—does it have anything to teach us now when we have to reconstruct Jewish life in America, a life emerging from different conditions in Europe. Thus we can have a series either of biographies or of critical periods.

There is another suggestion for a unified series. I tried it once. As a matter of fact, the book, *The Jewish Way of Life,* is just some of the notes edited of such a series of Friday night talks entitled "Judaism Looks at the World."

Or you may follow the *Sidra,* in a way that will have continuity of approach. This has the advantage, helpful in any study period, of a text. Let me give you an example of what can be done. I could mention a dozen topics for each *sidra* that would still make continuity of general theme, connecting a series of *Sidras.* For example, "Judaism Looks at the World," is the title for sermons based on the book of Genesis. Begin with *Bereshis,* the first *Sidra.*

This would be "Judaism Looks at Man." The second one would be "Judaism Looks at Nature." Why do I say Nature? Because in the *Sidra* you have a little noted statement, namely that the laws of nature do not change, and you can discuss miracles and kindred phases, what's natural and what is supernatural. Interesting! People are always interested in these questions. The next one, *Lech Lecha,* suggests the theme "Judaism Looks at Success." Now people are interested in success or greatness. You recall that the builders of the Tower of Babel wanted to make a name for themselves, and Abraham is told that his name would become great. We have these two stories for comparison or contrast to point out what Judaism thinks of greatness, or success, or standards of success. I need not give you the sermons now.

The next one, *Vayyera,* you can call "Judaism Looks at Sports" —that should be timely, always timely. There is the text, *Ben Hagar Metzahek,* the son of Hager is given to sports. This follows the statement that Sarah's son was named "Yitzhak." Note the same root, *Metzahek* and *Yitzhak,* just two sentences apart. Obviously there is a point. I need not give you the answer. "Judaism Looks at Marriage" or "Judaism Looks at Death" may be the theme for *Hayye Sarah.* These are topics which our people ought to know something about.

In *Toledoth,* you discuss "Judaism Looks at the Means and Ends." Was Jacob right in using some questionable means in obtaining his ends? The next, *Vayetze,* "Judaism Looks at Dreams," deals with the beginning of a series of dreams and dreamers. Incidentally, part of this sermon I gave in a coast-to-coast radio program, The Church of the Air, and I received about 400 fan letters, 394 from non-Jews and about 6 from Jews, 2 from relatives. *Vayishlah* is "Judaism Looks at Heredity and Environment." *Vayeshet* suggests "Judaism Looks at the Home." What was it in the home of Jacob that made the brothers act toward each other the way they did? Since *Mikketz* is always on Hanukkah, you can discuss "Judaism Looks at National Defense"—power; spirit— what is it? *Vayiggash* provides "Judaism Looks at Family Ties." What were the forces which made Joseph finally recognize his brothers and acknowledge his own identity? *Vayechi* offers "Judaism Looks at Wills," ethical and unethical—an opportunity to remind the congregation when they make their will to remember the synagogue and so forth, if nothing else. Now here you have covered a book. You can cover a complete philosophy of Jewish values in timely topics with up-to-date illustrations. There is continuity; there is a text; and there is enough novelty, with opportunities provided, as suggested before, to ask questions.

I have been experimenting, at the Sabbath morning service, with a very brief *She'ur*—a study period. Someday I may muster enough courage to transfer this method to Friday nights——the most informal method of teaching and yet the most effective—the Socratic method of questions and answers. I give the *She'ur* on Sabbath morning before the Benediction. We usually have a Bar Mitzvah. Our Junior congregation comes up for the second part of the service, so that there are always old folks and young folks. Theoretically, I am examining the youngsters, but only by the stretch of the imagination. Realistically I am imparting information—the type of information which somehow or other we never get around to transmitting to our people, yet information which helps them to understand the Jewish world around them.

Let me illustrate. This week we are reading *Shemoth*. Let me give an example on two levels; sometimes I use one, sometimes the other, sometimes a combination. I want to say that the old folks, especially guests move forward in their seats as they rarely do on Friday nights, to be sure that they will get the answer. It is at the end of the service and we are quite informal.

I begin: "This week we are reading the story of the birth of Moses. His mother, in order to save him, tried to hide him at the bank of the river. What is the name of that river?" Somebody will speak up. Sometimes it is a youngster. Sometimes a guest, an adult, will speak up. Invariably there will be hands; they will speak up. I continued: "Can You think of any other river that played an important part in Jewish history?" I go on just by association of ideas, to impart ideas or bits of information about Jewish life and Jewish history. Most of those present do not come to study groups. Here you have several hundred people—an opportunity! "Any other river?" Well, they'll think of the River Jordan; if they don't, we will help them out; somebody will think of it.

Here you have an opportunity to refresh their minds or to impart information and to teach them Jewish geography, which 99%

of your congregation, 99% plus, have no idea about. It is a mystery to them. They usually read about the Nile and Jordan as if they were of another world. Now the *Humash* becomes meaningful and they get an idea that the incidents happened in this world and that there is some relationship between the things they read and the values they cherish. It is an interesting lesson in Jewish geography. By association of ideas, you can go over from rivers to mountains. When you read about Noah's Ark on Mount Ararat, you ask for other mountains in Jewish history. You have Sinai, you have Zion. It is not strange to find how much confusion there is between Mount Sinai and Mount Zion. People haven't the slightest idea where those places are. Just mountains in Jewish history!

Now, on another level, take the next Sidra. Moses escaped; he was afraid of Pharaoh and so he ran away. You are dealing now with a moral situation. That's on a higher level. Was he justified in running away? You would be surprised that people right there in the synagogue get up and argue. That's fine; that's adult education. "Can you think of anybody else who ran away in a crisis?" "Elijah," "Jonah." If they don't recall, we will help them out. But, you see, we create a pattern and then there will be a connecting moral thought around the whole thing, and people become interested. They don't sit back and listen to what I may have to say. It is their study period and not mine. I am just the moderator, in a way. And it works. I have tried it for many years, and I can say that this is a most effective method.

These examples illustrate what I mean by informal education. Maybe rabbis ought to experiment on Friday night with this form of education. You can readily see that one can go on even for an hour this way. The congregation is interested, because there are always new thoughts, new facts, new areas for exploration, and they are interested because they get the feel of participants and not mere auditors. It may require at first very careful preparation, but after a while it will come easily. You can literally give *Kol ha-Torah kullah al regel ahat* in a very effective form of adult education.

I, for one, feel therefore that we ought to stress more and more the sermon and the pulpit as a medium of adult education. In the first place, some of the limitations of pulpit teaching can be obviated; in the second place, and that's important, the pulpit, no matter how relatively few may attend the service, the pulpit gets more people than all the study groups combined, in most synagogues. Thirdly, and this, too, is vital, when you study on Shabbas and you attend the service on Shabbas, you are not talking about Judaism—you are living Judaism. It is Torah in its historic sense, theory and practice. You can attend a study group Monday night for ten years and yet Jewish life will die out, because Torah becomes purely a theoretical discussion. If you can get the people in a Shabbas spirit you get Jewish living and not mere talk about Judaism.

I, therefore, urge that in our exploration of areas for the advancement of study hours for adults, more thought and consideration be given to the pulpit as an instrument—and potentially a very effective instrument—for adult education.

The Torch, Winter, 1951–52

Dr. Aronson, renowned Rabbi and leader in the West of Conservative Judaism, after serving as Rabbi of Beth El Synagogue, Minneapolis, Minn. for thirty-five years, is now Professor of Rabbinics at the University of Judaism, Los Angeles, California. He was formerly President of the Rabbinical Assembly of America. His book, The Jewish Way of Life, *has been widely acclaimed and used extensively in adult Jewish studies.*

FORMAL STUDIES FOR ADULTS

ISRAEL M. GOLDMAN

ADULT JEWISH EDUCATION
IN CONSERVATIVE JUDAISM

Adult education is as old as Jewish life itself. We in Conservative Judaism can be truly grateful that it fell to our lot to establish the first national agency for adult Jewish education in this country when in September, 1940 we founded the National Academy for Adult Jewish Studies. We blazed the trail and were soon followed by others. In February, 1943 the Union of American Hebrew Congregations established its American Institute of Jewish Studies and about that time a number of other national organizations, both secular and religious, broadened the scope of their educational activities. We helped to create what may properly be called an Adult Jewish Education Movement in America.

The growth of this movement within the ranks of Conservative Judaism has been most gratifying. Today there is hardly a Conservative congregation that does not at least recognize the need for providing Jewish educational programs for adults in the same way that it must provide a Jewish School for the young. During the last synagogue year 5709 (1948–1949), 120 of our congregations offered a total of more than 400 courses of study with an enrollment of over 10,000 people. The significant proportions of these facts can best be appreciated when they are contrasted with similar activities during the year previous, namely, 1947–1948 (5708), when 7,500 people were enrolled in 358 courses of study in a similar number of congregations. There is, therefore, a sharp increase of 25% in enrollments and a telling increase of 12½% in the number of courses offered. It is further worthy to note that during the year prior to that, namely 1946–1947 (5707), the number of adults enrolled were some 6,500 in 332 courses of study. This movement is only in its early phases and it is safe to

265

predict that it is bound to gain for itself a very significant place in the structure of Jewish education in Conservative Judaism.

Our immediate task is to discover ways in which to hasten this process. A number of pertinent questions come to the fore: How shall we approach the problem? What programs shall we offer? How can we succeed in interesting people? What are the best organizational procedures? In brief, what can we do to establish a school for adults in every one of our congregations?

A PEOPLE-CENTERED APPROACH

Before launching a program of adult Jewish education we should have the correct approach to the educational needs of adults. Some rabbis and educators, looking out upon their prospective students, start out with the question: "What *ought* they to know?" Of course the answer is quite obvious. They *ought* to know a great deal more than they know now, for the average Jew knows so little about his heritage. The usual procedure then is to present the following two types of educational offerings: (1) A Program of *Remedial* Education. Its purpose is to remedy the Jewish educational shortages of youth and to teach those things not previously learned. The type of courses developed would be in effect a duplication of the Hebrew school or the Sunday school curriculum. (2) A Program of *Supplementary* or *Extension* Education. The guiding purpose here is to add to that which may have been learned years ago and to extend the range of knowledge beyond the period of childhood.

There is much that is wrong with this approach and with everything that naturally follows from it. In the first place, adults are not children. You cannot tell them what "they *ought* to know." Then again, why start with a point in the *past* of adults? Why not start with where they are at *present*. And why start with *subjects*, either entirely missed or to be supplemented? Why not start with the *people themselves*. The correct approach, therefore, is to be concerned with such questions as "What Do the People *Want* to Know?", "What Problems *Bother* Them?", "What Ideas *Interest* Them?" With such an initial attitude, our objective would then be to develop what might be called a Program of *Re-*

lational Education in which we seek to *relate* the courses of study to the *present needs* and *interests* of the *people.* We now endeavor to establish a sense of *relevancy* between the subjects to be studied and the students. Our program thus inevitably becomes *people-centered* instead of *subject-centered.*

A LIFE-CENTERED PROGRAM

From what has been said above, it follows logically that the courses of study to be presented must be *life-centered in character.* This means that we should not start with a curriculum or with a catalogue of subjects. We should begin with *themes and with problems that touch the lives of people.* This applies not only to the content of the courses but even to their very titles. To illustrate:

(1) Instead of offering such courses as Hebrew I, Hebrew II, Hebrew IV, or Elementary Hebrew, Intermediate Hebrew, Advanced Hebrew, the courses should bear such titles as: "Keeping Up With Your Child's Hebrew Studies;" "Reading and Knowing the Synagogue Service;" "Words Every Jew Needs to Know."

(2) Instead of Bible I, Bible II, or the like, the course should be centered around such themes as: "The Pleasure of Bible Reading;" "Modern Problems in an Ancient Literature;" "The Bible as a Help to Modern Living;" "Great Passages in the Bible."

(3) Instead of Jewish Customs and Ceremonies, such titles as the following should be used: "Self-Expression in Jewish Home-Making;" "Understanding Jewish Home and Synagogue Life."

(4) Instead of such titles as Outlines of Jewish History, or Survey of Jewish History, or Bird's-Eye View of Jewish History, the following might be employed: "How the Jewish Present Came Out of the Jewish Past;" "Mirrors of Modern Jewish Life;" "Ten Jews of the Ages;" "Five Jews Named Moses."

(5) Instead of courses in Religion I, or Jewish Philosophy, these subjects should be presented as follows: "What We Jews Believe;" "Ways in Which Modern Jews Think of Themselves."

(6) Instead of Jewish Current Events, some such title as follows should be used: "Keeping Up With Jewish Affairs;" "What Is Happening in Jewish Life Today."

We stand a better chance of succeeding if we constantly bear in mind that the programs of Jewish study we offer to adults must be related to the basic needs of their lives.

ORGANIZATIONAL PROCEDURE

With the proper approach to people and to program we should now be ready to proceed with the establishment of adult Jewish educational activities in the congregation. We must bear in mind that it is our aim to have the entire congregation hold itself responsible for a school for adults in the same way that it is obliged to conduct a school for children. The following steps are therefore recommended: (1) Establish an Adult Education Council which is to be the counterpart in the field of adult Jewish education to the School Board in the realm of elementary or secondary education. This Adult Education Council should have the approval and support—financial if need be—of the Board of Trustees, and should be composed of representatives of the Board of Trustees, the Men's Club, Sisterhood, the Young People's League, and all adult auxiliary groups that are part of the congregational life. (2) The Adult Education Council should plan the programs of study and the promotional work necessary to arouse interest and to enroll students. (3) It has been proven that the most successful adult educational activities have all been centered in one night of the week. Just as we try to establish in people's minds the fact that "Friday Night Is Temple Night," so we should associate one special night in the week for the adult educational programs. A number of Congregations have as their slogan "Wednesday Night Is Institute Night." (4) The courses of study should be "Unit Courses" and should be conducted for a semester ranging from 8 to 10 consecutive weeks. Of course if in some Congregations it is possible to extend the length of the semester, then that should certainly be encouraged. (5) Experience has indicated that it is advisable to charge a nominal tuition fee and that text-books should be used wherever possible. (6) The School for Adults should bear a distinctive title such as "The Institute of Jewish Studies for Adults." (7) It is most urgent that the Institute of Jewish Studies for Adults in each congregation should become affiliated with the National Academy for Adult Jewish Studies which will issue a charter to each of its affiliated Institutes. This at once conveys the idea to the local congregations that it is part of a national movement for adult Jewish education and to the individual student that he is sharing in a nationwide program for Jewish learning which will give him recognition through various Certificates of Progress and of Achievement in Jewish Knowledge. (8) The issuance of a charter to a congregation, as indeed the opening and the closing of each semester, should be made the reason for a special convocation of special exercises to mark that event.

There are still many other problems to be considered. For example: How to interest people? How to discover their interests? How to administer an Institute of Jewish Studies for Adults? How to promote and publicize the work? What kind of teachers shall we have? I think, however, that enough has been said to indicate that much hard thinking and much hard work is needed to build adult Jewish education into the structure of Conservative Judaism.

The Torch, April, 1950.

Dr. Goldman is a distinguished Rabbi and leader in the field of Adult Jewish Education. Since 1948 he has been Rabbi of Chizuk Amuno Congregation of Baltimore, Maryland. He served as Director, National Academy for Adult Jewish Studies of the United Synagogue of America. He has been President of the Rabbinical Assembly of America and Vice President of the Maryland Commission on Interracial Relations.

THE LAYMEN'S INSTITUTE

An Adventure in Jewish Living

SIMON NOVECK AND LILY EDELMAN

The Laymen's Institute—in which a group of adults go off to share a few days of study, prayer and recreation—is essentially an adventure in Jewish living. In a few short but concentrated days participants are given the chance to refresh themselves at the fountains of Judaism. They read Jewish texts, discuss ethical and spiritual topics with religious leaders and scholars, observe rituals and practices, "schmoos" with new and old friends, enjoy good food and recreational diversion. And they discover, some for the first time in their lives, that Judaism is good, that it is meaningful, that it can enrich their daily living.

What is behind the enthusiasm expressed by businessmen, lawyers, doctors, accountants, engineers and other staid congregational "pillars" who have been attending Laymen's Institutes? How account for the fact that these week-ends or weeks are rapidly becoming one of the most popular adult education patterns in the Conservative Movement? The fact that more than thirty synagogues have offered their laymen such opportunities—and new Institutes are constantly being requested—would seem to prove that they are effective in bringing Judaism to life for a growing number of American Jews.

WHAT IS THEIR ORIGIN?

Laymen's Institutes are by no means new. Two months each year, around Passover and before Rosh Hashonah, in the Talmudic period, Jewish men traveled from all over that ancient land to meet and study Torah together in the Babylonian academies of Sura and Pumbedita. Such gatherings were called Kallahs. Among American Jews today, the Conservative Movement, in keeping with its philosophy of reinterpreting the old forms of Judaism in the light of modern experience, and the National Federation of Jewish Men's Clubs have taken the lead in reviving the traditional Kallah. Together with the National Academy for Adult Jewish Studies, the Federation arranged the first Laymen's Institute ever held in America, which, like the old Kallah, was a national gathering at a seat of learning. Meeting at the Jewish Theological Seminary in New York City, from August 4 to 9, 1944, it was attended by Men's Club members from Chicago, Detroit, Pittsburgh, Philadelphia, and metropolitan New York.

Two additional National Institutes were held at the Seminary, and were soon followed by regional Institutes, also spearheaded by the men's clubs, the first in Pittsburgh, in March 1946, and others in Detroit, Philadelphia, and Boston. All of these sessions were arranged for long week-ends, using the facilities of local synagogues.

TEL NOAR: PIONEER "AWAY
FROM HOME" INSTITUTE

The group-living concept of the traditional Kallah, where students were together night and day under the same roof, was added in June 1947, at Tel Noar Lodge in Hampstead, New Hampshire. This first "away from home" Institute was sparked by the Brotherhood of Kehillath Israel in Brookline, Mass., and organized by Rabbis Morris Dembowitz and Israel Goldman. Thirty-seven laymen from Boston, Salem, Malden, Chelsea, Springfield, Fall River, and Manchester studied *Pirke Abot*, the Book of Amos, and three folios of Talmud.

In June 1954 Tel Noar concluded its eighth year with a registration of sixty-five from the brotherhoods of fourteen temples. Its program still follows the original pattern set there in 1947, which has provided the model for most of the Institutes subsequently organized.

THE MOVEMENT GROWS

Camp Wohelo in the Blue Mountains, begun in 1948 by Dr. Goldman, and now in its seventh year, is the next oldest Institute, noteworthy for enriching men's clubs members from Chizuk Amuno and Beth El in Baltimore and Adas Israel in Washington. B'nai Amoona (St. Louis) and Beth Shalom (Kansas City) have joined forces for their Midwest Kallah for four successive years. The Long Island Laymen's Institute, established in May, 1953, and originally sponsored by nine Conservative congregations, has two sessions to its credit.

Some congregations, putting first the need to develop fellowship and potential leadership within their own ranks, arrange Institutes for their own members only. The annual Kibbutz of Shaarey Zedek in Detroit, for example, now in its eighth year, is limited to an "elite corps" of twenty-five men. Camp Oxford in Guilford, New York, has been the site of five annual Kallahs run by and for the Men's Club of Beth-El in Utica. The neighboring Men's Club of Temple Beth El in Rochester in 1953 started an Institute for its own people at Camp Markus on Lake Seneca. Other 1953 "firsts" include Institutes by the Men's Association of Congregation Shaar Hashomayim in Quebec, by the Men's Club of the Louis Feinberg Synagogue in Cincinnati, and an expanded use of the Camps Ramah of both Connecticut and Pennsylvania for adult study week-ends.

With new Laymen's Institutes constantly being born, 1954 has been a record year. Fifty Portlanders (Oregon) met in May with Rabbi Joshua Stampfer for "A Week-End in Quest," a group of upstate New Yorkers convened last June at Saratoga Springs under the sponsorship of the Capital State Region of the United Synagogue, while simultaneously Men's Club members of Adas Israel (Washington, D.C.) gathered at Plum Point, Md. about the same time the Men's Bible Class of Beth Torah (Orange, N. J.) went off for a Lag ba-Omer week-end.

1954 MODEL:
AT-HOME OR INDOOR KALLAH

The most interesting new development is the At-Home or Indoor Kallah, pioneered by the Men's Club, Sisterhood, and Rabbi Jerome Lipnick at Temple Beth El in Utica, New York. Shaar Hashomayim (Montreal) also offered a week-end of study "at home" to complement its annual Institute away at St. Donat.

Because this is a pattern which individual clubs may wish to sponsor, Rabbi Lipnick's description of the day-by-day program may be helpful. "At Friday Evening Service, our leader preaches, then an Oneg Shabbat and question period," he reports. "Our Kallah leader usually spends Saturday morning with the children of the Religious School and their parents. Between Mincha and Maariv I teach the Sedrah, and on Saturday evening our leader delivers his second lecture, which is followed by a social program. The final lecture and Siyum are held on Sunday morning, the climax of our week-end."

Dr. Max Arzt, who has been a most popular and devoted Kallah faculty leader, enthusiastically recommends the At-Home Institute, particularly to smaller congregations. "When there is only one faculty member," he says, "he can pour out his whole philosophy to a group, giving a consistent and sustained point of view. The cost is at a minimum since the indoor Kallah does not entail finding a resort or kosher food."

WHAT CAN LAYMEN'S INSTITUTES
ACCOMPLISH?

Raves from men attending such week-ends are plentiful, but we still know very little about carry-over. What happens when they go home? The Kallah may not be the cure-all for what ails today's Jewry, but its potentialities for lifting the level of Jewish life in America are many.

1) PERSONAL ENRICHMENT

Laymen's Institutes, offering glimpses into the satisfactions of study and prayer, are an excellent starting point for uninformed and hitherto unexposed individuals. For many, attendance has meant a moment of personal awakening, a rediscovery, as it were, of half-forgotten but still vital traditions. "My first real experience of the beauty of Jewish living," was how one layman phrased it. Such stirring at one's personal roots often leads to new flowerings of interest in Judaism.

2) DEMONSTRATIONS IN ART
OF JEWISH LIVING

In addition, Institutes provide workshops in Jewish living. Members actually take part in rituals and prayers. They participate in a Friday evening service, hear *Kiddush* and have a traditional Friday evening meal, say *birkat hamazon* (grace after meals), and sing the traditional *zmirot*, or Sabbath songs. They attend Saturday morning services and hear the *Havdalah* service ushering out the Sabbath. For many, these experiences mark the beginning of a desire to make Jewish practices a regular part of their lives.

3) STIMULATION OF SYSTEMATIC
STUDY

Laymen's Institutes or Kallahs have also demonstrated how much the Jewish classics still have to say about life's meaning. Participants discover that the traditional pleasure of study for its own sake can bring contentment where other experiences fail. By thus whetting their appetites for learning, adults are sometimes encouraged to continue study in their synagogues or at home.

An annual Laymen's Institute might be used to culminate any men's club's ongoing study program. The theme or text studied during the year could be approached from enlarged points of view at an Institute—and the members could then return to their synagogues for advanced study, creating cyclic, continuous patterns of Jewish learning.

4) A ROAD TO LEADERSHIP

Still another role of Institutes, and one of crucial concern to American Jewry today, is the development of alumni who can become a "hard core" nucleus or "cell" group out of which to draw club and synagogue leaders. All Jewish leaders, like Hillel, Akiba, Saadia, Maimonides and, in modern times, Solomon Schechter, have been scholars, and our people would do well to at least try to acquire a little learning, particularly before they accept synagogue offices.

NEED FOR FOLLOW-UP

If the heart of the Institute is deeper understanding of Judaism, its influence should shine into the lives of participants not for one, or five, or even seven annual week ends, but for all their years. The fine intentions chanted in the glow of the week end setting must not be allowed to fade in the lesser light of the work-day world back home.

The essential thing is that men's clubs and others responsible for Institutes make provision for follow-up. In-town Kallahs, like those described above, can help keep interest alive. Closer integration with regular synagogue adult study programs should be worked out. Indeed the full harvest of enthusiasms seeded in study sessions "away from home" must be reaped if we are to conserve the best of our tradition and develop an authentic Judaism in America.

The Torch, Fall, 1954.

Mrs. Edelman, a National leader in the field of Adult Education, is Director of B'nai B'rith's Department of Adult Jewish Education and Editor of Jewish Heritage. *She was formerly Executive Secretary of the National Academy for Adult Jewish Studies of the United Synagogue of America and Educational Director of the East and West Association. She has served as an editor of the U. S. Department of State's Overseas Information Program. She is author of* Israel: New People in an Old Land, Hawaii, U.S.A., Japan in Story and Pictures, *and* The Sukkah and the Wind.

FALL-OUT SHELTERS FOR THE SPIRIT

BERNARD MANDELBAUM

The most urgent problem which we face today is to start building individual fall-out shelters. It takes great effort and strain to build a shelter. Of course, what I am speaking about now is not a shelter to be built by engineers.

Each day finds our atmosphere increasingly polluted by a fall-out of panic, a fall-out of hopelessness. It is understandable that the irrational, explosive behavior of tyranny generates tension, apprehension. But hopelessness? Such feeling results not from the enemy's strength, but from our own weakness. This is our mood despite an America which is economically strong, militarily alert. What is wrong? Wherein are we wanting?

There is a lesson to be learned from a story by Zvi Kolitz about a document found in the ruins of the Warsaw ghetto. The overtones of one paragraph in the testament of one Yossel Rakover speak to America and the free world at this moment in history. He tells us that he clings to his faith—in his own words—

> ". . . not in spite of the cruel treatment of us, but precisely because of this treatment." He continues—"I should be ashamed to be one of those who spawned and raised the criminals responsible for the deeds that have been perpetrated against us."

When someone trying to do what is right, is the victim of forces that lie and deceive, then even the strongest of convictions can totter. When the wicked seem to prosper, then even good people may react by losing faith in themselves and begin to imitate the evil. Though engulfed by dark clouds of barbarism, Yossel Rakover did not lose sight of the divinity in man which enables him to know right from wrong. Despite the grave dangers, Yossel Rakover was not weakened by hopelessness.

Such strength is not inborn; it must be nurtured. Such conviction is not an accident of personal temperament; it must be cultivated. Such character is not genetically inherited, although it is part of a spiritual heritage.

"And the Lord said . . . Abraham shall surely become a great and mighty nation, and all the nations of the earth shall be blessed in him." Wherein is the greatness, wherein is the might? The Bible continues: "to the end he may instruct his children and his household after him, that they may keep the way of the Lord, to do righteousness and justice."

In Abraham's world of paganism and idolatry, to teach "the way of the Lord, to do righteousness and justice" was a revolutionary doctrine. Equally unique and forward-looking was a system of education in these goals of the good life:

"Thou shalt teach them diligently unto thy children, and shalt talk of them when thou sittest in thine house, when thou walkest by the way, when thou liest down, and when thou risest up."

How does one "talk of them," when sitting in the house, walking by the way, lying down and rising up? It is not only by the instruction in words, but by the eloquence of personal example. From this view of education—the home and the classroom, business and pleasure, the holy-day and the workday, private life and public—are all part of the school of life for the training of integrity, fortitude, faith. Such total education in character enabled many in the household of Abraham—no matter how outnumbered, no matter how out-maneuvered—to believe in themselves and to continue to teach truth and goodness. Such spiritual resistance against the evil in society was not only a rejection of what is bad. It was a positive dedication to ideals—a great love for what is good.

In another passage of his testament, Yossel Rakover reveals the source of his strength:

"I served God enthusiastically, and my single request to Him was that He should allow me to worship Him with all my heart, and all my soul, and all my strength."

To be committed to one's beliefs with enthusiasm, strength, fullness of heart—this is the great need of America today. Such commitment to the basic principles of freedom and human dignity is necessary, not only for the strengthening of our own character; it is necessary to guide a world which is in the throes of a new birth. For "the more perfect union" which Abraham Lincoln envisioned for America must now become man's program for the world. Our Declaration of Independence which affirms "man's inalienable rights, among which are life, liberty, and the pursuit of happiness," is, in Lincoln's words, "the immortal emblem of humanity." This vision of justice can stir the hearts of men the world over. This indeed is our spiritual heritage, but do we live it in the home and the classroom, in business and pleasure, in private life and public? Instead our view of success tends to define freedom more in terms of the opportunity to raise our material standards of living, and less in terms of raising the moral standards of life. Our desire for comfort defines democracy more in terms of equal opportunity to accumulate things that make life easy, and less in terms of the equal opportunity to accumulate ideas which make life meaningful.

And yet, there is no more urgent need than for us to recognize the qualities of a free man in terms of his own capacity to achieve strength in character by the practice of disciplined virtues, his capacity for sustained effort and deliberate sacrifice.

The extent to which we are confused about our goals, the lapses which find us occasionally imitating the ways of the enemy, point to our one pivotal weakness: we have neglected our own education in responsibility and consequently are not teaching "diligently" to our children. We act as if such education is worthwhile, perhaps even important. The hour calls for the realization that education in the values of the human spirit, education in character, is the most vital factor in our survival. In 1920, H. G. Wells predicted a race between education and catastrophe. What was then quoted as a vivid figure of speech is now a stark reality. Relating this to the challenge which faces us at the present moment in history, Paul Woodring said:

> "If education is to win out over catastrophe, we must find ways of diverting a larger portion of our national resources into it—even if that should mean some reduction in the amount available for tail fins, entertainment, and martinis. We must find ways of per-

suading more of our able young men and women to become teachers and more of our most brilliant adults to devote their lives to the solving of educational problems. Most important of all, we must re-define our goals, establish clear priorities, and promote a new sense of purpose in the schools and in the nation."

The roots of our program go back to the Patriarch Abraham. It is strengthened by the Abrahams in American history who give new vitality to the role of the mind of man in establishing equality, freedom and justice. Together we seek to cultivate in man "enthusiasm, strength and fulness of heart" in his devotion to the highest goals of a free, moral society.

Clarifying our goals, intensifying our commitments are trying tasks. It is all the more difficult when faced with opposing forces which seem to grow stronger. Yet this too we can learn from history: our greatest insights and achievements come from life's difficulties. A small boy once asked: "Why are all the vitamins in spinach and not in ice-cream where they ought to be?" We do not know the answer to this question, but vitamins are in spinach, and free men—only with proper concentration of energy and only with determination of purpose—can find it within themselves to rise to greatness when challenged. Free men have the powerful instrument of education which can fashion a society that advances the welfare of all its people. This truth, so vital for us today, was discussed some 1800 years ago in one of the great academies of learning in Lidda. This is a report of the exchange between Rabbi Tarfon and Rabbi Akiba. The question at issue was: Which is more important, education, or good deeds—which include, of course, caring for the health and welfare of society. Rabbi Tarfon spoke up and said—"deeds such as health and welfare." Rabbi Akiba spoke up and said—"education." And the Rabbis concluded: "education is truly more important, for education leads to good deeds—such as concern for health and welfare."

The conclusion of the Rabbis is no less than the definition of the highest goal in education. Much too often when we say the word "education", we think exclusively of "education for knowledge, education for science". Yet the greatest need is education for character, which is the proper use of knowledge and the wisdom in its application. Such perfection of character, the only appropriate goal for the individual, has implications for communities, for nations, for the world. World understanding which we seek, is achievable only in a society where individuals and nations are governed by such depth of character. The failure of others to seek this path of righteousness and justice, is never an excuse for our own inadequacies and weakness. Thus, while strengthening our physical posture, we must elevate our moral stature. America can become synonymous with the ideal formulated by a 19th century Rabbi who said: "Man must worry about his own soul and the next person's body, and not the opposite." The building of this strong shelter of character demands the immediate attention of each and every one of us.

The Torch, Winter, 1961–62.

Dr. Mandelbaum, scholar, administrator, and outstanding interpreter of Conservative Judaism, is President of the Jewish Theological Seminary of America. He was formerly Provost and Dean of Students at the Seminary's Rabbinical School. He served as program editor of the Seminary's Eternal Light NBC radio and TV series. He is also Director of the Religio-Psychiatric Center of the Seminary. He has published a critical edition of Pesikta de Rav Kahama d'Rab Kahema *and is preparing one of the* Midrash Tanchuma.

Part Five

AMERICA—ISRAEL

"We may freely admit that Eretz Israel and all that issues from there, will spur American Judaism, will enrich its content, will strengthen its verve. But Eretz Israel cannot be American Jewry's vicarious atonement. It cannot be a substitute for Avodah Atzmith, our own labor, our own responsibilities, our own achievements, our own intellectual and spiritual contributions, our own self-emancipation from servitude to the flesh pots, worship of gadgets, arrogance of ignorance, intellectual and spiritual sterility, emancipation from all these into inner freedom, into dignity and vitality, into a a worthy sense of values, a quest of Jewish knowledge, appreciation of Jewish scholarship, espousal of the duties of the heart and the endowments of the mind, inner security, in short, dedication to God and Torah."

—Israel Goldstein

INTRODUCTION

The Jewish people within the organizational structure comprising the Conservative Movement have consistently been in the forefront of the Zionist Movement. They were, like all other Jews in America, elated and invigorated by the powerful impact of the creation of the new State. They rallied to its support and gave it financial and material assistance in generous amounts.

Synagogue-minded Jews from the very beginning of the State felt the foundations of Israel had to be composed of the spiritual and cultural ideals which Jews had prayed for and dreamed about for the past several thousand years. There was no question about the State of Israel being a safe haven for stateless Jews or a permanent home for Jews who felt endangered or unwelcome in their former dwelling places. Israel finally gave the Jews a home of their own and this brought a feeling of comfort, security and self-respect to Jews all over the world. The task of rebuilding this "homeland" was primary, and once the processes for settlement had been established and the rebuilding of the land had proceeded at a healthy pace, thoughtful Jews began to think about the age old dream.

Jews in America had learned that material affluence, economic well-being and social acceptance alone were insufficient in themselves to guarantee the survival of Judaism. They had largely achieved these goals. The survival of Judaism however demanded a higher price—it required the devotion and adherence of the Jewish people to the religious traditions and institutions of Judaism. This had sustained the Jewish people during their dispersion in many lands over the past several thousand years. The Jews in America had gone through the agonizing experience of resettlement in a strange land and the difficult problems involved in achieving economic and social success, but their main challenge had been building a religious life in their new land. This challenge they had met and in the minds of many they were successfully resolving.

A new challenge arose with the destruction of the Jewish communities and the religious institutions in Eastern Europe. When these sources of scholarship and training had been destroyed new ones had to be developed. The filling of this cultural vacuum became the responsibility of the only community that had the resources, namely the American Jewish Community. Institutions of Jewish learning and centers of religious activities assumed the task of providing teachers and rabbis and scholars necessary, not only in America, but also in other areas of the world. American Jewry has begun to export its spiritual values to foreign lands including Israel. The question arises how best to transmit the cultural and spiritual values which America has to offer to Israel. The other side of this problem was how to have Israel accept the know-how which had been developed in America so as to make these values meaningful to the people of Israel. Israel, of course, had its own rich resources to give to the American Jewish community. We suggest that at this time the flow from America to Israel is more important than visa versa. Some may argue with this conclusion since they aver that now that Israel exists, the survival of Judaism is in its hands and diaspora Jewry, from the point of view of such survival, is expendable. History does not sustain this contention since diaspora Jewry sustained Judaism for two thousand years without Israel. This statement of course is not altogether true since the dream of a homeland in Israel gave powerful support to Jews wherever they lived.

Jews who are concerned about religious living in Israel feel that there is much to be done to create the atmosphere, the facilities and the desire there in order to create a Jewish state such as will be consistent with the eternal dream of a Jewish homeland. The great Jewish scholar and builder of the Jewish Theological Seminary of America, Solomon Schechter, fifty years ago voiced the fear that the establishment of the Jewish state might lead to disappointment if the leaders of such a State looked upon religion "as a negligible quantity." The political leadership of Israel and the nationalistic organizations outside of Israel which support the State have not entirely dispelled the possibility of that fear being realized.

These vital questions which concerned all thoughtful Jews stimulated the editors of *The Torch* to include in its pages articles discussing these problems. The samples which are included in this volume are typical.

The articles by Asher Block and Ben Zion Bokser, both of whom are eminent American rabbis, deal with the question of religious life in Israel. These articles express the opinion of religiously oriented Jews, that the State of Israel, to be meaningful, must develop a religious or ethical mode of living. Such Jews are concerned that the State should not emulate other states which concentrate merely on building a political entity. In this respect they suggest that America could be helpful. Rabbi Block talks about the creation of a relationship in which there would be "A dialogue between the communities of Israel and those of America as opposed to a monologue." Rabbi Bokser suggests that a healthy, meaningful Jewish life may also be maintained in communities outside of Israel and he buttresses his argument from examples in Jewish history. He further suggests that American synagogues can continue to be helpful to the State of Israel just as they were helpful to the Jewish community in Palestine before the state was established.

Rabbi Bokser sounds a warning that the culture emerging in Israel is "marked by pronounced indifference to the religious factors in life . . . The dominant groups in Israel have consciously rejected a religious outlook on life and have tended to replace religion with national values." He further suggests that the United Synagogue has been in a long struggle with secularism and can teach Israel how to combat it.

Another article which appears in these pages was written by a distinguished Israeli educator and scholar. This article presents a totally different point of view. Eleazer Rieger suggests that the only hope of Jewish survival is in Israel, and that diaspora Jewry will eventually disappear.

This article urges American Jews to recognize the importance of the Jewish State to Jewish life in America. He suggests that western society, including its Jewish component, has "lost its aim" and is suffering from "aimless drifting and confusion." He writes that Judaism has heretofore been preserved by external pressures. He does not believe that it can be sustained once those pressures are lifted. He makes a compelling argument, but hardly one which is acceptable to either the leadership or the great mass of Jews in America.

The Rieger article was included because it expresses the oft asserted idea that only by complete identification with Israel through settling there can a "Jewish life be constituted within the framework of a democratic progressive society and still be permeated with the light and glow of Jewish consciousness."

The same question which has been discussed in many forums and among different people came to an open debate at the 1959 Convention of the United Synagogue of America. Four distinguished Jewish leaders participated in a discussion of the issue: Shall the United Synagogue of America join the World Zionist Organization? In this debate, Mordecai Kaplan and Nahum Goldmann, in endorsing the affirmative of that proposal, gave their philosophy of Jewish life and their formula for Jewish survival. Simon Greenberg and Abraham J. Heschel, in upholding the negative of that proposal, each set forth his respective philosophy of the meaning and objectives of Judaism and the formula for its survival. These articles are reproduced in this volume because each man by his life, writings and action epitomized a philosophy of Judaism and in a concise form gave its essence and objectives —how the survival of Judaism could be guaranteed.

All of these men, it should be emphasized and underscored, wholeheartedly supported the State of Israel. The real issue was how best to serve it.

Mordecai M. Kaplan, the great teacher and philosopher of Jewish thought, in his dissertation, expresses a great fear that the failure of the religious groups to join forces with the Zionist organization would cause a "fragmentation" of the Jewish people and thus threaten its ability to survive. He urged that Judaism needed Zionism and Zionism needed Judaism and pointed out that the Jewish right to Palestine rested solely on a religious tradition. Without such unity, neither organization could achieve its aims, and Israel and diaspora Jewry would go their separate ways, to the great loss of both the Jewish people and of Judaism.

Nahum Goldmann, the brilliant organizer and lay leader of the

Zionist Organization, took a very practical approach. He stated that the very security and safety which diaspora Jewry now enjoys threatens its survival. He stressed that diaspora Jewry had thrived as a separate entity and had even grown strong as a people by reason of the hardships that it had encountered and the difficulties to which it was subjected in the various lands of its sojourn.

He postulated the survival of diaspora Jewry on unity with Israel. If a great center of Judaism were built in Israel, we would be assured of Jewish survival both there and in other lands, provided all Jewry was united. The vehicle for achieving this unity was the Zionist Organization, which he defined not as a political organization, but as a great unifying force.

Simon Greenberg, a brilliant teacher and rabbi, argued that the real question at issue was: What should be the proper conception of Jewish status? He asked the question—What makes one a Jew, irrespective of language, allegiance to state or political allegiance or residence? He answers this question thus:—"The institution which most adequately embodies that concept of Jewish status is the Synagogue." He further defines a Jew as one who is eligible for membership in the fellowship of the Synagogue. He concludes that ". . . the unity of the Jewish people has been and should be spiritual or religious in essence, rather than political, ethnic or cultural in essence." This concept he considers to be the foundation upon which "the whole structure of Jewish life everywhere, including the State of Israel, ultimately depends."

He admits that many Jews have challenged this concept, and have rejected the Synagogue and Judaism, but sought to remain Jews for other reasons. He is particularly concerned at such a nationalistic conception of Jewish life and emphasizes that relations with Israel should be "rooted in religious ties." Although he advocates the building of spiritual bridges between Israel and America, he nevertheless argues that ". . . Jewish life can and must flourish anywhere and everywhere in the world." The synagogue, he said, confers status on Jews and not the State of Israel, and therefore the synagogue must in no way be made subordinate to the state.

Professor Abraham Joshua Heschel attacks the problem from the point of view of the Jew as an individual. He says that "the supreme need of the hour is neither a definition nor a world organization of Jewish people, but a renewed personal attachment to Jewish thinking and living. Judaism, says he, will not perish for lack of organization or lack of definition, but may perish for lack of commitment, for lack of appreciation." He attacks the propositions involved in the debate by saying it would be suicidal to reduce Judaism to nationalism, and he suggests that the World Zionist Organization join the synagogue. He thinks that Judaism in America is having a renaissance. He optimistically writes that there is a real possibility of spiritual regeneration in America.

To religiously oriented Jews the cardinal foundation for the relationship between Israeli and American Jewry must be the spiritual and ethical values and principles of Judaism. In other words, emphasis must be on the relationship between two communities composed of co-religionists. The question as to which community will play the primary role is for history to determine. It is suggested that at this stage leadership lies largely with the Jewish people in America. The task therefore seems to be for American Jewry to give and for Israeli Jewry to receive whatever is necessary and valuable to build a strong and vital religious community in the State of Israel.

M. B.

THE RELATIONSHIP OF THE AMERICAN JEWISH COMMUNITY TO ISRAEL

✳

ASHER BLOCK

The main burden of Zionist ideology for many decades was that, if we are to take the plight of our European brethren seriously, we must be concerned not alone with religion, culture and philanthropy, but with politics as well. One of the central characteristics of Judaism itself is its attempt at integrating all facets of life —the so-called religious and secular, the personal and the social, the spiritual and the political. How, then, shall we draw the line when it comes to Israel? Is our obvious concern with the proposed Israeli constitution purely cultural and in no sense political?

We have strictly defined national commitments under which we are in extreme moments expected to dedicate our lives, our fortunes and our sacred honor, while (on the other hand) we have affinities, loyalties, and commitments which cut across all national boundaries and have no direct relevance to them. Zion, for us as Jews, can and should be one of these latter. It is, in at least some of its implications, a religio-political concept of the Kingdom of God on earth which transcends every national loyalty. But let it be understood that in this sense, Zion is not Israel, just as it is not the United States. It is a universal vision and standard of the Moral Law, in the light of which every unqualified loyalty to group or nation is a form of idolatry.

This approach, to my mind, represents the only way to resolve, honestly and basically, the perplexing question of dual or multiple loyalties. For myself I should have to say: I wish to be loyal to America, to Israel, to world Jewry, and to the rest of mankind. Should a conflict arise among them, then under the judgment of God I must strive to determine to the best of my capacity which loyalty or loyalties approximate more closely my concepts of Righteousness and Truth.

To what degree can one be true to any ideal religiously and culturally without standing by in a political crisis as well? Similarly, to what degree is our American allegiance only political, if loyalty to our country is to be understood primarily as a political, national loyalty, and to what degree can any such loyalty be "unquestioned?" Obviously we need a frame of reference which transcends both America and Israel, both culture and politics. Such reference I believe can be found only in religion. It would seem, therefore, that our particular contribution toward a solution of this problem ought to lie in that direction.

Another basic problem, which should be further explored, is that of the true cultural relationship between American Jewry and Israel. Culturally speaking, both communities ought to share in full and reciprocal equality. Each, we feel, has something essential and creative to offer in fashioning a total and well-balanced Jewish life.

The contribution of Israel (both actual and potential) to our partnership has been widely emphasized in recent years, and need not be rehearsed in detail at this time. Briefly stated, that contribution consists in demonstrating what Judaism can do when Jews are in a majority position and have the instruments of state at hand—instruments such as a congenial environment, a total culture, political power, and a national will-to-live.

The contribution of Diaspora Jewry, on the other hand, lies in the very opposite direction—in demonstrating what Judaism can do when Jews are in a minority position and do not have the instruments of state in their possession. (In the past, Judaism was apparently able to flourish under either of these conditions. Witness the fact that much of the Bible came into being when the Jews were on their land, while the Babylonian Talmud was created when they were stateless.)

It is this latter type of contribution with which we as American Jews are now especially concerned. For if Judaism can be lived meaningfully and creatively only in Israel, then we had better make it our conscious program to dissolve our identity or to emigrate to Israel. Logically or psychologically, why should one be content with a "second best," when the best is within reach?

I personally believe that just as the Talmud once conceived of מצוות התלויות בארץ—cultural opportunities that applied almost exclusively to Palestine—so we can now conceive as well of מצוות התלויות בחוץלארץ—cultural opportunities that apply primarily to the democratic Diaspora. There are, as I see it, five inherently valuable elements in non-Israeli Jewish life, which if developed by us, would redound not only to our benefit and that of our American neighbors, but to the benefit of Israel and mankind as well.

The first is the element of religion. By religion is here understood not a set of rituals or a formal manner of worship, but something vital to live for as a Jew. For a majority on its own land that "something" is in a sense optional, since it already has a structure of state to buttress itself; for a minority it is indispensable. A majority can often transmit to future generations almost any way of life—good, bad, or indifferent—by the sheer weight of numbers and a homogeneous environment. A minority usually stands or falls on its mettle. (For a minority has a tide to resist, and it will not long continue to do so unless it has something unique and outstanding which makes resistance worthwhile and effective. Dr. Leo Baeck, in his *Essence of Judaism,* says of the Jewish minority that it was always "compelled to think," compelled to be sensitive and progressive, and that was the "blessing of its fate.")

If the future of the State of Israel is to represent a meaningful —which is to say a "religious" or "ethical"—survival, not simply like that of so many other national groups, then we of the American Jewish community, whose rationale *must* be religion, should exert our full influence upon it.

Let it, however, be added in all humility that our native religion at the moment is hardly worthy of export. On the contrary, some of the Israeli spirit of hospitality and self-sacrifice, may be more deeply religious and should be emulated by us. Nevertheless, that spirit might ebb as the pioneer stage passes into history. We on our part will also undergo transformation as the vicarious excitement of recent Zionist history fades away. It is to that future, more permanent relationship—as well as to the present—that we must give thought.

A second beneficent influence that we as American Jews can exercise upon the people of Israel is in their attitude toward their own minorities. Paraphrasing the Biblical injunction, we must say to our Israeli brethren: "Ye shall love the minorities in your midst, for *we* are minorities in the lands of the world."

Here we confront one of the most crucial problems of democracy. Majority rule and minority rights are in truth contradictory concepts, yet we cannot cease from struggling to harmonize them. If American Jews, as a democratic minority, add their experience to that of the Jewry of Israel, a democratic majority, perhaps together we might help to achieve that sense of equilibrium without which democracy sinks either into tyranny, on one side, or into anarchy, on the other.

Certainly, from our minority standpoint, it would be unfair for the Jewish citizens of Israel to discriminate in education, in housing, or in business and community relations against their Arab or Christian neighbors. Likewise, if as a religious minority we should insist upon the separation of Church and State in America, we surely could not condone the union of rabbinate and government in Israel. In these and other matters, our experiences should be conveyed, for what they are worth, to the people of Israel, while we in turn should be ready at all times to benefit by whatever insights they have to offer.

Thirdly, our minority situation exposes us to the constant challenge of inter-group relations. As life in Israel exemplifies the values of cultural intensity, our life here can exemplify the virtues of cultural diversity. In the long run we do not know which is the more significant achievement. All we can say with certainty is that both processes seem essential to civilization. Cultures must be inwardly nourished, but like plants they must also be cross-fertilized lest they stagnate. We in America have a rich opportunity, as few countries have, to explore the avenues of cultural pluralism and inter-faith relations. As heirs to two great traditions, the American and the Judaic, our special job is to fashion a bridge between two civilizations.

Many conflicts and tensions will no doubt be thrust upon us in this task, the like of which Israeli citizens or non-Jewish Americans are spared. That is perhaps why so many American Jews wish to become "assimilated" into either a non-Jewish or a Jewish majority. However, the function of a minority is often a sacred one. Ultimately the very salvation of our society depends upon the successful disposition of values minorities represent.

The fourth element which I conceive as a primary contribution of ours to the total picture of Jewish life, is the emphasis upon non-violent techniques of social progress as opposed to what is commonly referred to as "power politics." I suppose it is almost within the very nature of statehood in our day to resort to physical force, both in internal and external relationships. Yet Judaism, if not altogether in theory, has at least in actuality for almost 2,000 years demonstrated group life without any of the instrumentalities of a power state. That is unique, to say the least. It is the kind of experience which should not be lost to future generations, as nations and people strive for a warless world. Prof. Simon of the Hebrew University, among others, has been calling our attention to the Israeli trend of idealizing the partisan fighter in place of the historic תלמיד חכם. We, whose success as Jews in the Diaspora cannot possibly be established militarily, must help to restore a proper equilibrium in Jewish values.

(Parenthetically, I might add, that American Jews run a corresponding danger. Here in this country our preoccupation with materialistic success threatens to put Judaism out of focus. Thus *we* stand in need of Israel's example of a "religion of labor," of economic cooperatives, and of a socially idealistic spirit. If as a result of a conscious interaction we should succeed in cancelling out our respective weakness, then perhaps we shall be more inclined to heed the prophetic truth—לא בחיל ולא בכח—not by "wealth" and not by "power," but by the spirit of the Lord.)

The final contribution that we as an American Jewish community are in a fitting position to make vis-a-vis the State of Israel, is in the realm of internationalism. As the largest, and perhaps the most significant, non-Israeli Jewish group in the world, we help to raise the concept and reality of Jewish peoplehood above the level of mere ethnic or geographic identity. Just as America is unique in that it is a nation of many nationalities, so Jewry is unique in that it is a people of many countries. And just as it would be unfortunate for minorities in our country who are not Protestant, white or native, to disappear somehow and leave America "like unto other nations," so it would be unfortunate for all non-Israeli Jewish communities to dissolve leaving Jewish civilization like unto other nationalisms. "Historical monotheism" (according to Prof. Baron), that is, the existence of a universal people, is as great a Jewish contribution as "ethical monotheism," the recognition of a universal God.

Progress, therefore, must somehow be made along these various fronts—toward a more spiritualized life; toward greater sensitivity for the rights of minorities; toward more intimate intergroup relations; toward a non-violent way of life; and toward greater universalism.

Our success as Jews in advancing these goals will, I feel, be greatly enhanced if the spiritual relationship between Israel and American Jewry will be that of a "dialogue," and not of a monologue. Together we can build a worthwhile future.

The Torch, October, 1949.

Rabbi Block is Rabbi of Little Neck Jewish Center, Little Neck, L. I. He has been editor of Hedenu, Jewish Youth Journal, Tidings, *(Jewish Peace Fellowship), and Associate Editor of* The Reconstructionist. *He has written and lectured extensively on Judaism and the philosophy of religion.*

ISRAEL AND THE AMERICAN SYNAGOGUE

BEN ZION BOKSER

The emergence of the State of Israel is the most revolutionary fact in modern Jewish history. The drama surrounding its birth has drawn our attention to its struggles and achievements of the hour. The permanent significance of a Jewish state functioning freely on the arena of world affairs has not yet registered fully upon us. But as the years flow on and the State of Israel is given the chance to work and to build in the quiet of peaceful dedication, the underlying facts and issues will become ever clearer. We who seek to meet events with a point of view that can give them coherence in a larger outlook on life must endeavor to explore the new realities which the State of Israel has brought into being.

The first great issue which we must be clear on is the status of Jewish communities outside of Israel. There is an attitude in Israeli circles which is occasionally expressed also by certain Zionist spokesmen in this country, disparaging the possibilities of maintaining a healthy Jewish life in the Diaspora. The dominant dream of the people in Israel is to "ingather the exiles," and to utilize the energies of world Jewry for the consolidation and the development of the state. It is an understandable dream, and within limits, we share in it also.

Jewish history testifies, however, to the possibility of maintaining Jewish communities that shall be culturally and spiritually creative anywhere in the world. The Babylonian center of Judaism flourished during centuries when the second Jewish commonwealth existed in Palestine. The golden age of Judaism in Spain and the intensely vital cultural and religious centers in Eastern Europe speak eloquently of the power of our tradition to live anywhere and everywhere, and to elicit from our people profound loyalties.

It may very well be that Jews whose Jewish interests consisted only in fighting anti-Semitism or relief for our stricken people overseas will find no more to do and thus drop out from Jewish activity. We, however, who stand identified with the synagogue recognize a conception of Jewishness which is born of no crisis and is therefore not limited to special circumstances in history. For us, Judaism is among other things a universal religion that offers man enduring answers to life's enduring problems. The disciplines of Judaism will therefore remain cogent for us in the Diaspora even as they are for those who live by them in Israel.

We thus visualize a continuing Jewish life in America to parallel the developing Jewish life in Israel. Indeed, we visualize a deepening Jewish life in America as the pressures of those problems to be solved in Israel will be removed, leaving us energies for the positive tasks of building for the American Jewish community. The two centers of Jewish life in America and in Israel will, however, have to seek forms of interaction if all the potentialities of Israel's birth for us and for the world are to be fully realized.

Interaction suggests a process in which the two communities will each give and receive. We envision a two-way passage in which two great centers of Jewish creativity will each benefit and grow through the unique resources of the other, and together seek to advance the cause of Judaism in civilization.

The American synagogue has much to offer Israel. The American synagogue has been the backbone of the material help that Jews in this country have rendered toward the creation of the Jewish state. We shall continue to summon our people to help in the building of the Jewish state. Our Religious Schools will continue to present the miracle of Zionism and its achievements as evidence of the divine providence which has ever hovered over our people and which enabled us to meet crises without being overwhelmed by them.

Some among us will seek to share more personally in Israel's rebirth, to invest of our substance in Israel's economy, and some will want to go to Israel as permanent settlers. These will be personal applications of the general ideal of identification with Israel which is bound to remain an indispensable element of the outlook represented by the synagogue. Because we have faith in American democracy and in American Jewish life, we shall not present our Zionism on motivations of fear either for our physical or spiritual safety. Indeed, such Zionism we shall resist wherever we shall meet it. But we shall present Zionism as a challenge and opportunity to share the greatest historic movement of our time which is transforming our people to new dignity and usefulness in the world.

But there are other areas of service which the American synagogue can render Israel, which are no less important. The American synagogue can help Israel meet its religious problem. The culture emerging in Israel is Jewish in the sense that the national experience of the Jewish people is its principal motif, but it is a culture marked by pronounced indifference to the religious factor in life. The dominant groups in Israel have consciously rejected a religious outlook on life, and have tended to replace religious with national values. And precisely because life in Israel is so fulfillingly Jewish in other respects, one does not feel the need of the synagogue unless one is consciously seeking the religious experience as such. The synagogue in America has a long experience in battling with secularism, and it can be of great value to our people in Israel. The utilization of the arts in the beautification of the synagogue edifice itself as well as of the act of worship, the utilization of the modern cultural idiom in presenting its message to the world, the grappling with the problems of the times, those that arise from world conditions as those that arise from the specific factors of life in Israel, the development of an active youth program—these would give the synagogue in Israel new power to assert its point of view in the face of the dominant forces of secularism which challenge it today.

The religious groups in Israel are today depending solely on political action for an improvement of the religious conditions in the country. But religion is one cause that is won or lost in the hearts of people rather than in the forums of parliament. It is significant that the one synagogue in Israel—the Yeshurun Synagogue in Jerusalem—which has the widest influence among the more cultured elements in the country is an American-inspired synagogue. It was built under the inspiration of our own movement, by the United Synagogue of America.

What can Israel give us in return? Israel has already given us some very precious things. It has given us new dignity as a people.

It has removed the despair from the mood of the Jew. It has opened doors to a new life for hundreds of thousands of our people who would otherwise have been doomed to stagnation and death. It has given tremendous stimulation to a revival in Jewish cultural creativity. It has given us a chance to demonstrate the validity of Jewish social values, for in Israel a society is in the making where these values will be incarnated in the living forms of social life. And out of the pressures of life, religious institutions too will in time move to new life and take on again the dynamism and the vitality that will make them sources of inspiration for our own religious needs in the Diaspora.

As life in the two major centers of our people moves freely and mingles freely, the unity of our people will be validated despite the sharp differences in status between them. For the essence of our destiny as Jews transcends nationalism and statehood, and will continue to make us one people. The State of Israel will then be the most deeply cherished asset in our larger cause, to serve God and man, and to work for the perfection of the world under the Kingdom of the Almighty.

The Torch, July, 1950

Dr. Bokser is the spiritual leader of the Forest Hills, N. Y. Jewish Center, where he has served for the past thirty years. He is Visiting Associate Professor in Homiletics at the Jewish Theological Seminary of America, and a member of the faculty of the Institute for Religion and Social Studies. He also is editor of the Seminary's "Eternal Light" radio program. Dr. Bokser is the author of Pharisaic Judaism In Transition, The Legacy of Maimonides, The Wisdom Of The Talmud, The World Of The Cabbalah, Judaism And Modern Man, *and* The Gift of Life. *He has edited* The Week-Day, Sabbath and Festival Prayer Book *as well as the* High Holy Day Prayer Book. *His latest work is* Judaism—Profile Of A Faith.

IMPACT OF THE STATE OF ISRAEL
ON AMERICAN JEWRY

ELEAZAR RIEGER

American Jews who believe that the implications of the establishment of the Jewish state for Jewish life in this country will not be of major importance, deceive themselves and others.

You in this country are now at crossroads together with your fellow-citizens in the democratic countries. Western civilization finds itself still in the throes of a crisis because it lost its aim, and hence the unrest and general bewilderment. A contemporary American historian compared modern society to a mill beside a brook whose waters have dried up. Everything needful seems to be at hand: the mill, the wheels, the wheat, the workingmen. Only one thing is lacking: the power to set and to keep the wheels going.

On top of this general confusion in American society at large, the American Jewish community suffers from its inner crisis, from aimless drifting and confusion. Jewishness has become void of real significance and vitality.

American Jewry is faced with an *unprecedented* problem. Hitherto, Judaism has been kept alive by discrimination and persecution. Indeed, the more the Jews were oppressed, the more intense grew their national consciousness. The crucial problem here is how to preserve Jewishness in the absence of high pressure from without. How can Jewish life be constituted within the framework of a democratic progressive society and still be permeated with the light and glow of Jewish consciousness?

It seems to me that this can and should be achieved with the help and under the impact of the Jewish State on three different levels: A) On the emotional level of vigorous Jewish life-experiences, B) On the cultural level of the Hebrew renaissance and

C) On the level of complete identification with Israel thru settling in Palestine.

Jewish life-experiences will provide for the Jewish masses the necessary *emotional* food. Nationalism is at root irrational, subconscious, emotional, and we have to cultivate the emotional background. We do not want to foster national chauvinism. Chauvinistic nationalism is the rickety offspring of perverted Europe. I trust that Jewish nationalism will uphold its *humanistic, creative character.* The necessary emotional background of Zionism will be achieved thru intensifying practices and experiences, which were common until now, and thru opening new avenues of thrilling life experiences. By practices and experiences, which were rather common in the last generation and require intensification, I am referring to the celebrating of Jewish festivals, customs and folkways, to the songs and dances of the New Palestine, to exhibitions of Jewish art, films, Israel's home-produce, etc. By new avenues of thrilling life experiences, I have in mind the renewing of the institution of pilgrimage to Israel on a much larger scale than ever before in Jewish history. Every Jew and Jewess will be expected—once in life—to pay a visit to Palestine, preferably within the impressionable years of youth. The crown of a life-experience on this level should be a year of service in Palestine as a student or worker.

The impact of the Jewish State *on a higher level* will express itself in the *rebirth* of the Hebrew language and culture in America. A common language is a most *tangible* tie. Nothing, absolutely nothing, can cement the inner bonds between Israel and Jewish America more than the introduction of Hebrew as a *second* language of every intelligent Jew in America. A generation ago a Jewish philosopher ventured a *bleak forecast* that with the establishment of a Jewish commonwealth in Palestine, a rift will be made between Jewry in Palestine and Jewry outside of Palestine; as a consequence, the Jewish people will split into divergent tribes, differing in language, attitudes and aspirations. Thus the unity and continuity of the Jewish people will—as a result of the establishment of the Jewish State—become disrupted. It is our task to make this forecast wrong and untrue. Whoever in America will speak, read and write Hebrew will help to uphold the *unity and continuity* of the Jewish people. The knowledge of Hebrew will be of some *practical* value for all those who will establish commercial contacts with Israel. For new settlers and visitors to Palestine, the knowledge of Hebrew will expedite matters. It is also possible that Hebrew as a second language, becoming the common denominator of all Diaspora Jewry, will help American Jews in their commercial relations with other countries. The cultural value of Hebrew will *enrich* every intelligent American by giving him insight into a *marvelous culture,* so different from that which he knows. I dare say that by getting acquainted with Hebrew he will better know the English language and the American culture as well. He who does not know any other language or civilization fails to appreciate fully and deeply his own language and civilization.

You in this country are surrounded by a magnificent, though possibly a too materialistic, civilization. In order to make the Hebrew language and culture functional in this country, it will have to be raised to a high level. American Jews will have to be not only consumers but *producers* of Hebrew cultural values. *Survival* in terms of the American scene does not mean, in its final analysis, the will not to perish, but to live a full, vigorous Jewish life. The Hebrew Renaissance depends on the creativity of American Jewry perhaps to a no lesser extent than on the cultural crop of Israel. The aristocratic culture of our ancient people is not yet in full evidence in Palestine. The spoken and written Hebrew advanced admirably but is still meagre. On the whole the danger of *Levantinization,* though far less serious than before, still looms over us. Levantinism, as you know, possesses the external trappings of civilization, but lacks depth, exactness and honesty. Intercommunication of personalities and ideas between Israel and American Jewry, and cross-fertilization between both, are not only welcome but most essential.

The impact of the Jewish State on Jewish life in America will be marked in still another direction: *Aliyah.* In this respect we expect drastic, colossal changes. Of the 800,000 Jews now in Palestine, only about 1% has come from the USA, though American Jewry constitutes *almost* one-half of World Jewry. Heretofore American Jewry had excuses: immigration into Palestine was *restricted,* and naturally non-American Jews were given priority. But now the gates of Israel are wide open and settlers from America are most welcome, not only leaders and experts, but many thousands each year. I expect 10% of American Jewry to settle in Palestine within the next generation. Settling in Israel—after the restrictions have been lifted—is not only a privilege but an *obligation*. Palestine is in dire need of settlers from the USA. There is no other country in the world that can serve as a *reservoir* of brain and brawn for Palestine, than the USA. The Halutz movement from Europe is nearing its end and the turn of America is approaching. It is not only a question of numbers but of the spiritual absorptive capacity of Palestine. The remnants of the concentration camps are most welcome in Palestine, but they should not be the only backbone of Jewish immigration. We need healthy men and women, enterprising, confident, with guts and driving power and we have to get them from here. The generous, the almost fabulous material assistance of American Jewry to refugees in Europe and to chalutzim in Palestine cannot replace the privilege and obligation of *personal participation*.

I am confident that the next stage of American Jewish education will be marked by an unprecedented revival of Hebrew and an upsurge of Aliyah to the Commonwealth of Israel.

The Torch, January, 1949.

Dr. Rieger, (1896–1954) Israeli educator, settled in Palestine in 1920 and was co-founder and first president of Hashomer Hatzair. *He was also founder-principal of* Beth Hakarem. *He organized the World Conference of Jewish Education in Jerusalem in 1946, and was president of the World Union of Jewish Education, 1946–1954. Dr. Rieger was Director General of the Israeli Ministry of Education and Culture, 1952–54 and Professor of Education at the Hebrew University, 1940–1954. He was the author of* History of Modern Times, Basic Word List of the Hebrew Language, Hebrew Education in Palestine *(2 vol.),* Vocational Training in the Jewish Community in Palestine, History of Jews in Modern Times, *(3 vol.), and* Everyday Hebrew.

SHOULD THE UNITED SYNAGOGUE OF AMERICA JOIN THE WORLD ZIONIST ORGANIZATION?

✳

"YES," says MORDECAI M. KAPLAN

The formation of the World Council of Synagogues marks the expansion of the Conservative Movement in Judaism. The Conservative Movement will no longer be confined to American Jewry. It will have adherents throughout the world. Insofar as the Conservative Movement is intended to strengthen Judaism, its becoming a world movement augurs well for the future of Judaism. All growth and progress, however, is shadowed by danger. This applies to the spiritual realm as well. The expansion of the Conservative Movement is no exception. The danger inherent in any movement that is sectarian or denominational in character is that of divisiveness. It breaks up the unity of the large body to which its adherents belong, be it nation, church or people. That danger was sensed by our Sages who forbade the formation of sects. The sovereignty of God, according to our Sages, is manifest only when Israel is united (Vayikra R. 30). So important is Jewish unity that it atones for the failure of most Jews to obey the divine precepts.

Having taken part in the organization of the United Synagogue in 1911–1912, I recall distinctly Dr. Schechter's fear that the United Synagogue which he called into being might become a denomination in Judaism. Our climate of opinion, with its social and intellectual freedom, renders uniformity in religious belief and practice even among members of the one religious body unthinkable. There must be room for diversity. The Conservative Movement in Judaism, like the Orthodox and the Reform Movements, is actually a coalition movement consisting of a right, a center and a left.

Nevertheless, we dare not disregard the warning of our Sages against the danger of fragmentizing the Jewish People. The unity of the Jewish People is not only essential to its survival, but even more so, to the *purpose* of its survival, which is that of promulgating the unity of God and the moral responsibility of nationhood. Now that the Conservative Movement is to have adherents in all parts of the world, its tendency to fragmentize the Jewish People is bound to be reinforced. We must therefore adopt a measure that will counteract the divisive influence inherent in the very process of expanding the Conservative Movement. Such a measure is the proposal to affiliate with the Zionist movement as represented in the World Zionist Organization. By identifying itself officially with the cause of Zionism, the World Council of Synagogues would prove that what *unites* it with the rest of world Jewry overshadows what *divides* it from the rest of world Jewry. The World Council of Synagogues would then be acting not only in the spirit of Jewish tradition but would also contribute to the fulfillment of Jewish destiny.

The time has come when the very existence of the Jewish People demands that all the Jewish religious forces identify themselves with the Zionist movement. Only thus can the common concern of all Jews for the State of Israel as the homeland of Judaism demonstrate the spiritual unity of the Jewish People. Only thus can that concern help World Jewry retain its spiritual solidarity. That is the inevitable conclusion which we arrive at when we realize how mutually indispensable are Zionism and Judaism. Judaism can have no future without Zionism; Judaism needs to render it viable in a world infinitely more complex than any that the authors of the Jewish tradition could even have conceived. On the other hand, Zionism without Judaism is subject to serious challenge: Zionism therefore needs Judaism to validate it and help it meet effectively all challenge and opposition.

So far the Orthodox are the only Jewish religious forces that are identified with the Zionist movement. The Conservative and Reform forces, while on the whole sympathetic toward Zionism, have not yet officially integrated Zionist activity into their respective programs. Being merely sympathetic toward Zionism is tantamount to wishful thinking, fearful of contamination by action. All you have to do is to spread the word that Zionism is a "political movement," and by association of ideas you suggest that Zionist activity carries with it a political taint from which a religious movement should keep aloof.

The truth is that the Zionist Movement has from its very inception been the synthesis of three Zionisms: Pre-Messianic, Spiritual and Political. Each has had its own rationale. Pre-Messianic Zionism is represented by the Mizrahi or the followers of Rabbi Zvi Hirsch Kalischer. It is based on the assumption that the destiny of the Jewish People is set forth in the traditional conception of a personal Messiah who will bring about the ingathering of the Jewish People in Eretz Yisrael. As a prerequisite for that to happen, however, the Jews must establish themselves in Eretz Yisrael in sufficient numbers and lay the foundation of a normal national life there.

Spiritual Zionism is represented by the followers of Moses Hess and Ahad Ha-Am. It views the destiny of the Jewish People as being the resumption of national life in Eretz Yisrael and the further development of the moral and spiritual or religious values there. As a prerequisite to the fulfillment of that destiny it is necessary to reawaken in the Jewish People its will to live and to live abundantly. To that end Jews have to settle in Eretz Yisrael where they can have the opportunity to foster to the fullest extent their own spiritual culture or civilization.

Political Zionism is represented by the followers of Herzl and Nordau. It maintains that the Jews constitute a people—one people, made such not by their own consent but through the irrepressible and universal character of anti-Semitism, whether latent or active. "We are one people," said Herzl, "our enemies have made us one without our consent" (The *Jewish State*, 1946, p. 92). Self-respecting Jews have no choice other than that of deciding to become once again a free and independent people. To carry out that purpose they need a land, preferably Eretz Yisrael. For the right to such a land they should engage in international negotiation.

If Zionism were merely a political movement, it would be unable to make out a case for itself. Granted that the Jews need a land of their own, for the simple reason they are not entirely welcome in any of the lands of the established nations. That puts them in the position of refugees in search of a haven. From a purely political standpoint the Jewish occupation of Eretz Yisrael must appear to the neutral observer as a solution of the Jewish refugee problem through the creation of an Arab refugee problem, and the granting of the Mandate over Palestine to Britain as essentially a thinly disguised form of 19th century Western imperialism. As a matter of fact, the fathers of political Zionism, Pinsker, Herzl and Nordau, had planned at first to secure not necessarily Eretz Yisrael but some uninhabited territory as a haven for the Jews. Moreover, from a political standpoint, Zionism fulfilled its purpose with the establishment of the State of Israel which alone has the right to engage in political negotiation with other states.

But, even as a *fait accompli* politically, the State of Israel is still in need of moral validation. That validation can come only from the historical claim on Eretz Yisrael which is put forward by the Jewish People on the basis of its religious tradition, a tradition honored as divine by the Christian and Moslem world. In the final stages of the political negotiations with Britain for the right to establish a Jewish homeland in Palestine, it was the historical claim advanced by Jewish People on Eretz Yisrael as the land of its origin and as the land to which its religion had taught it to look for the fulfillment of its destiny that tipped the scale. This moral and spiritual claim which we Jews have to Eretz Yisrael is far from being properly understood to say nothing of its being fully recognized. The task, therefore, of Judaism is to validate Zionism by calling attention to the full significance of the Biblical tradition concerning the place of Eretz Yisrael in the spiritual development of our People, and subsequently in that of mankind.

Unfortunately this identification of Jewish religion with Eretz Yisrael is still misjudged by Christian scholars, and all the more by Christian believers as a survival of ancient tribal or national religion. Hence the need to dispel that notion, and to make clear that the identification of Jewish religion with Eretz Yisrael carries a teaching of universal import of which mankind is sorely in need. What the Jewish People was to make of itself through its territorial civilization was what every nation in the world is expected to make of itself, what A. D. Gordon described as "a nation in the image of God." That means that every human society is expected to conduct its economy, its politics, its culture and its social life so as to enable all who belong to it to live reliable, responsible and creative lives. Such is the spiritual commitment or covenant which binds Jews to Eretz Yisrael. Those Jews who settle there are in a position to make good that commitment.

As for those of us who are destined to remain in the Diaspora, our role is so to influence the nations into whose body politic we have been admitted that their nationhood too shall reflect the image of God. That is the kind of living creative Judaism which is needed to validate Zionism.

On the other hand, Judaism, whether interpreted in traditional or in modern terms, is not viable and cannot have a future without Zionism. Judaism can live only as long as there is a living Jewish People. If Zionism had not come on the scene eight or nine decades ago, there might have been a formless conglomerate of people calling themselves Jews but not a history-making Jewish People. That would also have been the end of a salvation-bringing Judaism. For a salvation-bringing Judaism presupposes the existence of a history-making Jewish People, and not a mere unnamable, unclassifiable, status-less group of individuals identified as Jews. Hence, what Judaism needs first and foremost, even prior to a land, is an identifiable Jewish People, The most significant slogan in Judaism is: "Hear O *Israel,* the Lord our God, the Lord is One." To accept the teaching of the oneness and onliness of God in all of its depth and comprehensiveness one has to accept it, not merely as a philosopher or theologian, but as a member of the House or People of Israel. According to the great anonymous prophet, the Jewish People is a divine creation intended to demonstrate the power and glory of God. It is only through the Jews as a people with all the vicissitudes and opportunities of a collective life that Judaism can function as a spiritual force for the individual Jew as well as for the rest of the world.

Where, indeed, is there an identifiable Jewish People? There was a Jewish People during the centuries that Jews lived in enforced dispersion. The almost unbroken uniformity of belief and practice that obtained in the past made possible indivisible unity. We did not need our enemies to unify us without our consent. Came the emancipation and enlightenment and wrought havoc with the unity of the Jewish People. Emancipation has led to the integration of Jews into the body politic of the nations of which they are citizens. We have to adopt the language, culture and ideology of those nations. As a result, each local aggregate of Jews develops its own communal characteristics that render it incommunicable with every other geographic Jewish community. Mere memories of a receding past which has become irrelevant to the present cannot be expected to serve as a substitute for the live interchange of daily experiences that welds people into a People.

Even more disintegrative has been the Enlightenment which, as its very name implies, is a challenge to tradition. The response to the challenge of enlightenment even among those who are determined to remain within the Household of Israel has been various and divisive. If not for anti-Semitism which forced Jews to act in common for philanthropic and self-defense purposes, they would soon drift so far apart as to have nothing in common as Jews. "I think it is high time," wrote Arthur Koestler, "to liquidate this anachronism of a separate community dispersed all over the world, which cannot be defined either as a separate race, nation or religious sect."

Never in all our history have we Jews so experienced as we do today the tragic significance of the divine command to the prophet Hosea that he name his child Lo-Ammi—my non-people, in order to remind our ancestors that they had become a non-people. To mention only one or two dangerous symptoms of our non-peoplehood: in the series of volumes edited by Dr. Louis Finkelstein known as *The Jews: Their History, Culture and Religion,* there is a chapter by an eminent anthropologist entitled "Who Are the Jews?" The concluding sentence of that article reads as follows: "A word can mean anything to many people and no word means more things to more people than does the word Jew!" A second symptom is a symposium held recently in London. It was participated in by four Anglo-Jewish writers—two playwrights, one poet and one critic, who have by this time made a name for themselves. The theme of the symposium was "Is Jewish Society Bankrupt?" The main question which they had to answer was: Could their Jewish milieu nurture and stimulate them in their writing? Their unanimous opinion was that Jewish society in England was bankrupt because it gave the writer nothing worthwhile to write about. The fact is that Jewish religion in England enjoys government recognition. Why, then, is Jewish society there bankrupt? The answer is: there is no identifiable Jewish People with a culture and homeland of its own.

Since it is impossible to formulate a *descriptive* definition of the term "Jew," it is all the more impossible to arrive at a *normative* definition of the term Jew, i.e., a standard of what is an authentic Jew. When the question was raised some time ago in Israel as to who was a Jew, among those who dissented from tradition no two opinions were alike. In other words, once we deviate in the least from the Jewish tradition, we are left without any base for a norm in Jewish life. That leaves ninety percent of the Jews spiritually stranded.

The lack of such a standard is responsible for the irrelevance and consequent meaninglessness of most of what goes by the name of Jewish education, on whatever level. The recent ruling that the 600,000 children in Israel should be imbued with Jewish consciousness is intended to give them a sense of continuity with the Jewish People of the past and sense of unity with those of the Jewish People who live outside Eretz Yisrael. The intensive biblical and historical studies give the children an adequate sense of continuity with the Jewish People of the past. But as for cultivating a sense of unity of the Jewish People of the present, what is there to identify that Jewish People? Jewish education is a misnomer, unless it is a means of incorporating the child into the Jewish People. For that to be possible, the Jewish People must have some indisputably unifying factor to give it reality. In the absence of such a unifying factor the social heritage which is being transmitted can only have an antiquarian value for scholars of antiquity, but can have no interest for the average lay person.

Hence, the most urgent need of all Jews for their own self-respect and peace of mind is to reconstitute the Jewish People. That can come about only if some visible and tangible achievement be made the common objective of all Jews and therefore that which can unite them into a People. It is impossible to expect Jews who cannot subscribe to traditional Judaism in the form in which it has come down from the past to agree on any belief or practice other than on most of the ten commandments. That kind of agreement, however, would not distinguish Jews from non-Jews.

No matter how far apart Jews may be ideologically, religiously, culturally, or politically, a common interest in such an undertaking can certainly arouse in them a sense of solidarity. A common territory is to the life of a people what a catalyst is to a chemical compound. It brings about an interactivity among all the elements in a people's life and fuses them into an organic unity. Out of the community of spirit emerges a living tradition or social heritage, which is what we understand by a civilization. That kind of land-rooted civilization is normally a religious civilization, not because it happens to have religion, but because it itself is religion. Such a religious civilization is what Judaism is meant to be, and it can become that only through spiritual Zionism.

Thus far however spiritual Zionism has taken into account only those of the Jewish People who have or will have settled in Eretz Yisrael. It has not had the opportunity or the energy to think through in thoroughgoing fashion the problem of what is to become of the greater part of World Jewry that is to remain in a state of dispersion. Are they to be consigned to ultimate absorption and disappearance as Jews? By no means need that be the case. All that is necessary is to arrive at a new conception of Jewish Peoplehood. According to that conception, the part of Jewry that is in Eretz Yisrael in relation to the communities in the Diaspora would be like the keystone to the arch which it upholds. In other words, Spiritual Zionism can find a way of having the Jews in the Diaspora experience, even if indirectly, the catalytic effect of the Land of Israel. Jewish religious civilization with its homeland in Eretz Yisrael can achieve symbiosis, or living together, with the civilization of the countries where Jews live.

In order, however, to consummate that development of Judaism, Spiritual Zionism must unite with all the religious forces that exist in the Diaspora, whether Orthodox, Conservative or Reform. The World Zionist Organization and all who represent the religious forces in the Diaspora must unite for the purpose of achieving that spiritual Jewish unity which would embrace all of world Jewry, and which would derive its generative power from Eretz Yisrael. If the World Council of Synagogues would consider joining the World Zionist Organization, in accordance with the suggestion of Dr. Nahum Goldmann, I would suggest that the World Council of Synagogues adopt the following Platform that would clearly define its position with regard to the relationship of Judaism to Zionism:

"The Conservative Movement in Judaism from its very inception has regarded the fulfillment of the goals of the Basle Platform as indispensable to the creative survival of the Jewish People and the future of Judaism.

"Coordinate with the establishment of the State of Israel has been its recognition of the need for world Jewish unity.

"The World Zionist Organization which has been dedicated to the fulfillment of the Basle Platform has been the main symbol of world Jewish unity since the beginning of the Jewish emancipation. If the W.Z.O. is to continue as such a symbol, the Conservative Movement advocate the addition of the following principles in its platform:

"1. The existence of a democratically organized, spiritually sensitive and politically and economically secure State of Israel is indispensable to the creative survival of the Jewish People and to the future of Judaism.

"2. The creative survival of the Jewish People is predicated on the assumption that its unity is not of a political character but of an ethnic, cultural and spiritual character.

"3. Therefore, coordinate with the concern of the World Zionist Organization for the State of Israel should be its concern for the fostering of that spiritual unity."

The Conservative Movement should apply for affiliation with the World Zionist Organization on the basis of the foregoing Platform, without making the adoption of that Platform by the World Zionist Organization itself a prerequisite to joining the World Zionist Organization. The World Zionist Organization, on the other hand, is by no means precluded from admitting the World Council of Synagogues on the basis of the proposed Platform. That Platform is in keeping with one of the three main tasks of Zionism as defined in what is known as the Jerusalem Program which was adopted by the 23rd World Zionist Congress in August, 1951. Among its three main tasks, one is "the fostering of the unity of the Jewish People." Since it is entirely within the right of the constituent bodies or parties of the World Zionist Organization to define in specific terms what the World Zionist

Organization states in general terms, the Conservative movement is entirely within its rights from a Zionist standpoint in defining the unity of the Jewish People as eminently spiritual.

It behooves us to place the question at issue before the regional groups of the Conservative movement. The World Zionist Congress will meet in Jerusalem next summer. That gives those regional groups ample time to come to a decision.

Let us not forget that both Judaism and Zionism are at present in a condition of crisis. They are both in danger of being overcome by the disintegrative forces which emanate from contemporary civilization. If their adherents, realizing the danger, will merge their loyalties and their efforts, the outcome is bound to be both a greater Zionism and a greater Judaism. May we avail ourselves of the present opportunity of following up the establishment of the State of Israel with the reconstitution of the Jewish People as a spiritual and dynamic reality.

The Torch, Winter, 1960.

SHOULD THE UNITED SYNAGOGUE OF AMERICA JOIN THE WORLD ZIONIST ORGANIZATION?

✳

NAHUM GOLDMANN

My friends, I don't know how you feel about Jewish life, but I am very deeply worried. We are living in a situation where most of us are very easily fooled by the beautiful and prosperous facade of Jewish life, of organizations and presidents and vice presidents and executive directors and budgets of millions and buildings and centers and quarrels and conventions . . . and one would think that this Jewish life is overflowing with vitality, and the Jewish People is safe and secure in its position.

I know a little about Jewish life, not only in this country but all over the world; I am not exactly a scholar or an historian, but I believe I know a little about the Jewish past. I don't know of any period in our history when, in my humble opinion, the survival of our people was so endangered as it is today . . . despite this facade and despite even the State of Israel.

The simple reason for this—and Dr. Kaplan from another point of view has already said it beautifully and I can be short in repeating—is primarily the fact that we are no longer living in our safe separated life which we lived for centuries. As long as Jews lived in the ghetto or in a shackle, in whatever form it was, our entity and distinctiveness was assured. They lived a life which was dominated by the Torah and Jewish law. From the first minute when the Jew awoke until the last hour of the day when he went to sleep, his life was regulated. It was regulated by the same laws if the Jew lived in Russia or Spain or in Morocco or in the *Yemen;* they lived in what Henrich Heine once called "the imported fatherland of the Jews." This system of Jewish law which was religion and culture and nationalism, all together, guaranteed the distinctive existence of the Jewish people.

313

These conditions have passed away, and it's no use weeping about their having passed. We cannot change history. We have fought for emancipation. Now we are emancipated. Anti-Semitism is not a serious problem anymore in Jewish life compared to what it was. We are more or less integrated everywhere, not only in this great American democracy but nearly everwhere, even in Morocco and Tunisia, in countries where Jews thirty years ago were treated as slaves. We are integrated into the lives of the countries in which we live and we participate fully in them . . . And, with this, the main fortress, the main basis of Jewish distinctiveness has fallen.

I said on another occasion that we have managed in 2000 years of suffering and persecution to learn more than any other people in the world how to survive *tzores*. What we have not learned yet, and I have my grave doubts that we will learn it, and it will require a tremendous effort on the part of the Jewish generation of today to learn it, is to survive in prosperity and under economically and politically safe conditions.

Therefore, I say I don't know of any period in which our survival as a people was as threatened as it is today. The main task of these generations of Jews which we represent, the one which has witnessed the greatest tragedy of Jewish history and at the same time one of the greatest miracles of Jewish history in the same period, the great task is to secure the survival and the future of our people.

In order to do it, I think three great problems have to be solved. All of them together in my concept represent the meaning of Zionism today.

The first one (and I can again be very brief after what Dr. Kaplan said about it), the most central one, is to maintain the unity of our people. Once this unity breaks down, there is no future for our people.

There are three grave dangers to the unity of our people today. The first one is that they are being integrated into the various countries and civilizations, with the result of the danger of separatism, and of every Jewish community being on its own.

I would like to dwell for a few moments on this great American Jewish community which for a long time to come will determine, together with Israel, the delivery of our people. This great

Jewish community represents an over-organized chaos, with its multitude of institutions and organizations for which there is no unifying framework. There isn't even one platform in this country where Jews of various opinions can discuss their common problems. There was one attempt to create it—the American Jewish Conference, and it was destroyed. I tried a little in bringing together the presidents of various organizations for cooperation on problems of Israel, but it is difficult even to maintain this very shaky form of a loose platform where at least twenty or twenty-one presidents could discuss things together.

This danger of Jewish communities acting on their own and the various groups acting on their own is the first grave and permanent menace to the unity of the Jewish People.

There is a second menace which has very deep effect, the cold war. This cold war which has split humanity into two blocks has split more than anything else the Jewish people. Millions of Jews behind the Iron Curtain are separated from the totality of Jewish life . . . and I don't have to tell you what it means after having lost 6,000,000 Jews in the Nazi period to be menaced by the possibility of losing another 3,000,000 Jews as part and parcel of Jewish life, within one generation, half of the Jewish people. If the cold war would end, I believe that the Iron Curtain would disappear. But this does not depend on us and we have in the meantime to pray and do whatever we can in order to maintain at least some loose contact with these great Jewish communities in Eastern Europe.

Then there is a third menace to our unity as a people, which may appear paradoxical to you, the one created by the emergence of the State of Israel. If nothing will be done, a gap will develop between Israel and the Jewish people outside of it because of the totally different conditions of life they have.

So the first task is to avert the three menaces to our unity as a people. The second task is intimately connected with this first one. The second task is to build this center in Israel without which I cannot see a permanent future for our people. The great fortresses of Jewish spiritual existence in Eastern and Central Europe have disappeared forever—if tomorrow the regimes in Eastern Europe would change or if tomorrow the Soviet and other governments would give all facilities to live a Jewish life to their Jewish communities, never again will Russian and Polish and Galician and Hungarian and German Jews play the role in Jewish life which they played in the 17th and 18th and 19th Centuries, having served as the great sources and producers of nearly all leading ideas on which the Jewish people, wherever it lives, exists today.

Once these fortresses have been destroyed without any realistic hope of rebuilding them, there is one possibility only, to create a substitute and more than a substitute, something much more creative than a substitute, namely to create the new great center in Israel.

Let us not believe that this center is already secure and safe. Here, too, we are in great danger of living in a fool's paradise, in being seduced by the facade of Israel and being prevented from seeing through the facade to the real great unsolved problems of Israel. Just as we are being deceived by the beautiful institutions and organizations in the facade of Jewish life here in our country, we are also misled by the appearance of the facade of ministers and presidents and ambassadors and excellencies of Israel. Despite all that, none of the great problems of Israel on which its future will depend have yet been solved. Israel has not yet achieved either peace or economic independence, and it will require tremendous efforts to achieve both.

To build a center in Israel, without which, at least in my humble opinion, survival and a future for the Jewish people in the world is impossible, will require quite an effort on behalf of our generation, and it will require much more than giving money to Israel, which is the simplest and most primitive form of helping Israel. It will require a strenuous and great effort of this Jewish generation in order to enable Israel to solve these problems, because without the Jewish people in the world, there isn't a ghost of a chance that Israel will solve them, either politically or economically.

So, I say this is the second great task of our generation . . . cementing the unity of our people by creating this center of unity, to use the wonderful picture and notion which Dr. Kaplan gave you, creating the keystone in the arch, to make it secure, which is far from being secure. And this is tied up with the third problem, namely to tie the Jewish people to this center—one of the most difficult problems of our life and of our history. We haven't yet begun to realize the problem and certainly not solved it.

The problem of the relationship between Israel and the Diaspora is the most difficult problem of our life. It cannot be solved by campaigns and financial support. Great problems of people are not solved by money, however important money may be. They are solved by the development of spiritual and moral methods of dealing with them. How to bind Jewish communities in the world with Israel is a formidable problem for which there is no precedent in the life of other people because this problem doesn't exist for them. There is no parallel of a people in the world whose center represents a minority of the people whose majority lives outside of it.

These problems we have to solve without patterns, without precedents and if our generation will solve them, it will be a very creative and constructive generation.

In order to do this we not only must build Israel but at the same time build Jewish life wherever it is and in whatever form it expresses itself.

I am not entering into this for meaningless discussion. Is Israel equal to the Diaspora or has it priority over it? I understand the great theoretical fascination of this discussion, and I belong to those for whom Israel is Israel, Zion is Zion and *Gollus* is *Gollus,* in whatever form it is. But, this is my conviction . . . For all practical purposes both are of equal importance. Israel without a strong Jewish community in the world cannot begin to solve the essential problems on which its destiny will depend, and the Jewish people, the Jewish communities in the world without Israel as a great center of its pride and its inspiration and its creativeness can, in my humble opinion, also not begin to dream about the real solution of its essential vital problems.

So, we have to do both. For the Zionist Movement of today to take care of immigration to Israel is important, and to take care of Jewish education, of Jewish cultural values in the Diaspora, is no less important. Both are essential because in order to maintain a strong Jewish community we should be in a position to build Israel and enable those in Israel to solve their problems in order to secure Jewish survival. We have to engage in a process of educational and cultural activities which will require tremendous efforts.

We have made great progress, I know, in the last few years and maybe decades, but compared with the magnitude of the problem—it will require efforts much greater than anything we have done until now.

We must, in order to make this change, revise the fundamental policies of Jewish life, the order of priorities in Jewish life. We are a reactionary people. We are used to certain terms and methods and notions, and it's very difficult for many of us to change them.

Relief and philanthropy are no more the Number One problem in Jewish life, nor is fighting anti-Semitism. This was the case fifty years ago in the time of Russian Tsarism, of Polish or Nazi Anti-Semitism. The problem today of Jewish life is not to prevent Jews from starvation. We are not a poor people. The problem of Jewish life is no more relief and philanthropy and the artificial fight against anti-Semitism. The real problem is the internal problem . . . educating youth; securing the survival of the younger generation; developing Jewish spiritual and cultural values; giving the younger generation a justification for being Jews.

This can be done only through all the great values of our past and all the great values of Israel in the present and of the Israel of tomorrow, when it will be more secure and perhaps will have the possibility to develop its cultural creativeness not burdened by security problems and by economic survival.

Both parts of these activities, securing Israel through the full cooperation of the Jewish communities in the world and securing Jewish survival outside of Israel with the full cooperation and help of Israel are intimately tied up. These are equal aspects of the same one great problem of securing our survival; and the whole debate of which is number one and which is number two priority is a meaningless debate for those who are engaged in practical work.

Now this for me is Zionism. To secure the unity of the people by securing the center of our life in Israel, and to develop to the fullest Jewish survival and Jewish life outside of Israel, that is Zionism.

Now about the argument that Zionism is a political movement.

Here too there is a great danger in this clinging to words which have lost their meaning. What is political about the Zionism of today? Do we deal with the problems of Israel's internal, or external politics? You may rely on Ben Gurion that we are not dealing with this. And he is absolutely right. First it was a political movement, when it fought for a State; but then the movement was a Jewish government, so to speak, on the way, as Herzl once said. But once the State has taken over, what is political in this movement which arranges immigration and absorption of immigrants and settles them on the land and develops schools and helps Jewish youth and brings them to Israel and ties them up with Israel . . . What's political about it? It gives help to Israel politically in difficult moments; but so do all Jews, practically including your organization, with the exception of the Council of Judaism.

One last remark . . . For years I am of the opinion, and I say to my Zionist comrades with much greater frankness than I say it even here, that the Zionist Organization in its present structure cannot fulfill effectively its task.

In my opinion, 60, 70, 80 per cent of the Jewish people are potential Zionists today, but they are afraid to admit it. Those Jews who accept the principle of the unity of the Jewish people and accept the conviction that the center of Jewish spiritual development in the future will be in Israel, and who are ready to be tied up with Israel not only by giving money but by taking part in the development of Israel, economically, and spiritually, all those who believe in these activities are Zionists in my opinion.

I fully agree with Dr. Kaplan that unless this majority of the Jewish people who are theoretically Zionists will be brought together in one great organization, and I don't see at the moment a better one than the Zionist Organization, unless they are brought together in one framework, enabling united action, I am afraid we won't be able to fulfill this task.

I am making (if I may conclude on this personal note) for years the not easy attempt to convince my Zionist comrades of this necessity of enlarging the organization. It's not easy . . . old traditions and methods of thinking stand in the way.

But I think on the whole, the movement is ready to accept this. The decision arrived at at the last Actions Committee to enable new groups who are not yet officially Zionists to join in a new form, not being forced to affiliate with existing groups, and being given a recognized representation, is an expression of this readiness.

The success of this process depends less today on the Zionists than on the so-called non-Zionists. Will they (and permit me to conclude with this frank remark) primarily think of their own organizational vested interests and be afraid of a new alignment and of stepping into new fields of organizational life; will they primarily be influenced and guided by their own narrow, very legitimate, but narrow interests as seen in the context of the whole Jewish life? Then, nothing will happen; then the Zionist movement won't be enlarged. No other movement larger than it will be established because the same argument will prevail there too, and as a result the program for Israel will continue in a decentralized and over-organized, and at the same time disorganized way; and we won't be able to cope with these tremendous problems.

On the other hand, if those who are today outside the movement will be able to overcome their own organizational hesitance and be ready to see the problem from the larger point of view of Jewish life, of Jewish life after the Hitler period, of Jewish life after the emergence of the state, and see it in the context of the global world situation of the Jewish people, then, our generation could unite its efforts and concentrate on these three essential problems of our life, it then would be able to discharge its obligations to Jewish history.

Your organization could play a pioneer role in this process. I want to conclude only with the hope as a Jew that you will rise to the occasion and set an example for the whole of the Jewish people to create the one great framework of concentrated action to solve our problems. This generation of Jews is facing responsibilities which have confronted no previous generation. It is the generation which saw a third of its people disappear and couldn't do much to save them. But it is the same generation which has the opportunity of creating the state and implementing the dreams of many generations of Jews who were certainly as good as we, if not better ones, and may have deserved it more than we to see a State of Israel emerge but did not have the opportunity. We have the courage and the wisdom to use this opportunity and help this state emerge. I don't know of any generation so burdened, so faced with so many holy and sacred duties as our generation; and I only hope and pray that we will be a generation which sees the miracle and will be able to fulfill its task and leave a more secure Jewish people both in Israel and in the Diaspora to future Jewish generations.

The Torch, Winter, 1960.

Dr. Goldmann, world renowned Jewish statesman, has been President of the World Zionist Organization since 1956. He was a leading spirit in World Zionist conferences and has been President of the Conference of Jewish Material Claims against Germany since 1951. He instigated the Jewish-Israel Agreement with the West German Government and chaired the Commission for Jewish claims on Austria. He was initiator of the Law of Status adopted by the Knesset in Israel. He was formerly Acting Chairman of the Zionist Actions Committee, Member of the Zionist Executive, representative of the Jewish Agency for Palestine to the League of Nations, representative to the United Nations and Chairman of the American Section of the Jewish Agency. Dr. Goldmann is now President of Judaica Foundation, Geneva, Switzerland.

SHOULD THE UNITED SYNAGOGUE OF AMERICA JOIN THE WORLD ZIONIST ORGANIZATION?

✳

"NO," says SIMON GREENBERG

Our discussion rests upon a number of fundamental agreements. All of us have been confirmed Zionists for decades before May, 1948. All of us agree that the establishment of the State of Israel and its progress since then constitute events of miraculous proportions. All of us believe that in the world as at present organized, the continued existence of a politically democratic, spiritually sensitive, and economically and physically secure State of Israel is indispensable to the future welfare of Judaism and the Jewish people. All of us would like to see greater unity within the ranks of the Jewish people. Finally, all of us, I believe, agree that no group can function effectively in its own behalf without having a conception of its own status acceptable to the main body of its own members, and intelligible to the members of the groups with whom it comes into contact. The fact that in our day there is no conception of Jewish status universally accepted by Jews and understood by all others, is at the moment the greatest single impediment to long-term, concerted, constructive thought and action in behalf of the future of Jews and Judaism.

All of us, therefore, want very much to create an organization which would nationally and internationally:

a) mobilize maximum support for the State of Israel;

b) establish maximum Jewish unity; and

c) embody an acceptable concept of Jewish status.

While there are differences of opinion amongst us on how to best mobilize support for the State of Israel, or how best to achieve Jewish unity, neither of these two areas constitutes what I conceive to be the heart of our discussion. *As I see it, it is the question of Jewish status which is at the root of the most signifi-*

cant differences amongst us. I firmly believe that the establishment of Jewish unity or the mobilization of support for the State
of Israel which is achieved at the price of a false concept of Jewish
status in the world, is bound ultimately to undermine the very
existence of the people we seek to unite and in whose behalf we
desire the existence of the State of Israel.

What do I mean by the term "Jewish status?" Let me indicate
first what I do not mean. The term "status" is very often associated with such concepts as prestige, influence, power, "yiches."
These associations are clearly reflected in the phrase "status seekers," used as a title of a book currently very popular in America.
Now, there is nothing reprehensible about wanting to find favor
in the eyes of man as well as God, but when I use the term
"Jewish status" I do not have Jewish glamour or prestige in mind.

For me, the term "Jewish status" refers to that quality or characteristic which confers upon one his status as a Jew, and admits
him into the fellowship of the Jewish People, regardless of where
he resides, what language he speaks, or to what state he may owe
political allegiance.

The institution which most adequately embodies that concept
of Jewish status which I believe to be the only ultimately valid
one, is the Synagogue. *A Jew is anyone who is eligible for membership in the fellowship of the Synagogue.* I do not say that only
those who are *actually* members in specific synagogal congregations are to be accounted as Jews. I say that *only those who are
eligible for such membership are to be counted as Jews.*

There are differences of opinion amongst us on what constitutes such eligibility. But we are, I believe, all agreed that *birth
alone does not always determine eligibility.* Important as birth is
for the establishment of status within any group, it is not ultimately determinative. Within every group, a conscious act upon
the part of an adult member can change the status conferred upon
him by birth. Anyone born within the legal jurisdiction of the
United States is an American citizen. Birth alone can thus determine his status as an American for the rest of his life, regardless
of where he lives, what language he speaks, or what religion he
professes. But if he were to ask for and receive citizenship within
another political sovereignty, he would lose his status as an American, as far as America was concerned, regardless of how others

would consider them. Thus, also, anyone born a Jew acquires Jewish status for life, regardless of what country he lives in, to what government he owes allegiance, or what language he speaks. But even one born a Jew cannot by an act of free-will join another religious fellowship, and at the same time retain his eligibility for membership in the synagogue.

The Halakha may for formal, legal reasons, and within very narrow limits, continue to regard a Jewish convert as a Jew. There is the well-known Rabbinic dictum, ישראל אף על פי שחטא ישראל הוא. One born a Jew remains a Jew even though he may have sinned. Jewish converts belong technically, legally to this class of sinners who need only to do *Tshuva*—to repent—in order to be restored to their full status as Jews. They need not undergo any special ceremonies of reconversion. But Rabbinic law certainly does not bestow Jewish status on Jewish Christians, or Jewish Mohammedans, or Jewish Buddhists, as a class. No such groups are recognized as acceptable subdivisions of the Jewish people, similar in status to Hasidim, or Misnagdim, or Reform and Conservative Jews. Moreover, regardless of the fine distinctions Rabbinic law may have made in all these matters, the living, self-respecting Jewish community invariably severed its bonds with the Jewish convert.

On the other hand, *one born of non-Jews may acquire Jewish status, not by learning how to speak Hebrew or Yiddish, nor by becoming a citizen of the State of Israel, nor by marrying a Jew; he can become a Jew only by qualifying for membership in the Jewish religious fellowship, i.e., in a Synagogue.* It is the *Synagogue,* and not birth alone, nor language alone, nor any political, philanthropic or cultural institution which bestows Jewish status upon the individual, regardless of where he may reside. And it is to the Synagogue and to what it symbolizes in terms of man's relations to God, that we refer when we say that we believe the unity of the Jewish people has been and should be *spiritual* or *religious* in essence, rather than political, ethnic, or cultural in essence.

Any organization that implicitly, let alone explicitly, rejects this conception of Jewish status will, in the long run, undermine the foundations upon which the whole structure of Jewish life everywhere, including the State of Israel, ultimately depends.

This concept of Jewish status has, during the last 175 years, been repeatedly challenged by many distinguished men and women who were born Jews. They rejected not only the fellowship of any specific synagogal congregations, but also the theological and metaphysical foundations of the Synagogue. However, they did not seek to join any *other religious fellowship,* nor did they desire *to deny* or *to sever* their relations with the Jewish People. On the contrary, they loved deeply many aspects of the Jewish heritage. Some loved the Hebrew, others the Yiddish language. Some were attached to what they liked to call Jewish folkways, or patterns of living, while others were kept within the Jewish group merely because the outer pressures made it impossible to do anything else. It was but natural that none of them should want to think of themselves as inadequate or partial Jews. Hence they interpreted the Jewish historic experience and defined Jewish status in terms of that aspect of the Jewish heritage which continued to hold their own interest and allegiance. To some, therefore, Jewish status was associated with the *Yiddish* language. To others, with the *Hebrew* language. To some with works of *charity* and *philanthropy.* To others with *anti-defamation* activity.

The task set before the Jewish people by the Zionist Movement in the first paragraph of the Basle program, namely that of establishing a publicly recognized and legally assured home for the Jewish people in Palestine, was the one which attracted to itself, if not always the *greatest* number of these non-synagogue minded Jews, yet *always those amongst them* who were most zealously concerned with the preservation of the Jewish people as an identifiable group among the peoples of the world.

We, of the United Synagogue of America, never denied the significance of cultural, philanthropic, recreational and defense activities. *On the contrary,* the high *importance* we attached to them we expressed in our two-fold program: on the one hand we sought to incorporate *into the program of the Synagogue* as many of these activities as possible. Hence, we were the first to develop the synagogue center. On the other hand, both our local and national leaders urged the members of our synagogues to *contribute* to, and be *active* in these other non-synagogal groups. Indeed, our synagogue pulpits so often resounded with appeals for membership in other non-Synagogue organizations, and for contributions to non-specifically congregational causes, that one of the most common accusations brought against our Rabbis by those who have a narrow conception of what constitutes religion, was that they were neglecting their religious duties.

We, of the United Synagogue, acted as we did because we believe that those *born as Jews* have many *legitimate human needs* which the Synagogue, as at present organized, is not in a position to fulfill. They have need for physical and economic security. They have need to preserve all those spiritual and cultural treasures which as Jews they have inherited from their forebears. They have need for fellowship. They have need to express themselves in philanthropy and cultural creativity. They have need to engage in all those legitimate activities which give them a sense of dignity and self-respect as human beings known as Jews. But while the Rabbis, and lay United Synagogue leaders urged the members of their congregations to support all kinds of activities whose purpose it was to satisfy legitimate human needs experienced by Jews, they have consistently and strenuously opposed the *identification* of a *legitimate human need with the essence of Jewish being*. They have constantly warned against the tendency of every Jewish organization to attribute to the *specific need* it serves the power to confer *Jewish* status upon its *members,* and ultimately upon the Jewish People as a whole, among the peoples of the world.

The State of Israel unquestionably enables the Jews of the world in our day to meet the largest number of pressing, inescapable, legitimate and honorable needs that they have as Jews in the modern world. Hence, it is but natural that the organization most directly and completely devoted to the welfare of the State of Israel should feel that *its program* is sufficient to bestow Jewish status upon those who participate in it, and that it should want to become the symbol of Jewish status in the world.

The concern which we, of the United Synagogue, feel for the welfare of the State of Israel is, I firmly believe, as sincere and as profound as that of all others identified with the Zionist Movement. Indeed our concern goes beyond considerations of only the *secular* human needs which the State of Israel helps Jews everywhere to meet, important and legitimate as those are. Our relations to the State of Israel are rooted in *religious* ties to Eretz Yisrael, the nature of which I have at some length discussed elsewhere.

We see in the establishment of the State of Israel not only the response to the cry of the *Jewish heart* for a life of human dignity, creativity and security, but also a response to the longing of the *Jewish soul* for *Kirvat Elohim*, for the nearness of God, and the Kingdom of God upon this earth. Hence, we must be indefatigable in our efforts as individuals and as a United Synagogue to help our brethren in the State of Israel in every honorable way at our disposal, to build and defend their political, social and economic structure.

But we also believe that Jewish life can and must flourish *anywhere* and *everywhere* in the world where men cherish freedom and have respect for the religious conscience of their fellowmen. We believe that Jewish life can, and must, flourish in the United States and that even as a flourishing and free Jewish life in the State of Israel is indispensable to a flourishing and free Jewish life in the United States, so also does a strong, self-respecting, creative Jewish community in America have a contribution to make to the welfare of the State of Israel, a contribution which verges in significance on the indispensable. Hence, we believe that the Jewish communities of both countries must be tireless in their exertions to build spiritual bridges between themselves. The nature of those spiritual bridges, and how they are to be built, with special emphasis upon the roles of the Synagogue and the Hebrew language, I have indicated elsewhere.

In our concern for the welfare of the State of Israel, and for the building of spiritual bridges between us, we must, however, continue to be ever aware of the basic truth that it is the fellowship of the Synagogue that confers Jewish status upon us and not the State of Israel, and *that the Synagogue is in no way to be made subordinate to the State.* In the long and difficult era preceding the rise of the State of Israel, when no one ever questioned our allegiance to the Zionist Movement, it never occurred to anyone to suggest that the United Synagogue as an organization should seek affiliation with the WZO. The attempts that were made in some congregations to make membership in the Synagogue conditional upon membership in the ZO, proved abortive for the simple reason that Synagogue membership cannot be conditioned upon and subordinated to membership in any other group, without doing violence to Jewish status and causing irreparable harm to the future of Jews and Judaism.

Hence, the United Synagogue of America cannot as an organ-

ization join any other organization whose concept of Jewish status
or principle of organization relegates the Synagogue to a secondary role, or *even to the role of one among equals*. At no time
should the Synagogue, as such, become but *another member* of a
group whose chief concern is *not* the Synagogue.

The path that we, of the United Synagogue, must follow in our
effort towards achieving a maximum unity among our people we
have indicated by taking the initiative in the organization of the
World Council of Synagogues, and establishing its world center,
we hope ultimately in Jerusalem. The success of the World
Council of Synagogues as a unifying force in world Jewry will depend upon the means it will be able to muster to serve the maximum number of legitimate human needs. But its effectiveness as
the symbol of Jewish status in the world *will not depend upon
numbers,* but upon its ability to be the living *witness to the covenant between God and Israel.*

Finally, a brief word about the WZO. It came into being to
serve a specific Jewish need. That need it has served with phenomenal success. Since 1948 the WZO has been trying to formulate a program which would have at its core a need as widely recognized, as dramatic and revolutionary, as the one which was contained in the opening paragraph of the Basle program. It has thus
far failed in its efforts. I am quite convinced by now that under
present circumstances *it cannot succeed.* Nor will its failure be
due to lack of vision or devotion on the part of its leaders. It is
inherent in the historic situation. In the realm of secular Jewish
life no concept can have the emotional appeal, the electrifying
power of the concept, "Jewish State." The task of maintaining a
State can never be as *dramatic* as that of *creating* it. Moreover,
the State itself becomes increasingly the chief agency for its own
maintenance and every other group concerned with its welfare
must, of necessity, be *subsidiary* to it. Hence, the WZO, if it
wants to recapture its place of leadership in the world Jewish
scene, must formulate a program which goes *beyond* assistance to
the State of Israel, a program which contains a concept of *Jewish
status and destiny* in the world, to which the existence of the State
of Israel is made *subsidiary* and not ultimate.

This, I am afraid, the present leaders of the WZO are not prepared spiritually to do, for this inevitably leads to a concept of

Jewish status and destiny which cannot but be religious in nature. If ever the leaders of the WZO begin to think seriously in those terms, there will occur in the life of world Jewry as great a spiritual revolution as occurred in 1897 at the first Zionist Congress when the Basle program was adopted, a revolution that will set the course of Jewish history back onto the path divinely ordained for it from its very beginnings, the path beginning at Sinai with the shofar blasts calling upon us to be "a kingdom of priests and a holy people," and culminating in the shofar blasts announcing the Kingdom of God upon this earth.

Our people became conscious of itself as a distinct people among the peoples of the world when it became conscious of the peculiar, the unique relationship between it and God. In pleading to God to remain in the midst of the Children of Israel after they had made the golden calf, Moses says, "If *Thy presence* will not go with me, do not carry us up from here. For how shall it be known that I have found favor in Thy sight, I and Thy people?" Is it not *"Thy going with us, so that we are distinguished,* I and Thy people, from all the people that are upon the face of the earth."* (Ex. 33/15/16) God's presence in our midst—that is what gave and gives us status and significance in our own eyes and the eyes of our fellowmen. That presence, we have been told in the beginning of our history, is evidenced and made effective through the sanctuary.

"And let them make Me a sanctuary, that I may dwell among them," (Exodus 25:8)—ועשו לי מקדש ושכנתי בתוכם. We must ever be a people at the center of whose life is the sanctuary, both in the land of Israel and wherever we may dwell. The United Synagogue of America is dedicated to the task of preserving us as such a people. As *individuals* we *gladly* join hands with *all* who may be serving *any* of the legitimate *human* needs of our people. As an *organization* we cannot and should not do anything that might confuse or cloud or mar our status as a people distinguished by God as He revealed Himself to our ancestors in our Torah and as His *presence* is *experienced* by us *through* our sanctuaries, in our *homes* and in our *hearts.*

The Torch, Winter, 1960.

SHOULD THE UNITED SYNAGOGUE OF AMERICA JOIN THE WORLD ZIONIST ORGANIZATION?

"NO," says ABRAHAM JOSHUA HESCHEL

The issues I am about to discuss are: how do we understand ourselves as Jews? What are the ideas we stand for? What are the
thoughts the World Council of Synagogues has to convey to the
Jewish World? Should the United Synagogue of America join the
World Zionist Organization?

I must begin by expressing my appreciation to those who answer the last question in the affirmative. We share their concern
and anxiety for the survival of our people throughout the world
and the strength and welfare of the State of Israel. To us Jews
such concern and anxiety are *a part of our religious integrity*.

However, while there are so many issues on which we agree,
there is one practical issue on which we disagree. Most of us are
either a part of the Zionist Movement or at least view the work
done by the World Zionist Organization and the role it played in
the drama of building Eretz Israel with reverence and gratitude.
Yet, the proposal before us raises many problems.

Instead of discussing the proposal whether the United Synagogue should affiliate with the World Zionist Organization, I
should have preferred to discuss the idea of whether the World
Zionist Organization should not join a synagogue. From the perspective of history as well as from the perspective of the soul there
is eminently one place where we meet as Jews: the synagogue, by
which I mean the House of Prayer and the House of Study and
the House of Assembly. Organizations come and go; the synagogue
remains. Whatever is lasting in our charitable and political organizations derives its vitality from the synagogues of the past and
present.

There is no substitute for the synagogue. Deserting the synagogue, a Jew cuts himself from his roots. The goals of our tradition include as well as transcend the goals to which our political organizations are dedicated, and there is a profound difference between the function and methods of synagogue and the function and methods of the Zionist Organization.

The synagogue is the only institution that insists upon the truth that Jewish existence involves commitment to God and to Torah, attachment to the people Israel and to the land of Israel. Let it be said that for us Jews there can be no fellowship with God without the fellowship with the people Israel. Abandoning Israel, we desert God. Yet, Jewish religion is neither a coefficient of the Jewish people nor the product of our national spirit (Achad Ha'am) ; it is the heart and soul of the Jews.

Jewish existence means living in the spiritual order of the Jewish people, living *in* the Jews of the past and *with* the Jews of the present moment. It is a spiritual order in which the human and the ultimate, the natural and the holy enter a lasting covenant, in which kinship with God is not an aspiration but a reality of destiny.

The primary function of the synagogue is to inspire the soul and to instruct the mind; its task is to cultivate faith in God, love of man and understanding of Torah; its goal is holiness; its methods are personal, intellectual, spiritual. The primary function of a political organization is to serve the self-interest of the group it represents; its goal may be holy, yet its methods are adroitness, opportunism and expediency. We must shun any attempt to use political authority in order to achieve spiritual goals as well as resist involvement in activities that are determined by political tactics.

It is because of the sensitive nature of the spiritual substance of the synagogue and the high degree of corruptibility of anything as delicate as the spiritual, that we must prevent the synagogue from getting involved in any structure which may impair its autonomy and affect its integrity. I would be unhappy to see the Roman Catholic Church join the Democratic Party, or the National Council of Churches join the Republican or Democratic Party. Although I believe that it is the civic duty of every individual Jew, Protestant or Catholic, to identify himself with a political party which best represents his political views.

The analogy, of course, is inadequate. The synagogue unlike the church is not synonymous with the religious community of the Jews, nor is the World Zionist Organization a partisan movement, expressing as it does the aspiration of the overwhelming majority of our people. However, as an affiliate of the World Zionist Organization, the United Synagogue would be on a par with the political parties of which it is constituted.

The religiously motivated Jew would welcome a world wide instrument which would express the solidarity of the Jews throughout the world to defend the honor and security of the Jews wherever they may dwell and to raise the level of Jewish learning and observance in all lands.

While the priests of Jerusalem as individuals were loyal to the king, the Temple itself was not under the jurisdiction of the king. The synagogue is a small sanctuary, a precious corner in Jewish life, where we try to cultivate our understanding of the eternal insights of our tradition. Such insights are contingent upon the independence of the scholars, the autonomy of the priests, and the prophet's right of non-conformity.

This is a new age with new problems. The concern of Mr. Levi in Buenos Aires or Mr. Cohn in Rio de Janeiro is not to discover or to receive a definition acceptable in sociological terms. No one will succeed in defining Judaism sociologically. We may regret it, but it is a fact that Judaism defies definition. I cannot accept the equation of knowability and definability. There are many things that defy definition. And if the power to define is taken as a standard, what would be the estimation of Moshe Rabenu who taught us the meaning of God without giving us a definition of God? No one has succeeded in defining beauty, and there is no danger that beauty will vanish because of lack of definition.

The supreme need of the hour is neither a definition nor a world organization of the Jewish people, but a renewed personal attachment to Jewish thinking and living. Judaism will not perish for lack of organization or lack of definition; it may perish for lack of commitment, for lack of appreciation.

When I went to South America and spoke in various congregations, my task was not to teach them to become part of an organization. The Jews of Buenos Aires are efficiently organized in the framework of kehillah. The task was to set forth the conviction that there is an inner cosmos of meaning in our tradition to which the contemporary Jew can relate himself in the innermost part of his being.

The most urgent need of the Jews of the world at this hour is to gain new insight into the eternal validity and a new understanding for the immediate relevance of Jewish teaching and Jewish living. What the Jews of the world need is commitment and understanding.

The central problem of this generation is emptiness in the heart; the decreased sensitivity to the imponderable quality of the spirit; the collapse of communication between the realm of tradition and the inner world of the individual. The central problem is that we don't know how to pray, how to revere, or how to resist the hidden persuaders; and this is what we must try to do within our synagogues.

The central problem is *the personal problem*. At the heart of the Ten Commandments are the words: *Honor, Revere thy father and thy mother*. Without reverence for one's father and reverence for one's mother, there is neither culture nor Judaism. The problem we face, the problem I as a father face is why in the world should my child revere me? Unless my child will sense in my own personal existence commitments that evoke her reverence, the readiness to resist temptations, to overcome prejudices, to sense the holy in a secular world, why should she revere me? I repeat, without reverence for fathers and without reverence for mothers, there will be no Judaism and no survival, in spite of the will to survive.

This is a new age with new problems, and new approaches are necessary. Jewish thinking during the last three generations has had one central preoccupation. Speaking of the Jewish problem, the problem was the Jewish people, and legitimately so. The group, the community and its institutions received all our attention. The individual and his problems were ignored. We saw the forest, we forgot the trees. We thought about the community; we forgot about the person.

The time has arrived to pay heed to the forgotten individual Jew. Judaism is a personal problem. We have built magnificent organizations, but how Jewish is their membership? We have developed forms of living socially as Jews. Jews attend the Jewish meetings, belong to Jewish organizations, contribute to communal and national funds; but, when left alone, when they retire to their homes, they are devoid of Jewish spirit.

The American is known as a Joiner, and we Jews too have made a cult of belonging. Now, the true goal includes becoming a Jew as well as belonging; and this is a life-long task.

Now, it would be a fatal distortion to reduce Judaism to individualism. Separation from the people of Israel means detachment from the covenant with the God of Israel.

No Jew can live in isolation, in detachment. At the same time, it would be suicidal to reduce Judaism to collectivism or nationalism. Jewish existence is a personal situation, and the urgent Jewish problem today is the problem of the individual Jew. I repeat, attachment to our people, the love of Israel, the understanding and feeling for Jews everywhere are the well-springs of our strength. And sacred is the concern for their physical survival, for their political rights. But the problem is how to fulfill that attachment and that understanding in terms of individual existence, how to live in the morning and in the evening as a Jew— *personally, privately, intimately.*

Many of the cultural resources of the Jewish people in America have been depleted. Once upon a time other Jewish movements have filled the Jews of America with enthusiasm, and lent significance to their existence; but these movements have now lost their vitality.

This is the hour of the synagogue. The United Synagogue has contributed to a transformation in Jewish life. At the turn of the century, the synagogue was in danger of becoming an old folks' home, a מושב זקנים. Other institutions were invested with the role of leadership—Yiddish literature, the Yiddish theater, the Yiddish press, the Landsmanshaften, the political organization and until a few years ago the defense organizations were the leading forces in the community. All this has changed.

I speak with respect of these forces, particularly of the efforts to create a secular Jewish culture. Yiddish literature in particular represents a magnificent contribution to Judaism. So much soul, so many dreams, so much dedication have gone into the Yiddishist movement. It was a fatal error of the movement to detach itself from the Torah. It is a presumption to develop a Jewish secular culture to take the place of our religious tradition. In Jewish life nothing will abide in detachment from the Torah.

There would have been a future for Yiddish literature and Yiddish theatre had they worked in alliance with the traditions of the synagogue. A major factor in the disappearance of Yiddish from the synagogue.

What is the message that we can bring to the world? I believe we have something to say to the Jewish world. Something new has emerged on the American Jewish scene. It is, I believe, the image of a Jew who wrestled with an angel, and was not defeated. A new miracle is *slowly* emerging. A Jew who has been exposed to the challenge of the 20th Century and did not surrender. A Jew who goes to the synagogue to pray, trying to understand the meaning of the Sabbath and the meaning of the Day of Atonement.

We of this generation have seen the splendor of the great world civilization and have not become dazzled. We have gone through the doubts and the perplexities, and are slowly regaining a degree of the faith of our ancestors. This, indeed, is the task and this perhaps is also the image. We are a part of civilization, but try to learn how to stand above it and not to be lost in it, nor succumb to it.

This is the experience of many of us who have spoken to the American Jewish youth, and at this moment I would like to say that my experience in speaking to the Jews of South America as well . . . Deep calls to deep, and there is an answer. There is a longing in the hearts of many Jews.

I grew up in an awareness that Jews were running away from Judaism and religion. This was true in Poland, where I was born, in Germany, where I studied, and in America, where I found refuge in 1940. In those years, spiritual problems were considered irrelevant, but during the last seven or eight years I have been surprised by an extraordinary change. People are not running away any more, but, on the contrary, indicate concern for spiritual orientation.

This is a great hour in Jewish history, and one that probably occurs only once in two hundred years. In this hour we, the living, are "the people of Israel." The tasks, begun by the patriarchs and prophets and continued by their descendants, are now entrusted to us. We are either the last Jews or those who will hand

over the entire past to generations to come. We will either forfeit
or enrich the legacy of ages.

But the depressing aspect of the situation is that we have thus
far not succeeded in meeting the longing of our people for spiritual nourishment. The younger generation, which often seems
way ahead of us, is dissatisfied with what we are offering.

Something has changed on both levels. On the level of inwardness and on the level of action. There is a stirring in the hearts of
the Jews in many lands, particularly on this continent.

The possibility of a spiritual regeneration is real. Even those
who cannot pray are craving to pray. Many who cannot revere
feel a reverence. — אבן מאסו הבונים היתה לראש פנה: The stone that
the builders have despised has become a cornerstone. Let us stop
berating the American Jew. The American Jewish youth is one of
the wonders of Jewish history. They are ready to listen. For more
than 100 years Jews were running away from Judaism, and now
they are beginning to return.

My anxiety at this moment is that we may miss the opportunity, because there are so few who know how to speak in the
language of this generation and to convey the eternal wisdom and
commitment of all generations. Let us raise larger numbers of inspired teachers and we shall have a dedicated American Jewry.
Let there be Jewish scholars at every college and university of
America, scholars who not only know about Judaism but are in
love with our Torah and our people, and there will be a magnificent Jewry in America.

In his efforts to discredit Judaism, Spinoza advanced the thesis
that the Bible has nothing to say to the intellect. It was in the
spirit of Spinoza that the slogan was created that Judaism has no
theology. As a result, modern Jewish scholarship, with very few
exceptions, neglected the field of inquiry into the world of Jewish
thought. Jewish thought has been kept a well guarded secret. The
hundreds of books which reflect our people's wrestling with the
difficulties of faith, with the profoundities of biblical ideas, are not
even known by name.

Intellectual evasion is the great sin of contemporary Jewish
teaching. Vital issues are shunned, the difficulties of faith ignored.
We lost the sense for the relevance of Judaism, and run for refuge
to all sorts of substitutes.

Judaism is not a mood, a feeling, a sentimental attachment to customs and ceremonies. Judaism is a source of cognitive insight, a way of thinking, not only an order of living.

We must learn how to deal with the doubts, the confusions and the distortions. Our task is not to satisfy complacency but to shatter it. Our duty is confrontation rather than evasion.

Our future depends upon the realization that to be a Jew means not only to do certain deeds, but also to stand for certain thoughts. We must learn to discover the *intellectual relevance of Judaism* in terms of the moral and spiritual problems of human existence.

The synagogue is *not* what is ultimate in Judaism. Supremacy belongs to the Torah, and God is the ultimate. It is not enough to establish *the centrality of the synagogue;* the true goal is to live by *the supremacy of Torah* and *the ultimacy of God.*

The synagogue is *holiness in space.* But there is no holiness in space without *holiness in man.* Sanctity in the synagogue is derived from the sanctity in our lives. The life of sanctity includes commitment, sacrifice, illumination. The synagogue withers in an atmosphere of callousness, complacency, and conceit.

We do not go to the synagogue to find relaxation; we go to the synagogue to acquire religious insights, to learn how to be noble in a vulgar world. We go for information, as well as for appreciation; for the power of overcoming envy, resentment, conceit. We go to learn that shrewdness is not wisdom, that the ultimate standard is not expediency.

Efficiency of organization is not enough. What is needed is personal appropriation of Jewish thoughts, deeds and feelings. The synagogues must become a fountain of meaning to our personal existence.

No synagogue can exist as an island. The sanctity of the synagogue, I repeat, depends for its survival upon the holiness of the home. Ultimately it is not the synagogue that gives inspiration to the Jews; it is the Jew who brings inspiration to the synagogue.— ועשו לי מקדש ושכנתי בתוכם Let them make Me a sanctuary, that I may dwell among them. It doesn't say—that I may dwell in the sanctuary, but rather that I may dwell in them.

The purpose of the synagogue is not the segregation of God. According to Rabbi Yohanan, one must not pray in a house that

has no windows (Berachoth 34-b). The true sanctuary has no
walls.

Thus says the Lord:
Heaven is My throne,
And the earth is My footstool;
What is the house which you would build for Me?
And what would be My resting-place?
All these things My hand has made,
And so all these things came to be,
Says the Lord.
But this is the man to whom I will look,
He that is humble and contrite in spirit,
And trembles at My word.

Isaiah 66:1–2

The purpose of the synagogue is to help man to be humble and
contrite in spirit, and to tremble at His word. He whose soul joins
in the exclamation of the angels: "Holy, holy, holy the Lord of
hosts!" responds to the insight that "the whole earth is full of His
glory." We go to the synagogue to discover that God is present at
all times and in all places. We pray in a particular place at a particular moment in order to be able to pray at all places and in all
moments . . . Ultimately, unless we know how to pray when we
are alone, it is difficult, indeed, to know how to pray in the midst
of a congregation.

The life of the spirit is never static. It decays when standing
still. Its strength disappears, when ceasing to increase. We either
ascend or descend; we either resist or succumb. A day that passes
without sensing the meaning of אשר קדשנו במצוותיו Who has
sanctified us with His mitzvoth, marks a depletion of our individual existence and of the spiritual substance of the entire people. We do not survive by pride; we survive by attachment and
enrichment, by discipline and insight, by halakha and agada.

There is a profound Jewish theme of 36 hidden zaddikim by
whose merit the world exists. No one can name them, no one can
identify them, but everyone may meet them. Often when as a boy
I met a stranger, a poor man, of no comeliness and no distinction,
I thought, maybe he is one of the 36 hidden zaddikim. It is too

much to ask of anyone of us to be a pillar, to bear the burden of the whole world. Yet we are all called upon to remember that there is *a nucleus of a zaddik* in every one of us. ועמך כולם צדיקים

The synagogues that are built are visible and ostentatious; the nucleus of righteousness dwells in deep privacy, a still, small entity. It is important to contribute to good causes openly and publicly; it is equally important to contribute to *the supreme good cause* quietly, privately—מתן בסתר · לעולם יהא אדם ירא שמים בסתר ובגלוי—"Man should even be God-fearing in private as well as in public." The foliage is visible to the public, the roots are hidden from the eye. "Blessing rests only on things that are hidden from the eye." אין הברכה מצויה אלא בדבר הסמוי מן העין·

In earlier times when Jews lived clustered together in overcrowded towns, fires would frequently break out. With water resources limited and the streets narrow, it was only with difficulty that a fire was subdued.

As a result many old communities were devastated, with numerous manuscripts and other treasures gone forever.

Their first concern when a fire broke out in the middle of the night was to save the children, and the aged, and the next thing they did was to run to the synagogue and to save the *Sifrei Torah* (The Torah Scrolls). Thinking about Jewish history I have a picture in my imagination of fires raging in the world and Jews running to the synagogue to save the *Sifrei Torah*.

It was a great miracle that we assembled here have escaped from the holocaust of Europe. Our lives have been rescued; but did we save the *Sifrei Torah?*

When sent to South America to represent the United Synagogue, I didn't go in the name of a new God or of a new Torah. Our goals are eternal. Significant about the United Synagogue is the attempt to apply new methods in order to achieve ancient goals.

It is not enough to plead for the preciousness of *K'lal Israel* or the grandeur of the totality of our tradition. The task is to be concerned with the individual Jew, with his concrete situation, with the question of how he should relate himself to God, Torah, the people and Eretz Israel; of how he should understand our tradition and live it.

Torah as *a total way of living* has been abandoned by the multitudes of our people, and we cannot force it upon them. Only the Lord has a right to hold Mount Sinai over the heads of the people and to force them to accept the Torah. We have only been given the right to teach and to speak to the mind and the heart of a people who has the liberty and freedom of choice. We have only been given the power of love and the power of example. What we must do is to evolve a pedagogy of return, the art of *teshuvah*.

We must devise *a ladder of observance*. We have no right to abrogate the *halakha*, but we have also no right to abandon the Jewish people. Extremism, maximalism is not the way. Elasticity, flexibility is the way.

Ben Azzai used to say: "Do not despise any man, and do not consider anything as impossible; for there is not a man who has not his hour, and there is not a thing that has not its place." Even those who seem frivolous have moments of sensitivity, moments in which they will respond to those who combine *Ahavat Torah* with *Ahavat Israel,* depth of appreciation with the power of thinking. Both wisdom and love are necessary to show a way how to return.

What is the spiritual level of the multitudes of Israel? It is not on the heights of Torah but in the lowlands, in the valley. Like Ezekiel in his time, we also see the valley full of bones, and they are very dry. It is God who asks: "Son of Man, shall these bones be revived?" The answer is in our hands. Often we say in resignation: "Our bones have dried up." Now despair means paralysis. Indeed, we are spiritually poor. Instead of indulging in the sorrow and admission of our failures, let us undertake a new effort to revive the dry bones.

The mountain of full Jewish living is very high, and few are the men who know how to leap out of the valley to the top of the mountain. If we assert that a Jew has no status unless he lives at the top of the mount and fulfills all the details of all the commandments, the masses will remain in the valley. Rabbi Judah Ben Baba said: "Not all men or all places nor all times are equal."

For the benefit of those who are able to return, we should set up *a ladder* in the valley, *a ladder of learning, a ladder of observance*. To each individual our advice should be: "Observe as much as you are able to, and a little more than you are able to. And this is essential: a little more than you are able to."

For such a pedagogy to be effective, it will be necessary to prevent the *tendency to minimalism*. The level of Jewish living must never be stationary. It is the task of religious pedagogy to instill an awareness that there is no standstill in the life of the spirit. We either *ascend* or *descend*.

One of the early Hassidic leaders and the founder of the HaBaD movement was HaRav Schneur Zalman of Ladi. As a result of their hatred of the Hassidic way, the Misnagdim went to the Russian government and denounced him. When the police arrived at his home, they found the Rav sitting in tallis and tefillin and praying. His prayers went on for hours, and, the police stood there, overwhelmed by reverence, and did not dare to approach him. It was only after he finished his praying that they carried out their order and arrested him.

The Rav was sent off to jail. Only after a prolonged time there was he released and sent home. On his arrival, he discovered his Hassidim talking about the miracle:

> The police had come to arrest the Rav, yet out of great reverence, did not dare to approach him.

The Rav called in his Hassidim and said to them:
"This was no miracle.

"Moses blessed Israel, saying: 'And all the peoples of the earth shall see that the name of the Lord is (called) upon thee; and they shall revere thee' (Deuteronomy 28:10). What does it mean: 'The name of the Lord is upon thee?' This means wearing the tefillin of the head— תפילין שבראש (Berachoth 6a), says the Talmud. When the people shall see the תפילין שבראש they will revere thee.

"You see, it was no miracle. They saw my tefillin. That is why they had reverence."

Thereupon the Hassidim said to the rabbi:
"It happened many times that the police came to arrest the simple Jew. He wore tefillin, but they did not pay any attention."

Again, the Rav corrected them:
"You see, the Talmud says *Tefillin Shebarosh,* tefillin within

the head. It does not say *Tefillin sheal harosh*, tefillin on top of the head. (Shebarosh means within the head). The tefillin has to be in the head."

When the Rav finished, the Hassidim began to understand the meaning of tefillin.

This is our hope and our prayer: for all Jews to achieve both: תפילין של ראש and תפילין שבראש.

Moses entreated the Lord: "Show me, I pray, Thy glory." And the Lord said to him: "You cannot see My face; for man shall not see Me and live, you shall see My back, but My face shall not be seen."

What did Moses see? According to Rabbi Simeon the Hasid: The Holy One, blessed be he, showed him the knot in the band of the tefillin (resting on the back of the head) (Berachoth 7a).

The secret of Judaism is in the knot where time is interlaced with eternity, the outward with the inward, habit with insight, the simple with the sublime.

He who has not seen the knot in which all threads of Jewish existence are intertwined has failed to grasp the meaning of Judaism. The power of תפילין של ראש is in its being תפילין שבראש.

The Torah as written in the Scrolls has no vowels and no marks of cantillation. It is the reader who must bring breath to the consonantal letters; it is the reader who adds chant to the words. Without the person, the word is silent; without the music in the person, the word is dormant.

To keep alive the wisdom of the past we must try to cultivate the voice of the present, the freedom of the heart.

A harp was hanging above David's bed. As soon as midnight arrived, a north wind came and blew upon the harp, and it played of itself. He would rise at once and study the Torah until the break of dawn.

A harp is hanging above our heads. A wind arrived, and without our understanding it, there is an awakening. The harp is playing of itself.

What did David do? It was dark and midnight, and he would arise to study the Torah. We too have heard the chimes in the middle of the night, The hour is dark and dreary, but we must arise and try to follow God's trace in the world of His words.

The Torch, Winter, 1960.

Part Six

SIGNIFICANT FACTORS IN CONTEMPORARY JEWISH LIFE

"There are those who believe that we cannot hope for the development of greater piety and saintliness. They regard the effort to seek such a goal as visionary and unrealistic. But if we cannot translate the dilemma in which man today finds himself into a means for deeper spiritual insight, is there any hope for misled and confused millions who must be won back to faith in God and love of man, if our world is to be saved from destruction? If it be visionary to hope for our own betterment, is it not futile to expect the betterment of others? Thus the deepening of our faith and the raising of our own standards become, in a sense, the test of our ability to guide mankind."

—Louis Finkelstein

INTRODUCTION

As the Jewish community in America during the first half of the twentieth century grew in numbers and became more closely integrated into the general community, many changes became apparent in its makeup. Those who were identified with the religious groupings in the Orthodox and Reform camps proceeded with their respective approaches to Judaism. The Conservative Movement was just beginning to search for its medium of expression in the synagogue, home and community. In addition there were large numbers of Jews who were members of *landsmanshaften,* Zionist groups and Jewish labor bodies, who were unaffiliated with synagogues. As the process of crystalization of the Jewish community went on a number of factors emerged which were responsible for new approaches both within the Conservative Movement and within the Jewish community at large.

Three major factors influenced the American Jewish community which had swelled to a population of about five million by the middle of the century. First of all they were brought face to face with living in two civilizations. Secondly, the scientific and secular influences presented new challenges to traditional religious patterns and concepts. Thirdly, new sociological factors were affecting the synagogue, home and individual, and forcing a re-evaluation of their respective roles.

Rabbi Stanley Rabinowitz posed the problem of living in two civilizations in this way:

"We Jews live in two status systems, one based on the aristocracy of wealth and the other on the aristocracy of learning. The question is: How can we balance living in the Jewish social structure as well as in the American social structure?"

Rabbi Jack J. Cohen also asserted that "no pattern for Amer-

345

ican Jewish living . . . can be of lasting value unless it is cut from the cloth of religion."

However, he says "the problem of Jewish living today is fundamentally one of trying to find the happy medium between a complete worship of the group and the equally extreme clinging to doctrine, to the exclusion of diversity and change."

Rabbi Cohen believes that "those of us who want to perpetuate what is worthwhile of our inherited values and to create new ones must do all in our power to fashion a Jewish community life which will embrace in an organic fashion, all Jews who want to be Jews." According to the latter, in the organic community the loyalty of each Jew will be first to the community as a whole rather than to a particular organization in the community. It will so function as to care for the interests of individual Jews and channel them to the advantage of the whole Jewish people both religious and secular. It will not conceive of Jewish religion solely in terms of so-called religious institutions and personnel and will see Jewish religion in any activity which embodies the highest ideals of Jewish life."

Rabbi Cohen also stresses the need for "a much greater spirit of inquiry in Jewish life . . . and experimentation. It means that in wide areas of Jewish life we shall have to substitute trial and error for Halakha." He relates the Jew in the Diaspora to Israel by urging "it is time we begin to bridge the ever-widening spiritual status in the United States and the democratic socialist character of the Yishuv. If the values of cooperation, service, mutual help and equality are to be considered Jewish, then they ought to be ours as they are those of Israeli Jewry. Why not incorporate them into our prayers, our curriculum, our community organization and our participation in the American social scene?"

The religiously oriented American Jew who is facing up to the materialistic and secular influences about him has to seek an honest rapprochement between himself and Judaism both at worship in the synagogue and in his religious practices at home and in the community. Naturally this has already resulted in some new experimentation in the realm of religious practices.

Rabbi Jacob Agus analyzes the situation in this manner: "Jewish loyalty has been directed, heretofore, in the channels of the preservation of the Jewish people. The life of our people was threatened by the twin-headed hydras of anti-Semitism and assimilation. We countered by means of the Zionist program, on the one hand, and the Anti-defamation on the other hand. The emergence of Israel as an independent, self-governing nation makes the twin expression of the Jewish will to survive obsolete . . . By the same token, Anti-Semitism had been robbed of its unique sting and quality of universality."

Rabbi Agus then asserts that "in terms of the realistic endeavor to build Jewish personalities, the Sabbath is the logical beginning. For if it be observed, even in part, Judaism becomes part of one's routine . . . properly interpreted and accepted, it aids us to make the most of our lives."

He seeks to relate the observance of the Sabbath to our needs of the day. He says, "in our age of tensions and neurosis the most important therapeutic institution is the Sabbath. Thus Eric Fromm, who writing from a purely psychiatric viewpoint in his latest book "The Forgotten Language," declares that the Sabbath is the most profound symbolic language of religion. He recommends it as of unique value for the good life."

The search for a satisfying approach to Judaism is also touched upon by Rabbi Max J. Routtenberg, who weighs the complaints of many laymen "that there is no set or fixed pattern of worship either liturgically or musically in the Conservative Synagogue." Commenting on this he says "I believe that the state of fluidity in which we find ourselves is a source of great strength for us and not a manifestation of weakness . . . This approach is not even revolutionary but is quite endemic to Jewish religious life." Nevertheless, he adds, "in my abhorrence of uniformity with its accompanying dullness and deadness, I am not pleading for chaos . . . these restraints and disciplines which we impose upon ourselves in a real sense derive from what we regard as the emerging consensus in the Conservative Movement as it is reflected in the developing pattern of our public worship, as it is expressed in the ritual of our synagogue. That pattern is triple stranded . . . Hebrew . . . Congregation . . . Ceremony . . . anchored in the tradition."

As the American synagogue has grown to be the major bond

between the Jew and his people, the Prayerbook, which is the basic instrument of synagogue worship, takes on even greater significance.

Dr. Robert Gordis has pointed out that "it is a basic principle of modern research in the fields of natural and historical sciences that everything that lives, grows and changes, and only that which is dead is fixed. The modern scientific study of Judaism during the past century and a quarter has shown that this truth applies to Jewish life and institutions as well . . . and the creative process must continue in the modern age, if Judaism is to live. That is the historic function of Conservative Judaism . . . It regards Jewish tradition as dynamic, to be preserved in largest measure, to be sure, but also to be created."

As a manifestation of this process, Dr. Gordis then stated that "an important milestone in the coming of age of Conservative Judaism has been the issuance of the new Sabbath and Festival Prayerbook. This work was issued by the Joint Commission of the Rabbinical Assembly and the United Synagogue of America." He said further that "certain fundamental principles emerged which we believe are significant for Conservative Judaism as a whole. First is the principle of continuity with tradition, second is relevance to the ideals and needs of our own generation, and third is intellectual integrity. In order that it may truly live, Jewish ideas and ideals must be reformulated anew in every age."

During the past decade the Rabbinical Assembly has published *The Weekday Prayerbook* and *Selihot*. The Prayerbook Committee of the Rabbinical Assembly is now preparing the publication of a *High Holy Day "Machzor"* and a new edition of the *Sabbath and Holiday Prayerbook*.

The sociological changes which have taken place in the twentieth century have affected Jewish communities here and abroad and are reflected in the changing attitudes toward the community, home and synagogue. Professor Abraham Joshua Heschel describes it in these words: "The masses of East European Jews repudiated emanicipation when it was offered at the price of disloyalty to Israel's traditions. Both pious and free-thinking Jews fought for a dignified existence, striving to assure the rights of the community, not only those of the individual. In a spiritual confusion of the last hundred years, many of us overlooked the incomparable beauty of our old poor homes . . . We preached in the name of the twentieth century, measured the merits of Berditshev and Ger with the standards of Paris and Heidelberg."

Dr. Heschel then notes "in the last decades there has developed a longing for accord between the present and the past . . . gradually the inner beauty of the old life and the emptiness of the present day civilization have been disclosed. . . . we have bartered holiness for convenience, loyalty for success, wisdom for information, prayer for sermon, tradition for fashion."

He warns us that "a world has vanished, all that remains is a sanctuary hidden in the realm of the spirit. We of this generation are still holding the key." "The alternative to our Jewish existence is spiritual suicide, disappearance, not conversion into something else." The synagogue must serve as the power house for preserving the spiritual values of our people.

What is the relationship of the Jew to the synagogue today? "While methods of the synagogue have been improved," writes Dr. Arzt, "the essential purposes of the synagogue have been almost forgotten. The general membership . . . faithfully pays the dues and promptly ignores the duties, the personal spiritual commitments involved in the synagogue affiliation."

Among the steps recommended by Dr. Arzt to improve this situation are special "orientation courses for officers and board members, exemplification by the latter of the purpose of the synagogue life, cooperation of the home, adult education, greater participation in public worship, and relating teachings of Judaism to the personal mundane life of our congregants and to the larger ethical problems of the community, country and the entire world."

The mad pace of life in our times has crowded out the home from its central place in fashioning the individuals who dwell within it.

The late Rabbi Charles I. Hoffman has stated that "it is in the Jewish home, in its integrity, in its purity, in its observances, in its principles and ideals, it is there that the final stand for Jewish existence and worth is to be made." Rabbi Hoffman's words have a most contemporary ring when he writes that "the Jewish home would regain its ennoblement if material advantages were made not the means of spiritual growth, but were utilized in the elevation of the family ideal." His son, Dr. M. David Hoffman, a lay educator, places the responsibility of moulding wholesome Jewish lay leadership upon schools of higher Jewish learning, such as the Jewish Theological Seminary of America.

He suggests five ways in which the Seminary could help to accomplish this task: "It calls for a Jewish philosophy, a Jewish education, a Jewish *welt-anschauung*. It must be rooted in Torah and Jewish experience. Modern in method, sensitive to present needs, it must give meaning and purpose and direction to Jewish living."

The twentieth century Jews in the Diaspora and particularly those in the Western Hemisphere are fashioning a new identity for themselves based on the pluralistic society in which they live and upon the currents which affect them religiously, culturally and socially. They are becoming the responsible guardians of Judaism. As Professor Heschel so aptly put it, "in this hour, we the living are the people of Israel."

J. S. G.

LIVING IN TWO CIVILIZATIONS

STANLEY RABINOWITZ

If the theological challenge of our day is the resolution of the tension implied in the I-Thou relationship of God and man, the sociological challenge of our day, especially for the Jew, is the resolution of the tension between the "we-us." For man is both subject and object of society. He is both the creator of a tradition and at the same time the bearer of a tradition. He is the molder of a culture while being molded by that culture.

But every Jew is a special case; he must learn to create and to be influenced by not one, but two cultures. He is both the subject—"we"—and the object—"us"—of two civilizations.

And the essence of our culture as American Jews is to develop the dignity and the wisdom to live in two civilizations. Which means to develop the sensitivity to be true to the values of two civilizations.

Of this challenge, much has been written. Most noteworthy are the writings of Dr. Mordecai M. Kaplan. Others have pondered the challenge in fiction and in autobiography. Worthy of note are Chaim Raphael, *A Special Case;* Alfred Kazin, *A Walker in the City;* S. N. Behrman, *The Worcester Account;* David Daiches, *Two Worlds;* Leslie Fiedler, *An End to Innocence.* But the differences are important. M. M. Kaplan wants to live in two civilizations. Too many of the others are concerned with the question, how to live between two civilizations. Living in two worlds is not the same as living between two worlds. The latter alternative implies being at home neither in the one nor the other.

This is our problem. It requires sensitivity and delicate balance. It's an art to be felt as well as a skill to be learned.

The relationship between the two cultures in which the American Jew walks must not be seen as two opposing goal posts so much as the two uprights of the same goal post. In order to main-

tain the crossbar in its position, the two uprights of the goal post
remain in a position rather than in opposition to one another;
they must face each other in a state of coordination.

These two cultures need not be in conflict, though between
them there may be a state of creative tension. I would prefer to
think in terms of creative harmony.

Creative harmony results from the fact that both the Jewish
people and the American people are the only important groupings whose being is an outgrowth of a covenant rather than that
of biology and geography. The diverse tribes of the ancient Israel
were welded into one group by virtue of the covenant which they
entered with God; the diverse colonies of the United States were
welded together by a covenant which they entered with that aspect of man which we consider to be the reflection of the Divine,
that aspect which gave rise to the statement, "We hold these
truths to be self evident: that all men are created equal; that they
are endowed by their Creator with certain inalienable rights: that
among these are life, liberty, and the pursuit of happiness."

It is no accident, therefore, that a president of the United
States could face the challenge of a devastation with the words:
"We are united by a faith that goes all the way back to the first
chapter of the Book of Genesis, which says that man is created in
the Divine Image." It is no accident, therefore, that Judaism has
flourished most comfortably in this land in which we are equal
partners and citizens.

A Jew who lives in two civilizations lives in two social structures. Let's look at each social edifice.

The American social system had its origins in England. It was a
closed class system. You stayed in the position of your birth, be it
gardener, blacksmith, butler, or lord of the manor. American colonists came from this environment. Most of them were sturdy yeo-
men from the lower strata of British society. Their positions in
the Colonies were reshuffled, but the system remained just as
closed as it was in England. Even in colonial days, the English
peerage was at the top and the indentured white servant was at
the bottom. The system was frozen into law. The colony of Connecticut prescribed appropriate dress for each class and stipulated
where each should sit in church.

The closed class system was challenged by two wars. The Revolutionary War was not only a war of independence; it was a civil war between classes. The pro-British colonists were the Tories. They were largely upper class, while the Whigs were lower class. The Tories went down in defeat, forcing a reshuffling of class positions.

The Civil War was not only a war between North and South, but also a struggle between the upper class plantation owners, mostly, but not all, Southern, and the lower classes . . . mostly, but not all, Northern.

The Civil War has not ended. It is fought every day in Congress, especially in the Senate, and whenever the legislative rules of procedure are questioned. States rights is a symbol of the struggle. The Negro is the victim as well as the excuse.

The plantations were destroyed by the Civil War as was Southern wealth. There was further reshuffling and gradually the closed class system of America gave way to the American dream, a society in which aristocracy was to give way to industriousness . . . a way of life which preached that there is always room at the top for the able and the hard working. It didn't matter where you were born. The philosophy of the open frontier preached that achievement, high status, success, and fame were open to all who earnestly worked for it. Horatio Alger became not only the national myth hero, but a national aspiration as well.

This is the American Dream. It is certainly a step upward in the system of human social organization.

There is after all something revolting in the feudal system with its closed class, dooming a man to the level which his father achieved, or keeping him there even when he didn't deserve an exalted position.

But at least this much must be said of the English or European system—it was an honest system. There was little room for pretense or fakery. There was no neurotic rejection of one's place. A man was born either to royalty or to the common fold. And, if he were a commoner, he didn't aspire to be royalty, and he didn't think that he could become royalty simply by purchasing a jewelled crown, or by sending his daughter to the finishing school that the princess attended, or by buying a chariot from the same livery stable that served the royal house, or by having his suits tailored by the tailor who served "by appointment" to the king.

There may be more to our taste in an open system which allows every man to try to emulate Horatio Alger, and to progress from rags to riches if he can, but there is something wrong in a system which only pretends to be open but which in reality is as closed and as rigid as were the societies of Europe.

In America we still have our royalty. We have assigned status of royalty to the families of great wealth and long-standing prestige: the first families, the top 10%, the blue blood 400, the patricians who sponsor coming-out parties, the people the society columnists write about. We are urged to share their status. And we are led to think that we can share their status by driving the cars they drive, living in the neighborhoods in which they live, decorating our homes the way they do, belonging to the clubs to which they belong, sending our children to the schools which their children attend, affiliating with the churches to which they belong, and shopping in the stores they patronize.

We make these choices not because these represent our tastes, and not even because we think they are superior, but simply because these are the things that America's royal families do or own.

If you join a club, church, synagogue, neighborhood, if you acquire an automobile, house, tailor, hairdresser, French poodle, or Picasso because this represents your own taste, this is your commendable right.

But if you make this choice because you want to do that which is done by the class to which you think you belong, you have only acquired a symbol of status and not membership in that status. You have abdicated your right of decision to other people.

There is something ludicrous if not pathetic in people who sell their souls, their dignity, and their birthright, in order to identify with a class or a group that they deem desirable and who think that they have achieved that identification simply by the acquisition of the symbols of that class.

Closed system had its place; open system is the goal. But what we have is something else. We have a closed system that pretends to be open and we have created a society of frustrated social climbers.

What about the Jewish community? Is it free of class? Of course not. The Jewish community, from its earliest beginnings, had its class structure. In its most ancient form, it was based on birth. It survives today in the concept of the Kohane, the Levi, and the Yisroel. The Kohanim were the early aristocrats. They were also quite reactionary. Nothing more than a vestigial remain exists today in the priority of the order of being called to the Torah.

But the class struggle was a factor in the struggle of Pharisees and Sadducees. The struggle between them was more than theological; it was social as well. Sadducees were the priests, the aristocracy. They were also Fundamentalists and quite narrow in their interpretation of the Bible. The Pharisees were liberal interpreters of Biblical tradition. Their Talmud made the Bible flexible. For the most part, they were laborers, artisans, and keepers of vineyards.

The Pharisees had contempt for the priesthood and the determining factors of birth. They attempted to dethrone the class system based on birth, and to set up a class system based upon learning and knowledge.

They said: a learned gentile has merited greater reverence than an ignorant high priest.

They said: A man cannot become a priest or a Levite no matter how he might wish it, unless his father was one. But he can become righteous, even though he be a heathen, because righteousness does not depend on ancestry. To become righteous entails only the resolve to do good and to love God.

But they did not establish a classless society. They simply changed the basis of the class structure. Note its basis as reflected in the Talmud:

"One should sell all one has in order to marry one's son to the daughter of a Talmid Haham. If one cannot find a suitable daughter of a Talmid Haham, he should marry a daughter of a leader in the generation in piety and in good deeds. If one of this type is not available, let him marry a daughter of a head of a synagogue. Or if that is not possible, the daughter of a head of a charitable institution. If that, too, is not possible, the daughter of a teacher of children. But in any event, let him avoid marrying the daughter of one who is lacking in piety and culture . . . The am-ha-arets. . . ."

It was a long struggle. The Prophets rebelled against the priests, but the priesthood regained dominance.

The Maccabees rebelled against the aristocratic priest Hellenists.

The Maccabees themselves became such rigid and snobbish aristocrats that the Pharisees rejected them and actually refused to observe the Festival of Hanukkah, a Maccabean festival.

The Pharisees resumed their rebellion against priest-class Sadducees. The priesthood was finally destroyed by Roman destruction and only the Pharisees remained. But Pharisaism itself became rigid and obsessed with a *yichus* of intellectual snobbism which rejected the ignorant masses.

The revolution of the Baal Shem Tov that emerged into Hassidism captured the loyalty of the lower classes, poor and unlearned, to whom Hassidism gave dignity and status. The period of the Misnagdim and Hassidim involved that kind of a struggle.

For the most part, however, the Pharisee revolution prevailed even over Hassidism and it persisted into the days of the ghetto, where the ignorant stood in awe of the learned, and the rich exerted themselves to find scholarly though poor husbands for their daughters.

It has persisted until today and has provided us with the momentum that gives us more than our share of men of learning, scientists, winners of Nobel and Pulitzer Awards. Whether it will persist or whether it has lost momentum remains to be seen.

But our question remains to be answered:

What happens when two class systems with different bases exist side by side, which is the case today? This is the sociological essence of the Jewish dilemma.

We see the results of this conflict in adjustment in the way we live as Jews in America. It is evident in the names we give our children. It is evident in the way that we have molded our rabbis, for we prefer rabbis with a smooth, Protestant bedside manner and social polish. His ability in public relations is prized more than his learning. We are molding our rabbis into the shape of a minister. He is expected to be an expert in delivering invocations, an expert in visiting the sick, and more of a psychiatrist than a teacher.

We garb him in a monk's robe and a bishop's hat. Our synagogues imitate the forms and status of the upper class-dominant church. For in religion as in all other things, the powerful at the top influence those below the top. We mold our children as a "wasp"—White-Anglo-Saxon-Protestant.

This is not said so much in criticism as in honest analysis.

It is not evil to seek higher status and higher recognition, for higher status gives you the power to influence others instead of being influenced by others.

Seeking higher status becomes evil only when we sell our souls to acquire the symbols of higher status.

A status system is inevitable, not necessarily evil.

A status system becomes evil when the basis for the system is evil.

If the basis for the system is strength, as it was for centuries, then the gymnasium and golf course will be our temple of worship as it was with the Greeks. If the basis is wealth, then there will be no limits to the lengths that we will go to acquire wealth. If we can't acquire it legitimately, then we'll do so illegitimately, and we'll justify what we do with such cliches as "business is business," or, "everybody is doing it." But if the basis is learning, the school will become our most sacred institution, as it has been in Judaism at its most creative best.

We Jews live in two status systems, one based on the aristocracy of wealth, and the other based on the aristocracy of learning. We may have one position in the Jewish scale, and another position in the general. But how long can you balance yourself?

The question is: How can we balance living in the Jewish social structure as well as in the American social structure?

These are the considerations that I would suggest:

1. Be true to yourself rather than to your class. Be true to your own standards. The evil in class consciousness is that it allows other people to make decisions for you, and in a class system which is based upon wealth, it makes materialistic considerations the determining factor in reaching a decision.

There is wisdom in the Jewish observation—"Who is wealthy? One who is content with his lot."

2. Do not confuse high and low with good and bad.

3. Don't be a social snob in reverse.

Don't reject the values of a class because you are not of it. Just because you may not be in the upper class, do not reject its values if they are good values.

4. Wealth is not necessarily evil. Therefore, don't apologize for what you own or the car you drive or where you live. Don't apologize for a color TV set, even though it has come to be a symbol of success. Seeking and possessing wealth is not an evil. Jews have never regarded poverty as a virtue and wealth as a sin. Nor have they regarded poverty as a crushing burden and wealth as a sign of God's favor.

In truth, the values of America's real upper class are not in conflict with Jewish values, for Judaism has said: "If you are wealthy, let your good deeds show your wealth."

5. Don't reject the values of the Christian world just because they are Christian. Just because you are a Jew, don't reject the values of a non-Jew, if they are consistent with Judaism.

Many people reject the glamour treatment given Hanukkah because they correctly observe that it reflects the influence of Christmas. This is not the point; the point is: is it inconsistent with Judaism to glorify Hanukkah? It is not inconsistent. There is nothing evil in accepting a good idea from another culture. And Judaism also maintains that the customs we observe should be observed with the joy of beauty.

6. Root your child in the richness of the Jewish tradition and he will be able better to resist the corrosive influence of materialism.

You will dull the pernicious effects of class consciousness if you allow norms of Jewish religious behavior to be part of your lives and the pattern of your home, because the Jewish religious culture will serve to insulate your child against the false gloss and glitter about him.

7. If you want to dull the effects of pernicious class consciousness on your children, be careful how you refer to those in the lower classes, to those who work for you, and those who serve you.

Never speak disparagingly of them or of their color. They are not your "help." They are not hired hands. They are children of God before whom you must stand in reverence. You are indebted to them because they are doing things that you can't do or won't do. And they give you the leisure to do the things that you would like to do. You owe them more than wages; you owe them dignity. The woman who sweeps your office is as worthy of your respect as the man who pays your salary. Teach that to your children.

8. And let's not lose sight of the Jewish class system which is based on the intellect. Let's try to retain it. What has made the Jew and his class system unique is that it has given high status to the man of learning. Learning has always been the passion of the Jews.

9. Let's not be afraid to challenge the social structure of our community. History is made by those who have had the daring to espouse values which they considered beneficial for total society, even if it meant rejecting their class. History has been shaped by a Roosevelt who dared espouse values that were not shared by the conservatives of his class, by a Lincoln who aspired beyond the aspirations which were his class heritage by virtue of his lowly birth.

And let us not forget an Abraham who dared challenge the mores of his pagan parents, or a Moses who turned his back on the luxury of the Egyptian court, where he was accepted as a prince.

10. And finally, let us look with pride upon our origins, whatever they may be. On Passover we remind ourselves that we were once slaves in the land of Egypt.

The Daughters of the American Revolution do their best to forget that they were revolutionaries. A revolutionary is always of the lower class. They have nothing to lose but their chains. Aristocrats never rebel. But we Jews remind ourselves year after year that we were slaves in the land of Egypt. We should understand that out of slavery can come greatness, just as there can come greatness out of every class.

One can live in two civilizations, and not only in America. The process, however, is facilitated in America whose cement is made up of the mortar of Jewish idealism and links the dignity of man to political forms.

In both is there a passionate devotion to the ideal of social justice.

In both is there the aspiration for the achievement of God's kingdom on earth.

This cannot be achieved by rejecting either culture. If you reject America, your children will reject you.

And if you reject your origins, you will reject that which America today needs most.

To blend the two takes delicacy and conviction and integrity. It requires resilience, but it can be done.

The Torch, Fall, 1963.

Rabbi Rabinowitz occupies the pulpit of Adas Israel Congregation in Washington, D. C. Previously he was Rabbi in New Haven, Conn. and in Minneapolis, Minn. He served as Field Director and Acting Executive Director of the United Synagogue of America. He is Vice-Chairman of the B'nai B'rith Youth Commission.

A PATTERN FOR
AMERICAN JEWISH LIVING

❄

JACK J. COHEN

In "The Meaning of Evolution", George Gaylord Simpson points out that "It is neither the change in environment nor the lack of change in organisms that causes extinction; it is the two together." Those of us who want the Jewish people and Judaism to continue to survive on the American scene would do well to remember Simpson's words. For although his thought refers to physical evolution alone, it takes no great stretch of the imagination to see its relevancy to social evolution as well. There is no certainty about Jewish survival; it is a matter of choice and wise planning. And in our planning we had better consider both the environment in which we live and the resources we have inherited and can create.

Let us start with our environment. Our American environment today is, generally speaking, a far cry from that of any previous period of Jewish history. Up until the last 150 years or so of Emancipation and Enlightenment, our people was everywhere oppressed—economically, politically, socially and even physically. I should like to emphasize that despite the challenge of this hostile environment, it was comparatively easy for our people to adjust to it. The fact is that the very oppression helped strengthen our people's moral fibre. Convinced as they were of their own spiritual worth, the oppression suffered by our ancestors served only to confirm their conviction that their ethical tradition was superior to that of their tormentors. God, as the Midrash told them, is always on the side of the oppressed.

In addition to this psychological factor, there was an intellectual resource which also facilitated our ancestors' adaptation to their environment. Both Jews and non-Jews alike found the source and method of their way of life in the same basic approach to reality; namely, the religious approach.

Until the rise of secular nationalism, the Western world was a religious one, and religion in those days meant a way of life interpreted for the masses from the revealed tradition by ecclesiastical authorities. In each of the traditions, whether Christian, Mohammedan or Jewish, God was assumed to have revealed His will to mankind in particular times and places. God's requirements were conceived to have been set forth in detail in the sacred texts and in the traditional principles of interpretation. The Jews, of course, even enjoyed an advantage, because their tradition was assumed by both Christians and Moslems to have been initially valid until superseded by the later revelations.

It can be seen from this all too brief sketch of our ancestors' environment that, however they may have suffered physically, spiritually they were as secure as the majority peoples among whom they lived. Thus the pattern of Jewish living until modern times was determined not only by the native genius of our Torah-centered tradition but by the intellectual and spiritual soil in which that tradition was planted.

Imperceptibly, and then with the force of a flood breaking through a levee, the rising tide of experimental science inundated the Western world. The first faint glimmerings of reason in Europe were seen by our people from the perspective of their physical condition. They saw in the rule of reason and enlightenment an opportunity for their physical emancipation. Only gradually did it dawn on them that this same instrument of reason which they hoped would secure their social, economic and political freedom was cutting away their spiritual security. Many of our people, when they recognized that danger, sought refuge in a self-imposed spiritual ghetto. They preferred the promise of revealed salvation to the agonizing experience of re-thinking their Judaism in a world of free exchange of ideas. For those who chose to accept the consequences of emancipation and enlightenment, the path was blocked by the inherited prejudices of the Middle Ages. Emancipation turned out to be an illusion. Many of our people were forced to live in a physically oppressive environment and in a rarefied intellectual atmosphere which they had not yet learned how to breathe. Their faith in their tradition had been weakened, if not destroyed, but they were still physically attacked. No longer did they have a psychological fortress behind which they could find security. For the first time since the destruction of Jewish national independence at the hands of the Romans, our people suffered a severe blow to their morale—a blow from which we have not yet recovered. Even in the United States, where the physical emancipation of our people has reached its highest point, Jewish morale is still at a low ebb, if we are to judge by the apathy of the Jewish masses to Judaism.

Thus is set the stage for a new adjustment in Jewish life, (and I confine myself now to American Jewish life) an adjustment to a free society in which the winds of new doctrines are ever penetrating into the cracks of our own tradition. Our problem is how to take advantage of good ideas, no matter what their source, without doing violence to that which is unique and precious in the Jewish heritage.

No pattern for American Jewish living, it seems to me, can be of lasting value unless it is cut from the cloth of religion. We shall help ourselves if we distinguish clearly between two approaches to religion.

There are and have been two fundamental types of religion to which men have subscribed. One I call conceptual religion and the other, historical or group religion.

Conceptual religion, represented most clearly by Protestant Christianity, consists of a series of tenets about the world and man, about God, revelation, etc. It is usually created in the mind of a single man or by a small group of men and is then offered to the world for acceptance. Those who accept the system of belief become adherents of the particular religion. That was the way in which Christianity was initiated and adopted, although later on many conversions to Christianity were imposed by force. American Protestantism today is typical of this conceptual approach to religion, for one is a Protestant, at least nominally, by accepting a particular theology and its associated beliefs. An interesting corroboration of this thesis is the fact that the Unitarians who view Jesus only as a great prophet are not considered Christians by orthodox or even liberal Protestants. A Christian, by definition, must accept the divinity of Jesus. Needless to say, this conceptual approach to religion has failed to unify the Protestant world. Testimony to this fact are the hundreds of sects which often express extreme opposition to one another. Protestants, in recent years, have been searching desperately for some basis of Protestant unity.

There are many Jews who believe that this conceptual approach to religion is the only valid one, and that what differentiates a Jew from a non-Jew is what each believes. Such Jews would, therefore, have us organize Jewish life around universal acceptance of a particular Jewish religious viewpoint. I submit, however, that even if such a procedure were possible (which I do not believe), it would be out of keeping with the nature of Jewish religion. For Judaism is the example, par excellence, of the group or historical approach to religion.

An historical religion is the repository of ideals, aspirations and sanctified modes of behavior (the mitzvot of our tradition) which grow out of the experience of particular people. (Compare the Old and New Testaments). There was, of course, a close tie between the Jewish historical religion of the past and the conceptual outlook of almost all Jews. A harmony and a uniformity pervaded the atmosphere of Jewish life. Whatever disagreements existed among individual Jews about certain tenets of theology rarely challenged the fundamentals. Jews could disagree about the reasons for *kashruth,* but not whether *kashruth* had to be observed.

The problem in Jewish life today is fundamentally one of trying to find the happy medium between a complete worship of the group, and the equally extreme clinging to doctrine, to the exclusion of diversity and change. It seems to me that we can steer our course accurately if we would remember two things: One is that problems are being solved in the modern world, not by mere assertions, but by experimentation and trial and error. The second is that the Jewish religion of which we are the heirs is a function of the community as a whole.

It follows from this second interpretation of Judaism that those of us who want to perpetuate what is worthwhile of our inherited Jewish values and to create new ones must do all in our power to fashion a Jewish community life which will embrace, in an organic fashion, all Jews who want to be Jews. By organic, I mean:

(1) That the loyalty of each Jew will be first to the commun-

ity as a whole rather than to a particular organization in the community.

(2) The organic community should so function as to care for the interests of individual Jews and channel them to the advantage of the whole Jewish people. It means, to cite one concrete example, that both the secularist and religionist must recognize their primary loyalty to the Jewish people, and that the organic community, by using its total personnel (rabbis, center workers, educators, etc.) will be able to bring them together for a healthy and essential exchange of views. The present separation of educational and cultural activities of religious and secular Jews in the synagogue and the center can only perpetuate the misunderstanding between them. Only by bringing the varieties of Jewish opinion into creative contact will a really vital Judaism emerge.

(3) Organic community means further that we must not conceive of Jewish religion solely in terms of so-called religious institutions and personnel—like synagogues and rabbis. We must learn to see Jewish religion in any activity which embodies the highest ideals of Jewish life. Is it any the less religious if a lay organization collects and distributes funds for the alleviation of the suffering than if this activity is supervised by the synagogue? Is it any the less religious if the social ideals of Zion are discussed from a lecture platform than if they are presented from a pulpit? We must learn to think about religion from the standpoint of its inherent meaning rather than its auspices.

Let us synagogue Jews, therefore, take the initiative in calling upon our fellow Jews, whatever their persuasion, to pool their mutual love for the Jewish people and their intellectual, spiritual and material resources for the purpose of constructing a Jewish community for all American Jews.

It stands to reason that there are many architectural plans which might be drawn for such a community. I, for one, would not like to hazard a guess as to its ultimate appearance. But I should like to impress upon you the method of construction and the spirit in which the problem ought to be approached.

We need a much greater spirit of inquiry in Jewish life. I shall concentrate henceforth on the synagogue (for this is our own chief concern), but this same spirit is needed in other areas of Jewish life as well. Less than one third of American Jewry—and that means men, women and children—are to be found in the ranks of the synagogue. Only a small percentage of that number is active in the spiritual life of the synagogue. This is not something that has happened in the past few years. It has been a chronic complaint for decades. What have we done about the situation?

In the first place, we've preached old-time religion. If it was good enough for our parents and grandparents, it should be good enough for us.

Secondly, we have talked about change in the abstract. We have worked under the assumption that change should not be rushed and not be artificial, that it should fall within the framework of *halakha*. We are still talking. And meanwhile the synagogue, the house of worship, is empty of young people, while those who do come to pray often do so out of a sense of duty rather than because of the inspiration to be found.

Thirdly, we have sought to discourage any independent action. There must be group discipline, we said. So we denounced those who took the bull by the horns; instead of criticizing objectively the quality of their work we attacked their motives. If I may cite one example close to home, when the New Haggadah was published eight years ago by the Reconstructionist Foundation, the Jewish world gave forth with a crescendo of denunciation. The fact is that there is much in that Haggadah to be improved upon. But its effect on making the *Seder* significant to thousands of Jewish families has more than justified its publication. But why was it necessary to have to defend the very right to publish a religious text?

Now what do I mean by a spirit of inquiry? I mean that we must stop preaching chiefly about the glories of the past and encourage our people to ask the questions that are on their minds. For example, we must not try to justify the stand of Jewish tradition concerning women, but should seek to devise means by which women might have a greater creative role in Jewish religious thought and activity. We have to ask ourselves not only whether the prayers we recite can be logically interpreted, but whether or not they actually help create pious Jews or provide a satisfactory spiritual expression for those who are already pious.

Secondly, a spirit of inquiry implies a method of answering the questions one raises. It means, in short, experimentation. It

means that in wide areas of Jewish life we shall have to substitute trial and error for *halakha*. It may be that we can draw up a
new code of practice based on *halakha* and legislated by the rabbis. But I cannot help feeling that this procedure will be ineffective. It fails to take into consideration, what should be apparent
to all, that those who are expected to live according to a certain
pattern of life, must not only find it acceptable, but must also
help to shape it. Without such participation by the masses of Jewry in revitalizing our tradition to fit their needs, there will be little motivation for the average Jew to live Judaism every hour of
every day. Spiritual life for the lay person cannot and must not be
the creation of the rabbi alone.

Certain implications follow inevitably from an acceptance of
such an inquiring attitude to Jewish spiritual life.

(1)   Instead of preaching, we ought to analyze our problem, set
our objectives and work cooperatively on achieving them. As I see
Jewish life now, we each work in our own little synagogue and
repeat the same mistakes year after year. When we meet together
at conventions, we raise questions and then proceed to forget
about them until next year. Even our professional leaders give
the impression of working as individualists, if not in outright
competition—thereby failing to benefit from each other's experience. Our lay people, in their management of our synagogues, often act as though they were conducting businesses. There is competition for members, insistence on separate schools whether or
not they are efficient, etc.

(2)   This same spirit, I feel, is reflected in our higher institutions of learning. I take it that the Seminary, Hebrew Union College, Jewish Institute of Religion and Yeshiva want to train leaders on the highest level of scholarship and understanding of the
Jewish scene. Yet we deliberately segregate our students from one
another so that they are insulated during their student years from
diverse opinions and practice on the part of students and teachers.
Where is the spirit of inquiry and openmindedness in our seminaries?

(3)   The time has come for Jewish laymen to stop passing the
buck. If it is true that we, the rabbis, have not lived up to our responsibility, it is equally true that our laity has encouraged us in
this laxity. You have expected the rabbi to be the repository of
ritual observance and Jewish values. You may ride to synagogue

and eat non-kosher food, but the rabbi is expected to adhere to traditional standards. You expect the rabbi to teach you all you need to know about Judaism, but you want no part of study. And you want the rabbi to get together with his colleagues and to agree on change, but you see no need to assume any responsibility for yourselves in bringing about that change. Yet Jewish religion was not meant to be a rabbinical prerogative. If you want a vital Judaism, you can no longer duck your share of the work. Which means, you have to study and you have to press for those changes in Jewish life without which Judaism is meaningless to you. If there is to be a new regimen of Jewish observance, it must come from the combined efforts of lay and professional workers.

(4) The spirit of inquiry also demands a readiness to try new paths in thought and observance. It is true that our brothers in Israel, particularly in the secularist kvutzot have made many mistakes by their radical departure from tradition. It is nevertheless certain that their daring and resourcefulness has breathed new life into many old practices and has whetted their appetite for further effort to find a spiritually elevating Judaism. We need this same courage.

While on the subject of Israel, it might be well to point to one lesson we ought to learn from our Israeli brothers. One thing which is lacking in American Judaism is the social application of our heritage. We have seen our ethical heritage once again sink its roots into the soil of Israel, and we have seen it enriched by the fertilization of the cooperative experiment. I realize full well that one cannot transfer social systems from one environment to another, but every social system which is humane creates universal values that can be implemented in different settings. It is time we began to bridge the ever-widening spiritual gap which has been created between our middle class status in the United States and the democratic socialist character of the Yishuv. If the values of cooperation, service, mutual help and equality are to be considered Jewish, then they ought to be ours as they are those of Israeli Jewry. Why not incorporate them into our prayers, our curriculum, our community organization and our participation in the American social scene?

The Torch, July, 1950.

Dr. Cohen, Rabbi, educator, interpreter of the Reconstructionist Movement, is Director of the Hillel Foundation in Israel. He formerly was Educational Director, Cleveland, Ohio, Jewish Center, Director of the Jewish Reconstructionist Foundation and Rabbi of the Society for the Advancement of Judaism in New York City. His writings include The Case for Religious Nationalism *and* Jewish Education in a Democratic Society. *He has served as Editor of* The Reconstructionist *and* The Synagogue School, *and was Chairman of the United Synagogue Commission on Jewish Education.*

THE SABBATH REVITALIZATION EFFORT

JACOB B. AGUS

I. THE URGENCY OF THE PROJECT

A. Why is the revitalization of the Sabbath an immediate problem? Haven't we been talking about the Sabbath for years? Why the sudden sense of urgency?

B. To be sure, problems do not cease to be urgent and timely because they have been faced before. Nevertheless, to prod people into facing a problem with earnestness and determination, a *dramatic* factor must be introduced. Indeed, something has happened which brings the Sabbath into the forefront of consciousness. Always *timeless* in significance, it has suddenly become a very timely, up to the minute task for our generation.

C. That epoch-making event is the emergence of the State of Israel.

1. Jewish loyalty has been directed, heretofore, in the channels of the preservation of the Jewish people. The life of our people was threatened by the twin-headed hydras of anti-Semitism and assimilation. In opposition to these pressures which attain their climax in our time, those of us, who refused to give up in despair, countered by means of the Zionist program, on the one hand, and anti-defamation, on the other hand. Zionism was primarily the collective response of Jews to the corroding challenge of assimilation. Anti-defamation was the response to the painful crescendo of hate propaganda.

2. The emergence of Israel as an independent, self-governing nation, makes the twin expressions of the Jewish will to live obsolete. The survival of the Jewish people is now no longer subject to the day by day challenge of life. It is no longer charged with a character and a quality that is unique. As a nation, Israel now faces and solves its problems as do other nations, taking its normal chances in the universal struggle for survival. The will to live

of the other immigrant nationalities does not prevent their continuous absorption into the life of the American nation, because
the continued existence of their home-nationality does not depend
upon their stubborn resistance to the assimilating powers of the
American "melting pot." Now, that Israel has taken its place
among the governments of the world, Jewish national loyalty is
bound to seek the "normal" level of other national groups.
Hence, the Zionist dream can no longer function as a motive for
Jewish living.

3. By the same token, anti-Semitism has been robbed of its
unique sting and its quality of universality. The Jew was previously in a class by himself, subject to the stigma of being different
as a nation from all the peoples of the world. Now this stigma has
been removed. Anti-Jewish feeling may continue to manifest itself from time to time, fluctuating in intensity, but it can no
longer appeal as a "philosophy." The debacle of Hitlerism contributed to the same end, by demonstrating the inhuman madness
of anti-Semitism.

II. WHY BEGIN WITH THE SABBATH?

A. The logical procedure for a religious revival seems to be
one which begins with faith in God. If a powerful faith in the living God of Judaism is reborn in the hearts of our people, they
will not hesitate to accept such rites and ceremonials as are implied in a program of Sabbath observance. Thus, too, the Christians in their evangelistic crusades focus their efforts upon the acquisition of "faith," in the sense of an overwhelming emotional
experience.

B. The answer is that in Judaism faith is conceived not as a
dogmatic assertion, but as the reflection of a good and holy life.
We say not only "faith without works is dead," but faith is the
verbalization of a life, sanctified by "works." The "holy" to us is
not so much an awareness of the "ineffable," as it is the consciousness emerging out of a life molded by the compelling attraction of
the good, the beautiful and the true.

1. In all fields of culture, the act precedes the judgment. Good
music is that which good musicians sense to be good. "Good
taste," in all spheres of life, results from living in accord with

good taste. Culture is that which cultured people prefer. Religion is the acquisition of a taste for the highest expressions of the human soul. "Taste and see that the Lord is good."

C. The second answer is a practical one. In terms of the realistic endeavor to build Jewish personalities, the Sabbath is the logical beginnning. For if it be observed, even in part, Judaism becomes part of one's routine. Also, if attendance in the synagogue is accepted as an integral part of the Jewish way of life, every significant ideal in every aspect of life will receive its proper impetus thru the service and the sermon. Whatever effort or institution is needful at any one time will be analyzed, evaluated and conveyed to the nuclear elements of our people thru the synagogue. For Judaism is an all-embracing pattern of life, deriving its inspiration from religious faith, not merely a collection of "spiritual" doctrines, and the rabbi is not merely a purveyor of pious ideas, but an architect of Jewish living. Hence, nothing that is intrinsically and soundly Jewish is outside the scope of the rabbi's message and the synagogue's interest.

D. The Sabbath, accepted in this sense, would make an end of the diverse vulgarities in Jewish life.

1. The resort by congregations to undignified tricks, in order to secure attendance at services.

2. The search for the flashy and the popular and the interesting instead of the truly substantial in congregational activities.

3. The unseemly competition of a multitude of organizations, each claiming to preempt Jewish loyalties, is one of the manifestations of the prevailing confusion as to the meaning of being a positive Jew. It is for the synagogue to discover and to evaluate the "holy spark" in each organization.

III. WHAT CAN THE SABBATH DO
FOR THE AMERICAN JEW?

A. This is the most central question, for Judaism is not a burden imposed upon us from without but our dearest possession. Properly interpreted and accepted, it aids us to make the most of our lives. Let us see, therefore, what the Sabbath can do for us.

1. The Sabbath responds to the rhythm-principle that governs

every aspect of life. We breathe rhythmically, our blood flows and ebbs in spurts, our energies need release and tension, our highest ecstacies require periods of relaxation and indifference. In keeping with this principle, we need not only periods of cessation from work, but we must have a time when the entire secular bent of our personality is redirected and reoriented. All week long we express the basic drive of "self-assertion;" on the Sabbath, we give vent to our yearning for "self-surrender"—surrender to God, who is our Master.

2. All the detailed laws of the Sabbath were intended to express the principle that "the earth and all its fullness belong to the Lord." In their Conservative interpretation, these laws may serve today as the means of inducing the spirit of "self-surrender."

3. We all know of the basic drive of "self-assertion," but few people have ever heard of the opposite and corresponding drive, the yearning for "self-surrender." Yet, all dictators know it, and our time has furnished ample proof of the evils of surrendering to the false gods of race, of clan and of the state.

4. In our age of tensions and neuroses, the most important therapeutic institution is the Sabbath. Thus, Eric Fromm, writing from a purely psychiatric viewpoint in his latest book, "The Forgotten Language," declares that the Sabbath is the most profound symbolic language of religion. He recommends it as of unique value for the good life.

5. "Self-improvement" is one of the most powerful motivations in the lives of Americans. But, what is our self?—Is it merely the sum-total of our ambitions, drives and aspirations?—Is there not a deeper level, where our self truly dwells? We say "I" so glibly, but we rarely pause to reflect what we mean by it. Surely, our self is not a momentary desire, but an enduring entity. We become aware of it only when we reflect on our position in the total scheme of things. Our impulses live in our selves, our selves live in time, but time dwells in eternity. What do we mean for God?

The Sabbath induces us to become conscious of our selves, and of the need of improving ourselves through prayer, reflection and the spirit of fellowship.

6. We tend to think of "self-improvement" in terms of sharpen-

ing our wits for the arduous battles of life, but life is richer and nobler by far than a relentless race. On the Sabbath, we think of "self-improvement" as the task of polishing the windows of our souls, so as to appreciate the nobler aspects of life.

The Torch, Winter, 1952.

THE RITUAL OF THE SYNAGOGUE

MAX J. ROUTTENBERG

One of the recurrent complaints of laymen, familiar to all rabbis and cantors, is the charge that there is no set or fixed pattern of worship, either liturgically or musically, in the Conservative Synagogue. Each congregation appears to be a law unto itself and no attempt is made by the national rabbinic and cantorial bodies to establish a uniform service for all the synagogue bodies in our movement. Without having personally attended the services in the 800 or so synagogues affiliated with us, I have little doubt, from my own limited experience, that the charge is substantially correct. Despite all the unifying factors within our congregations, a majority of rabbis who have received the same rabbinic training, cantors who receive direction and guidance from the Cantors Assembly, the use of the same prayer book and mahzor in most of our synagogues, nevertheless, we have considerable variety and a wide range of differences in the forms and practices of our public worship.

I plead guilty to the charge, yet at the same time I number myself among those who regard our present condition as a virtue and not a calamity. I believe that the state of fluidity in which we find ourselves is a source of great strength for us and not a manifestation of weakness. The time will come, I am afraid, when our variegated ritual and liturgical practices will coalesce into a fixed and formal pattern of worship, in accepted prayer and musical modes which will become "traditional" in our Conservative synagogues. I hope that day is far off. We are living through a period of great creative accomplishment in our liturgical and musical development and we are really only at the beginning of this process. I do not know how many new prayer books have been edited by rabbis and cantors for use in Conservative synagogues during the past few decades but I, personally, have rejoiced every time one has appeared. Each one has added something to our liturgical heritage; I have found something of value in each one of them, some new approach to the order of the service, some new insight into the meaning of the prayer. Many new liturgical compositions have appeared in recent years, many new musical settings for Friday night or Shabbas morning or Festival services. Whatever their quality or intrinsic merit, I am certain that in one way or another they have enriched the musical repertoire of every cantor and have brought fresh and, at times, exciting musical experiences into the Synagogue service. All this has been possible precisely because we have not striven for standardization of the ritual and because we have encouraged and made room for the creative works of gifted colleagues in this field of endeavor.

This approach is not even revolutionary but is quite endemic to Jewish religious life. One has only to consider the bewildering variety of *minhagim* and *nushaot* which have come down to us through the centuries. We speak broadly of the Ashkenazic and Sephardic rituals as the two main divisions of the synagogue. But you and I know how each of these is divided and subdivided by ethnic, geographic and historic circumstance in a multiplicity of differing ritual practices. Any one who has been in Jerusalem and taken a tour of the synagogues and visited the many religious establishments in the Holy City knows that among the many unquestioned virtues of the traditional heritage, uniformity in religious ritual certainly was not one of them.

I am afraid that the cry for uniformity and for standardization is being heard too soon in our circles. We need more time and more freedom for experimentation, for innovation, time for hospitality to new ideas, new forms, new expressions, before we settle down into a comfortable old age, set in our ways and fixed in our habits. But I would not be misunderstood. In my abhorrence of uniformity with its accompanying dullness and deadness, I am not pleading for chaos. In my advocacy of liberty I do not condone libertarianism. The early days of *hefkerut,* each one doing what is right in his own eyes, is over and done with. We have organized our chaos and we have put some fences around our freedom. We have developed a sense of discipline, of group responsibility; we have consultation with each other and are not prone to wild, extravagant, individual action. That's why we are "conservative." These restraints and disciplines which we impose upon ourselves, in a real sense, derive from what we regard as the emerging consensus in the Conservative movement as it is reflected in the developing pattern of our public worship, as it is expressed in the ritual of our synagogue. That pattern is triple-stranded, and I would like to describe each strand briefly.

The first strand is that of Hebrew. Worship in Conservative synagogues is definitely Hebraic-centered. This is our historic link with the Jewish communities of the past, it is our link with "K'lal Yisroel" of today, it is our badge of authenticity in our claim of full citizenship in the Jewish people. We must reckon with the fact that large numbers of our constituents do not understand Hebrew, many cannot recite the Hebrew prayers. We need a vast educational program for them. In the meantime, we shall have to have responsive readings and unison prayers in the vernacular, interspersed through the service. This is a temporary expedient; this is a concession to the uninitiated; it is not a principle that Conservative Jews must have English in their prayers. Our principle is that Conservative Jews must learn to pray in Hebrew, must study Hebrew, so that some day the synagogue service will be predominantly Hebrew. But certainly, in the chants of the synagogue, in the cantorial recitatives, the choral compositions and the congregational songs and hymns, these ought to be based exclusively on Hebraic texts. Here the uniquely Jewish flavor of worship, here the emotional response and involvement of the worshiper, is possible only in the classic Hebrew formulations of our prayers.

The second strand is that of congregation. Worship in Conservative synagogues has become increasingly congregation-centered. In the older traditional synagogues, it was *davener*-centered. A worshiper came to be with the fellow Jews who davened alone. In the more recent traditional synagogues, the service became largely cantor-centered, though certain rabbis have begun to take the lime-light away from them. Certainly, in most Reform congregations, the service is rabbi-centered; and for a time, it appeared that this is the way our Conservative synagogues would go. Fortunately, the trend in our movement would seem to be largely in the direction of congregational participation. The daveners have largely disappeared from our congregations, the lure of the "star cantor" has largely diminished, because now all the cantors are stars, and it is becoming increasingly unfashionable for rabbis to play the role of prima donna—so, willy nilly, the congregation, as a congregation, has become the center and focus of the worship experience. There are the prayer readings which, in Hebrew and in English, in unison and responsively, keep the worshipers actively occupied. But it is in the area of congregational chanting that you feel the emotional stir and excitement as the worshipers achieve a degree of religious fervor and even ecstasy that mark the genuine religious experience. We have made some advances in the field of cantorial recitatives and choral compositions and that is all to the good. They have an important place in the ritual of the synagogue. But we must increasingly devote ourselves to the crucial and central field of the congregational chant. We must enrich the repertoire of our songs and hymns; we must encourage composition in this field; we must develop proper techniques for teaching and conducting the congregation in its participation in the service. We are moving in this direction because we have to; because in the Conservative synagogue, the congregation is the center of the service and our best efforts must be concentrated in making the congregational service as spiritually rewarding as possible.

The third strand is that of ceremony. As worship in our synagogues becomes more routinized and formalized, there has developed a great need for vivid and dramatic moments to high-light certain events or experiences, whether of individual or a group nature. We have unashamedly used all the techniques of pageantry and staging to enhance the beauty and heighten the interest of the service for taking out the Torah and returning it to the ark. Our processionals and recessionals are all carefully planned and rehearsed. In addition to some of the ceremonies we have inherited, to which we have contributed numerous embellishments, we have added many new ones. We have done a great deal with highlighting events that center around great milestones in the lives of our congregants. The naming of a child, the Bar and Bat Mitzvah, the blessing of the bride and groom, recovery from illness, significant anniversaries, have been invested with beautiful and meaningful ceremonial and ritual that involve the active participation of those directly concerned. We need, for the proper performance of these ceremonies, more and better prayer and musical settings, to enrich and intensify the experience for the entire congregation. We would love to see a genuine outpouring of musical expression on the part of our cantor-composers in this developing area of conservative ritual which is occupying such an important part of our worship service.

Let me say this final thing. During this period of flux and change through which we are going, it is imperative that we do not permit ourselves to be swept away by the tides of change and novelty for their own sake. We must remain rooted in and faithful to the ideals and values which have been the hallmark of Conservative Judaism. Our ritual and ceremonial, developing and evolving as they are, must be anchored in the tradition. Rabbis, cantors, educators have a tremendous responsibility in this free-flowing, creative age in which we are living. Thus, at all costs, we must maintain the highest standards of learning and scholarship in our rabbinical school, our Teachers Institute, our Cantors Institute. A Judaism based on Torah must not become a mockery and a derision in our own eyes. We must possess not only an understanding of the tradition, but a deep love and reverence for it. The Sabbath, the festivals, the Mitzvot, the action-symbols of our religious beliefs, the Hebrew language, not simply as language, but as *Loshon Kodesh,* the holy tongue of prophets and seers and sages, the land of Israel and the people of Israel—all these must be sacred to us, in thought and in deed.

Above all, we must rear a generation of Jews who will turn to the religion of their fathers with love and reverence, with understanding and appreciation of its rich treasure-troves which can bless them and their children and all future generations. Such a program is possible here in America; such a program will vindicate the faith and fulfill the hopes of our founder and teacher Solomon Schechter who believed in the emergence on these shores of a Judaism rooted in the Torah and tradition, harmonizing with the culture and civilization of the western world, flowering as a living faith in the lives of a living people.

The Torch, Spring, 1965.

Dr. Routtenberg is Rabbi of Temple B'nai Sholom of Rock-
ville Center, New York. He previously served as Rabbi in
Reading, Pa. and as Chaplain in the U. S. Army. He is a past
president of the Rabbinical Assembly of America. At the
Jewish Theological Seminary he is Visiting Professor of Hom-
iletics, Vice Chairman of the Board of Overseers and of the
Rabbinical Cabinet, and member of the Board of Directors.
He has been Chairman of the Committee on Jewish Law
and Standards of the Rabbinical Assembly.

A JEWISH PRAYER BOOK
FOR OUR TIMES

ROBERT GORDIS

ges, the Prayer Book has been the comfort and
w. To its pages, every generation contributed its
irations and noblest thoughts, and from them, it
... and faith in God. As we have seen, the Prayer Book
grew with Israel, always remaining the deeply cherished treasure
house of the Jewish spirit.

During the long centuries of the Dispersion, Jews had their
share of troubles, to be sure, but few found Judaism a problem.
Everywhere, Jews lived within their own communities, were governed by their own laws and practiced the Jewish way of life. This
period continued for East-European Jewry almost until our day.
For the Jews of central and western Europe, it ended about 150
years ago. The modern period may be dated somewhat arbitrarily
but conveniently with the French Revolution, which began in
1789.

As a result of the far-reaching political, industrial and social
changes set in motion in the eighteenth century, two great forces
made their impact felt upon Jewish life. One was the Enlightenment, which in the name of reason, subjected all traditional ideas
and institutions to critical observation and found them wanting.
The other was the Emancipation, which declared in the name of
"Liberty, Fraternity and Equality" that Jews were human and
should be admitted to citizenship in their respective countries.
While these movements were, by and large, a boon to the individual Jew, their effect upon Jewish group-life was far from an
unmixed blessing. The Enlightenment undermined the authority and power of the Jewish religion for many Jews, while the
Emancipation dissolved the cohesiveness of the Jewish community.

381

These negative effects were not noted at the beginning. The political rights and economic opportunities that were now being offered West European Jews as citizens of France, Germany or England, seemed to them the drawn of the Messianic age. They did not stop to notice that there were strings attached to these rights. There was the understanding, nearly always implied and often explicitly stated, that Jews would in return reduce and, if possible, eliminate the Jewish loyalties and practices by which they lived. Only time revealed one fatal lack among the rights bestowed upon them—the absence of the right to "spiritual self-determination."

II

Thus, the modern age confronted both the Jewish people and the Jewish religion with a far-reaching challenge. For perhaps the first time in Jewish history, Judaism became a problem. Various patterns of behavior and thought now emerged. There were those who preferred to desert Judaism completely by conversion and intermarriage, for whom the problem ceased to exist altogether.

Many other Jews were unprepared to surrender their Jewish identity completely and began instead to "adjust" Judaism by reducing its rich tradition and elaborate way of life to the dimensions of a cult, and converting the Jewish people to the status of a "denomination."

This movement, called Reform, naturally turned to the Prayer Book, for public worship is the most obvious form of Jewish life. Conscious as well as unconscious motives were at work in the process. There was a desire to shorten the service and hence the Torah reading was drastically reduced, while the Psalms and the medieval *piyyutim* were almost completely eliminated. Hebrew was less and less known and appreciated, and the demand arose for prayers in the vernacular, with the result that ultimately Hebrew was virtually eliminated from the ritual, at least as far as the congregation was concerned. The traditional chanting of the service and of the Bible readings were abandoned. Since Jews were no longer members of a people, but solely German, French or British citizens of the Mosaic persuasion, prayers for the restoration of Israel to its homeland, the rebuilding of the Temple and the re-establishment of the Government of David had to be eliminated.

When all these and countless other changes in content and in form were carried through, a new Prayer Book emerged, the resemblance of which to the traditional *siddur* and *mahzor* was scarcely more than coincidental.

This extreme action with regard to the Prayer Book led to an equally passionate reaction. Faced by the wholesale dissolution of Jewish life, a new party arose in Germany, the neo-Orthodox, headed by Rabbi Samson Raphael Hirsch, a man of great spirituality and warm-hearted love for Judaism. Declaring that Judaism was divine, this school of thought insisted that it was fixed, unchanged and unchangeable throughout time. Reform had played havoc with the traditional Prayer Book. Its retention without change now became the mark of loyalty to tradition.

III

It was precisely here that Orthodoxy, for all its great virtues, made its fundamental error. It is a basic principle of modern research in all fields of natural and historical sciences that everything that lives grows and changes, and only that which is dead is fixed. The modern scientific study of Judaism during the past century and a quarter has shown that this truth applies to Jewish life and institutions as well. Jewish customs and ceremonies, Jewish laws and religious ideas all have changed with time, exactly as the youth differs from the child, and the man from the youth. The stages of this development are mirrored in the Bible, the Talmud and medieval Jewish literature, and the creative process must continue in the modern age, if Judaism is to live.

There was need for a new, vital and historically sound approach to Jewish tradition, which would neither stand pat on the past nor run riot in the present. For easily understandable reasons, this tendency was the last and the slowest to emerge. It is much easier to hold on to the old without change, at least in theory, or to cut loose from the past altogether. It is a far more arduous task to evolve the principles and the techniques necessary for conserving and revitalizing a four-thousand-year-old tradition, and there are countless pitfalls along the way, for life is always dangerous.

That is the historic function of Conservative Judaism, as has become evident from the three decades of its history in America. It regards Jewish tradition as dynamic, to be preserved in largest measure, to be sure, but also to be created. To use Dr. Finkelstein's fine phrase, it speaks of Jewish tradition as "in the making."

IV

An important milestone in the coming of age of Conservative Judaism has been the issuance of the new Sabbath and Festival Prayer Book. This work was issued by the Joint Prayer Book Commission of the Rabbinical Assembly and the United Synagogue, of which the writer had the honor to be Chairman, and which included on its roster such distinguished rabbis and scholars as Dr. Max Arzt, Associate Professor of Practical Rabinics at the Jewish Theological Seminary, and Dr. Simon Greenberg, Provost and Professor of Education at the Jewish Theological Seminary, both of whom have had long and fruitful careers in the active ministry; Dr. Jacob Kohn of Temple Sinai, Los Angeles, California; Dr. Israel H. Levinthal of the Brooklyn Jewish Center; Dr. Louis M. Levitsky of Congregation Oheb Shalom, Newark, New Jersey; Dr. Abraham A. Neuman, President of Dropsie College; Rabbi Morris Silverman of Congregation Emanuel in Hartford; and Dr. Elias L. Solomon of Congregation Shaare Zedek in New York.

In the Fall of 1944, the Rabbinical Assembly and the United Synagogue entered into an agreement with Rabbi Morris Silverman to use the manuscript of a Sabbath and Festival Prayer Book that he had prepared as the basis for an official Prayer Book for our Movement. All the material was subjected to careful study by the Commission, which had full authority to revise, supplement and delete the material. All decisions were carefully weighed at nearly forty meetings which lasted for many hours over a period of two years. Between meetings, sub-committees studied important problems and supplementary notes were pre-pared by individual members.

As the work progressed, certain fundamental principles emerged which we believe are significant for Conservative Juda-ism as a whole. First is the *principle of continuity with tradition.* This is basic for two reasons. First, loyalty to tradition is the strongest bulwark the Jewish people possesses against dissolution; second, and at least equally important, Jewish tradition, which is the product of our best creative spirits through the ages, is still rich in meaning and inspiration for us.

Relevance to the ideals and the needs of our own generation is the second basic principle, for our prayers are addressed to *Elohenu Velohei Avotenu,* "Our God" and not merely "the God of our fathers."

The third principle is *intellectual integrity.* We dare not evade the difficult problems posed by an ancient tradition in a new world. In order that it may truly live, Jewish ideas and ideals must be reformulated anew in every age. We must neither say what we do not mean, nor fail to say what we do mean.

V

Obviously, the application of these three principles to any issue and their harmonization is not easy. But as the work progressed, it was an inspiration to see how viable Jewish tradition is, when approached with sympathy and insight, and how superbly the prayerbook of the ages can serve as the spiritual treasure-house of our day as well.

In by far the largest number of instances, Jewish tradition needs only to be properly understood, in order to be appreciated and accepted. This is true even of aspects that have been under fire. The idea of the "Chosen People" is a striking illustration. Time and again, it has been attacked as an expression of national chauvinism or racial superiority. Doubtless, this idea has often been misunderstood and vulgarized by those who took it to mean that the Jew regards himself as better than his neighbor. But the ignoramus and the vulgarian are not our source for what Judaism means, any more than the professional patrioteer is a guide to true Americanism. If we wish to understand the meaning of patriotism, we turn not to the rabble-rousers, but to Washington, Jefferson and Lincoln. If we wish to comprehend the doctrine of the Chosen People, the Prophets and the Sages must be our guides. When we consult the Bbile and the Talmud, we quickly discover that the Chosen People means, in Zangwill's striking phrase, that the Jews are a "choosing people." The election of Israel means not greater privileges, but higher responsibilities for each Jew, who is called upon to be a witness of the Living God and an exemplar of His law. Hence, the Prayer Book invariably links the idea of a chosen people with the Torah and the commandments, for these constitute the patent of Israel's nobility, as well as the pattern of his life.

Similarly, there is no need to eliminate references to the House of David or the Messiah from the Prayer Book. For whether we conceive of the Messiah literally, as a personal redeemer, or as a symbol of the Messianic age, the figure of the Messiah, son of David, expresses in matchless form the unshakable faith of the Jew in the restoration of Israel to its homeland and the establishment of justice, freedom and peace for all men.

VI

In some instances, tradition needs to be re-interpreted to be meaningful for our age. To cite an example, the Hebrew word *avodah* means "service, religious worship." For our ancestors, religious worship centered around animal sacrifices in the Temple. There are many sincere Jews who still look forward to the restoration of the sacrificial system. But even those of us who regard animal offerings as a past stage in the history of Judaism, and consider prayer, study and righteous living as the highest forms of the worship of God need not change the ancient prayer, "Restore the worship to Thy sanctuary." For we too look forward to the re-establishment of a Temple on Zion's hill as the spiritual center of our faith.

Another phrase which may legitimately be re-interpreted is *mehayyeh hammetim,* which literally means "who gives life to the dead." In Biblical Hebrew, this idiom means "to restore to health those near to death." In later times, it was taken to refer to the physical resurrection of the dead. Whether we conceive of man's immortality in these terms or otherwise, the phrase serves admirably as a statement of our faith that man's spirit is deathless, and we praise God "who calls the dead to everlasting life."

VII

There are other cases *where tradition needs to be supplemented to meet our contemporary outlook and situation.* Thus, there is an ancient prayer in the liturgy written in Aramaic, *Yekum Purkan,* in which we pray for the scholars and leaders of Israel in the communities of Palestine and Babylonia. Though written in the heyday of those communities centuries ago, the prayer voices a thought perfectly relevant today. All that is required is to add the phrase, "and in all the lands of our dispersion."

Similarly in the *Mi Sheberakh,* which is a prayer for the welfare of all who serve the Jewish cause, we have added a phrase bespeaking God's blessing also on those "who engage in the rebuilding of the Land of Israel," because we see in it a cardinal mitzvah of Judaism today.

VIII

Finally, there are a few instances where the traditional formulation must be modified, if we are to be true to our convictions and not distort the meaning of the text. Thus, in the *Musaf Service* there is a prayer for the restoration of Zion and the re-establishment of the sacrificial system in the Temple. Even if we no longer look forward to animal sacrifices, it is clear that to delete the Musaf completely would mean to throw the baby out with the bath, for there is much of great value in this Service which should be retained and even emphasized.

Ranke called Jews the most historical of peoples, by which he meant that the past is always vivid to the Jew. Sacrifice was an important and central feature during long periods of our people's history, and it is entirely proper for us to recall the ancient Temple in all its glory. But the Musaf is more than reminiscence. Our movement is deeply devoted to the upbuilding of Eretz Yisrael, which we should like to see once more as the homeland of our people, the center of Jewish culture, and perhaps once again a source for the religious and moral inspiration of mankind. Finally, the Musaf Service recalls the importance of sacrifice as an expression of man's love for God, and as the indispensable instrument for the fulfillment of all worthwhile goals in life.

For all these reasons, neither the deletion of the Musaf nor its retention unchanged would satisfy our needs. To express our ideals, a few minor changes in the text were introduced. Instead of saying, "these sacrifices we shall offer up," the text reads, "these sacrifices our ancestors offered up before Thee." To give vivid expression both to our recollections of the past and our hopes for the future, two new prayers in Hebrew and English, one for the Sabbath and one for the Holidays were introduced, which it was the privilege of the writer to compose, with the advice of his colleagues. These prayers may be read by the individual worshipper, by the Cantor or by the Rabbi.

Another problem was posed by the three Preliminary Blessings at the opening of the Service. Here the Jew thanks God for the high privilege of observing the Torah and the commandments. Since non-Jews, slaves and women were not expected to observe all the commandments, the traditional liturgy contains three blessings in which the worshipper thanks God "who has not made me a Gentile, a slave or a woman." Obviously, such a formulation is easily subject to misunderstanding, and does not do justice to the increasingly important role of Jewish women in modern life. Interestingly enough, some of our very oldest liturgical texts, as well as early printed editions of the Talmud, offer a basis for rephrasing these blessings positively rather than negatively. Our prayer book now contains the blessings in affirmative form, thanking God "who hast made me in Thine image, free, and an Israelite."

IX

Other features of the Prayer Book can only be briefly referred to. To make it increasingly relevant to modern needs, over 100 pages of supplementary readings and hymns have been added, gathered from ancient, medieval and modern Jewish authors who

UR HERITAGE FROM EASTERN EUROPE *

ABRAHAM JOSHUA HESCHEL

) be sure, in the life of the East European Jews there was not
ly light but also shadow—one-sidedness of learning, neglect of
nners, provincialism. In the crowded conditions in which they
ed—persecuted and tormented by ruthless laws, intimidated
drunken landowners, despised by newly enriched city dwellers,
mpled by police boots, chosen as scapegoats by political dema-
gues—the rope of discipline sometimes snapped. In addition,
ked misery and frightful poverty deafened the demands and ad-
onitions of religious enthusiasm. The regions of piety were at
nes too lofty for plain mortals.

Not all the Jews could devote themselves to the Torah and ser-
ce to God, not all of their old men had the faces of prophets;
ere were not only Hasidim and Kabbalists, but also yokels and
mps. But even in the mud of their little towns there were
arling, tender flowers, and in the darkness, sparks smoldered,
iting to be kindled.

There was hardly a Jew in whom respect for the spirit had died
t completely. There were always moralists who publicly
anded the abuses that arose in the Jewish communities and
rled flaming denunciations at those who sat above, uncon-
rned with justice. The faults were in the limelight; *schnorrers*
read far and wide the knowledge of their unsavory qualities.
The record of quiet self-sacrifice, of unpublicized charity, of in-
ardness and devotion of the plain folk, of those who patiently
re their poverty and did not run abroad to seek their fortune
ill probably remain forever untold.

It is easier to appraise the beauty of traditional Jewish life than
e revolutionary spirituality of modern Jews. The Jew of older

* Editor's Note: We consider it a great privilege to be permitted to present this,
 concluding chapter of Professor Abraham J. Heschel's book, *The Earth Is the
rd's*. Abelard-Schuman.

speak to the modern mind. In addition, an accurate
has been sought, while the Aramaic portions of the
for the first time been purged of the grammatical er
they generally abound.

The English version is clear, direct and in the n
We have sought to avoid the pitfalls confronting
translators, who either make the Hebrew confor
style, or reproduce the Hebrew idiomatic usages l
English. In dealing with Biblical passages, we hav
the most modern Biblical scholarship and found
improve upon the translation of many passages. Fir
word, several supplementary notes, the indices and
seek to supply the background required for the re
telligent use of the Prayer Book.

That nearly one hundred congregations have
Prayer Book within a few short months of its appea
cast of the growing sense of unity binding the links
chain of Conservative Judaism. The popularity of
us hope that to some degree, at least, it meets the
presses the outlook of our movement, which striv
serve and recreate Judaism as a living and growing
Sabbath and Festival Prayer Book seeks to mak
meaningful in the life of the modern Jew, so tha
the joyous affirmation of our ancestors, "Happy are
ly is our portion, how pleasant our lot, how bea
itage!"

The Tor

days often overlooked this world because of his preference for the other world. Between man and world stood God. In the meantime, however, persecutions, pogroms, and murders shattered the ground under the feet of the people. There was no peace, no security, and the means to gain a livelihood were systematically taken away. The Slavonic masses, dominated by self-complacent landowners, feebly responded to the impulses of the industrial revolution that swept through the northern countries in the nineteenth century. Lacking the drive to enterprise, landowners, civil service, and peasantry alike ignored the challenge of the shaking transformation. The average man preferred to live on the public payroll as a state or municipal official rather than to be exposed to the risks of free commerce. As a result of failure to exploit natural resources and to substitute modern for antiquated methods in farming and trade, the people lived in misery and poverty. The increasing pauperization affected particularly the Jewish population, engaged to some extent in agriculture, but mainly in handicraft and trade, which for want of capital and because of systematic oppression by the state had scarcely any hope of recovery. Pioneers in city building and in developing important industries, the Jews encountered a mounting well-planned system of curbs and obstacles. Jewish youth, restless, alert, and flexible, eager and full of dynamic impulses, looked for a way out of the gloomy and over-crowded streets, where no chance of improvement, no conditions for development could be found.

Then came young men with new tidings; they refused to accept misfortune passively, they wanted to build their existence on their own soil. They no longer wanted to live on miracles, they wanted freedom, a natural way of life. They did not want to live spiritually off the past; they refused to live on bequests; they wanted to begin anew.

The cosmopolitan breeze of enlightenment blowing from the West with its optimistic message of emancipation for all people brought a flash of hope into the Jewish communities. The romanticism of poets and students, aspiring to bring about a revival of the Hebrew language, concurred with the post-Mendelssohnian activities aiming at rationalizing and unraveling the contents of Jewish life and lore. There arose the Enlightenment movement (Haskalah), Zionism, the Halutzim movement, Jewish socialism.

How much of self-sacrifice, of love for the people, of Sanctification of the Holy Name are to be found in the modern Jews, in their will to suffer in order to help! The zeal of the pious Jews was transferred to their emancipated sons and grandsons. The fervor and yearning of the Hasidim, the ascetic obstinacy of the Kabbalists, the inexorable logic of the Talmudists, were reincarnated in the supporters of modern Jewish movements. Their belief in new ideals was infused with age-old piety. They could see a "daughter of heaven" in the message of rationalism, a holy temple in the revived Hebrew language or the essence of Judaism in Yiddish, the "mother tongue."

They believed in Europe and extolled the "twentieth century." To absorb the culture and ideas of Western civilization was their passionate desire, their dream of happiness. Yet, unlike the ancient sects, even those who felt that for the sake of adopting the modern they had to abandon the old, even those whom the revolutionary impetus had carried to the antithesis of tradition, have not severed the ties from the people; with few exceptions, they have remained within the fold. The powerful urge to redemption survived in their souls. The allurements of assimilation were, indeed, seductive; but the Jews who did not capitulate, who did not flee from Jewish poverty, who gave up careers, comfort, and fame, in order to find healing for the hurt of their people, who left the sacred books or the universities to till the ground and dry the swamps of Palestine, were like old wine in new bottles.

The masses of East European Jews repudiated emancipation when it was offered at the price of disloyalty to Israel's traditions. Both pious and free-thinking Jews fought for a dignified existence, striving to assure the rights of the community, not only those of the individual. They manifested a collective will for a collective aim. With lightning rapidity, they straightened their backs and learned to master the arts and sciences. Gifts for abstract dialectical thinking, developed in the course of generations, were carried into scientific research. Hasidic enthusiasm was sublimated in the noble profundity of musical virtuosos. Three thousand years of history have not made them weary. Their spirits were animated by a vitality that often drove them into opposition to accepted tenets.

In the spiritual confusion of the last hundred years, many of us overlooked the incomparable beauty of our old, poor homes. We compared our fathers and grandfathers, our scholars and rabbis, with Russian or German intellectuals. We preached in the name of the twentieth century, measured the merits of Berditshev and Ger with the standards of Paris and Heidelberg. Dazzled by the lights of the metropolis, we lost at times the inner sight. The luminous visions that for so many generations shone in the little candles were extinguished for some of us.

In the last decades, there has developed a longing for an accord between the present and the past. The antithesis of the Haskalah had gradually begun to change into a synthesis. Gradually the inner beauty of the old life and the emptiness of present-day civilization have been disclosed. But the time has been too short and the will too weak. Clarity and solidarity have been lacking not only in spiritual but also in political matters. When confronted with a world of misery and indifference, our will and our vision proved inadequate. In our zeal to change, in our passion to advance, we ridiculed superstition until we lost our ability to believe. We have helped to extinguish the light our fathers had kindled. We have bartered holiness for convenience, loyalty for success, wisdom for information, prayer for sermon, tradition for fashion.

A world has vanished. All that remains is a sanctuary hidden in the realm of spirit. We of this generation are still holding the key. Unless we remember, unless we unlock it, the holiness of ages will remain a secret of God. We of this generation are still holding the key—the key to the sanctuary which is also the shelter of our own deserted souls. If we mislay the key, we shall elude ourselves.

In this hour we, the living, are "the people of Israel." The tasks, begun by the patriarchs and prophets and continued by their descendants, are now entrusted to us. We are either the last Jews or those who will hand over the entire past to generations to come. We will either forfeit or enrich the legacy of ages.

Judaism today is the least known religion. Its rare splendor has been so frequently adjusted to the trivialities of changing opinions that what is left is a commonplace. There are only few who still perceive the vanishing *niggun* of its perennial yearning.

Mankind does not have the choice of religion and neutrality.

Irreligion is not opiate but poison. Our energies are too abundant for living indifferently. We are in need of an endless purpose to absorb our immense power if our souls are not to run amok. We are either the ministers of the sacred or slaves of evil. To be a Jew is to hold one's soul clean and open the stream of endless striving so that God may not be ashamed of His creation. Judaism is not a quality of the soul but spiritual life. With souls we are born; spirit we must acquire.

Judaism is the track of God in the wilderness of oblivion. By being what we are, namely Jews; by attuning our own yearning to the lonely holiness in this world, we will aid humanity more than by any particular service we may render.

We are Jews as we are men. The alternative to our Jewish existence is spiritual suicide, disappearance, not conversion into something else. Judaism has allies, partners, but no substitute. It is not a handmaiden of civilization, but its touchstone.

We do not live in a void. We never suffer from a fear of roaming about in the emptiness of Time. We own the past and are, hence, not afraid of what is to be. We remember where we came from. We are endowed with the consciousness of being involved in a history that transcends the interests and glories of particular dynasties and empires. We were summoned and cannot forget it, winding the clock of eternal history. We are taught to feel the knots of life in which the trivial is intertwined with the sublime. There is no end to our experience of the intense, stern import of the dangerous grandeur, of the divine earnestness of human life. Our blossoms may be crushed, but we are upheld by the faith that comes from beneath our roots.

Our life is beset with difficulties, yet it is never devoid of meaning. The feeling of futility is absent from our souls. Our existence is not in vain. There is a Divine earnestness about our life. This is our dignity. To be invested with dignity means to represent something more than oneself. The gravest sin for a Jew is to forget what he represents.

We are God's stake in human history. We are the dawn and the dusk, the challenge and the test. How strange to be a Jew and to go astray on God's perilous errands. We have been offered as a pattern of worship and as a prey for scorn, but there is more still in our destiny. We carry the gold of God in our souls to forge the gate of the kingdom. The time for the kingdom may be far off, but the task is plain: to retain our share in God in spite of peril and contempt. There is a war to wage against the vulgar, against the glorification of the absurd, a war that is incessant, universal. Loyal to the presence of the ultimate in the common, we may be able to make it clear that man is more than man, that in doing the finite he may perceive the infinite.

The Torch, April, 1950.

AMERICAN JEWISH LEADERSHIP

M. DAVID HOFFMAN

The record of leadership in American life is colorful and almost
fantastic. It is a product of a dynamic society, youthful, uninhib-
ited, drawn from all the cultures of Europe and Asia, transplanted into a new soil which had not been prepared. American
leaders at times have been well educated, but more often have
been "self-made" men. They have been drawn from all walks of
life. Occasionally they have been profound thinkers, but more
frequently they have been fanatics, opportunists, unscrupulous
seekers after power. Unfortunately there are no generally accepted qualifications for leadership in this country. The equali-
tarian tradition, the influence of the frontier, the tides of immigration, the growth of industry, the common school, universal
suffrage—all elements of our democracy—have thus far made leadership a matter of chance or a product of the times. Our robber
barons and our more recent gangster leaders, our Coughlins and
our Huey Longs, are a part of our history of leadership as well as
the great spirits of Washington, Jefferson, Jackson, Lincoln, Emerson, and Whitman, Wilson and the Roosevelts. Our changing
social order bred religious fanatics, abolitionists, "Know Nothing" leaders, railroad builders, exploiters of natural resources,
and titans of capital, in greater number than poets and philoso-
phers and scientists. The Log Cabin to the White House legend,
the poor boy who becomes a multi-millionaire story, was characteristic of our nineteenth century development. Material success
was worshipped. Power was sought and secured without much regard to the means of securing it.

Into this fluid, and, at times, almost unpredictable and chaotic
social order came the various streams of Jewish immigration.
Each brought with it old world traditions, some from a so-called
emancipated Western Europe, some from the Ghettos of Eastern

Europe, some with interest in Jewish social life, others with strong religious and racial loyalties. The old values gradually became less significant and the American-born generation grew up confused as to the requisites for group leadership. The break with the past was so pronounced that even in the synagogue wealth and social position were qualifications of greater importance than learning, piety, or character.

Almost all of our Jewish leaders secured the support of those who had similar European backgrounds, who came from the same country, spoke the same language, ate the same food, worshipped in the same manner.

The Jew in America has not yet developed a way of life or sense of values which integrates his religion and his culture with American civilization. He is confused by the eloquence, by the wealth, or other prestige symbols, by which Jews seek power among their own people. He is usually ignorant as to things Jewish, and is unaware of the standards which the Jewish people have set up throughout the ages. With a minimum of Jewish education, with only a nominal affiliation with the synagogue (and often without it), he aspires to leadership through devious paths of politics, philanthropy, fraternal organizations, and nationalistic propaganda.

It is time that American Jewry should grow up. Our contribution to American life will be significant only if our spokesmen are a credit to us. Our lay leaders will have the characteristics that the American Jewish community demands of them. If learning be requisite for leadership, those who aspire to position in the community will qualify themselves accordingly. If respect for our religion and observance of Torah be expected, it is likely to be forthcoming. If loyalty to the Jewish people and to Eretz Israel be demanded, it will follow. This problem is one of public opinion. It is the creation of an intelligent Jewish laity, possessed of religious sensibilities and a sense of direction. In our democracy the influence of the clergy or statute law is not as likely to be effectual as is the climate of opinion.

Historically this has not been the case. Up to the so-called period of emancipation of Jewry in the Western World the Jewish people demanded learning and piety and character of its leaders. Our prophets and sages spoke in the name of God. They identified themselves with the manifold institutions of Jewish life. They were loyal to Jewish tradition. Maimonides, Mendelssohn, and Moses Montefiore were genuine representatives of their people—not by virtue of a referendum, to be sure, but because they were interpreters of the Jewish spirit, because their roots were in Jewish soil. They were products of the Jewish genius flowering in alien ground—but they were linked with the Jewish past—their inspiration grew out of the experiences of their people, their aspiration was the preservation of that way of life which has justified the continued existence of the Jewish people throughout the ages.

We must not allow Jewish leadership to be irresponsibile and quixotic if we hope to build a wholesome Jewish community life in the United States—if we wish to be self respecting and to be held in esteem by our fellow citizens.

We have in the Jewish Theological Seminary of America and similar academies of higher Jewish learning the institutions best fitted to meet this need. As a matter of fact, of the half dozen recognized lay leaders of our people in this country, five have been identified with the Seminary—Louis Marshall, Jacob Schiff, Felix Warburg, Cyrus Adler, and Henrietta Szold. These great personalities recognized the important contribution of the Seminary to the enrichment of Jewish life among us, to the strengthening of our religious life, to the development of morale, and esprit de corps—an enlightened catholic Israel in America. Under the spell of the magnetic personality and the erudition of Dr. Solomon Schechter, this leaderhip flourished for a time. The Seminary library and museum, the Israel Friedlander classes and the Teachers Institute, the Institute of Jewish Affairs, the Institute of Religious Studies, and the National Academy of Adult Jewish Education—all are indicative of the role the Seminary plays in Jewish life. Dr. Finkelstein, through conferences, is trying to bring home to increasing numbers the resources of the Seminary at our disposal. The Seminary as the training school of Rabbis and teachers, as the seat of Jewish learning, is well known. It has also a function in a democracy to reach the whole Jewish people and to guide them. If the Seminary is to meet this great responsibility, its support must come from the whole Jewish community in America and not from a few more fortunate Jews of means. The

Seminary must become the center of our Jewish life—it must represent K'lal Israel. Along with widely diffused financial support, should go democratic representation in administration. We Jews of the Twentieth Century America are not creating a religious hierarchy such as exists in other faiths, but we are looking to our Rabbis and scholars to counsel and lead.

There are five ways in which the Seminary might contribute further to the training of lay leaders.

1. In the training of Rabbis and teachers more attention should be given to the American scene—to study and research and experimentation in various phases of Jewish Community life. Knowledge of Jewish law and ritual, of language, literature, and history, is not enough to make vital contact with many of the American Amorazim, the Jewish innocent and woefully ignorant generation that is characteristic of our times. The needs, the fears, the hopes, the problems we lay Jews face in our everyday life are different from those of the Rabbi. He now monopolizes religion and religious authority to a large extent. There are techniques of group discussion, there are social issues which we face in common with non-Jews—all of which should be more familiar to the Rabbi.

2. There should be a means by which lay leaders would be brought in contact with the distinguished faculty of the Seminary —through speaking tours and regional conferences and through a Summer Institute for laymen held at the Seminary, and possibly at other points throughout the country.

3. The National Academy of Adult Jewish Education should be strengthened. Perhaps specific syllabi for training, for leadership could be developed, giving historical, psychological, and sociological studies of American Jewish life—at least making less academic the approach to the courses now offered.

4. Further assistance in the form of publications, counsel, and speakers should be given to the lay groups affiliated with the Seminary, such as the United Synagogue of America, National Federation of Jewish Men's Clubs and the Women's League.

5. Finally, to raise the tone of Jewish life—to give it substance and character there must be provided an opportunity for exchange of ideas and a development of real democratic community spirit. The popularization of Jewish learning and its wider diffu-

sion, need not mean spreading it thin. Democracy depends upon the education of mind and spirit of the whole people. The Jewish group living in a democracy cannot make a healthy adjustment by doing its own thinking on problems of the general community, and accepting without challenge the disciplines of Jewish life. Creative Jewish life in America set in a new, free, dynamic society, inspired by contemporary Jewish life in Palestine—this the Jewish Theological Seminary of America must foster, because out of it will come the leadership which can contribute to Jewry throughout the world the sympathy, the support, and the vision for which it looks to us today.

This requires courage and independence. It calls for a Jewish philosophy, a Jewish education, a Jewish *Welt-Anschauung*. It must be rooted in Torah and Jewish experience. Modern in method, sensitive to present needs, it must give meaning and purpose and direction to Jewish living. In developing it and in training leaders of it, the Seminary will make its greatest contribution to American Jewish life.

The Torch, February, 1944.

Dr. Hoffman, educator, editor and communal worker, retired in 1963 as Principal of Simon Gratz High School after 48 years of service in the Public Secondary Schools of Philadelphia, Pa. He has been officially associated in various capacities with the United Synagogue of America since 1915, recently as President of the Board of Jewish Education in Philadelphia. He was Co-editor of The Torch *for ten years and helped to establish the first Laymen's Institute at the Jewish Theological Seminary. Among the anthologies he had edited are* Literary Adventures in a Modern World, Leadership in a Changing World, Life in America, Readings for the Atomic Age, *and* Readings in Democracy. *He is Co-editor of this volume.*

INCREASING EFFECTIVENESS OF
OUR SYNAGOGUES

MAX ARZT

Great strides have been made in recent years towards transforming the American synagogue from a poorly administered, precari-
ously financed insitution into one which makes full use of the
best techniques of our age. Mortgages are being liquidated, sound
systems of synagogue finance have been introduced, fine buildings
have been erected, and still better ones are being planned. The
synagogue office is now properly staffed, its public relations department functions more smoothly, the bulletin appears regularly
and everything spells administrative efficiency. Yet we are tormented by a feeling that while the methods have been improved
the essential purpose of the synagogue has been almost forgotten.

Many lay leaders of the synagogue seem to think that a balanced budget equals spiritual achievement. Often I am invited
by the proud president of a congregation to "come and see our
fine plant and our excellent record files." The general membership, sharing this attitude, faithfully pays the *dues* and promptly
ignores the *duties*, the personal spiritual commitments involved
in synagogue affiliation. The synagogue *is* commanding increasing
loyalty in terms of financial support from a numerically aug-
mented membership. But measured by more appropriate standards, the story is sad indeed.

Synagogue attendance is falling off, even on Friday evenings
when almost all adults in the congregation can attend. In many
congregations the officers and board members of the synagogue,
who so faithfully conduct the fiscal affairs of the organization,
teach the membership by example how to administer "absent
treatment" to God's house. With the virtual disappearance of the
pious grandfather of yesteryear, the Sabbath morning service is on
the verge of being abolished. Only the artificial stimulus of a so-

cially popular Bar Mitzvah ceremony enables it to show sporadic signs of life.

Religious schools are not showing increased registration and teachers see more and more evidence of the chilling influence of the dejudaized home atmosphere. We have better textbooks with more attractive pictures, more regularly appearing report cards, well appointed classrooms and better school organization. But results achieved are not at all satisfying to the rabbi or to the spiritually alert and religiously sensitive layman.

In the face of this gloomy picture it is a tall order for me to offer suggestions on "how to increase the effectiveness of our synagogues." One is tempted to blame the sorry situation on the intellectual climate of our age, which is not exactly conducive to the religious life. One can point to the distractions of the radio and to the cacophonous appeal of commercialized amusements as formidable deterrents to synagogue attendance. One could easily list the economic, environmental and other negative factors which militate against the realization of the spiritual objectives of the synagogue. I believe, however, that these obstacles call for greater determination and a clearer perception of the duty of the hour, rather than for a hopelessness which discourages and almost paralyzes remedial action.

Let me, therefore, proceed to list a series of steps which can be taken to bring about a revitalization of the synagogue as an institution devoted to the advancement of the ethical and religious knowledge and conduct of the men, women and children of the community. I shall list a number of suggestions, each of which deserves amplification and modification through multiple experimentation.

1. Make the leadership of the congregation aware of the historic and contemporary role of the synagogue. Rabbis receive their training under the guidance of world renowned scholars. On the other hand, officers and board members are not exposed to any form of educational orientation to prepare them for their synagogue responsibilities. Often when a rabbi contemplates his well-meaning but uninformed lay leaders, he is depressed by their almost complete estrangement from the religious life. They are ostensibly his partners in a spiritual endeavor, but he feels, to use a Biblical phrase, "that my thoughts are not their thoughts." I am

a firm believer in the redemptive power of a sound and persistent educational approach. We need special "orientation courses" for officers and board members of our synagogues. The Laymen's Institute has given its students a heightened perception of the richness and relevance of our Jewish heritage. Such institutes should be established and held periodically in every part of the land and our lay leaders should be strongly urged to attend.

2. The time must come when the officers and directors of our synagogues and its auxiliary organizations (such as the Sisterhood and Men's Club) must live according to the Rabbinic dictum "Perfect thyself before thou proceedest to perfect others." It is they who by example can establish a public opinion for dependable synagogue attendance, against card games and movie shows on the Sabbath, and for a home life enriched with Sabbath and holiday observance. They must be the first to evidence their belief in elementary and secondary Jewish education by enrolling their own children in the religious school and by evincing a personal interest in the problems and progress of the school. They should be the first to enroll in courses for adult education. Thus they will set the tone for the entire congregation and will lead many new members to emulate their example and to avail themselves of the spiritual opportunities offered by the various cultural and religious activities of the synagogue.

3. The alert minded members of the congregation should be offered membership on permanent commissions dealing with the following phases of the synagogue and Jewish life:

a. Commission on Synagogue Worship and Attendance.
b. Commission on Elementary Hebrew Education.
c. Commission on Secondary Hebrew Education.
d. Commission on Adult Education.
e. Commission on Synagogue Endeavor Among the Youth.
f. Commission on Cooperation with the Jewish and General Community.
g. Commission on Strengthening the Religious Influence of the Home.
h. Commission on Synagogue Finances and Administration.

The chairmen of these committees should be carefully chosen after a consideration of their aptitudes and qualities of leadership.

These commissions should meet four or six times a year to consider the theoretical phases of their problems and to initiate practical steps toward their solution. Under the guidance of the rabbi and other experts in religious life and thought, they should become thoroughly acquainted with the specific problems facing their commission and should consider the areas in which the habits and thought processes of the congregants need to be changed and redirected. Participation in the diagnosis of a problem and co-operation toward its solution will stimulate an abiding interest. The decisions of the commission should be carried out by a smaller executive committee responsible to the larger commission and the board of the congregation.

4. The annual meeting of the congregation should be a major event and should dramatically and realistically portray the nature, scope and direction of the synagogue's multifarious activities. It should take the form of an annual convocation on a Sunday afternoon and attempts should be made to attract a large attendance. An opening inspirational address should set the keynote for a series of Seminars into which the membership can then be divided. These Seminars should deal with the problems and plans of the various synagogue commissions. The Seminars should provide for general discussion and the conclusions reached at each Seminar should be formulated in a statement of about three to four hundred words. At the closing or plenary session of the convocation, held in the evening or in the late afternoon, the brief Seminar reports should be read, followed by an address on "The Road Ahead in Our Synagogue Endeavor." The entire membership should later receive a printed or mimeographed copy of the addresses and Seminar reports.

5. In the early days of my rabbinate, I delivered frequent appeals for the reinstatement of Kiddush in the home. After one of these pleas, a layman, instead of telling me how much he enjoyed my sermon, revealed to me how unrealistic and naive I was. He said to me, "I am moved to obey the mandate of your sermon, but I can do nothing about it. I cannot read the Kiddush nor do I know the melody." Jews to whom Hebrew is Greek and who are completely estranged from the Siddur will not make Kiddush, conduct a Seder or regularly attend services even if some of the prayers are recited in English. We are all familiar with the man

who, upon entering a synagogue on Saturday morning (to pay a social call at a Bar Mitzvah service), extracts a promise from the gabbai that he will not be given an aliyah since he does not know the benedictions. There will be no appreciable increase in dependable "weather-proof" attendance at worship unless we raise a generation familiar with the prayerbook, fluent in its reading and acquainted with its noblest affirmations and aspirations. Its sacred language, its tunes and its overtones must become the vehicles for the articulation of the "dominant desires" of our souls. To live an expressive religious life in the synagogue and the home, our children must be equipped with what I would designate as "skills of Jewish living." Here are the skills which should be taught:

a. How to chant Kiddush and Havdalah on Sabbaths and festivals.
b. How to chant Grace after Meals.
c. How to use a Hebrew calendar.
d. How to conduct a Seder.
e. How to chant the daily, Sabbath and festival services.
f. How to chant the Haftorah and the benedictions preceding and following the reading of the Torah and the Haftorah.
g. How to chant the Torah and the Megillah.

Not all children will master all these skills. The first four listed above should be the indispensable minima expected of a child receiving week-day Hebrew instruction. The other skills should be mastered by a substantial minority and should be generally familiar to the rank and file of the pupils to allow for joyful participation in congregational worship. To achieve these aims, the cooperation of the home must be enlisted so that once a skill is learned, the child will experience the satisfaction of practicing it. Through the Junior congregation, children can be given opportunities to utilize the synagogue skills which they master. A series of awards and forms of public recognition can be devised to encourage voluntary and enthusiastic acceptance of the rote process of learning involved in acquiring these skills. We can learn much from the system of merits devised by the Boy Scout movement.

6. I am not ready to write off the adult membership of our congregations as an irretrievably "lost generation." Tested experience has proven that adults are capable of learning what was

neglected in their early education. Young parents, stimulated by a concern for the spiritual welfare of their children, can be induced to attend classes aiming to equip them with some of the basic skills of Jewish living. I remember vividly how a group of men and women learned to read and chant the Hebrew prayers for the Friday evening service in the course of three months and how thrilled they were when they realized that at last they could participate in a synagogue service. Texts like Doctor Greenberg's "Ideals of the Jewish Prayerbook" (published by the National Academy for Adult Jewish Education of the Jewish Theological Seminary of America) can help enhance the appreciation of the religious and ethical values of our liturgy.

7. Jewish observance is colorful, inspiring and best induced by example. In each community there are homes which on Friday evenings are permeated with the sanctity of Sabbath observance. One of the students at the Laymen's Institute made the excellent suggestion that people who conduct such homes invite young couples to a Sabbath meal. They are bound to be impressed by such an experience. Likewise, if all who believe in the edifying habit of regular synagogue attendance would tactfully but persistently urge their friends to accompany them to the synagogue, they would in many cases meet with the response implied in the Psalmist's exclamation, "I rejoiced when they said unto me, come let us go together to the House of the Lord." Most Jews may be indifferent to the synagogue. Few are really hostile. Indifference can best be dissolved by a contagious zeal.

8. Greater emphasis must be placed on greater participation in public worship. The congregation must not become a passive audience. We must urge the Rabbinical Assembly to establish a National Commission on Synagogue Worship which should enlist the coooperation of laymen in introducing means of making our public worship more decorous, more stirring and more conducive to zestful participation by the congregation. The first step in this direction is already being taken in the preparation of an authorized prayerbook by a joint commission of rabbis appointed by the Rabbinical Assembly and the United Synagogue of America.

9. The "late" Friday evening services afford all men and women an opportunity to attend public worship and to sense, at least in part, the sublimity and sanctity of the Sabbath. But the

God of Israel deserves to be worshipped also in broad daylight. In every congregation there are many men who can arrange to be in the synagogue during the major part of the Sabbath morning service. Almost all the women and the boys and girls of high school age can attend. It is a mockery to initiate a Bar Mitzvah on one Sabbath morning into a congregation which fails to conduct worship on the very next Sabbath. This is not a problem to be solved by the rabbi alone. He must have the cooperative thinking, sincere planning and personal participation of the leading men and women of the congregation if the Sabbath morning service is to be revived and restored.

10. The teachings of Judaism must be related to the personal "mundane" life of our congregants and to the larger ethical problems of the community, the country and the entire world. We must learn to think of Judaism as governing our life, "when thou sittest in thy house, when thou walkest by the way, when thou liest down and when thou risest up." The synagogue should initiate the formation of groups and the conduct of forums and classes dealing with the clarification of ideal Jewish standards of ethical behavior in business, in the professions, and in our relations to Negroes and others who suffer from discrimination. Such activities should induce a clearer perception of the duties of responsible citizenship and of the striving of all high-minded men for a more just social and international order. Judaism will then become a law of life rather than a sanctimonious escape from life's highest duties.

I am fully aware of the difficulties involved in carrying out these suggestions. Herculean efforts and iron determination will be needed to achieve these objectives. The desire to go to the root of the problem will be stimulated by a frank appraisal of the present situation in our synagogues. Most of European Jewry has been decimated by those who are determined to destroy Judaism as well as the Jews. American Jews have become the responsible custodians and standard bearers of Judaism in the Diaspora. They must be made to realize the historic role they are called upon to play, that of perpetuating the faith for which so many have died and by means of which all of us can achieve life's most enduring satisfactions.

The Torch, February, 1945.

THE JEWISH HOME

CHARLES I. HOFFMAN

The home is the expression of the individual. In it his personality is developed, enlarged, and perpetuated. In the family, in the institutions and customs of the home, the individual's character is seen. It is nature's original provision for his shelter, and protection; for his care and nurture; for his usefulness and happiness.

To the development and safeguarding of the home man has at all times given his utmost devotion. He has protected it from invasion from without and corruption and disruption from within. The home is at once the sanctuary, the castle, the refuge, the abiding place of man. Therein he has found comfort and support when all else seemed turned against him. It is the last entrenchment, even as it was the first provision, for human life and growth.

While the integrity of the home has been maintained at all times and by all peoples, to the Jews it has appealed with special significance as the nursery of childhood. The Greeks to a large extent surrendered the child to the State, for the development of its mental, spiritual and physical powers. The natural ground for the child's growth was, to the Jew, the home. The patriarchal home was the place where the great principles of life were to be implanted. Abraham's great virtue was declared to be, "I have known him that he will command his children and his household after him that they may keep the way of the Lord, to do righteousness and justice."

The home was to be the natural store-house of the customs, the institutions, the traditions that were to be preserved and developed and transmitted from generation to generation. From the home the influence was to be extended to the outside world. Against the diversions and alien influences from without, the home was to be the bulwark and fortress. In a very real way the home was to be the microcosm representing in principle and aspiration what the individual and the world was to attain.

Owing to the conditions by which the Jewish people was surrounded and, especially, after its dispersion when land and government and central sanctuary were taken away, the preservation of the Jewish home gained in importance. It became the refuge from hardships and degradation to which the Jew was exposed. The word home was associated with all that was considered sacred. The home land in Judea was surrounded with the halo of sanctity as the place where Jewish life could flourish in all its freedom and vigor. In the individual Jewish home, the Jew could be himself, could regain his dignity, could find understanding and rest and happiness.

In the modern world, the Jew among the nations is subjected to a constant attrition that wears down and out his personality. The economic and social world in which he moves constantly calls for assimilation and obliteration of differences. Even in his religious life, even in the synagogue, the secularizing forces from without tend to weaken and change Jewish identity. Amidst the varied calls from without, the voice of the synagogue grows indistinct and uncertain, less clearly discerned and hearkened to. It is in the Jewish home, in its integrity, in its purity, in its observances, in its principles and ideals, it is there that the final stand for Jewish existence and worth is to be made. From there it will again gain strength and enlargement.

This place of the Jewish home as the basic and final power to maintain the Jew's identity suggests the struggle against the Romans in the siege of Jerusalem. The Enemy had already taken the two walls that surrounded the City, but were amazed when confronted with a third wall which they endeavored in vain to storm. In our days many of the ramparts of Judaism, Synagogue and School, have been impaired and recourse must be had to the third entrenchment, the Jewish home, which we hope to fortify and maintain. External influences and the stress of economic needs cannot prevail when the internal provisions have been made secure.

What is the Jewish concept of the home and family that we can offer to the world and maintain and exemplify by our conduct as a living tradition and ideal? It is the place where one feels in harmony with the fundamental, pervading influences. This gives a sense of security and peace. The scriptural vision of contentment is: "To sit under one's vine and under one's fig tree with none to make him afraid" (Micah IV, 4). While the actor in the Jewish home is the individual, the action and objective is to carry out and realize the great purposes of human life and high human endowment; to live in consonance with the Divine Will and to realize on an individual scale the height to which mankind is to rise in the final development of the world.

This ideal is represented by the religious institution of prayer. Prayer has been termed "the service of the heart." It is the soaring of the human soul in communion with its Maker. It manifests itself in spontaneous declaration as well as in set phrases of the liturgy. It rises to great dignity in the swelling anthem of the public service, but finds its deepest meaning in the outpourings of the individual in the privacy of the home. It responds to every emotion of joy or sorrow, of gratitude, or remorse; of lamentation and hope. It is present in health and illness, in youth and old age; in life and death. It becomes all seasons and times, morning, noon and night, and includes the lying down at night and rising up in the morning. It represents the sacred and illumines the secular. It gives comfort, consolation, and hope to human life. The warning is against making prayer a mechanical and burdensome task and the injunction is to imbue it with sincere devotion and supplication. It is present, not only at fixed times, but also at the various events in human life, at birth and death; at the festivities of weddings and at the sorrows of mourning.

There is a relation between public prayer in the synagogue and private prayer in the home. The one is occasional, the other is constant and regular. The private prayer in the home prepares for and finds its consummation in the public worship in the Synagogue. The influence of the Synagogue is seen in the private devotions in the home. Unless there is this constant devotion in the home, the service in the House of Worship will lack in fervor, depth, and sincerity, will tend to become formal and perfunctory. The daily prayer, adorned in the uniform of prayer (phylacteries or tefillin) maintains the continuity of the higher life of Communion with the Divine. There is the divine assurance of reciprocity: if you will come to my (God's) house then I (God) will come to your house. Unless there is this correspondence of the synagogue and the home, both will fail in their influence and objectives.

It is not merely in the solitude of the individual but rather in the assembly of the family group that prayer in the home exercises its beneficent influence. It was a beautiful custom for the family on arising in the morning to gather together for devotion, but even when this morning assembly is absent, the practice prevails that on the occasions when the family gathers together as at the meal, there a prayer is offered in common. Especially is this the case on holy days such as Sabbath and festivals. The Mother's uplifted hands accompanied by Sabbath blessing, the Father's raised cup of wine ushering in the Sabbath and festivals (Kiddish) is profoundly impressive and of marked influence upon all the family. The practice of prayer gives a higher tone to these gatherings and affords a pervading atmosphere of family unity and devotion.

This pervading influence of prayer that elevates and refines the home life, is only one of the means in which the Jewish tone is expressed. There is the cleanliness that is enjoined as a religious not less than a hygienic duty. The care of the body and purity of the family life as well as the attention to the dietary regulations leave their impress. Then too, the observances connected with each festival and sacred season, the use of unleavened bread and the prohibition of all leaven food on the Passover, and the great family service of the *Seder*, as well as the social features that grow up about family observance, make a deep impression. Each festival has its own peculiar features and its deep spiritual importance. The festival of deliverance and freedom, Pesach, leads up to the festival of Revelation, Shabuoth, and especially on the festival of Tabernacles, Succoth, the Succah calls to mind the original home of Israel with its divine protection, as well as the simplicity and rugged austerity of the beginnings. The kindling of the lights on the festival of Dedication (Hanukkah) and the merrymaking on the festival of Lots (Purim) are only highlights in the Jewish life in the home throughout the year. Much of the value of these observances will be lost if they are performed in a perfunctory way. The religious life in all its observances has its full effect only when entered into with love and understanding and presented in a form of beauty that indicates and instills high esteem. When so observed, the "beauty of holiness" (*hadras kodesh*) will be truly indicated.

The larger opportunities that are now opened to the Jewish woman in common with her sisters of other faiths should not be at the expense of her primary duty in the home. Rather should they conduce to the elevation of the home, and a deeper, truer understanding of the religion that has given it and her true worth and position. After all, it is the home that is the true test of the character and worth of the individual and of the real merit of his public work. It is in the refinement, the devotion, the purity, the intelligence and the elevation of the home that the real life and character of the individual is most truly seen. It is a sad reflection upon the real value of the rearing of our children, and upon the merits of our boasted educational system, if this is manifested in various other directions, but is neglected in its most essential discipline, the training of the human soul. Time was, when this was the highest, the all-absorbing interest of the Jewish home; when Jewish knowledge and the Jewish sage were the highest embodiment of Jewish life. To make this influence again prevail in the Jewish home, is the great endeavor to which Jewish womanhood should direct itself. The neglect of this has been most evident in the rearing of the Jewish girl. The development that freedom has brought with it, ought to manifest itself most clearly in her spiritual training. The knowledge of the long and exalted life of Israel, the ennobling influence of the Bible, and the deep spiritual experience of communion with God in prayer in all the exigencies of life, ought to form again the basis of character-building. The Jewish home would regain its ennoblement, if material advantages were made not the means of spiritual growth but were utilized in the elevation of the family ideal.

The home represents in miniature what the community and society stand for in the world and prepares for the larger duties that these call for. This is seen in its simplest and purest form in the relation of marriage. It is based upon the permanence of marriage, not in a merely formal or legal sense but in the essential understanding and good faith upon which it is founded. The covenant between man and wife is likened to that between Israel and God. The wife and husband are dedicated (*Mekudesh*) to each other. This permanent union is cemented by the production and rearing of offspring. This consecration of the marriage relation finds its definite expression in the mutual duties of husband and wife. "The heart of her husband trusteth in her. She doth him good and not evil all the days of her life." The Bible itself prescribes the basis of the duties of the husband, support and conjugal affection. To the wife is practically accorded the conduct of the home and the rearing of the children. "I call my wife, home," declares one of the Rabbis. She is to sustain him in his larger undertakings both spiritual and civic. "Her husband is known in the gates when he sitteth among the elders of the land." Nor is her work entirely confined to the home for she is the economist and the almoner of the family. Hers it is to lend beauty and dignity to the home for we read: "Strength and beauty are her clothing." The breach of this consecrated relation during life cannot be made without guilt on the part of the offender or the total failure of the marriage relation, while its termination in death is the great calamity to which either spouse is subjected.

The parental relation includes the bearing and the protection, the care and rearing of children. It extends to the physical as well as the spiritual nurture of the child. The great objective is to transmit human life in its growing development from generation to generation. To be without children and disciples is to defeat the purpose and is cause for sorrow. This care of the child is directed towards his spiritual growth and hence his religious and moral education is given special attention. The duty of the parent is extended, however, to his physical well-being and to his economic maintenance through training for a vocation. He is to be provided also against accidents by land and water.

While the primary duty of education is reposed in the parent, that undertaking is in part delegated to the teacher at an early age and should be guided according to the child's ability and age. While tenderness should be the guiding principle, the coddling of the child is to be avoided. The parent is to be especially on his guard in the presence of the child to avoid by word or deed setting a bad example. It is this transmitting of the great spritual heritage that is likened to the giving of the law on Sinai and its establishment in the life of the progeny vindicates and establishes the value of the parent. The filial relation is expressed in the

Fifth Commandment that connects duties to God with duties to man. The natural love of parents is given this particular aspect of respect, guidance and reverence. In this it partakes of the relationship to God Himself, of whom the parent is the earthly and human representative. The only limit to this acceptance of parental influence is when, if ever, it conflicts with divine direction.

Honor and reverence are not confined to material provision for parental needs but extend to the utmost consideration and attention to their feelings, and convictions. Honor is shown in continuity of thought, of effort and activity. When a great and sacred purpose in life has been continued for three generations, we are taught, it is safety established in the character of the family. Regard for the good name of the parents should enter into the actions of the children, that by their deeds it may not be brought into disrepute and bring shame to the parental heart. So it is related of Joseph in Egypt that the thought and love of the patriarch Jacob saved the son from sin and degradation. Nor is this regard confined to the actual presence of the parent on this earth, but is extended to reverence for his memory even after death.

This continuity of purpose so wonderfully marked in the past history of Israel as a people is the ideal also for the future, when the hearts of parents and children will be in accord and the one generation shall enlarge and perfect what was undertaken and established by the other. It is this purpose, to continue and perpetuate the honor of the family name, that will stimulate and ennoble the action of the descendant. The home and family relation is not confined to parents and children but is extended not only to other relatives but also to those engaged in the service of the family, to the guests and neighbors. It thus widens out into general social duties, to associations, to state and country. The family and the home becomes the nucleus and epitome of the world.

The Torch, October, 1947.